The Talent Sourcing and Recruitment Handbook

Source better, smarter, faster, and cheaper than the competition

By Shally Steckerl

Printed in the United States of America.

ISBN: 978-1-928734-79-6

WEDDLE's
www.weddles.com

WEDDLE's
www.weddles.com
2052 Shippan Avenue
Stamford, CT 06902

Where People Matter Most.

Contents

What People Have Said About Shally Steckerl

Being in this business for over 20 years has afforded me the chance to see numerous speakers and trainers, many of which would not want to spend a single minute with you unless you bought their "system". Not Shally! He took the time on each day to answer a non-techie's questions about how to be more successful in an ever-changing technical world. He opened my eyes to some ideas and insight that were missing from my day-to-day operations and never blinked twice when I continued to pick his brain.

– John Randolph, GM at Resource Staffing

Shally trained our National Recruiting team and it was the most relevant, on point training I have ever had. He was funny and could relate to our daily challenges.

– Meaghan Brown, Recruiting Manager at Pitney Bowes

If you ever get a chance to see Shally present, you should grab that chance with both hands. Any time spent listening to his depth of knowledge and passion for his specialized area is time well spent. Truly a pioneer, Shally is generous with his ideas and expertise. The next time Shally is anywhere in Australia, I'll be in the front row (again!)

– Robert Godden, Author, Speaker, Tea Merchant

I've been a Recruiter for over 12 years and can say that Shally is not only one of the best recruiters in the U.S. but one of the nicest ones as well. The search strategies of Shally's that I've taken back to our recruiting team at REI have produced excellent, immediate results.

– Bruce Bobzien, Recruiter and Social Media Strategist at Accenture, Former recruiting manager at REI

It is great to have Shally in my direct LinkedIn™ network. He adds real, positive value to my network, growth and development. Thank you for your help and efforts. I give my highest recommendations!

– Steven Burda, MBA Senior Financial & Business Professional. Strategic Thinker. Entrepreneur. Most connected person on LinkedIn™

As one of LinkedIn's most highly connected 'uber-users', Shally Steckerl should be familiar to anyone that takes professional networking seriously. (If you're not familiar with the name already, I strongly recommend checking out his profile immediately).

In addition, the resources and information available on his website are an invaluable compendium of resources. Shally is an absolute fountain of knowledge (which he shares generously & freely) and radiates charisma and intellect.

– Stan Relihan, Principal Consultant at Propenso Executive, Australia

Lots of people have high visibility on the Web...but few – if any – have the unbelievable skills that Shally brings to the table. More than anyone I've ever met, he's able to use the Internet/Web 2.0 as a web-like collection of specific talent, people just hiding behind something that Shally can show you how to very simply brush away.

– Jack Cage, President, Cage Talent

Shally is passionate about teaching his searching methodologies via various search engines on the Internet. His presentation is fun and will yield quick results for anyone interested in hiring top talent. Thank you for sharing your vast amount of knowledge and enabling me to become a more valuable recruiter.

– Joe Perez, D&B (Dun&Bradstreet)

Shally led several members of our team through a well thought out presentation regarding using the Internet to source candidates. He has proven methods that are easy to understand and put into practice and have already provided us with results. I would highly recommend anybody take an opportunity to connect with Shally...it will be a good investment of your time.

– Joseph Hart, Talent Acquisition Consultant at CIGNA

Although Shally is what you could call an "old timer" in this business because he's been doing it so long, he certainly brings to the table "ahead of the game" thinking/tactics and leaves his clients with a "why did it take us so long to do this" feeling. His training and strategy consulting services are highly recommended.

– Sean Rehder, Director, Global Recruitment Operations & Inclusion at Sony Pictures Entertainment

Shally is AMAZING! I truly value his expert insight, knowledge and navigation of Sourcing the web. I personally have taken his courses and it has improved me and given me success in my work that I do every day! I constantly look forward to attending every event he speaks at. Shally is able to teach and share his knowledge to others in a very professional, engaging manner and makes challenging Sourcing matters become fun and easier with the tips he presents. He is a true master and extremely smart and resourceful in uncovering multiple ways at finding talent! If you are looking to take your Sourcing to the next level Shally is the ultimate one to learn from!

– Dan Harris, Talent Acquisition at Yahoo

Shally provided specific training for our Talent team. This was the best 3-day training seminar I have ever received. His in-depth knowledge and workarounds for all the recruiting/network/search engines was unbelievable. He also continues to provide support for the "Hard to Find" people in the market.

– Darren McCloud, Technical Recruiter at Adecco

Shally has a wealth of knowledge when it comes to the art of Sourcing qualified candidates. He also has a solid recruiting background which makes his one-on-one training even more valuable. I highly recommend his services.

– Mark Cruz, Sourcer/ Recruiter, Korn Ferry

Shally is a master of deep Sourcing and sleuthing on the Internet and possesses a clear and concise ability to take apart the specific requirements of online searching and map out a logical, comprehensive attack plan that delivers results. I'm extremely comfortable in recommending Shally for any deep web/net Sourcing or training.

– Barbara Ling, Master Trainer at Virtual-Coach.com

I just returned from one of Shally's training seminars. It was the most informative and captivating presentation I have ever attended. He is a true master of the Internet and has such enthusiasm to share his knowledge with all who have interest in learning. I highly recommend Shally's seminars and a visit to his website is a must.

– Patty Martin, Sr. Technical Recruiter, humcapinc.com

It has been my privilege to work closely with Shally. The depth of knowledge I was exposed to had me treading water very quickly, but Shally was always happy to extend a lifeline to keep me afloat. Quite simply, Shally is a true expert in his field. Fortunately for us he is willing to share his experiences.

– Simon Townsend, Manager Innovation at Deloitte Australia

First off Shally's trainings are the best in the recruiting business. Second, I consider him a dear friend & a wealth of wisdom. The original CyberSleuth and, in my opinion, one of the greatest Sourcing gurus of all time.

– Jeremy Langhans, Global Brand & Talent Attraction Leader, President of the Northwest Recruiters Association

I've known Shally since the beginning of his recruiting career. Since then, we've stayed in contact. Through the years, he's trained my recruiters and has provided great tools and advice to me and my organization. If you're looking for a top notch recruitment expert, Shally is the one to call. He's the best.

– Jose Carbia, Director, Talent Acquisition at Manheim

I had the extreme privilege to work with Shally Steckerl while he was recruiting for Google. I found Shally to be very professional and well versed in finding the resources they needed to accomplish their recruiting goals.

– Tom Eckhart, Vice President at DirectEmployers Association

Shally is the quintessential Internet search guru. He reads everything...he knows everything. Through our training with Shally, our recruiters and researchers have grown professionally and are excited to be on the leading edge of Internet Sourcing and recruitment strategy for the 21st century.

– Paul Jesselson, Senior Talent Acquisition Leader

Shally is a legend. A true guru who brings together technology, the Internet and sound recruiting practices. I am fortunate to call him a friend and recommend him without hesitation. A true gentlemen and an outstanding industry leader.

– Bill Vick, Founder, Recruiters Online Network

Leaders aren't measured by words but by execution & ability to enthuse others with their vision. And yet, even with these qualities, without compassion for those one serves & with whom one works, there is zero. Kindness, empathy, focus & an ability to instill confidence....all of the above is what I have both experienced & observed in Shally!

– Emily White, LMSW, Medical Social Worker

Extremely creative and innovative with advanced "Thinking Out of the Box" techniques for all industries and all situations in Sourcing. Very quick and bright and interesting.

– Barry Geiman, Consultant, Futurestep, a Korn/Ferry Company

A premier recruiting guru in the industry with in-depth Internet search knowledge. I am impressed with his generosity in sharing a technique or skill to assist you in finding.

– Rithesh Nair, Talent Acquisition Recruiter at Ernst & Young LLP

I have interviewed hundreds of professional recruiters; I consider myself well versed in the recruiting skill set. When it comes to Sourcing, research, candidate generation and competitive intelligence, Shally is among the top 1 percent of recruiters who understand the function thoroughly.

– Carmen Hudson, Leader in the Recruiting Community

Shally is one of the most knowledgeable people I know in the recruiting industry. Whether you need a referral, information on how to find a specific type of candidate, or knowledge about a process, Shally is a great go-to person.

– Kim Rutledge, Vice President, Global Talent Acquisition and Human Resources at SunPower Corporation

Shally is a true researcher, who fully understands how to execute both a position-focused and a high volume Sourcing effort. There are very few people within the HR/Recruiting industry who "gets it" like Shally does. If you are looking for a solid researcher, be sure to leverage Shally when conducting, competitive intelligence, target market research, talent and more.

– Tracey Friend, VP of Solutions Design, Agile 1

Shally is THE most brilliant Internet search and research technologist I have ever come to know. I have worked with him directly when I was CEO of The Breckenridge Group and I can tell you first hand that he is a real innovator in the field.

– Frank Scarpelli, Director Talent Management, CISION

I have known Shally for a few years now and can comfortably say that he is in the top 5 percent of Internet research/Sourcing experts. Shally also understands the benefits of the Internet tools and tricks from not only the technical perspective but on the business implications.

– Rob McIntosh, Senior Vice President Global Talent and Recruitment at Avanade

Skip headlines, read the fine print. I've interacted with Shally for years now and have only great things to say about him...though most folks connect him directly to recruiting-related projects (based on many of his contracts), he is in fact an all-around top notch industry research guy with a strong grasp of other areas of applied research (competitive intelligence, research applications and software/tools, etc.)

– David Carpe, Principal, ReedShay & Company

I am amazed by Shally's ability to grasp the big picture and yet stay focused on the details. He constantly looks for new and innovative ways to tackle problems and bring solutions to the table. Most importantly, he knows how to treat people with respect and understands what drives them to success. This translates into a contagious motivational spirit.

– Andrew Middleton, Infrastructure Consultant at Applied Information Sciences

I have worked closely with Shally for many years. He consistently delivers powerful training sessions, and is in my opinion a true recruiting industry expert in the fields of Sourcing & recruiting for top talent. Shally has presented training presentations on many topics including "How to use GOOGLE for candidate Sourcing" for up to 250 of my recruiters as well as webinars, workshops, and recorded podcasts. His content, delivery and handouts have been highly praised by my recruiting teams. If you are looking for up-to-date material, with step-by-step directions that really work, then I suggest you tap into Shally and his best practices

– Craig Silverman, VP, Middle Enterprise Sales @ Proofpoint

Preface

Recruiting remains a "people business" at heart. Nonetheless, recruiting has evolved into a unique ecosystem where visible human presence has been replaced by a digital mouthpiece. In this technology-laden industry, thinking time has emerged as a discrete and key instrumentality. The overarching goal of this book is to concretize these industry shifts into daily sustainable practices that will maximize a professional recruiter's day-to-day productivity. Of particular note is an expansive discussion on the topic of Sourcing, signifying the (r)evolutionary leap forward in web-based recruiting. This text is designed to satisfy two key questions in a comprehensive manner.

Do You Always Know What You're Doing?

Perhaps it would take you a lifetime to master on your own the multitude of specialties found in all aspects of recruiting. To balance competing forces, an effective modern recruiter is increasingly compelled to become a true Project Manager, a prospect that can be daunting to even the most seasoned of professionals.

Rest assured, if you read and apply this text as intended, you will know exactly what to do in the course of your job, or the component of your occupation that entails the attraction, identification, selection and subsequent recruitment of talent. The recruitment industry ebbs and flows at an outrageous pace. From one day to the next you may be faced with the unexpected, and to adjust you will need to make radical shifts. Regardless, this book should help you create a process and put separate mechanisms in place so that you can navigate through expected and unexpected events easier, wasting as little time as possible. In short, you can answer the question "What's next?" with confidence.

Note that references provided in this book are informational only; they do not constitute my endorsement of any websites or other sources. Please be conscious that the websites listed in this book may change, and that I receive no compensation from them in exchange for their inclusion in this book.

How Does Technology Make My Job Easier?

Any hiring manager or labor attorney will tell you that the cost of correcting a hiring mistake is more than the cost of hiring the right person in the first place. In addition to the financial expense of hiring, training, onboarding, and mal-affected performance, there is the human cost of time, emotional toil, and basic dignity. Moreover, while any hiring decision requires the expenditure of time, life stewardship demands that individuals not spend time performing one task that could be better spent on another. Technology is the excellent means through which recruiters manage valuable limited resources. In addition to reducing the time and energy spent on logistics, technology makes it easier for recruiters to focus on people, appropriate because recruiting is, in fact, a people business.

"It's easy to find a needle in a haystack – you use a magnet. But finding a needle in a stack of needles is another kind of challenging."
–Shally Steckerl

GK Chesterton, a prodigious mystery writer and poet, notes: "Where does a wise man hide a pebble? On the beach." This handbook contains in depth commentary on the value of Sourcing, on finding the right pebble on the beach. The "Hidden in Plain Sight" trope applies quite well to the profession of Sourcing and recruitment. Sourcing is the process of interpreting massive amounts of raw data (e.g. resumes, job postings) into actionable intelligence (i.e. hiring) at lightning speed. Another way, spending days sifting through a pile of resumes to produce a list of unfiltered candidates from your Penny Saver pool is merely recruiting. Spending ten minutes piloting the right channels to produce a list of the best candidates from the global pool is Sourcing.

In answering these questions I address or mention many of the same concepts throughout the book. This is done intentionally with the expectation that you will consult the book regularly through the course of your work. Not everyone will pick up the book at the same chapter, or read it front-to-back in one fell swoop.

I designed this book as a working guide, a reference to provide helpful information during the execution of your duties, but please bear in mind, every company is different. The advice and strategies I discuss may not be suitable for your situation. If you are interested in customized strategies, find out more about how you can retain my advisory services at 4sct.com.

Acknowledgements

"We are like dwarfs standing upon the shoulders of giants, and so able to see more and farther than those before us." -Bernard of Chartres, circa 1130

Before the end of the 20th century I arrived at the conclusion that Sourcing was more than a way for me to meet my recruitment goals by finding talent unavailable in mainstream sources. It was to be my chosen career, my calling, and my legacy. The path leading from that epiphany to the completion of this book was not plotted overnight, nor was it completed in isolation. So many before me have illuminated the trail I now follow, and have lent to me their strong shoulders on which I stand. I take this opportunity to acknowledge those who continue to go out of their way to make an enormous difference in my life. People whose encouraging words have lifted me many times from the darker corridors, pointing the way back to my main pursuits.

My faculty for research may never have been discovered, much less applied, if not for the hand of Harriet McCormick. Early in my career, Harriet saw something in a young recruiter with only one year of experience. What she saw prompted her to take a chance and bring me into her organization to help identify passive candidates, before I even knew they were different than the "active" ones in my first database. I started recruiting as a rookie at a traditional staffing firm. Even after breaking 11 company records, my colleagues refused to acknowledge that my online efforts were the source of my productivity because it simply did not fit into the "way things had always been done".

Sourcing back then hardly existed as a function, much less a dedicated role. Harriet recognized this new skill would become very important so she recruited me away from my first job in this business and brought me in under her wing. I was fortunate to receive Harriet's tutelage for a few short months before her passing, but even in such a brief time she left an indelible mark. Harriet was the spark, and just as sparks ignite, they also expire unless they find fuel for a fire.

My wife Stefanie nurtured that spark, and through her encouragement provided the fuel that blazed a path for my freedom to pursue what many thought was impossible: A successful career built entirely upon Sourcing. Since my very first entrepreneurial foray (JobMachine.net in 1998), Stefanie was elemental. Without her I would have had no shelter from the stresses or protection from the endless assault of urgent tasks, nerve-racking fire drills and tense situations that spontaneously consume a recruiter's life. She patiently supplies the cover that gives me room to pull off all-nighters, provides the revitalizing salve that protects me from permanent damage, and selflessly administers the guidance that steers me back to sanity after I lose my way. She continues to be indispensably involved in countless aspects of our business from testing techniques to creating our websites, running our technology, supervising our accounting, and keeping me on track with projects like writing this book. In great part, this book owes its existence to her belief in me, as much as it does to my publisher Peter Weddle's firm leadership and encouragement.

In the ever-changing, fast-paced world of the Internet, content is king. When it comes to those who have most profoundly influenced my Sourcing knowledge there is none I esteem more, or feel a deeper sense of solidarity with, than Glenn Gutmacher.

No other individual has done more in helping me promote the role of the Sourcer and elevate our profession's standing within the ranks of recruiters. Since the moment I recognized I wanted to leave a professional mark in this world by inspiring a generation of Sourcers, and raising the overall level of our industry, Glenn has been right there with me. Over the years he has never ceased to be a pragmatic colleague and fervent contributor to Sourcing lore. Throughout our work together we have collaborated vastly, the end product being greater than a sum of its parts. Not only has his intellect endlessly inspired me, but also he has so tirelessly tested the limits of what can be done with many of the practical techniques discussed in this book that many would likely not exist without him. His influence, therefore, is strongly felt. However, his greatest impact cannot ultimately be measured because in writing this book, I have so liberally, and with permission, borrowed from him. To the extent that I have stolen from others, I've probably stolen more ideas from Glenn Gutmacher than from anyone else. My one regret is not having recorded all our conversations.

There are two others who in a short time have written an indelible chapter of my life. Without Rob Delp and Suzanne Salsbury I would not have stayed my professional course through the uncertainty of the past few years and would no doubt have succumbed to precipitous chaos. Each in their own way continues to make sacrifices to provide me with a sense of stability, and encourages me to follow my entrepreneurial bent while silently paving the way forward. Their counsel alone would be enough to secure them a place in this book, but it is their tireless cheerleading behind the scenes that makes them rock stars.

In my travels I have been fortunate to benefit from sage heroes of our industry like Peter Weddle and Gerry Crispin, and to count among my friends passionate visionaries like Bret Hollander, Eric Jaquith, Anna Brekka, Dean DaCosta and Dan Harris who's boundless energy and constant contributions to our trade fan the embers of my creativity.

Besides being boorishly boring, citing a long list including all the names of all the champions who have given me of their sharpened steel and resolve would be lengthy if not utterly impractical, but if you are inclined to read such a thing, I have made my best attempt at tipping my hat to all those who deliberately or inadvertently influenced me in a section at the end of this book.

To everyone else who has ever taken a moment to share with me an idea, suggestion, question, critical comment, challenge, kind word, or an opposing point of view, this book is dedicated to your success.

Introduction

"To recruit is to replenish, maintain or increase the talent ranks of an organization." - Shally Steckerl

Recruiting is a vast, misunderstood topic. More art than science, the original "people business" has existed in many forms over the centuries. Just as no two people are completely identical, so too hiring organizations. Each has their own DNA. Modern recruiters play a multidisciplinary role, masters of basic human psychology, well versed in business rules and requirements, savvy in the use of tools and technology, and cognizant of the nuances of the industry and its unique business "ecosystem". Because the recruitment industry changes dramatically from day-to-day, today's recruitment professionals must truly be Project Managers. No individual could learn how to handle the multitude of specialties found in all aspects of recruiting on their own or in one lifetime. This text is an overview of and introduction to the foundational skills, such as organization, communication and business acumen, needed to build a strong Sourcing and recruitment practice.

Demand for specialized labor continues to outstrip supply and many enterprises face long-term challenges in hiring the mission critical talent they need to meet their objectives. A company's growth is reliant upon its ability to fill key positions with experienced workers, drawn from similar industries, companies, and direct competitors.

How Are Recruiting and Sourcing Different?

Differentiated from recruitment, Sourcing is the specialized discipline of proactively identifying and engaging with talent not found via traditional means. Sourcers focus more on research activities than their recruiter counterparts. While sometimes involved in other aspects of talent attraction, most Sourcing revolves around creating and managing a prospective candidate pipeline comprised of individuals who have not initially expressed an interest in the company. These individuals are known as "passive candidates". This activity always includes identification, initial qualification or pre-screening, and usually also extends to some form of initial outreach.

The act of Sourcing for candidates is performed either as part of a recruiter's regular duties alongside all other tasks, or sometimes by a dedicated, specialized recruiter exclusively focused on the research components of the function.

Sourcing needs to be clearly defined by what it is, as much as what it is not. Candidate Sourcing activity typically ends once the name, job title, job function and contact information for the potential candidate has been identified by the Sourcer. To develop a list of previously sourced names further, some companies have a second person then reach out to the names on the list to initiate a dialogue with them with the intention of pre-screening the candidate against the job requirements and gauging candidate interest for new job opportunities. This activity is called "candidate profiling" or "candidate pre-screening".

In some situations, a candidate Sourcer can perform both primary and secondary research to identify candidates, as well as execute profiling protocols to further pre-screen candidates. There is a growing market for experts solely focused on primary research in the form of telephone Sourcing, Internet researching and candidate profiling.

Primary research: *original information obtained first hand through conversations, interviews, telephone calls, surveys, or otherwise not openly available to others.*

Secondary research: *information obtained from indexes, abstracts, articles and other written or oral information supplied by a participant or eyewitness.*

How to Use This Book

This book is intended for use as your trusted "go to" resource for proven tips to enhance your effectiveness over the years. Each time you pick it up select one idea to study and practice until it becomes instinctive. Even something that may appear trivial when mastered will exponentially increase your efficiency.

Psychologist Anders Ericsson put forward the idea that practicing something for 10,000 hours is what it takes to make you an expert. Working 40 hours a week with two weeks off, you would work for approximately 2,000 hours a year. According to the "10,000-Hour Rule" you would then be an expert after Sourcing and recruiting for five years. Yet, I have spent over 40,000 hours learning, practicing and developing what is in this book, and to this day I continue to discover new ways to apply it and hone my trade craft. I encourage you to do the same.

To facilitate your discovery, this book is organized into the following parts:

> **Part I - Define:** The book begins with an introduction to Sourcing and recruitment, including definitions of the various roles and components. Much more than an overview, this chapter explores organizational models, explains the workflow and makes strategic recommendations on building the function.
>
> **Part II - Find:** The largest component of this book is a comprehensive examination of talent identification techniques, paying particular attention to the dominion of Internet search for passive candidates. Numerous methodologies are illustrated along with cutting-edge search techniques like natural language, peer regression, referral Sourcing and social recruiting. Also take a virtual journey around the world to explore how these techniques apply to international recruiting.
>
> **Part III - Attract & Engage:** Having identified the potential candidate, we will turn our attention to methods of candidate attraction and engagement. From their initial impression of your employment brand to your advertisement and social media, the third part of this book couples proven best practices with emerging candidate contact techniques. The commentary within these sections draws upon established marketing principles

while providing keen insights into cutting edge practices and trends. Careful instructions, explanations and examples are provided to alleviate your concerns or fears around professional, interpersonal communication with strangers, bringing a distinctive personal touch to your professional recruiting process.

Part IV – Achieve: Once you have sufficiently practiced the principles and techniques discussed in the previous three chapters it is appropriate to step back and review your progress. At the same time, it is important to look forward so you know what changes lie ahead. The chapters contained in this part of the book will help you look backwards and forwards by addressing performance assessment, the good habits of effective recruiters, and the future of recruiting technology. A brief look at privacy issues in the digital age is also presented. The material will place your head in the game, spin the wheels in your head and direct your eyes toward the future.

The Evolution of Recruitment

Recruiting has evolved rapidly in the last decade, but has existed for centuries before the industrial revolution. The Town Crier, a role which still exists in some parts of the globe, may have been the first advancement in recruitment technology since smoke signals and drums. Short lived because of its even shorter range, it served the function of advertising "help wanted" and was assisted by the rumor mill that would carry the message via word of mouth.

Messaging in larger volumes later became possible through the rise of print media, generating the classified advertisement. At trading posts and traveler's inns, it was possible for "help wanted" messages to be distributed, and with the advent of speedy postal services, these messages could bridge distances rapidly enough to be of more immediate use to recruiters. Shrinking the globe further, the telegram briefly led the charge, followed closely by the telephone and in short order the telex, fax, email, the Internet, and of course mobile Short Message Service (SMS).

Then along came social media...

After the printing press, anyone could publish ideas and distribute opinions widely, but popularity or recognition of expertise was still hard earned.

Combining the broadcast ability of the press with the personal nature of the Town Crier, blogs and social media seem to grant nearly instant popularity or the semblance of expertise.

Prologue

While traditional Human Resources disciplines are well represented within academia, the recruitment specialty, and Sourcing in particular, remains greatly underserved by educators. Like a developing nation, our trade's starvation for knowledge has thwarted its growth.

I feel there is greater thrill or higher reward than knowing I contributed to the lighting of a light bulb above someone's head as they learn something new. That moment of discovery is exhilarating for coach and student alike. This is why I have a hard time understanding why there are so few leaders in our industry willing to share their knowledge. Of those who do share, an uncomfortable majority does so by standing above the audience, looking down at them from a pulpit or in a position of seniority, and not as mentors, coaches, or facilitators. While there is a place for lecture and for reverence such learning already permeates conferences and webinars.

Wisdom gained through experience seldom finds its way into lecture halls and virtual conference rooms, much less onto a book about recruitment. In the age of information where people's talent, thoughts and ideas are a company's most treasured product, those who replenish, maintain or increase the talent ranks of an organization play an essential role in generating profit, yet are provided almost no education, coaching or mentorship.

Further complicating matters, every company has its unique set of idiosyncrasies, political and environmental challenges, and resource constraints. Consequently one organization's successful formula seldom works within another's. Too often recruiters must fend for themselves. Despite minimal guidance, recruiters are expected to solve complex business problems. It is my hope that this book finds its way into the hands of all those who could use a few more light bulbs lit up over their heads.

Part I: Define

Chapter 1
Recruiting & Sourcing Primer

What started out as the responsibility of office managers to place job advertisements in newspapers or help wanted signs in storefronts has now grown into a multi-billion dollar industry. Many enterprises face long-term challenges in hiring the talent they need to meet their objectives. Often, the identification of talent requires internal corporate recruitment departments or independent employment agencies focused solely on this transaction through both proactive and new reactive recruiting techniques.

Section 1. Recruiting

The Talent Crunch

As mentioned above, prospects for organizational growth are dependent upon the organization's ability to identify, attract, engage and retain experienced workers. The majority of these workers inevitably must come from similar industries or companies and even from direct competitors.

There are many other market forces that contribute to the increase in demand for talent:

- Strong economies favor experienced candidates, making it harder to recruit them.
- Weaker economies enable employers to increase required qualifications and encourage desirable, experienced candidates to value job security and remain out of the job market.
- Older, more experienced workers tend to change jobs far less frequently than younger, less experienced workers.

- An entire generation of experienced, baby boom workers has already begun exiting the workforce with no plans to return.
- Universities do not produce enough skilled graduates in many high-demand fields.
- Many experts and industry surveys report that the number of hires from job boards and corporate career sites is declining or flat for most companies.

None of these trends comes as a surprise. Nonetheless, a company's success has become inextricably tied to their success as employers and recruiters. Recruitment, the ability to attract the skill set that will help companies achieve their objectives, has now evolved into the most critical function at the core of employment concerns for most companies. With this new emphasis on recruitment, continued business viability and endurance require organizations to rethink their human talent development. Companies using the same approach to recruiting they used a mere 5-10 years ago will lose the fight for talent.

Modern Forms of Recruitment Strategy

The recruiting process is highly variable from employer to employer. Variations are driven by the markets they serve, the type of hiring they do, the strategies of their recruiting leadership, and the skills and dedication of their direct line recruiters. When hiring highly skilled workers, there are three broad categories in which corporate recruitment processes may be grouped: Conventional, Contemporary, and Cutting-edge. The categories are based on how much a given company's recruiting process and practices have evolved to meet market conditions.

Conventional Hiring

Conventional hiring has often been described as "post and pray". Companies advertise available positions, watch as the resulting resumes pour in, and pray that within the pile of resumes they receive, they will find someone who can do the job. This model can be attractive because it shifts most of the work of recruiting to candidates. The problem with this model is that it leaves much control and thus room for poor decision-making in the hands of outsiders.

Making matters worse, many conventional hiring companies make it difficult for potential hires even to apply for a job. Some corporate websites require a login and password, and even ask candidates to complete a 30-minute profile and application just to submit their resumes. For high volume hiring of low skilled workers, this approach might work at times, but the more options a candidate has, the less likely they are to invest the time in such a process.

An additional problem with conventional recruiting is the way candidates become lost and forgotten after the initial hiring decision is made. Hiring managers at these companies may consider several candidates for one position and then never revisit them after making the initial hiring decision despite the fact that the other finalists may be well qualified for similar or other positions. The truth is that virtually no companies actually consider old resumes for new openings although they tell candidates they will keep their resumes on file for future opportunities.

These instances contribute to a "do not call us, we'll call you" attitude which is perceived by candidates as the "HR black hole". The subliminal message being conveyed to candidates is "do not apply", and as a result, many do not. This conventional recruiting style is typical of companies who view relationships with candidates as unimportant. In the end, this style will backfire on them because in limiting the pool of candidates from which they can recruit. In time, they will be left with drawing from the slate of candidates that more aggressive recruiting organizations have already rejected.

Contemporary Hiring

Companies which have figured out that conventional recruiting is insufficient to attract top talent will turn to Sourcing candidate resumes directly from major job boards. In this way, they gain access to a wider pool of talent. These are candidates who may never have heard of the company, are uninterested in jumping through all the "old school" hoops, or never hear back from employers. Many contemporary companies are also increasing hires coming from employee referrals. Unfortunately, they do not maximize the power of referrals by incorporating formal programs to solicit them proactively. The most common referral programs are ones in which employees are rewarded when someone is hired and not when they merely generate candidates. Use of this approach means employees need to keep tabs on which of their contacts are job hunting and what jobs are actually open at their company. This requirement involves more time than most employees are willing to spend. Finally, many companies are increasingly turning to agencies for hard-to-fill positions, even as they greatly expand the number of positions in the hard-to-fill category.

Because contemporary hiring competes with cutting edge hiring as discussed below, three challenges arise that are distinct to the contemporary model.

Challenge #1: Timing

Timing is critical in recruiting. Searching a database for qualified candidates can take hours each day. A recruiter can view hundreds of resumes and find perhaps one or two potentially qualified candidates. This is a labor-intensive process that lowers the yield per recruiter and drains valuable time. When a strong candidate enters the job market, only a short window opens during which they are accessible before they reach the offer stage with other employers. If a recruiter does not reach candidates while they are actively looking, therefore, all of the recruiter's effort is wasted.

Challenge #2: Cost

A related issue is cost. Access, agencies, referrals, and recruiters all drive up the cost-per-hire. This outcome occurs because the two essential parts of this model are paying for more resumes, and then paying for more people to read them. These expenses would be justified if these mechanisms resulted in better candidates or faster fills, but they usually do not. Instead, there are merely more gatekeepers to the decision-maker for whom the employer bears the cost.

Challenge #3: Quality

Similar to "post-and-pray", the contemporary hiring model assumes that candidates will arrive after the job has been posted. The time span between the opening of a requisition and a hiring manager's review of resumes may be a couple of weeks or more. Many of these resumes are slowed down in the selection process, and candidates are usually off the market before they are ever contacted. This type of delay in filling positions inevitably leads to compromises around the skills needed, which results in a weaker candidate pool.

Cutting Edge Hiring

Recruiting challenges have already taught growing companies that they must evolve in order to survive. These companies understand the need to be proactive about seeking and attracting top talent and are arriving at the conclusion that centralized Sourcing is one of the best ways to bridge the gap. Modern technology enables forward-thinking organizations to automate the gathering and processing of information about potential hires.

Forward-thinking companies apply a more progressive approach to recruitment. The characteristics of this approach include proactively Sourcing from the broadest markets for available talent, and then using technology to ensure recruiting remains nimble and cost-effective. These organizations recognize that a broad Sourcing strategy is critical in today's market and set their sights on candidates who take little to no initiative in their job search yet would be open to opportunities if contacted about the right one, at the right time.

The other aspect of cutting-edge hiring today is the adoption of tools and technology to automate or eliminate low value-added tasks. Tools like Internet spiders and resume search engines enable recruiters to search multiple databases simultaneously. Such tools have improved significantly in the past few years. Now, the process of retrieving a thousand resumes off a job board and generating a shortlist of the best ones can be done in a completely automated fashion. A recruiter can spend twenty minutes instead of twenty hours and have a better, fresher list of prospects to call.

Danger still lurks in cutting edge hiring models, however. If recruiting leadership merely acknowledges the problems with other models but does not devote resources to support cutting edge methods, then this model retains many of the inefficiencies of other models. Despite the interest in untapped pools, many obvious sources of candidates remain untouched. Resumes from past candidates are rarely used as Sourcing tools. Employee referral and agency resumes that do not match the specific job they initially come in for are often discarded and subscriptions to resume databases like Monster®, CareerBuilder® and LinkedIn™ remain unused by the companies that sign up for them.

Cutting Edge Recruiting

Transitioning to a cutting edge recruiting stance involves rethinking the flows of information from beginning to end. The way resumes are managed and treated should reflect the tremendous value they hold for the company. The way candidates are managed and treated should convey they are respected and valued. This rethinking means changing the tools and processes that have been in place since the introduction of the conventional recruiting model.

The Talent Reservoir

The first step in forward-thinking recruiting is to take an expansive view of building a talent reservoir. Resumes represent the pool of talent a company can approach when recruiting. They are a valuable asset, and need to be treated as such.

Many companies have made it difficult to submit resumes, and most have failed to create a usable, centralized database of these resumes once they have been received. Companies should take the approach that more is better. Resumes from candidates, agencies, employees and other sources should be consolidated into one talent pool. Robots like infoGISTTM Platinum Recruiter, TalentHook and DaXtra can be used to scour public databases for resumes, expanding the reach of companies far beyond simply those who applied. Any of these candidates could be right for a position at some point. Additionally, these candidates may also be able to point the way toward other candidates.

There are additional benefits to a consolidated talent pool. One is the entire history of a candidate can be seen, including when they previously applied, and the result of that process. In the event agencies submit resumes that are already in the company database, fees can be avoided. Finally, turnover and change in the recruiting department does not damage the long-term ability of the company to recruit. The asset remains even in the event that a recruiter leaves.

Tap Your Reservoir

A talent reservoir is useless without an effective means of understanding the talent it holds. Traditional search tools have generally been ineffective in helping companies take advantage of their talent pools. Keyword searches fail frequently because they are simultaneously too broad and too specific. Asking for all the resumes with "marketing" yields too many results, while asking for all the resumes with "marketing programs" generally overlooks many qualified candidates.

To effectively take advantage of a talent pool, therefore, companies need to use intelligent search technologies that can apply human-like criteria to resumes. This strategy entails looking at factors such as total years of experience, breadth of knowledge, educational background and work experience. At a minimum, such intelligent search tools should have the following capabilities:

Conceptual Search

True conceptual search means looking beyond synonyms to understand related concepts. For example "financial analysis" as a skill might include variance analysis or cash flow projections. Conceptual search means finding the skills you want and not just the words.

Contextual Search

Contextual search places values on items like dates of employment and duration at each job. With the ever-expanding keyword sections on resumes today, it is important to look past the presence of a word, and evaluate candidates based on appropriate levels of experience.

Learning

People react differently to the same resumes. What is a top school to one hiring manager may be very different to another manager. As the talent pool grows, a learning system can provide more distinction between candidates based on what it has recognized that different managers like.

Automated intelligent systems will never replace the need for humans in the recruitment and Sourcing function but will aid in processing what is coming to be known as "big data" and improve efficiency.

The Advantages of Intelligent Search

Intelligent search does not just mean less time spent reading resumes. The real value is in better knowledge and communications about the real-time state of the talent pool. It is the shared awareness of the state of the market that leads companies to more targeted and better recruiting.

With traditional recruiting, it is common for recruiters or agencies to take a listing, post the job, and then wait a week or two before presenting resumes to the hiring manger. If misunderstandings have occurred about what type of person can fulfill job duties and responsibilities, then additional time in the hiring process is required.

Social Sourcing and the Internet as Talent Reservoir

Taking advantage of the proliferation, low cost and ease of use of cloud-based technology (applications, services and resources available to uses on demand via the Internet), a new breed of Sourcing tools has emerged. These "social Sourcing" applications and cloud based services like SwoopTalent.com, Gild and many others provide an advantage simply because their data is kept up to date by the prospects themselves, instead of growing stale over time as it does in traditional static databases.

Set Expectations about the Skills that Exist

With traditional recruiting, it is common for recruiters or agencies to take a listing, post the job, and then wait a week or two before presenting resumes to the hiring manger. This creates an inherent delay resulting in friction. Great candidates move on to more nimble employers, or hiring managers end up waiting another two weeks for a position to be reposted due to an initial lack of response. If misunderstandings have occurred about what type of person can fulfill job duties and responsibilities, then additional time in the hiring process is required.

With an intelligent search tool, discussions about what the talent pool holds can take place before the requisition is even opened. Expectations about what is needed and what might be available are set early in the process. By realistically reviewing what is likely to happen during the search, recruiters and hiring managers spend less time learning about the market and more time focusing on a solution.

React Immediately when Right Candidate Shows up

When companies have numerous openings that require similar skill sets, candidates do not always know which job they are the most qualified for, and recruiters do not always have time to review all the resumes received. It is critical to use technology to match candidates to the jobs for which they are most qualified and not just the job to which their resume may have been attached. Intelligent search and screening processes solve this problem by evaluating every resume the moment it arrives, and notifying the recruiter and hiring manager immediately if any candidate represents a strong match for their position. Recruiters can focus on the real work of recruiting – talking to candidates about the roles they are right for – instead of the manual work of reading resumes of individuals who are not a good fit.

Reduce Cost Through an In-house Staffing Agency Function

Many staffing agencies find candidates by closely monitoring job boards like Monster®, CareerBuilder®, and LinkedIn™ and then moving fast when a candidate indicates availability by updating their resume. They earn their commissions simply by finding and acting on publicly available information faster than other agencies and companies. Intelligent search and screening, when combined with automated tools like those discussed in The Talent Reservoir, automate this process and do so faster than any human. A resume posted on Monster® will be routed to the right recruiter within 24 hours. This means candidates receive the right phone call before other employers engage them.

Recruiting Technology Boosts Your Competitive Advantage

Again, as the availability of talent shrinks, workforce management becomes a critical competitive arena for all employers. In today's economy, people are the single most valuable asset in a corporation, and unlike physical assets, individuals generally gain value over time as workers accumulate experience. Recruitment of experienced personnel is as important as retention, but unlike retention specialists with direct access to employees, recruitment it is much more difficult because recruiters do not have easy and direct access to prospects.

Forward-thinking companies know that while various individual components may be impressive, but it is not until they are all used together that a bigger, more consequential picture emerges. The ideal technology solution should enable you to concurrently:

- Reduce cost, or increase hires without increase in cost
- Hire more people with fewer resources
- Automate repetitive and time consuming tasks
- Reduce tedious tasks thereby reducing labor

In addition to lower overall headcount costs, there should also be a reduction in the number of accounts purchased for paid database access and other services.

Hire Faster than Competitors

As soon as a new prospective candidate profile is available, it should be injected into the pipeline without delay and immediately matched against current and future openings.

One of the most effective ways to beat competitors is to reach top talent first. Companies able to attract the most top talent will inevitably have a competitive advantage and those adept at recruiting talent away from their competition will gain an even more significant advantage. Through the appropriate use of technology and automation, organizations can access talent quicker and stretch their horizons to include the worldwide talent landscape.

Four Types of Job Seekers

Job seekers can be classified into four distinct types. These four types are not distinguished by a prospect's suitability for a new role. They are instead stages separated by the direction of initiative (weather interest in the candidate originates from the recruiter or interest in the employer originates from the candidate) and further divided by the amount of time or effort a prospective employee will invest in search of that new role.

These four types can occur in anyone at different times in their career, and individuals frequently shift from one type to another during their careers or even during the recruitment process.

1. Suspect

Leads (name and contact details) for whom there is little background information but who are suspected to be a fit for the role and who may potentially be recruited or interested in considering opportunities.

Suspects have not been officially recruited and would likely retreat from an opportunity if they are prematurely presented with the amount of time they would need to invest in interviews and paperwork. Potential employees may enter this process at any of the four points, or they may traverse through all four, but evidently they must be treated differently at each stage. The most passive applicants begin as suspects (leads) who do not initiate the process themselves. Instead, they receive an initial cold call from a recruiter or another intermediary. Upon their active recruitment, they become prospects because they believe the recruiter's presentation is a compelling opportunity, and it is the right time to explore it. If it is not the right fit or the right time, the lead will never become a prospect.

2. Prospect

Contacted suspects who show promise to be a good fit for the role and who are interested in exploring the opportunity.

Prospects are willing to consider investing some time to participate in exploratory phone calls. Further along the initiative scale, candidates will invest much more time into the process and will more readily attend interviews yet may balk and lose interest if confronted with all the required processes upfront.

In comparison, prospective employees entering the process directly into the applicant stage are frequently willing to jump through all the hoops and complete lengthy forms online even when they feel they have only a slim chance of receiving a call back from a recruiter.

3. Candidate

A prospect formally considered by a hiring authority.

Once you have established two-way communication with a prospect, and completed the initial screening process, you must make a decision. Is this person still someone you would like to present to the hiring authority? If so, they may now be considered a candidate. If the candidate themselves is not interested, then you track their lack of interest as such in your applicant flow log, or in your ATS. This is referred to as a candidate disposition of "no interest". Someone you spoke with, but decided was not a fit for this particular role, must still be tracked as a candidate, with a note made as to why they did not match the qualifications. In this case the candidate disposition in an applicant flow log would be "not qualified" accompanied by a brief note regarding which minimum requirement was not met.

Smart recruiters treat individuals who never make it past the suspect phase as resources even if they do not become candidates, keeping them in their network so they can produce referrals or be re-approached once their situation changes or the timing is right. Converting suspects into applicants is a resource-intensive task. Leads must be first identified by an expert researcher and then pursued by a knowledgeable recruiter who persistently follows up with several time consuming attempts to contact, one of which leads to an initial recruitment conversation. Of course, the candidate must also invest plenty of their own time in calls, interviews, and the application process.

4. Applicant

A candidate who has completed all the requisite employment application activities as defined by the company's standard practices, or one who meets the EEOC's standard definition of an applicant.

Prospective employees may apply directly, without an initial approach by a recruiter, and proceed in the manner standard to the company. Whether this avenue begins in an online process or a walk-in application, these individuals take the full initiative themselves, thus entering immediately into the Applicant stage. They are **active candidates** who eagerly apply for opportunities regardless of whether the time or fit is right. **Passive candidates** then are really no more than applicants who must be approached directly and actively recruited for the right opportunity at the right time.

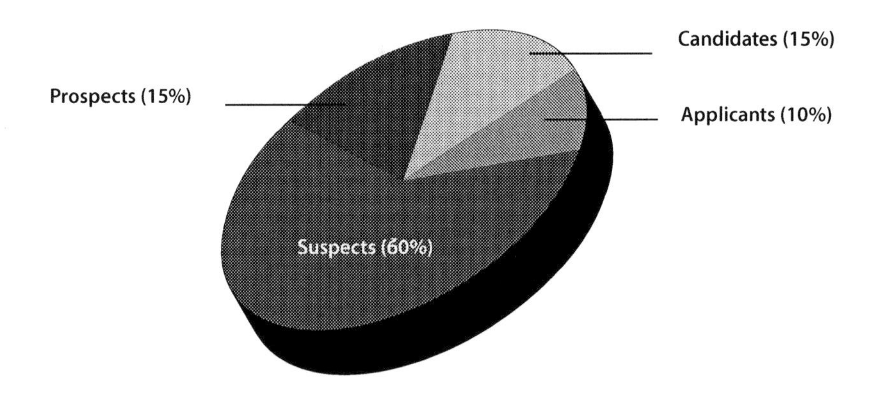

Figure 1 Suspects, Prospects, Candidates, Applicants

Top talent may come from any piece of this pie, but the largest population of untapped high quality talent can be found at the point where a modicum of effort is required on behalf of the recruiting organization. There is an area awash with ambiguity where candidates take varying degrees of initiative depending on their perception of the opportunity or prospective employer, but it is precisely because of that ambiguity that this middle area is where the largest return on investment of recruitment activities can be found.

Section 2. The Talent Pool Equation

The Economics of the Talent Equation

Some companies are looking at the job market of the future, and adapting their recruiting strategies to match market conditions. This activity generally involves turning to other sources for talent and applying more money to the problem. As a solution, this approach does not address root weaknesses in traditional recruiting strategies that still cause good candidates to fall through the cracks. Money spent on bringing candidates to the door is still lost if no candidate is hired. At the crux of the problem with most recruiting models is the fact that the right candidates do not apply to new jobs because their excellent work is already recognized and rewarded by their current employer. Forward-thinking companies are modifying their hiring and recruiting processes and broadening their reach beyond traditional methods to find candidates to which other employers are not talking. The following illustration depicts a simple formula for reaching the largest pools of talent.

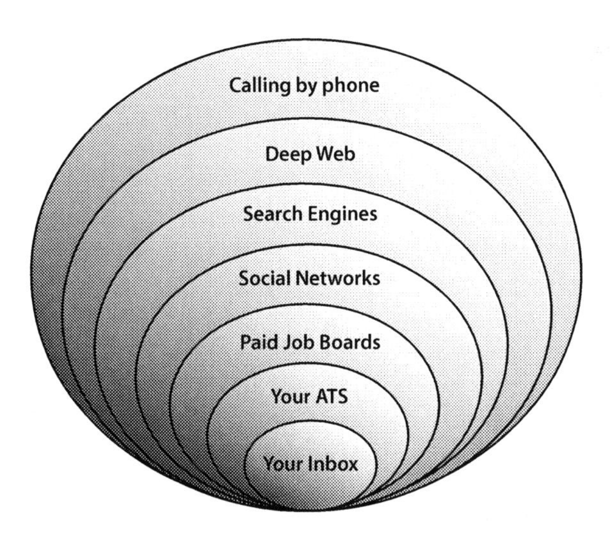

Figure 2 Time + Effort = Talent Pool Size

Defining the Talent Pool

It is important for an organization to define their talent landscape and identify the critical points where recruitment should focus. In the following diagram, follow the straight line from the bottom left corner to the top right corner. This line represents the fictitious **perfect talent landscape**, where the size of the talent pool available to an organization increases proportionately with the amount of time, effort and money put into recruitment.

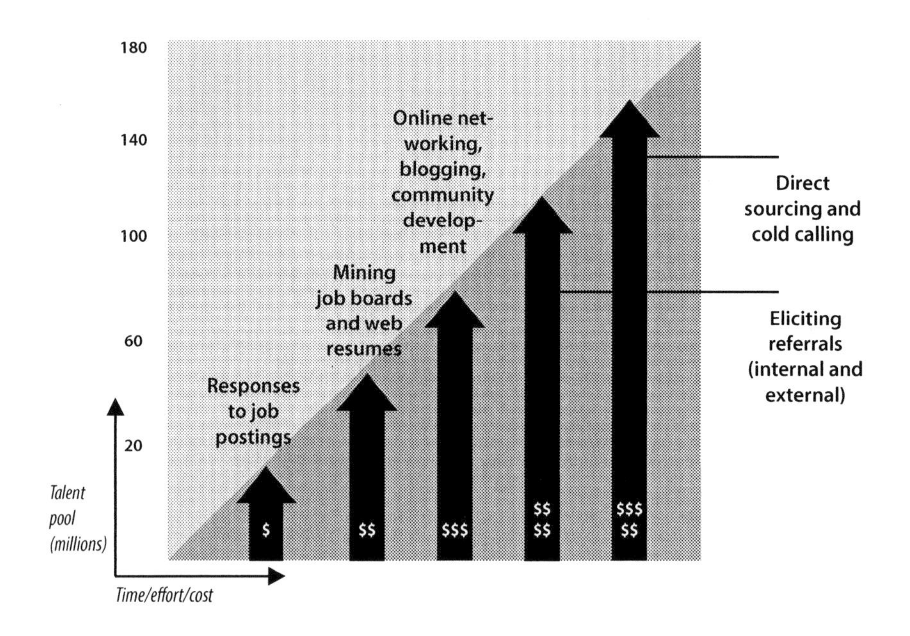

Figure 3 US Talent Pool Reach

Moving from left to right along the X-axis represents an increase in the amount of time, effort or money required to recruit talent. Increased cost is due to the diminishing amount of initiative prospective candidates will take when shopping for jobs, making the organization intent on hiring that kind of talent invest more in identifying, contacting, and recruiting. The diminishing initiative in turn can be due to many environmental factors: The difficulty of locating and contacting those types of candidates, particularly diversity candidates, geographic or relocation issues, and competitors who recently increased demand for similar talent.

At the far right of the X-axis, in the deepest part of the candidate pool, candidates are almost completely unwilling to participate, at least initially, in typical applicant activities like completing forms. In fact, they are, for all intents and purposes, uninterested in exploring opportunities. These candidates are the most difficult, expensive and time-consuming to engage, yet recruitment efforts here frequently yield the highest ROI.

As in Figure 3, the next graph shows a pool of available candidates that grows vertically along the Y-axis, with the largest talent pool at the top. Some talent pools are much smaller than others, a fact that is represented in the A and B example curves, which terminate on the right-most end of the graph without ever reaching the top.

In actuality, there is no real linear relationship between the talent pool and the amount of resources required to tap into the pool. Talent landscapes are represented by various curves that depict aspects of this wide and varied relationship. These curves portray the return on investment realized from varying degrees of recruitment activity. Macroeconomic factors and demographics also play a big role in changing the shape of these ROI curves. Different segments of the working population produce different curves depending on experience level, education, location, and job function.

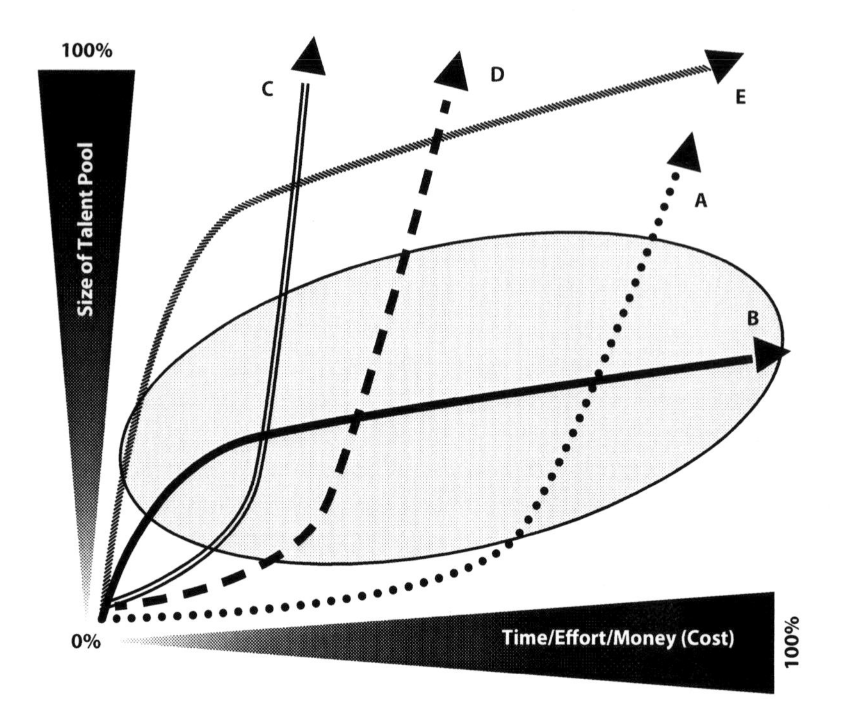

Figure 4 Ideal Zone for Size of Talent Pool vs. ROI

As a result, some job functions will map differently at different times, so care must be taken to re-evaluate the talent landscape regularly and adjust strategies as appropriate. With that in mind, here are a few example curves and explanations of what they represent:

Curve A

This is a typical profile for recruiting highly specialized technical talent like engineers, programmers, auditors and consultants. In these industries or job functions, it is imperative to initiate communications with suspects. This is the costliest talent pool to expand, but the size of the talent pool will increase after investment, and so long as the potential talent pool continues to increase, organizations should correspondingly invest additional resources and time. This curve also demonstrates a smaller maximum talent pool population than the others though not as small as that of Curve B.

Curve B

This curve can represent many of the highly skilled professional fields like doctors, lawyers, researchers and scientists as well as other employment wings in which career changes happen less frequently as with upper management and leadership. Curve B is a very limited talent pool because most candidates seldom take the initiative to seek out opportunities unless a recruiter first contacts them. Moreover, candidates in this pool usually know exactly where to go when they do decide to make an employment change, resulting in an initial spike in the size of the talent pool correlating to little investment. However, following the curve, it quickly becomes apparent that large increases in time and effort lead to small increases in the size of the talent pool. Tapping into a larger talent pool quickly becomes very costly in this curve. The best return on investment for this example is at about the point where the size of the talent pool no longer accelerates as quickly as it had done initially.

Curve C

This curve depicts many blue-collar talent landscapes and even some business or office jobs. A moderate initial investment, like that of standard job advertising for example, dramatically increases the talent pool. A little more investment like targeted or niche job advertisements, social media, or recruitment marketing and PR campaigns will quickly increase the talent pool available, so in this example, it is appropriate to invest as much as the curve allows to obtain the largest possible talent pool.

Curve D

This curve exemplifies a different subset of the blue-collar professions, including more of the skilled or technical job functions like nurses, skilled technicians and operators, or specialized mechanics. These fields require a mid to high-level of investment, but once reputations and relationships are well established, the talent pool quickly broadens through referrals and word of mouth. The best return on investment here is right after the end of the curve as it moves up. This point occurs when word of mouth picks up momentum, and quicker increases in the size of the talent pool are realized without significant increases in invested time or effort.

Curve E

One of the examples that this curve represents is university recruiting. Regardless of the kind of degree, organizations hiring large numbers of graduates and post-graduates right out of college find that, with a small-to-moderate and fairly consistent investment, they can forge relationships with select educational institutions and recruit many top students from each graduating class. Small increases in time, effort, or funds invested will quickly broaden the talent pool. However, recruiters must increase their investments to secure graduates who are the "cream of the crop" from the most competitive institutions.

Another example that fits this curve profile occurs when a large, highly branded "employer of choice" recruits mid-level professionals for its corporate headquarters. When a city's most reputable employer takes some initiative to recruit for job functions like Corporate Finance, Accounting, Marketing, HR, PR, Legal, Sales, or any other corporate HQ kind of role, professionals in the city take note, and word spreads fast. A small-to-moderate investment of time and effort opens the floodgates, and people who normally do not apply for jobs will apply directly and complete the application process.

> ***Bottom Line:*** *Obtaining access to the largest talent pools simply does not scale. Blindly driving to maximize talent pools at any cost for every single role is time consuming, expensive and ineffective. Efficient recruitment efforts focus on the most productive parts of these curves where cost and size of talent pool are balanced.*

Increased Demand Meets Decreased Supply

Recruiting challenges have already taught growing companies that they must evolve in order to survive. They understand the need to be proactive about seeking and attracting top talent, and are arriving at the conclusion that centralized Sourcing is one of the best ways to bridge the gap. Modern technology enables forward-thinking organizations to automate the gathering and processing of information about potential hires.

The Recruitment Funnel

One of the most commonly used metaphors to describe how organizations filter applicants is a funnel. With a wide mouth at the top that allows volumes of people into the screening process, the idea is that the selection of candidates shrinks as recruiters move down the funnel until the very best candidate falls out of the narrow end and becomes an employee. While this is a useful metaphor when dealing with near infinite numbers of applicants, it is absolutely useless for a model where there is a limited talent pool. There is simply no way that the funnel can be infinitely and repeatedly filled from the top each time a new requisition is opened. Even if that were possible, after a few attempts most of the available candidates will have been through the funnel once before and will be unsympathetic to organizations who ask them to go through it time-after-time.

A modern recruitment process operates more like a renewable hopper than a funnel. In this metaphor, people are brought into the process or come in on their own at different stages of the recruitment life cycle, but they can just as easily be moved around, put on hold, or brought back into the process again at a later date, adjusting for both their needs and those of the employer.

> ***Recommended Practice:*** *To achieve the delicate balance between retaining the interest of prospective talent yet not setting unrealistically high expectations, organization must begin by empowering recruitment to be connected at all levels of the company.*

The hopper represented above is a pipeline of candidates, which is constantly filled with suspects. As new suspects are identified, they are evaluated to see if they show potential and if they do, contact is initiated. If they are interested, then a new candidate is fed into the application process. If they are not interested, additional suspects may be solicited from that individual, or the suspect is simply put on hold, kept warm, and brought back in at a later time. Suspect and prospect data is kept separate from candidate data so that they can be treated more like leads and not tied to a specific requisition until both the timing and the opportunity are a fit. Another form of building a talent pipeline is where Sourcers conduct extensive competitive intelligence research and identify exactly where to go when talent is needed, but do not contact prospects until there is an immediate need. For more information on pipeline development, please see Chapter 6.

Many search firms and RPOs scrape only the big job boards (including LinkedIn™) and compete fiercely for the same candidates. Expert research teams will dig into the over 40,000 niche job boards and micro communities that serve the needs of specialized workers in a way the broad databases cannot, thereby finding talent that is not combed over by hundreds of recruiters or dazzled with multiple offers.

It is widely accepted that on average about half of experienced, external hires come from traditional sources such as employee referrals, the company's career website, and responses to job board advertisement. The percentages of hires from the other half of experienced, external hires break down as follows:

- 10 percent Direct Sourcing (increasing)
- 5 percent Print Ads (decreasing)
- 5 percent Re-hires
- 4 percent College hires
- 3 percent Agencies (decreasing)
- 3 percent Temp to Perm conversions
- 2 percent Career Fairs (decreasing)
- 1 percent Search Engines
- The remainder come from endless other sources including numerous variations of "I do not know" *Source: CareerXroads Annual Surveys*

Direct Sourcing makes up an average of 10 percent of experienced, external hires, and that number continues to grow at a rate of about 2-3 percent per year, and even faster among technical and specialized functions. Hires from company websites, print ads, agencies, career fairs and job boards have continuously declined for the last five years, and the trend is clear that they will become even less significant.

Finding talent and making connections with them directly is necessary for critical roles that would otherwise go unfilled. Yet, most estimate that about 20 percent of critical talent does not respond to marketing efforts. Sourcers working in a centralized research team can support a large group of recruiters, and fill the talent pipeline with the absent 20 percent of talent who are otherwise unreachable. Leads uncovered via Sourcing often come not in the form of a resume but rather just a name, title, company and phone number or email address. While the research team focuses on pipeline building, the recruiter focuses on working that pipeline into hires and addressing the 80 percent found through established hiring channels.

Section 3. Steps in the Staffing Lifecycle

What follows is a general guideline designed to give you an overview of all the steps involved in filling a position.

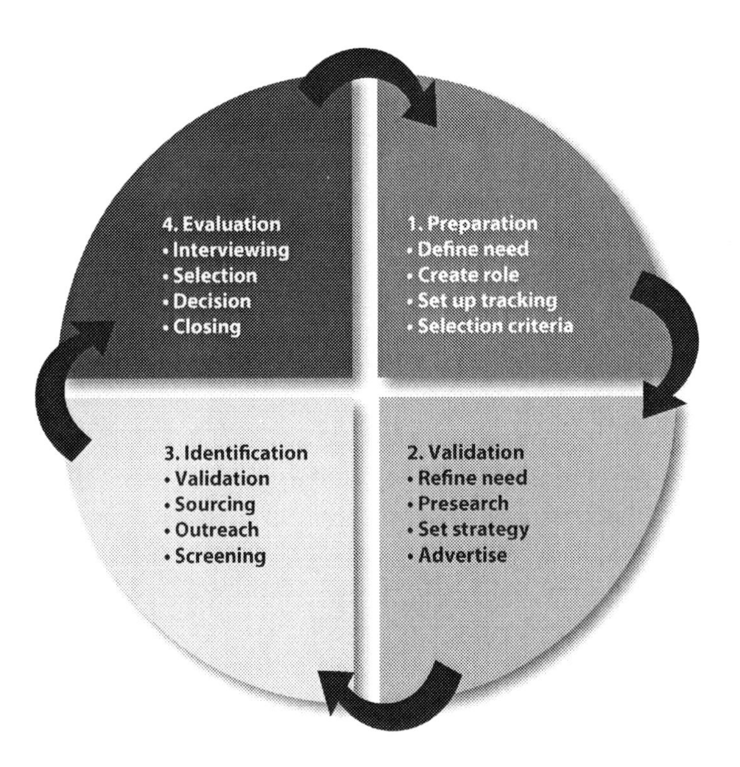

Figure 5 Staffing Lifecycle

Preparation: Define the Need and Create a New Role

The hiring authority collaborates with the HR organization to determine the need for a new hire, examine internal equity, define the role and job title, and arrive at an appropriate compensation band or level for this new hire. Note that if this position is frequently replicated or was recently vacated, the process begins with the next step.

Tracking and Compliance

Four organizations enforce the Uniform Guidelines on Employee Selection Procedures (UGESP), which require employers to solicit race, gender, and ethnicity data from applicants. These four agencies are:

- Equal Employment Opportunities Commission (EEOC)
- Department of Labor (DoL)
- Department of Justice (DoJ)
- Office of Personnel Management (OPM)

In addition to the above four agencies, employers holding Federal contracts in excess of $10,000 are subject to the jurisdiction of the Office of Federal Contract Compliance Programs (OFCCP). If your organization is a government contractor or subcontractor, the regulations implementing the civil rights requirements enforced by OFCCP apply to your entire company, even parts of the business that have no contact with the Federal Government.

While logging and tracking the ethnicity, gender and veteran background of each candidate is completely voluntary, it is a recommended practice that you keep an Applicant Flow Log chronologically listing applicant records. Include the name of the applicant, date of application, their race/ethnicity, national origin and gender as well as the job title they applied for, the source of the referral, if they were interviewed or not, and the disposition (action taken). Even if you believe this does not apply to your organization, you may be asked to present these records as part of a compliance investigation so it is best to be prepared ahead of time. As an additional resource, review the example Affirmative Action Program provided by the Department of Labor at www.dol.gov/ofccp/regs/compliance/pdf/sampleaap.pdf

Internet Applicant Final Rule

Electronic Applicant Tracking Systems characteristically include features that automate compliance with these regulations, but the ATS only tracks incoming applicants that end up in your internal database, not ones resulting from new proactive Sourcing or outreach. The OFCCP has published a final ruling on what they consider to be an Internet Applicant and address the recordkeeping required by Federal contractors and subcontractors at www.dol.gov/ofccp/regs/compliance/faqs/iappfaqs.htm.

Quick Tip! *Contractors need to maintain only those search criteria that produce job seekers to be considered further in the selection process, and they do not need to maintain records of futile search criteria.*

This ruling states that you must retain a record of all expressions of interest for candidates you considered, even if they are not entered as applicants into your systems. It affects searches of external databases such as Monster® and LinkedIn™ and requires that you maintain copies of resumes meeting the basic qualifications of the specific position for which you considered them. It also requires that you keep a record of all of the basic qualifications used to develop your applicant pool.

Recommended Practice! *Although companies with less than 150 employees must only retain applicant records for one year, it is recommended that you keep the data for two years.*

When it comes to external searches, you are only required to maintain information associated with the search itself. In other words, you do not need to track every Web page resulting from a search. It also means you do not need to track all the bios, profiles or resumes you read but did not consider because they lacked minimum qualifications. On the other hand, if you downloaded the resume, it is now part of your internal database, and you do need to track it.

Due to this last requirement, you would be wise not to download massive numbers of resumes from job boards and social networks. Instead, consider reviewing the resumes online, and only downloading the ones that match qualifications and will definitely be considered. This approach should result in a more manageable number of resumes in your internal database. Or, instead of downloading resumes, you could contact the individuals directly via email, phone or social media outreach, and invite them to apply for the position. Refer to the Appendix for a practical example of a Sourcing Tracking spreadsheet.

☞ *CROSS REFERENCE BOOKMARK: REFER TO CHAPTER 15, HABIT #1*

Nota Bene: If you think using an external recruiting firm relieves you of recordkeeping obligations, think again. As the employer, your organization is held accountable if your search partner does not maintain adequate records.

Quick Chart! EEO Codes Occupational Categories for the EEO

- Administrative Support Workers
- Craft Workers
- Laborers and Helpers
- Officials and Managers
- Operatives
- Professionals
- Technicians
- Sales
- Service Workers

EEO Race/Ethnicity Identification Codes

- American Indian or Alaska Native

- Asian
- Black or African American (Not of Hispanic Origin)
- Hispanic or Latino
- Native Hawaiian or Other Pacific Islander
- White (Not of Hispanic Origin)
- Persons of Two or More Races

SOURCE: EEOC GLOSSARY. Full descriptions can be found at www.eeoc.gov/federal/reports/fsp2011/appendix1.cfm.

Validation: Refine the Need

The hiring authority works with a representative of the recruitment department to fine tune details such as salary and other compensation, availability of relocation assistance, specific work requirements and responsibilities, and any applicable diversity inclusion needs or visa statuses that may apply. At this point, there should be a formally written Job Description or Position Summary, from which a Job Posting is created.

This is the best time for the recruiter to look closely at the requirements and help hiring authorities identify similar skills or synonyms that may return better search results.

Pre-Search and Recruitment Strategy

During the Intake Meeting you and the hiring authority discuss expectations and Sourcing strategies and review the Service Level agreement (SLA). Come prepared with preliminary research conducted on this requirement, and findings from similar positions you worked in the past. Introduce the hiring committee to whatever process, method, or model your company uses for fulfilling staffing needs. Getting this right is the most critical step of all, yet one frequently ignored and seldom standardized.

☞ ***CROSS REFERENCE BOOKMARK: SEE DETAILED SLA EXAMPLE IN APPENDIX ADVERTISE THE OPPORTUNITY***

Broadcast and market the opportunity early to have a better chance at garnering interest. While you proceed through the remainder of the steps, advertising should begin taking effect and give you an idea regarding how much Sourcing you will need to do in order to bolster the slate of candidates.

☞ ***CROSS REFERENCE BOOKMARK: REFER TO CHAPTER 10, SECTION 1***

Identification: Sourcing Commences

Sourcing begins with running a few broadly sweeping searches in your ATS, on job boards, through social networks and in the open web to identify the talent landscape.

> ***Recommended Practice:** A recommended practice is to send a sample resume or two for quick review by the hiring manager along with your intake meeting summary notes.*

Screening

Reviewing and ranking resumes of potential candidates is one of the key differentiators between a recruiter who just "processes paper" and one who adds significant value. Part of your role as partner in the hiring process is to reduce the amount of time hiring managers have to spend reviewing resumes.

Outreach

Utilizing every outreach method at your disposal ensures you reach enough candidates in a short period of time, further adding value to the hiring process. The fastest way to reach enough prospects is to 1) email them, 2) call those who do not reply, and 3) send social media messages or text/SMS to those who do not call back or reply via email.

Evaluation:

Interviewing

Neatly packaging and fluently presenting your candidates to hiring managers provides you with yet another way to become indispensable. Creating easy-to-digest summaries and a standardized presentation saves everyone time and effort throughout the remainder of the process. Assist your customer in reviewing the slate of candidates and deciding which should be invited to interview. External organizations can be of assistance in setting up appointments and making travel arrangements. It may also be prudent to inform the legal and relocation departments if you expect you may need their services.

Selection, Hire/No Hire Decision

Staying involved through the interview process ensures you will be in the best position possible to assist with the hiring decision were any snags to come up. If you have done your job well, the hiring manager or team will have an excellent choice of applicants from which to choose and have a tough time deciding which is the best. Guiding the hiring managers through your organization's hiring policy and relevant regulatory or compliance requirements protects both your work product, and your organization.

Closing the Opportunity

Some applicants are hired, but of course many are not. At the end of the recruitment process, great recruiters are involved with the offer process, bring closure to those who were not hired, wrap up any loose ends, and confirm all required records were kept.

Making the Offer

While some hiring managers may prefer to make the offer themselves, others may ask you to do it. If they are new to the role and want to make the offer themselves, provide assistance and support to them in avoiding counteroffers or falling for unusual negotiation tactics. Before you make an offer, even if it is just verbal and not in writing, en sure you are authorized by your employer to make the offer you are going to extend. Like other sections of this handbook, making offers is a topic that could fill its own book, but the following provides what is essential.

Wages are, of course, the main component of compensation, but starting pay is not the only piece that can be negotiated. Hiring bonuses, relocation benefits, first-year bonus guarantees, sign-on bonuses, and vacation days are among what is typically negotiated but there are other possibilities. For example, do they need time off to complete an advanced degree? What education or training is available to employees that may benefit their career? Maybe they want to learn a new skill, program or process and this opportunity grants them the ability to do that. Reinforce the value your organization brings to them as an employer and how they fit into the employer's big picture.

Offer Declined

The first step in closing out an opportunity is to ensure the offer is accepted by those selected. All parties involved in the process have invested a great deal of time at this stage so when made, offers are typically accepted. Look for your acceptance percentage to be about 90 percent and never allow it to drop below 80 percent. In other words, no more than 20 percent of your offers should ever be declined. More than that may indicate issues with the compensation range, interviewing and selection process, or even with the way offers are being made.

Offer Accepted

Even once an offer has been accepted, there remains a possibility someone could fail to begin work on his or her first day. For our purposes in this book, it is sufficient to acknowledge that there are circumstances where this risk may be acceptable, and many situations where it could be averted, but either way, the possibility remains. Therefore, it is a recommended practice that you leave the door open to future conversations with "silver medalist" or runner-up candidates.

Offer acceptance traditionally marks the end of a recruitments' involvement in the hiring process, with a few trailing items which may need to be finalized. For example, sending Thank You notes to others who interviewed but were not selected, letting them know of your continued interest in them in the future while also informing them that they are no longer in the running for this particular position. You may also be involved with requesting the processing of reference checks, background verifications, education and employment verification or other forms of investigation. At this point, you may interface with the onboarding function if there is one, or alternatively, simply hand the individual off to the relocation or legal departments for paperwork around contract, visas or other agreements. You may also need to notify security for identification and badging and IT for the creation of their user ID.

Of course, some of this activity may be happening simultaneously, just as it you should continue your Sourcing until the offer is formally accepted, in case things do not go well.

Provided on the following pages are two visual representations on all the steps involved. The first is an overview of the entire staffing process, the second provides additional detail including a breakdown of the task dependencies associated directly with candidate identification and Sourcing.

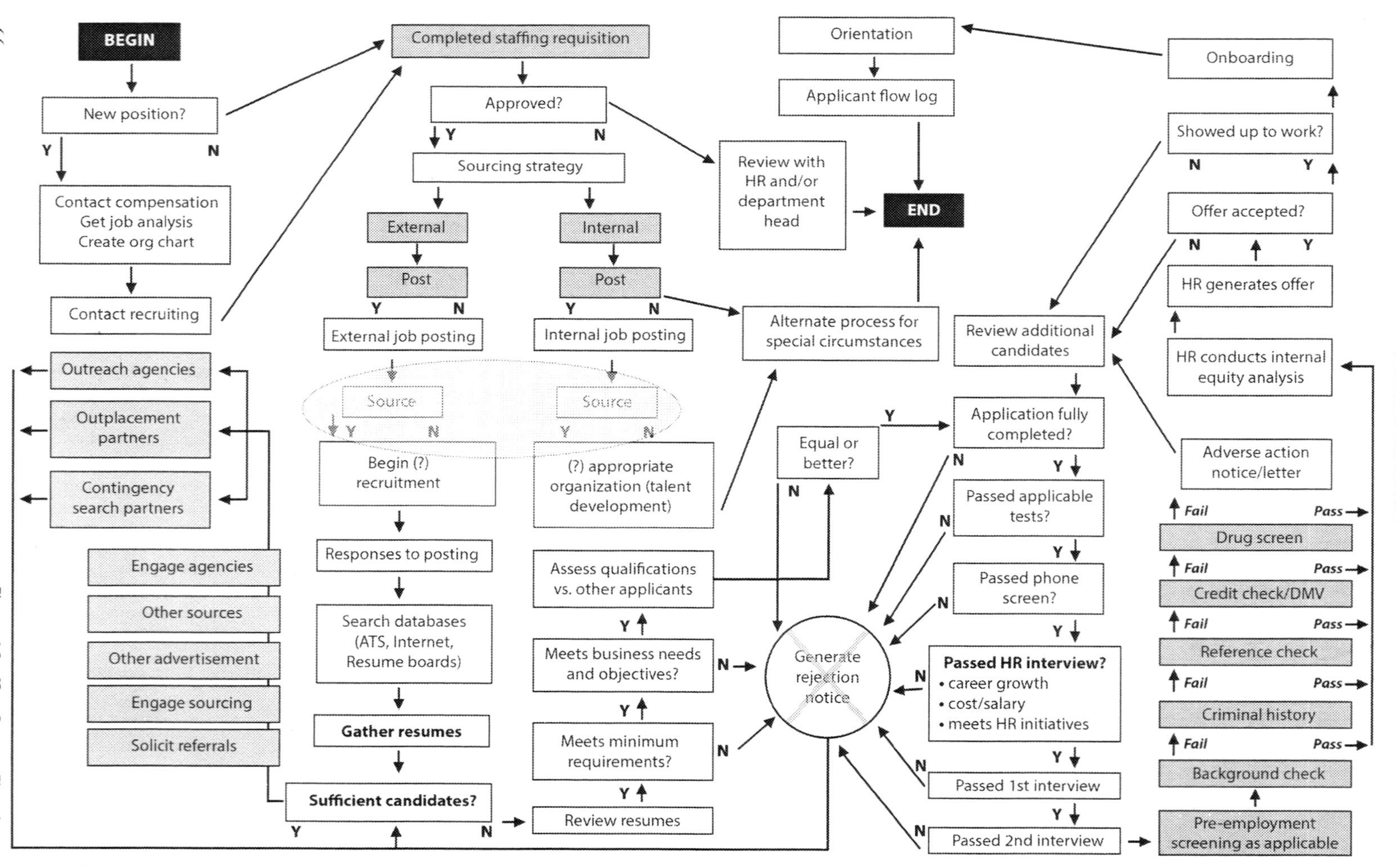

Figure 6 Staffing Process Flowchart

1. Preparation

- **Pre-search**
  - Evaluate and select sourcing methods to utilize
  - Identify initial set of keywords to test
- **Intake**
  - Select keywords to be discussed with hiring manager (HM)
  - Conduct Intake Meeting with hiring manager
- **Message**
  - Craft two emails to be used in email campaigns, one to active candidates the other to passive candidates
  - Create and run A/B variations of subject lines to use in each campaign

2. Validation

- **Verify**
  - Validate requirements after meeting with HM
  - Create and test initial search strings
  - Clarify or negotiate search terms with HM as needed
- **Summarize**
  - Prepare executive summary of intake meeting
  - Present to HM and obtain their commitment
- **Marketing**
  - Write and publish compelling job posting that is SEO and social media friendly
  - Create and run A/B variations of job posting headlines

3. Identification

- **Search**
  - Search initial resources, ATS, resume boards
  - Run search strings (or use Custom Search Engine) and include target company names, associations, job titles, social networks, etc.
  - Complete a Sourcing Tracking template or add to an existing one
- **Lead Generation**
  - Find about 250 leads using sourcing techniques
  - Identify 50 potential prospects from among those leads

4. Evaluation

- **Outreach**
  - Email all 50 top suspects/leads
  - Call those who don't reply
  - Use social media to reach those who don't return calls
  - Phone screen prospects
- **Selection**
  - Narrow the 50 choices down to 7
  - Develop full bios on selected finalists
  - Select the top 3 candidates among
- **Presentation**
  - Package the top three candidates
  - Present top 3 candidates to HM

Figure 7 Sourcing Task Dependencies and Timing

Section 4. Definition of Sourcing

What Is Sourcing...Exactly?

Sourcing is the specialized discipline of proactively identifying and engaging with talent not found via traditional means. Historically, Sourcing was the sole and inclusive responsibility of the recruiter along with other job responsibilities including:

- Screen and interview candidates against the position requirements
- Work closely with the hiring manager on hiring activities
- Help with the "offer letter" and interview

Now, recruiters are increasingly focused on account management responsibilities. In fact, practically speaking, a typical recruiter is bombarded with calls all day from vendors, busy in meetings with hiring managers, interacting with employees, and processing candidates. As a result, there is all too often very little time left to conduct primary research and initial candidate development or to specialize in these critical job responsibilities.

To ensure an adequate volume of potential candidates, the growing trend is for corporate recruiting departments to assign Sourcing activities to individuals dedicated to the function or to engage third-party recruitment agencies specializing in Sourcing. Sourcers remain focused on the search and development of leads just as recruiters must remain focused on maintaining communication with candidates in process, enforcing HR policies, attending meetings, negotiating, and handling the hiring from initial offer to onboarding. Indeed, specialization in recruitment is on the rise as evidenced by the number of corporate recruiting departments and agencies who are Outsourcing even these other non-Sourcing responsibilities to Recruitment Process Outsourcing (RPO) vendors.

What Do Sourcers Do?

Sourcing always includes identification, initial qualification or pre-screening, and may also extend to some form of initial outreach. The actual act of Sourcing for candidates is performed by either a recruiter, whether an internal corporate recruiter or agency recruiter, or a dedicated recruiter who is focused on the Sourcing function, the **candidate Sourcer** or just **Sourcer**. While sometimes involved in other aspects of talent attraction, Sourcers specialize in managing or identifying a prospective candidate pipeline of individuals who have not initially expressed an interest in the company.

To find job candidates, Sourcers spend more time on research activities like complex Internet searches, online and professional networking, organizational mapping, and cold calling than their recruiter counterparts. Candidate Sourcing activity typically ends once the name, job title, job function and contact information for the potential candidate is ascertained and finalized by the candidate Sourcer.

Sourcing for candidates proactively identifies people who are either **passive candidates**, those not actively looking for job opportunities, or **active candidates**, those who are actively searching for job opportunities. The status of being an active or passive candidate is fluid and changes depending on the circumstances, including the position offered. Despite debate within the staffing community exactly whom to include under each label, typically either term is irrelevant to a Sourcer as the status of any particular candidate can change from moment-to-moment or with the simple presentation of a job opportunity. **Active candidate Sourcing** refers to utilizing candidate databases, job boards and other depositories where the candidates themselves submit candidate information.

Pre-Screening Candidates

Sourcers are uniquely positioned to sell or "pre-close" candidates before the candidates enter the rest of the recruitment process, because Sourcers are also often the initial point of contact with candidates, qualifying whether candidates are real job seekers or just "job shoppers". They accomplish this task by initiating a dialogue with individuals on the candidate list with the intention of pre-screening them against the job requirements and gauging their interest level in hearing about new job opportunities. This activity is called **candidate profiling** or **candidate pre-screening**. Generally, several recruiters can rely on a single Sourcer to generate leads and fill all their pipelines with pre-screened or pre-qualified candidates.

☞ *CROSS REFERENCE BOOKMARK: FOR FURTHER DISCUSSION REFER TO CHAPTER 12, SECTION 7 INTERPRETING RESUMES*

Putting forward the best quality candidate has quite a bit to do with a good resume. Good resumes need not be as "pretty" as they need to be informative. What you present to your hiring authorities should contain everything they are expecting to see. In the section on working with hiring managers, there is an explanation of how a good resume, particularly one that is provided to the hiring team as a sample, is in actuality a very useful Sourcing tool because it allows you to "find more like this".

On occasion, you will not have the luxury of unique, rare or abstruse keywords to use in searches yet will still be tasked with finding resumes. In such situations, it is imperative that you are able to understand exemplary resumes in order to identify other ways of finding similarly skilled people.

This section addresses two essential questions. First, is the resume you found really a match to the requirements? And second, how do you find more like it?

Speed Reading

A great bulk of what Sourcers and recruiters do is to read and interpret resumes. If, like most people, you do not have an eidetic or photographic memory, being able to scan content quickly and without having to pause at each sentence or word will greatly accelerate your recruitment cycle time.

Scan First and Last Sentences

Scanning the first and last sentences of each segment of the resume will quickly give you an idea if you want to proceed with that individual as a prospect. One of the main sections of a resume, of course, is the Experience segment, though it may not explicitly be named as such. The first line of this segment typically includes important items like their most recent employer, job title and dates of employment. Read the line for their current or most recent job, and then skip to the oldest job listed on their resume which matches your requirements. The last section of a resume often is an abbreviated listing of skills.

Turn Headlines into Questions

Headlines on a resume entail section headers such as summary, experience and education and sub-section headers. Under the experience section, for example, subsection headlines are often job titles. Turn these headlines into questions such as "What is their summary?" or "What degree do they have?"

Scan Text for Answers

Each of the headlines-turned-question should have one primary answer within the body of the text. Scan the text only long enough to pick out that answer, then move to the next section.

Skim the Left Edge

Glancing quickly down the resume in a vertical direction, read just the first and second words of each line of text. By browsing the resume in that fashion, you may not understand much, but your brain will process enough information to start identifying patterns.

Fill in the Blanks

If you have not moved on to another resume at this point, now would be the time quickly scan the whole document top-to-bottom.

Speed reading provides another advantage, and that is the ability to synthesize all the information from the resume pages into a pithy summary paragraph you can include when introducing the candidate to the hiring authority. Putting that summary together with the information provided in the following segment will enable you to interpret resumes rapidly and more accurately judge if and how they fit the requirements.

Word Clouds: Keyword Frequency Visual Aid

Have you ever been on the receiving end of a hiring manager brusquely and repeatedly stating something like this?

"That's NOT what I am looking for; why can't you find what I asked for?"

If so then this segment is especially dedicated to you. When disconnects of this magnitude occur, word clouds are a measure worth applying to aid in resolving any disparity between your interpretation of the position and the hiring manager's description of it.

You may be surprised at how well this device works, even though at first, it may strike you as nothing more than a cute ornament, so hold your disbelief until you have applied it at least once in a real situation.

There are many Word Cloud websites out there, but one of the best is WordleTM as it is among the fastest and simplest to use for resume analysis. This self described toy generates a picture of words you provide (such as resume content), drawing with greater prominence, words that appear more frequently than others. At wordle.net, access the free word cloud generating tool by following the "Create your own" link immediately below the introduction paragraph.

The "bunch of text" you are to provide here is what you copy and paste from several resumes identified as matching the requirements. You could obtain exemplary resume directly from the hiring manager, or by referencing resumes previously considered by that interview panel, or by looking at previously filled requisitions in your system. Paste the text from all of the resumes into the box as one big run-on text. A larger amount of samples increases the accuracy of your results, so be sure to select five to ten resumes to provide as samples.

Wordle Data Confidentiality: *The information you paste into wordle.net never leaves your workstation. It is neither stored nor used by WordleTM in any way other than to construct a word cloud on your computer. Submitted data is destroyed as soon as you navigate away from the website, unless you save the image to the public gallery. In that case, only word counts are saved, from which it is impossible to reconstruct the original document(s).*

Figure 8 Wordle Example

The visual you obtain from this exercise will vividly display which words appear most frequently among the resumes provided. Those words are likely to be a broad departure from the "must have" keywords identified in the requirements, but are amazingly accurate representations of what the hiring manager wants to see on a resume. Write down the ten largest words and search a resume database or even on the open web for all of those words together. You will be astounded at the accuracy of results given a collection of seemingly unrelated words.

Push vs. Pull

Sourcing activities in recruiting can be categorized as either **push** or **pull**. Push activities occur when Sourcers reach out proactively to the target audience and include headhunting, HTML mailers, and referral follow-ups among others. In **pull activities**, the burden of reaching out to recruiters and employers rests on the applicants themselves; in other words, applicants come to know of an opportunity on their own. Pull activities include advertising in many forums: On a microsite (this technique makes search engines index the ad), in newspapers, on Radio or TV, in flyers/leaflets, or on job portals.

Proactive Sourcing: *Using major search engines and other websites to identify potential candidates who might meet the criteria of the position to be filled based on targeted keywords. This approach includes searching for candidates in job board resume databases using keywords related to the position requirements, networking with others to uncover candidates including the use of social networking tools and sites such as LinkedIn, and "Phone Sourcing" or cold calling into companies to identify individuals who match the key requirements.*

In summary, a push activity is akin to a direct marketing activity whereas pull activities are more like indirect marketing within the same concept. Ideally, both push and pull activities result in candidate attraction and using their interest to trigger a response (applying, referring, calling, sending an SMS, etc.). These action triggers are also sometimes referred to as **Call To Action (CTA)** steps. Calls to Action must be determined before any outreach commences so that Sourcers can anticipate the range of possible responses.

Reactive Sourcing: *Techniques such as reviewing candidates who have applied to positions through the corporate/agency website, processing employee referrals, and receiving candidates from external partners such as employment agencies, are generally not considered to be part of Sourcing.*

Examples of Sourcing

The actual act of Sourcing candidates is generally split out into two clearly defined categories based on the techniques used: Primary Sourcing and secondary Sourcing. There is a third category, diversity Sourcing, but this category is defined by purpose rather than technique.

Primary Sourcing AKA Phone Sourcing

In recruiting and Sourcing, **primary Sourcing** means the leveraging of tools, namely the phone, to identify the majority of the existing workforce who are not locatable. "Not locatable" means that potential candidates cannot be located or tracked on the Internet because they have not left digital footprints large enough to link them to a specific online location. Phone Sourcing should not be confused with the practice of finding information elsewhere such as via the Internet and then using the telephone for verification purposes (Does this person still work at the company? Has this person's title changed?) Instead, phone Sourcing refers to using the telephone as the preliminary means of discovering information.

Primary Sourcing uncovers candidate information by calling directly into organizations to obtain data on people, their roles, titles, and responsibilities. True phone Sourcing is practiced by a minority in the personnel Sourcing community and requires a mastery of verbal communication techniques. Just because someone can pick up the phone does not mean that person is qualified for phone Sourcing. The level of verbal communication skills needed here requires either years to develop or an extremely high degree of intuition. This skill is similar to the ethical telephone elicitation of information as described by the reputable Society of Competitive Intelligence Professionals (www.SCIP.org), and to the methods employed by investigative journalists. Like human hackers and social engineers, **telephone Sourcers** or **names Sourcers** generally rely on direct conversation in person or virtually as their means to obtain information.

Secondary Sourcing AKA Internet Sourcing

Secondary Sourcing is the utilization of techniques primarily revolving around Internet research and the use of advanced search operations to identify candidates or manipulate database search results. Internet Sourcing is a highly specialized field that takes time to master. Sourcers develop deep expertise in uncovering talent from the harder-to-reach places on the Internet such as forums, blogs, alumni groups, conference attendee lists, personal home pages, social networks, or anywhere else candidates may have an online presence. Many of the best Sourcers started as recruiters who found they enjoy the "thrill of the hunt" more than the rest of the process and became successful because of their heightened research skills and abilities that border on hacking. Another common origin for strong Sourcers is from professions where research or investigative skills are an imperative: Journalism, library science, fact checking, and academic research.

Diversity Sourcing

Some recruiters specialize in Sourcing candidates for inclusionary purposes, to broaden the diversity of the candidate pool. This could be a proactive initiative, such as a company seeking to better represent their customer base among their staff, or it could be a response to governmental regulation such as audits, fines, or mandates. Either way, intentionally increasing the diversity of candidates by generating interest from a population segment not typically attracted to the organization is a formidable task. Identifying talent based on gender, race or other protected status can be very difficult, and when not carefully done, could also have compliance ramifications. For all of these reasons, diversity Sourcing has become a specialty. Methods include searching for specific keywords found on resumes, Sourcing from affinity groups and researching distinct communities.

Section 5. The Sourcing Value Proposition

The Criminal Defense Lawyer Analogy

Imagine you have been charged with murder and are facing impending trial. You need to hire an attorney and have two choices: A general practice attorney who has successfully defended one murder defendant with a $200/hour rate and a criminal defense attorney who has defended 9 murder defendants successfully and unsuccessfully with a $400/hour rate. Further, each attorney has excellent online reviews. It may be tempting to choose the general practice attorney because of cost concerns, but is that the most financially prudent choice? And which attorney will provide your best defense?

Most likely, the general practice attorney has several areas of practice: Criminal, civil, business, immigration, and family law. Even if the attorney has provided excellent service to other clients, in order to defend you, this attorney must still spend several hours researching criminal procedure and case law to get educated and defend you properly. For the criminal defense attorney to defend you, she most likely does need to spend nearly as much time on research or knows exactly where to go to supplement their knowledge. Further, this attorney most likely has established relationships in the criminal courts that can expedite your matters. In the end, you will most likely pay less for the criminal defense attorney than the general practitioner because the criminal defense attorney has more relevant experience and a high degree of specialization. More importantly, your criminal defense attorney has a deeper, more varied experience that can enhance the quality of your defense and minimize the risk of critical errors in the process.

Where Does Sourcing Economic Value Lie?

In periods of economic contraction, many organizations undertake austerity measures to limit expenditures and preserve capital. Austerity policies often render exclusive Sourcing functions vulnerable to downsizing or elimination because they are often characterized as an amenity to big budget recruiting departments. Smaller firms that have limited budgets or a smaller company size may also share a similar perspective. Understanding the value of Sourcing requires an examination of two key factors: Cost savings and quality of results.

When organizations create in-house exclusive Sourcing functions, they do not have to incur the expense of Outsourcing the work to vendors that include a profit margin and operational costs in their invoices. This type of cost savings is direct. Additionally, internal Sourcing enables recruiters to streamline their activities, which should decrease the number of hours required in the recruiting department and fewer bodies in the unit, particularly for larger organizations. Similarly, when using the services of a third party agency devoted to Sourcing functions, organizations pay for the most efficacious masters of Internet research instead of the "jacks of all trades" found in ordinary recruiting agencies, which can provide savings similar to that described in the analogy above. When functions are assigned separately, the group operates with the efficiency and specialization as described by traditional economic models portraying divisions of labor.

A qualitative examination is important because of the economic truth that, in the real world, the cost of something is very different from its value. Dividing recruiting activities, including Sourcing, among multiple individuals allows them to specialize in those tasks. With increased specialization, their skill-sets improve while the time to complete a task diminishes, all of which results in more qualitative pop when they accomplish an objective. Freed from laborious research, recruiters can focus on maintaining communication with candidates in process, enforcing policies, attending hiring manager meetings, negotiating, and handling the hire from offer to on-boarding. Dedicated Sourcers have more time to utilize techniques such as search engines, new media, and social networks. Furthermore, dedicated Sourcers have the time to pursue lesser known, esoteric methods such as **Search Engine Optimization** or **Search Engine Marketing** (SEO & SEM) and deep web penetration to create a more comprehensive suspect list. Plus, pre-screening prospects winnows out non-serious job shoppers and spoon feeds recruiters or hiring managers with two important categories of individuals: Pre-screened passive candidates for the organization's talent pipeline and pre-closed candidates ready for the recruiter's engagement.

Five Hidden Benefits of Sourcing

There are less obvious benefits of Sourcing that affect cost savings and quality of results.

1. Economies of Scale

A Sourcer who produces leads for several recruiters requires only one license to databases, job boards, software, etc.

2. Viral Marketing

Many Sourcers are skilled at online networking, so this is one of the easiest and least expensive ways to build an employment brand using grassroots efforts.

3. Competitive Intelligence

Researchers generate information about competitors and "who's who" in the industry.

4. Barometer

Through their online presence and conversations with passive talent, Sourcers can assess a company's reputation among potential candidates in the marketplace as well as the reputation of the company's competitors.

5. Talent Community Assessment

Sourcers can collect information about the types and availability of talent communities, and create/maintain purpose-built ones for the organization.

General Data Sources

No one single Sourcer could cover the entire Internet. There are simply too many resources available. It is difficult to find someone who knows how and when to use every single Sourcing technique available to ensure they are covering all possible channels. Possible channels are divided into two types: 1) static channels that rely on just one person, the Sourcer, to obtain data, and 2) non-static channels that require contemporaneous human interaction.

☞ *CROSS REFERENCE BOOKMARK: REFER TO CHAPTER 3 STATIC*

Sourcing Channels

- Deep web research (direct Sourcing)
- Resume databases
- Resumes from search engines (Google, Bing, etc.)
- Traditional job postings and job board resumes
- Online social networks (LinkedIn™, Facebook, Twitter, Ning, etc.)
- Other social media (blogs and micro blogs)
- Online communities (mailing lists, user groups, forums)
- Specialized leads databases (Zoominfo, Jigsaw, etc.)
- Professional associations, conferences, and non-profit organizations
- University and corporate alumni organizations
- Diversity communities and affinity groups
- Resumes from a company's ATS and/or CRM
- Recruitment marketing (SEO/SEM, direct ads, mobile)

- Purchasing white papers, proprietary publications, and other independently created research
- Company press releases and news outlets
- Public information (SEC filings, non-profit tax filings)

Non-Static Sourcing Channels

- General networking
- Cultivating industry contacts
- Employee and non-employee referral solicitations and campaigns
- Professional networking events with industry peers and contacts

Section 6. Sourcing Introduction Final Words...Team Effort!

"It is amazing how much you can accomplish
when it doesn't matter who gets the credit."
– Abe Lincoln

Much ado is made about the differences between Sourcing and recruitment, and the distinction in value between the two. Such an argument is nothing but a distraction, since both roles have the same common objective: To serve the organization's need for hiring the best possible talent. In any job function with role

specialization there will always be a certain competitive tension between areas of responsibility. This is healthy so long as it leads to doing things better. When that conversation derails the ultimate goal, it becomes an impractical academic debate.

Sourcing and recruitment are a team sport and relay race. For the purposes of this book, I define the Sourcer as the researcher who builds a pipeline of ready candidates and the recruiter as the closer who works that pipeline into hires. Some Sourcers are perfectly comfortable in Candidate Development, making the initial contact via telephone "cold call" and/or email to pre-screen, while others may prefer to leave initial contact up to the recruiter. Where the line is drawn is something that needs to be worked out on an individual basis between the Sourcer and recruiter, or at a team level, allowing team members each to play to their strengths. Organizational differences, the volume of leads needed, and the types of candidates being recruited may also have an impact on when the baton is passed from Sourcer to recruiter.

Chapter 2
Strategic Principles

For recruitment to evolve beyond a simple administrative function and make a contribution to leaderships' strategic goals, there are ten key initiatives that must be undertaken. While each of these activities illustrates separate components of the talent equation, they must all be considered together as a whole in order to align strategy with tactics and operations most effectively.

Section 1. Ten Key Initiatives

Senior leadership holds the organization's strategic vision. You need their support in order to implement key initiatives necessary to improve results. To get that support you must first present your initiatives in ways they will understand, then be able to effectively communicate which one are most likely to immediately address their strategic business goals, and how they will do so.

One major step in this direction is to relate your key initiatives in terms of outcomes rather than actions. The largest obstacle preventing you from effectively communicating your initiatives in ways senior leaders understand is an operational perspective. Because operations revolve around process, and processes are activities not outcomes, you must learn to translate your processes into outcomes. For example, candidate interviews are a process, being able to hire the ten sales people your company needs in order to meet their revenue projection is an outcome.

Communicating the business case for your recruitment initiatives begins with having the metrics necessary to gain credibility with leaders, but to maintain that credibility you must be able to show progress towards the desired outcomes. Time, money and risk are factors that lend themselves very well to presenting your progress in ways leadership will understand. What follow are some examples of how you could present your case using those three universal factors.

Time

Is hiring faster a primary business objective? Or perhaps it is closing more deals, or making more widgets?

1. Increasing Speed

Save time by specializing research into channels. Prequalify or "screen" those candidates who are serious job seekers from those who are merely "window shoppers".

2. Improving Branding

Increased online presence elevates your brand, grows your talent pool, and reduces time-wasting friction. Participate and engage with prospects on others' Facebook pages, LinkedIn™ Groups, Twitter accounts and blogs.

3. Raising Quality

Knowing where the good people are already working means spending less time finding them. Avoid mainstream sources and find qualified, experienced people directly from competing employers.

Risk

Is there pain caused by positions going unfilled? Is there a risk competitors may find out what you are doing tomorrow based on who you are recruiting today? Are there critical projects such as new product lines that your initiatives would be well suited to solve?

4. Gathering Intelligence

When necessary Sourcing can identify talent with secrecy and confidentiality. The Internet is replete with "word on the street" so another value added would be to gain industry buzz or competitive intelligence on where the talent pool is headed, the types and availability of talent communities, and "who's who" in the sector.

5. Increasing Engagement

Online communities allow members access to each other via email or other contact information. Make direct and reciprocal contact with specific individuals of interest instead of broadcasting your confidential hiring needs.

6. Pipelining Talent

Fill pipelines with pre-screened passive candidates. Sourcing is greatly about online networking, an easy and inexpensive way to build employment brand. Initiate and maintain contact with all viable candidates in both purpose-built talent communities and other already existing networks – engaging future prospects "just in time".

Money

Would saving money, or increased hires within existing budgetary constraints better serve strategic needs? Is there a push to increase sales, or acquire new customers, or operate more efficiently?

7. Reducing Cost

Online activity results in favorable organic ranking by search engines, driving traffic to your online presence therefore reducing advertising budget. Lowering the amount spent on staffing firms and job boards can be done by proactively and continuously soliciting referrals from online contacts.

Cost reduction is not only about reducing spending; it is also about getting more results from the same budget. Sourcing economies of scale plug the money sinkhole of unused resources.

What about measuring the cost not to hire? Take the productive output of an average day in this role then extrapolate that out to a full year's worth of productive days (approx. 260 working days / year), how much revenue is lost due to this role's vacancy?

8. Reaching New Channels

Through search engines you can access the deep web, social networks and other Internet data and leverage the "friends of a friend" effect. Each online contact becomes a gateway to a broader community, this is known as the viral networking effect, and in turn it builds referral networks (i.e. LinkedIn™ connections, friends on Facebook, "followers" on Twitter).

9. Increasing Efficiency

Pre-closing candidates before they fully engage reduces time waste. Another reduction in cost can come from conducting the laborious task of finding qualified candidates ahead of demand so, when ready, recruiters can focus on maintaining communication with candidates. Use every source available to develop a database of future prospects, even if you do not contact them all.

10. Retaining Knowledge

Sourcers can be subject matter experts, and typically make good librarians. Enable them to share their knowledge and give them the power to coach others. Establish a center of excellence or knowledge repository so your organization retains the collective experiences of recruiters/Sourcers so you will not have to spend again to build the same resources in the future.

Section 2. Organizational Structure

Four distinct types of organizational models can be employed to respond to hiring needs. While not every recruitment effort requires all four, many utilize two or three of them simultaneously. Before diving into each of the four organizational models, it's important to separate out two principal distinctions based on volume and complexity of recruitment needs.

Four Distinct Sourcing Schemes

Vast distinction exists between low and high complexity recruitment, and low and high volume. Complex requirements are where the candidates sought must have particularly specialized or otherwise technical skills. Specializations are not limited to high-tech; they exist even in the mainstream corporate job functions. For example, in the accounting discipline, consider areas like Forensic Accounting and Audit. Within marketing, there are fields like Loyalty Rewards marketing. Requirements may also be complex because of the environment in which employees perform their duties. For example, many people can weld but not many can do so at the great depths required to maintain oceanic platforms. A third type of complexity arises from relative scarcity of talent due to severe geographical conditions, relocation or travel requirements. Volume is also relative and can be difficult due to location, plus it introduces complications associated with resource constraints, ramp up time and processing capacity.

1. High Complexity Low Volume

Approximately 25 percent of requirements necessitate this most intense type of requisition-based passive candidate Sourcing which typically consists of outbound engagement. The primary deliverable for this model is a slate of qualified and pre-screened candidates based on a specific requisition. Variations of this model could include medium complexity, medium volume or both. These are the types of requirements where Sourcing and research have the highest return on investment.

2. Low Complexity High Volume

These requisitions have a higher requirement for advertising and lower direct or passive candidate Sourcing needs. Engagement is primarily through inbound response. The principal deliverable expected from these models is a constant stream of active candidate and applicants.

High Volume Low Complexity	Low Volume High Complexity
Operational, some tactical	**Tactical**, some strategic
Requisitions with multiple openings, each or many openings with closely similar skill requirements	Hard-to-find skills
Extensive utilization of repetitive activities	Market research, industry knowledge
Pipeline building involves maintaining an active database of candidates and prospects	Pipeline building involving mapping out the talent landscape in order to be able to reach appropriate resources when needed
Coordinators assisting with logistics	Sourcers aiding in identification
Plans include: Job advertisement distribution Searching your ATS and paid resume databases Long term drip marketing efforts to attract pipeline Employee referrals	**Plans include:** Non-employee referrals Direct Sourcing via both primary and secondary Sourcers (phone & Internet) Dedicated cold calling for passive candidate development Industry networking resources

This volume-complexity spectrum contrasts widely differing methods of recruitment. Somewhere between the opposing sides of the scale are two others dissimilar enough to warrant their own mentions, but not discrete enough to be considered extremes.

3. Executive and Management

Though typically low in volume, and relatively straight forward, these types of requirements are more relationship intense, take longer to fill, and the strong emphasis is placed on fit rather than specialized skill. High level, passive candidate searches conducted through traditional channels such as advertising are less effective. This type of requirement typically requires exclusive outbound engagement. The deliverable is a fully vetted, interested and motivated candidate for a unique role that may not even have an associated requisition.

4. Mid Complexity High Volume

These requirements necessitate relatively less direct Sourcing of passive talent, but do require continuously building ongoing pipelines based on multi-incumbent profiles instead of individual requisitions. Outbound initiation of contact is less intense or extensive, and some inbound response is possible. The deliverable is a pipeline of qualified candidates by profile, and may or may not be requisition based. The pipeline consists of candidates who have been previously contacted. These are maintained as a sort of ad-hoc talent community of people potentially interested in the right opportunity at the right time.

Three Dysfunctional Operational Models

Within each distinct Sourcing scheme appear four operational models that are not mutually exclusive. Many recruitment organizations are host to two or more of these models in response to various pressures and environmental factors.

1. Reactive/Defensive

***AKA Inbox Recruiting:** Mainstream recruitment, inbound ad respondents, career portals, job boards, events, and employee referrals.*

The reactive model ("post and pray") consists primarily of outbound recruitment marketing with broadly automated job advertisement distribution resulting in a high volume of inbound candidate flow that must be managed. This model shifts most of the work of recruiting to candidates. Adequate for high volume hiring, this might work at times for skilled labor, but the more options a candidate has, the less likely they are to invest the time in such a process.

☞ *CROSS REFERENCE BOOKMARK: REFER TO CHAPTER 1, SECTION 1. CONVENTIONAL HIRING*

2. Reactive/Responsive

***AKA Advisor, Partner:** Specialized job ad distribution, viral marketing, contest, mobile apps/SMS; SEO, SEM, PPC (pay-per-click advertisements, also known as (pay for results"), contextual ads via Twitter, Facebook, LinkedIn™.*

For positions where conventional recruiting is insufficient, recruitment turns to Sourcing candidate resumes directly from the major job boards. In this way, recruiters gain access to a wider pool of talent.

☞ *CROSS REFERENCE BOOKMARK: REFER TO CHAPTER 1, SECTION 1. CONTEMPORARY HIRING*

3. Reactive/Anticipative

> ***AKA Agency:*** *Pipeline ahead of demand, business aligned high-grade corporate recruiters, consultative approach, and existing and purpose-build talent communities.*

For "hard-to-fill" roles that are high level yet of low criticality or unlikely to recur frequently, turning to agencies shifts the labor burden and increases the speed to hire. Time is critical in recruiting. Searching a database for qualified candidates can take hours each day. In this model a recruiter can view hundreds of resumes and find perhaps one or two candidates who qualify. This is a labor intensive process that lowers the yield per recruiter. The cost incurred in paying for more resumes, and then paying more people to read them, makes this model attractive to contingency based firms who can afford to specialize in niche areas and work with a wide spectrum of clients with similar hiring needs, thus maximizing their investment. When a good candidate in this quadrant decides to job hunt, there is only a short window to obtain their attention before they are considering other offers. So if a recruiter does not connect with the candidate when they're still looking, all effort is wasted.

An Optimized Operational Model: Proactive/Strategic

> ***AKA Sourcing:*** *Expert researchers and callers conducting lead generation and identification, non-employee referrals; ATS searches for silver medalists, offer declined candidates, re-hirable former employees.*

Strategic research/Sourcing consisting of industry experts with low requisition volume focused on building critical talent pools 20 percent of an organization's hires are critical, yet these are the jobs that remain unfilled the longest, cost the most to fill, and when they go unfilled, impede growth the most. Hiring organizations generally agree that to fill these jobs they must turn to passive talent.

☞ *CROSS REFERENCE BOOKMARK: REFER TO CHAPTER 1, SECTION 1.CUTTING EDGE RECRUITING*

Summary of the Four Operational Models

Three of the four distinct operational models discussed are in fact dysfunctional and reactive. The following diagram plots all four:

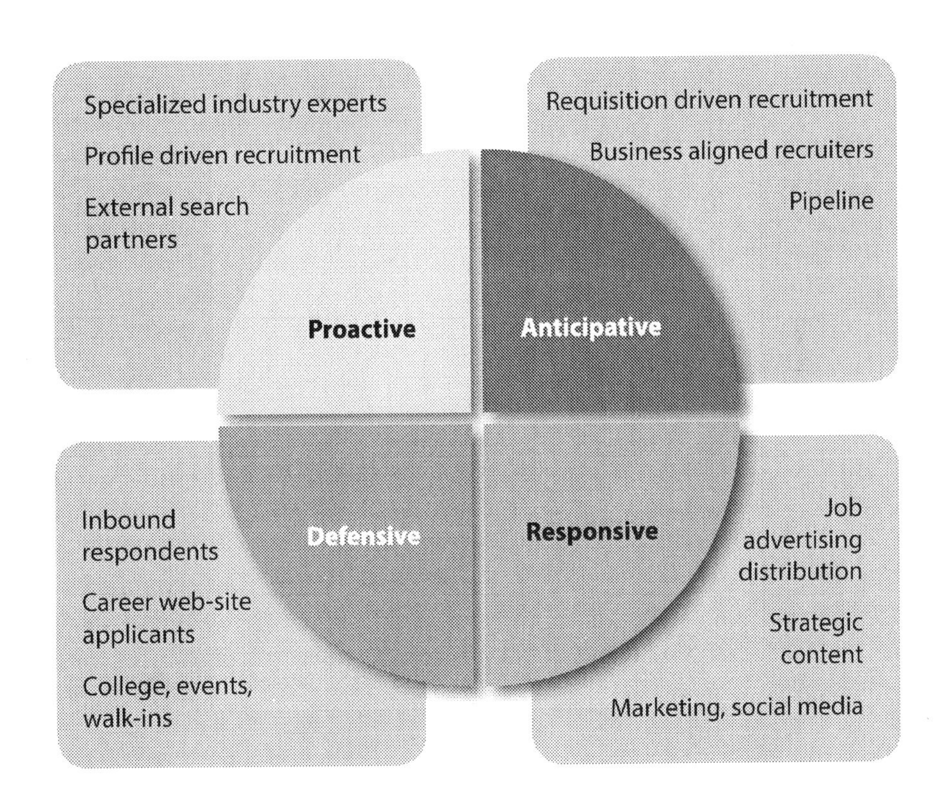

Figure 9 Operational Models

QUICK LIST! Examples of resources used in Strategic Recruitment Models:

- Social Networks: Blogs, Facebook, Twitter, Google+, Tumblr, Pinterest, Instagram, LiveJournal, Live Spaces, Xanga, Imeem, Beebo
- Professional Networks: LinkedIn, Ning, Plaxo, Xing, Viadeo, eCademy, Affinity Circles, Talent Circles, Select Minds, MyWorkster
- Job Advertising Distribution: SmashFly, JobTarget, Broadbean, eQuest

- Recruiting Exchanges: Dayak, Bounty Jobs, TalentHire, HotGigs, Work-Giant
- Leads Databases: Zoominfo, JigSaw (Data.com), Hoovers, Spoke, Swoop-Talent
- Search Engines: Search for alternate Job Titles, Company Names, Skills, Licenses, Degrees, Certifications, Locations and geographic criteria; Advanced search techniques using syntax such as intitle:, inurl:, site:, filetype:, linkdomain:, anchor: Etc.; Former employee and corporate alumni groups
- Deep Web Data Capture: Broadlook Suite, eGrabber, InfoGIST, DaXtra, TalentHook, SwoopTalent
- Social Media: Search engine optimization, pay-per-click ads, search marketing, social ads, contextual ads, Twitter ads, Facebook ads, LinkedIn ads, online discussion groups, forums, conferences and associations, wink.com, pipl.com
- Talent Communities: Skills-based sites, LinkedIn Groups, Facebook Pages or Ning Groups geared to your most challenging candidate skillsets

Section 3. Scalability

At the center of scalability lies specialization. Highly specialized, experienced recruiters who have become researchers conduct suspect identification or lead generation. Their passion is for the hunt, the identification of primary and secondary information that leads to pockets of talent previously unidentified. Researchers' single focus is to identify potential talent and obtain their contact details, information which is then fed into a Contact Relationship Management (CRM) application and could then be assigned to another highly specialized recruiter, a "cold caller" or "closer". These recruiters take the suspects or leads generated by researchers and evaluate them for specific roles, then initiate contact with those who are a fit. Callers specialize in generating interest. Akin to sales people, these recruiters are passionate about pitching the opportunity to prospects and engaging their interest. Callers may also work with other sources of prospects like employee referrals and leads generated through special projects or campaigns. When callers identify new prospects or suspects, they share that new information with researchers who in turn may use them to source additional leads for the callers, or to find updated contact information. Frequently callers will obtain pieces of information or competitive intelligence while on the phone with prospects that complement the work researchers are doing and enable them to penetrate deeper into untapped sources of talent.

In the event that during the phone conversation there is no interest from either the prospect or the caller, or the prospect is simply not a fit, callers then attempt to make the prospect into a resource from which they can obtain additional leads. They can also choose to make a note to revisit the prospect at a later day when situations have changed and there may be a fit. If a

prospect is interested and willing to go through the interview process, they are then presented to the hiring authority and the traditional evaluation process begins. At this point, they are typically defined to be an applicant in the hands of either HR or the hiring authority.

Because of this specialization, if hiring needs grow beyond the output capabilities of the researchers and callers, then additional resources can be brought in. Due to the sensitive nature of Sourcing research and competitive analysis, the ideal situation is one where researchers are full time employees. Callers may be full time staff, contracted labor or vendors. This allows for the flexibility of being able to bring on board enough callers to scale up recruitment efforts while the researchers simply increase their output. Since the pipeline, or the hopper, should be constantly filled in this model, the callers simply revisit any contacts which have been kept warm, and work the leads researchers generate.

One researcher should be able to keep from one-to-three callers busy. In models where the amount of labor needed to identify talent is initially much higher, the ratio could be one researcher per caller. In other models where obtaining a high volume of leads is a bit less labor intensive, the ratio could scale up to as many as five callers per researcher. For example, if a researcher can generate four leads per hour of Sourcing and spend six hours per day solely on the task of conducting research, that would result in 24 calls for a recruiter to make.

Leads that go through the process from suspect to prospect are phone screened by the callers, then sent to a principal recruiter or someone else serving as the employer's point of contact who then presents them to the business units' hiring managers and staffing leaders. Some candidates may arrive directly into the candidate stage because they are the "runner up" from a previous interview round, or they received an offer in the past but declined it and are now willing to consider opportunities again. Applicants may also

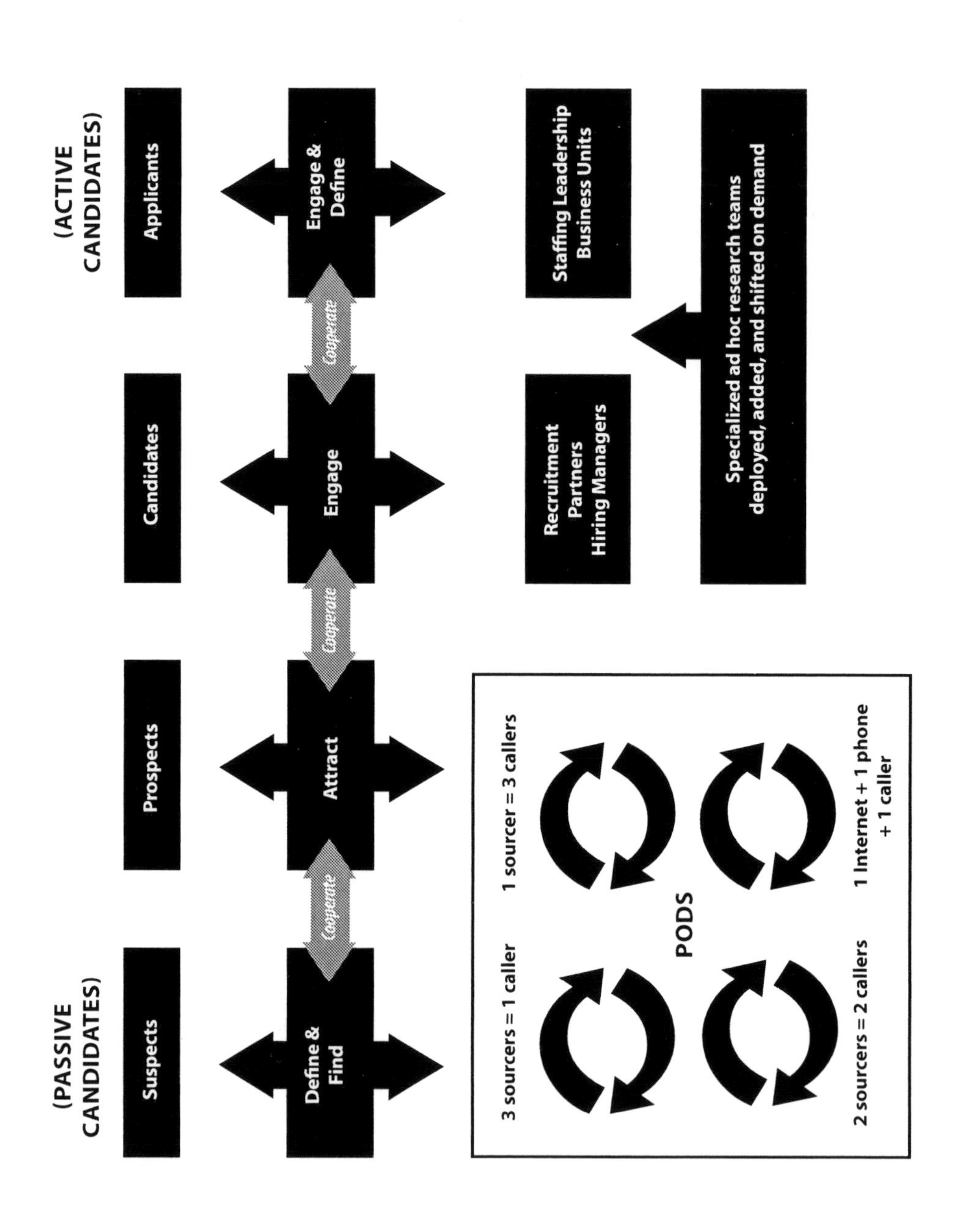

Figure 10 Sourcing Pods Structure Diagram

arrive in the process by applying directly through the company's standard process, but in this case they would typically go straight to business aligned recruiters, skirting the "suspect to prospect" dynamics of this model. Below is an example organizational structure for research pods, teams of ad-hoc, fully deployable, highly specialized recruitment researchers.

These Sourcing pods have proven to be the most successful Sourcing model implemented by organizations. This model is a combination of just-in-time batch processing and how small teams of specialized U.S. government intelligence analysts process massive volumes of collected information. A pod consists of three or more team members with highly specialized Sourcing skills supporting one major type of candidate recruitment such as a functional or technical expertise.

Experienced candidates in specialized functions are much more resourceful today than ever before. They seek to connect, not just be "talked at". Yet typically, only 15 percent of recruiters use blogs as a source of talent, despite the fact that they are among the largest sources of information online. The best researchers participate and source from blogs along with other sources competitors do not reach.

Specialized Activities

Research pods focus on engaging future prospects ahead of demand for roles that are much harder to fill and have a longer life cycle because those candidates are more difficult to reach and engage. Best practices and sophisticated Sourcing protocols are applied to identify and engage with rate talent. As part the process, Sourcers select from a vast array of tools and techniques as needed to satisfy each project requirements. These may include but are not limited to:

- Creating and nurturing a talent community through staying in touch with and continuously re-visiting viable candidates in the pipeline
- Mining resumes from search engines like Google and Bing
- Identifying experienced prospects directly from competitors and similar organizations using advanced deep web research techniques
- Tapping directly into professional associations, conferences, university and corporate alumni organizations, diversity communities and affinity groups, and other online communities like mailing lists, user groups and forums

- Using specialized leads databases such as Zoominfo, JigSaw (data.com) and dozens of others
- Deploying creative and unusual searches on job boards such as Monster and LinkedIn™ to identify people who are not typically found by recruiters
- Aggressively pursuing non-employee referrals through vigorous online networking and employment branding
- Developing search marketing tactics in the fast-changing space of search engine advertising, and social media, direct marketing and micro-advertisement platforms like Facebook and LinkedIn™
- Implementing search engine optimization methods to increases employment brand visibility by increasing the chances of jobs being found among organic (unpaid) search engine results
- Increasing speed to hire and decreasing process friction by centralizing and automating tasks such as posting and distributing jobs, downloading resumes, and processing or filtering information found on the Internet
- Staying abreast of evolving search techniques such as natural language search, semantic search, and peer regression search
- Rolling out purposely-built, skill- or job function- based sites, blogs, virtual private networks, LinkedIn™ Groups, Facebook Pages, Ning Groups and other talent communities geared uniquely towards the most challenging candidate skillsets to engage such talent in their natural habitat

Sourcer Job Description

A competent Sourcer possesses the following qualifications:

- Experience rapidly gathering difficult-to-find passive candidate and competitor company data
- Expert knowledge and proven track record tapping traditional and non-traditional online data sources such as Job boards, internal databases (ATS/CRM), employee referrals
- Expert knowledge of search engine syntax for at least three search engines
- Expert knowledge of social networking tools like LinkedIn™, Facebook, and Twitter

- Proficient at time management and organizing large quantities of information
- A strong sense of urgency, flexibility, and adaptability
- Proficient in primary and secondary intelligence gathering
- Command of search automation tools, RSS feeds and search engine alerts, rapid data entry or parsing tools, and desktop efficiency tools
- Proven track record of delivering sufficient, high-quality pipelines for multiple complex searches simultaneously
- Ability to read between the lines and decipher job descriptions, analyze complex, multi-faceted information and grasp new ideas
- Persuasive and effective email and phone communication skills

Quick Distinction! Role Differentiation

Sourcers (researchers) can save your organization money by providing your recruiters passive candidates who may never have applied directly through your company's website or online with one of your job posting partners. Because of a broader set of job responsibilities, not all recruiters are able to dedicate sufficient amounts of time during the workweek to the time consuming task of finding new candidates. Sourcing works for the early stage of the recruitment process, covering the outbound activity of finding leads and sometimes making initial contact, and therefore is a function separate from recruiting. The two primary reasons to separate Sourcing from recruiting are:

Mastery

Sourcing and Internet research is a highly specialized field that takes years to master. As previously noted, many of the best Sourcers started out as recruiters who found they enjoy the discovery aspect of research more than the rest of the process and became successful because of their heightened research skills and abilities. Sourcers are often the initial point of contact with a candidate. As a result, Sourcers are uniquely positioned to "pre-close" candidates before they enter the recruitment process in earnest.

Natural Habitat

By nature of the position, most recruiters do not have the time to conduct primary research and initial candidate development. A typical recruiter is bombarded with calls all day from hiring managers, candidates being considered, and employees. Those distractions can throw off an otherwise excellent Internet search. Sourcers must remain focused on the search and development of leads just as recruiters must remain focused on maintaining communication with candidates in process, enforcing HR policies, attending meetings, negotiating, and handling the hiring from initial offer to on-boarding.

Sourcer	Recruiter
Goal = Hire	Goal = Hire
Conducts research	Closes candidates
Special teams perspective	Coach perspective
Build pipeline	Turn pipeline into hires
Focus on skills and qualifications	Focus on responsibilities and job environment
Easily makes logical leaps	Manages expectations
Technologically savvy	Manages process and policy
Endlessly curious	Business savvy
Intuitive (read between the lines)	Customer Partner
Tenaciously, tenaciously persevering	Strategic hiring Partner, Coach
Effortlessly coachable	Insightful communicator and interviewer
Continuous learners	Gatekeeper, Evaluator, Match Maker
Natural Problem Solver	Diplomat, Negotiator, Closer

Section 4: Considering a Dedicated Sourcing Function

Five Questions to Ask

Best practices are nothing more than models for avoiding a collection of mistakes previously made in other models. What works for one organization does not necessarily work for another, even if it is considered a "best practice". There can be no single one-stop-shop solution for structuring a successful centralized Sourcing team, but a few key questions should be answered while in the design process. If your organization has decided to build an internal Sourcing team, here are some things to consider:

1. What metrics do you use to measure the team's success?

There are myriad ways to measure yet only a few experts who totally understand them. The best advice is not to forget to establish a baseline and track trends over time, not just take snapshots in "mid-air".

☞ *CROSS REFERENCE BOOKMARK: REFER TO CHAPTER 14, DETERMINING SUCCESS*

2. How does the team interact with the client?

Carefully. Not all of your customers are going to want multiple points of contact (recruiter, Sourcer, account manager, staffing manager, HR contacts, etc.), yet some will want to know who to go to for each function. Negotiate what is best for your customer group (business unit, branch, division), but include your hiring managers, business leaders, staffing leaders, and the recruiters in this discussion.

3. What service-level agreements are put in place between the recruiters and Sourcers?

The short answer is to keep it simple. The more complex answer is to provide a simple commitment that explains what is needed, what you guarantee to deliver if you are provided what is needed, and a promise that "if we deliver that, then this is what you promise to do in return" works best. If you need an attorney to decipher your SLA, then your customers will not know what to make of you.

☞ *CROSS REFERENCE BOOKMARK: REFER TO APPENDIX FOR SAMPLE SLA*

4. When do the Sourcers hand off the candidate?

When the candidate indicates. In some industries, candidates do not mind being approached by Sourcers, but in others they would prefer the first call to come from a hiring manager or even a business leader. Only you know your industry well enough to answer this question.

5. What is the major challenge centralized Sourcing will run into?

No discussion about a business topic would be complete without the requisite analysis of where things can go wrong. Sourcing has four weaknesses that commonly cause catastrophic failure, and not all of them are directly tied to recruitment. This reality can be a very complex sell in the organization. Common roadblocks are:

> **Short-sighted:** Expecting Sourcing to deliver a short-term solution to what is a long-term problem such as a broken interviewing, pre-boarding/onboarding or hiring process, dismal employment brand reputation, obstinate hiring managers intent on opposing change, and so on.
>
> Stopping and starting an internal Sourcing team each time hiring objectives move can result in fractured teams that do not collaborate.
>
> Finally, treating Sourcing like an entry-level position, which results in the Sourcers gaining experience then promptly moving on to a role where they are adequately rewarded for their specialization.
>
> **Disconnected:** Relying on recruiters to pick up the phone and follow through with sourced leads means the leads do not receive calls. This situation also happens when recruiters expect hiring managers to know what to do with passive candidates who have been aggressively recruited and still need more encouragement.
>
> Similarly, over-relying on email as the only initial outreach method results in the hands-thrown-up-in-the-air apathy of "I'm not getting responses". This is a problem easily solved by picking up the phone.

Abandoned: Inadequate contact management brings about chaos and often resentment among candidates, recruiters and hiring managers alike. Lack of follow up on future-interest candidates results in the pipeline drying up, the employment brand eroding, and candidates declining to interview for positions the "next time around".

Abandonment refers not just to the leads but also to the souring team itself. Not investing in the development and training of the Sourcing team leads to Sourcers leaving, or becoming obsolete and ineffective.

Marginalized: Burdening Sourcers with administrative duties normally delegated to a coordinator means they cannot fulfill their function of generating leads.

Combined with Sourcers receiving little or no feedback on candidates submitted, this creates a unilateral feedback system where only negative results are communicated, making it impossible to improve. Not allowing Sourcers adequate time with hiring managers to completely understand search criteria is another form of marginalization and one that results in losing more time later on in the process.

Obtaining Upper Management Buy-In

But how do you pay for all this?

Getting Funded

To separate the Sourcing specialty from that of recruiting you may need to make room in your budget. Here are some ideas you can use to make your case to your leadership when requesting funds for the creation of this function:

Cost-not-to-hire

Figure out the cost of open positions, or "cost-not-to-hire" which can be estimated by adding up the revenue lost each day those positions go unfilled. For example take the productive output of an average day in this role, and extrapolate that out to a full year's worth of productive days (approximately 260 working days per year). If a vacancy results from attrition, add to this figure the commonly accepted replacement cost of two times the annual salary of the vacated role.

Time, Money, Risk

Identify what motivates your business leadership, and make your case in that language. They could be motivated by a number of factors so paint your picture according to what is most important to them. For example:

- Is it reduction of cost? (money)
- It is reduction of time to fill? (time)
- Is it pain of positions going unfilled? (risk)
- Is it to increase the quality of hire?
- Is it secrecy or confidentiality?

Critical Projects

Are there any critical projects (e.g., a new product line) or situations that would cause your company to seek an entirely new kind of talent, which the organization has never worked with before?

Metrics

Other metrics that could have strong value when proving your case to management include:

- Reduction in overall cost per hire
- Improved performance evaluations
- Decreased time to perform (from recruited to hired and productive)
- Reduction in cost per source (job boards, purchased research, etc.)
- Increase in quality of hire as measured by lower turnover and higher internal promotion rates

Surviving

Change is inevitable, and corporate Sourcing teams are among the first to be demolished when it happens. To remain a going concern within the organization, the most important aspect to maintaining sustainability is to evangelize. That's it. Just TELL someone! Spread the gospel of Sourcing among the business leaders, executives, and influential stakeholders.

To begin, identify a couple of business champions who will help you spread the word on the good work you and your Sourcing team do. These individuals should be your champions who will defend your case in the event of a leadership change, or other major environmental changes.

Cultivate relationships with hiring managers - specially your repeat customers. They can be your number one advocates. If your leadership changes, make sure your hiring managers remember you and go to bat for you, or at least ask the new leadership to keep the Sourcing team going. Happy hiring managers have often volunteered to fund Sourcing projects from their budget.

Section 5. Managing the Sourcing Function

Sourcing is a growing industry, but Sourcing experts are increasingly difficult to find because they are so highly specialized. Once your organization is ready to utilize Sourcers, follow these tips to build a world-class recruiting and Sourcing team.

Understand the Difference: Sourcers and Recruiters

Recruiters lean more towards the traditional HR role, and they enjoy the people and process aspects. Experienced Sourcers, on the other hand, generally have a recruiting background but choose to specialize in the front-end candidate research aspect because they enjoy the "thrill of the hunt". These two positions have become differentiated enough that they now represent two completely divisible skill-sets. When you hire a recruiter to work as your Sourcer, take measures to ensure that they fit Internet Sourcing profiles. For example, the individual's experience should show a proven track record of successful candidate identification using extensive primary and secondary research. Furthermore, the individual should be able to explain in-depth the resources utilized in each campaign.

Respect This difference

Highly competent Sourcers will save you tens of thousands of dollars in placement fees that you would otherwise spend on external, traditional candidate search firms. This value that they bring deserves your respect. Avoid viewing Sourcers as junior recruiters, especially when the Sourcer may have as much traditional recruiting experience as many recruiters. In addition, expect that you will have to pay competitive compensation to these specialists; good Sourcers are in demand just much as good recruiters. If you decide to hire a Sourcer and label the opening an entry-level position, be prepared to invest significantly in training and mentoring. Otherwise, regard the Sourcer's position equal that of a recruiter with a similar amount of years of experience.

Use the Right Sourcer

Not all Sourcers are created equal. Depending on the volume of your hiring needs, consider hiring several Sourcers specializing in different channels. It is difficult to find someone who knows how and when to use every single Sourcing technique available to ensure they are covering all possible channels. After all, no single Sourcer could cover the entire Internet, much less all the other resources available.

Maximize Sourcing Talent

If you are investing in a Sourcer, then maximize the Sourcer's services. Sourcers are skilled in producing a high volume of leads in a short period of time, which is why a single Sourcer can support multiple recruiters. If your organization has the scale to support more than one Sourcer, then organize the Sourcers into teams where they can divide up different channels, helping to prevent duplication of labor.

Sourcer Performance

Like recruiters, Sourcers can be motivated or de-motivated by their business environment. Here is a representative sampling of the environmental factors that could enhance or inhibit the performance of your Sourcers:

Boost Performance

- Having autonomy in planning their workday, Sourcing plan and search strategy
- Given the encouragement to experiment constantly
- Granted access to some paid resources/databases
- Receiving acknowledgement for contributions

Inhibit Performance

- Insufficient feedback on leads submitted

Metrics and Keeping Sourcers Accountable

What ultimately matters in all recruiting efforts is that good candidates fill open requisitions. Because Sourcing is only half the recruiting process, it can be easy to lose track of the effectiveness of Sourcing efforts. Standard hiring metrics rarely capture Sourcing efforts because Sourcing work – Internet research and lead generation – is often not viewed as separate and apart from recruiters' work.

The following are some ideas to help you distinguish Sourcing contributions and keep your Sourcers accountable:

Know What They Are Doing

You may be hiring a Sourcer whose knowledge and tactics are much more advanced than your own, but it is important that you take their pulse frequently enough to understand the gist of what they do.

Use Research Forms

Tracking methods becomes much easier if you use a research form that creates a map of where your Sourcers have been and what they have accomplished. The research form also allows you and your Sourcers to identify which methods can be improved upon and repeated, and which ones have inefficiencies that can be eliminated the next time a similar position is open.

Measure Results

On the research form, there should be columns that contain some measure or qualitative assessment of each search method. One column could measure the total number of leads found, while the other column could measure the number of resulting qualified contacts. This simple process documents the methods' yields and compares quality to quantity. It also allows you as the manager to see where the ratios need improvement. For example, if you see that a specific method is yielding hundreds of leads but only a handful of qualified contacts, you could spend some time mentoring your Sourcer on that method or lead them to some specialized training.

Set Expectations

Clear and realistic expectations are important. Each type of search has different time investment requirements. For example, finding candidates with very specific technical keywords like J2EE or SAMBA on their resume may be quicker than identifying candidates with soft skills such as leadership or account management. If you know in advance that a type of search will take longer or have a lower "leads-to-candidates" ratio, you can appropriately manage the hiring manager's expectations.

Monitor Ongoing Searches

Generally if the Sourcer isn't conducting Candidate Development, they should be able to carry a workload of anywhere from 20 to 30 separate searches any given month. This number can be significantly increased if the searches are repetitive and simple in nature, but the opposite is also true if the searches are unique and highly specialized. For example, generating leads for thirty open medical technician positions a month is not the same as for thirty neurosurgeons.

Productivity can really only be measured if you have historical data. Over time, you should be able to see how well your Sourcers are doing based on how many positions they can effectively fill in comparison to other similar positions in the past. Once you have a baseline, you can adjust expectations based on the difficulty of the search. This benefit is another reason the research form is invaluable in setting expectations when it comes time to perform similar searches in the future.

Track Fill Rates

Sourcing is critical in assisting with hard-to-fill positions. However, a widespread reason these positions are hard to fill may correspond to volume. For example, generating enough leads to fill one hundred wireless telecom account manager positions in a mid-sized market like Seattle can present unique difficulties. Similarly, identifying prospects for a single super specialized position such as that of a long haul optical networking architect with experience in both Japan and South America also presents a unique set of difficulties. Therefore, measuring Sourcers' performance based solely on the total positions they fill is misguided unless you have metrics on filling those same positions over time. If you know how much time and money it took to find someone for that position last time, then you can measure those figures against your current Sourcer's efforts.

Section 6. RPO AKA Recruitment Process Outsourcing

When an organization needs assistance with filling open requisitions, they may turn to outside partners. Recruitment Process Outsourcing companies, RPOs, are sometimes utilized as external partners. BPO or Business Process Outsourcing providers may also offer some Recruitment Outsourcing services, and a few HRO or Human Resources Outsourcing organizations also provide such. MSP (Managed Services Provider) and VMS (Vendor Management Services) are onsite agents or systems that handle the recruitment of large volumes of people through centralizing the management of all external recruitment partners. Regardless of what it's called, Outsourcing is basically the delegation or transfer of responsibility for the daily management of a specified business process to an external provider. Anything from a single task to complex processes can be outsourced.

To be an RPO, an organization must be capable of Outsourcing if not all then at least most recruitment processes. Many staffing firms and other talent supply vendors have adopted the term RPO to describe a new kind of service that partially covers some of the tasks in the recruitment lifecycle. That kind of work is more akin to what Business Process Outsourcing offers, and they are not truly RPOs, replacing from one to several tasks but not an entire departmental function.

The decision to outsource should be made because it is the best decision for the business, not solely as a cost-cutting measure but also to maximize efficiencies or to compensate for a lack of internal resources and capabilities. Here are some common reasons RPOs are hired:

Why Utilize an RPO?

Save Time

Hire faster by removing rules-based administrative and repetitive tasks from your recruitment process. You can assign easy-to-follow tasks to your RPO or BPO vendor. For example: data entry, duplicate checking and removal, reference checking, resume formatting, responses to basic inquiries, high volume initial contact to prospects, and so on.

Save Money

Assign those tasks to a workforce that does it not only faster but also for less money. Why pay an experienced recruiter a decent salary for the time it takes to manually process some basic activities that require little experience? Pay your recruiter to do what they do best – recruit – and save money by having fewer recruiters who focus on critical activities with the support of Outsourcing vendors that manage trivial yet time-consuming tasks.

Improve Agility

Accelerating global competition drives a need for agility like never before. Your organization may be in a position where they simply must engage a flexible Outsourcing partner that can ebb and flow as growth spurts speed up and slowdown in your industry domestically and particularly as you expand to foreign markets. This organizational flexibility can be the key to survival in a fluctuating economy, particularly in industries suffering from radical or unpredictable trends.

Compliance

From Six Sigma to Sarbanes-Oxley and points in-between including the Equal Employment Opportunity Commission (EEOC) and the Office of Federal Contracts Compliance Programs (OFCCP), companies are being scrutinized to provide process transparency like never before. Outsourcing partners should excel in process and internal controls, and with a refined process be able to provide clear metrics, as well as evidence, that can substantially mitigate risk in the event of an audit from any of the regulatory bodies.

Maximize Recruiters

Let recruiters spend more time impacting the business and driving the hiring process, instead of slowing them down with repetitive, menial tasks that sap their focus and attention. A boost in performance will allow your organization to employ a smaller number of recruiters who are of a much higher caliber and capable of advanced project management, who will in turn yet again improve yield.

Your recruiters become experts and focus on what they do best, adding value during a much higher percentage of their productive work day.

Quick Guide! What Is Outsourced?

Some organizations choose to outsource only certain parts of the process. Here is a short list on the pieces that some companies have elected to outsource:

- High volume non-exempt positions, temporary or seasonal roles, administrative or manufacturing positions, and/or other hourly personnel hiring
- Recruitment marketing, advertising and branding
- Background checking, drug screening, reference checking, employment verification
- Interviewee travel, relocation and immigration
- Mining resume boards for resumes, direct Sourcing, lead generation, or interest generation
- Initial candidate contact and pre-screening, coordination and scheduling of interviews
- Data entry, data formatting and standardization
- Record processing, duplicate checking and removal, moving records

Section 7. Twelve Steps to Sourcing

Candidate Continuum

Imagine a straight line. On the left end of the line is the extreme passive candidate. On the right end of the line is the extreme active candidate. The line represents the amount of time and effort per week an individual spends on the initiative of searching for a new job. A truly passive candidate makes no such initiative and spends zero amount of time each week on their job search. They are not looking at job postings or Sunday classifieds, nor have they posted a resume or profile on a career database. However, if contacted about the right opportunity and in the right way they may be interested in pursuing it.

As one moves to the right of the continuum, there appear candidates who exercise more initiative. They are somewhat active in their job search. Maybe they post a resume confidentially to see what comes their way, or spend an hour or so looking at job postings while sitting at their desk over lunch hour.

They could also be checking with their trusted industry contacts to see if there are any appealing openings at other companies. At the far right are those job seekers with great initiative treating their job search as a job itself, spending a great deal of time finding employment opportunities.

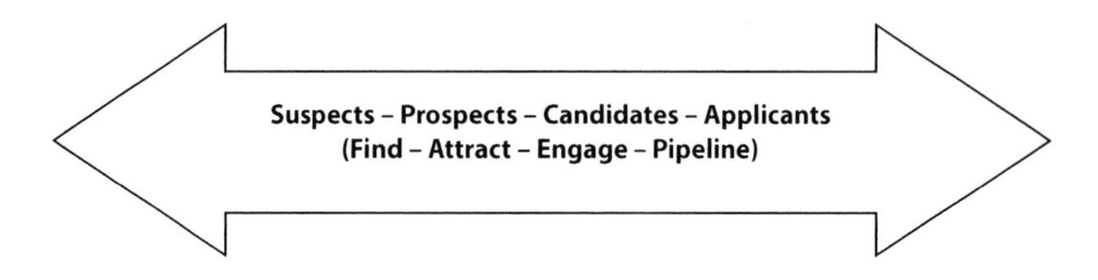

☞ *CROSS REFERENCE BOOKMARK: REFER TO FOUR TYPES OF JOB SEEKER IN CHAPTER 1*

The Twelve Steps

This twelve-step summary takes you through the process of conducting research. As you progress down the list, each step involves more time and effort than previous steps, so it is important to plan your approach, and of course, work your plan.

- ***Find: Source leads through primary & secondary research, via Internet and phone; referrals, lists***
- ***Attract: Convert marketing response, selection and assessment, pre-screen bios, resumes, CV's, etc.***
- ***Engage: Initiate outbound contact via phone, email or social media, obtain interest, pre-qualify***
- ***Pipeline: Add to continuous process, push to targeted recruiters, clients, hiring managers***
- ***Not interested now? keep warm, develop into resources, get referrals***

Figure 11 Sourcing Funnel

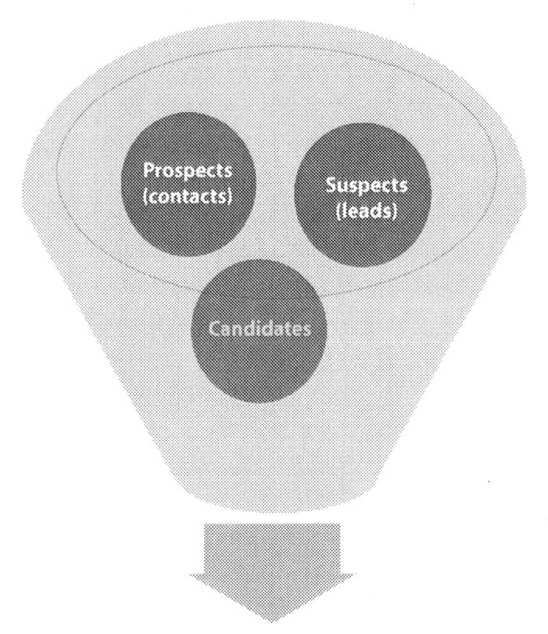

Applicants
Qualified and Interested

1. Gather your search keywords

This step is the most critical. Better keywords translate into better search results, while poor keywords will send you in all kinds of time wasting directions.

☞ *CROSS REFERENCE BOOKMARK: REFER TO CHAPTER 3, SECTION 1*

2. Broadcast the job

This step is when you do your advertising and job posting in as many places as appropriate. Because it takes time for people to read and respond, you want to start out with this first, so by the time you complete your research you will have results from your job postings.

☞ *CROSS REFERENCE BOOKMARK: REFER TO CHAPTER 10, SECTION 1*

3. Search your internal databases

Your Applicant Tracking System, your leads database, your contact manager, your previously saved searches, and your email inbox easily contain leads and previous referrals that you can tap into. Because they are people you have probably already contacted, these are the quickest hits.

4. Tap into you current contacts

Once you gather people from your internal databases, call them or send them an email, but be sure to include candidates and other people you have already worked with! This is the time to solicit referrals. You should build a running list of people who have agreed to help you with your searches. Send them an email with a brief description of the type of candidate you need and let them help you.

5. Search the resume boards

Scan through all the free and fee-based subscription databases that provide you resumes. Since these are potential candidates who have actively posted their resume, you can easily call or email them and obtain quick results.

6. Find industry information

Collect intelligence so you can prepare for the deep searches. Begin by researching your industry, reviewing all kinds of publications, websites, and periodicals to see if you missed any keywords, buzzwords, job posting sites, or resume databases. Once you understand the industry landscape you are ready for the competitive intelligence steps.

7. Identify and locate competitors

Apply the knowledge you learned in step 6 to identify companies that employ people similar to the kind of people you seek. Once you have a list of target companies you can conduct specific searches for people from those companies. A great place to do this is the vertical search engines like Indeed, SimplyHired, and JobCentral. View the RSS chapter for more information.

8. Search for candidates from competitors

Use the names of your target companies to go back through all your contacts, internal databases, resume boards, and other resources to find potential candidates associated with your target companies. Contact those people and ask for referrals.

9. Search for resumes on the web

Searching for resumes online can be a very time consuming process so it should be one of your last steps. If you have exhausted all of the leads from previous steps, then when you can, use the search engine techniques to find resumes, home pages, and bios.

10. Search for people from your competitors

It's easier to contact candidates who have published their resumes online, but once you have found as many as you can, it's time to begin looking for leads from your competitors. Using the list of target companies, apply your search techniques to find the names of people who are employed by your competitors and are participating in communities like mailing lists, forums, groups, associations, social networks, and blogs.

11. Communicate with new contacts

Once you have collected all the leads, initiating contact with the people you found is the most time consuming activity of all, so it should be your last step. You can build a mass email or cold calling campaign and contact as many of the new leads as possible. In addition, by now, your job posting or advertising should be yielding results.

12. Reset

If all of the previous steps fail to yield results, then it's possible you are using the wrong keywords, targeting the wrong leads, or sending the wrong message. Adjust your keywords and start over from step one using new keywords and a refined message.

Be sure to revalidate your keywords, refresh your outreach message and reset expectations with hiring managers.

Chapter 3
Workflow

Quick Sample! Sourcing Workflow

So, what does the recruitment workflow look like when the specialized function of Sourcing is applied? Use the following ordered steps to build your workflow model. In this model, the Sourcing Team may be either an internal recruiting arm or external third party. Additionally, this workflow takes participants up to the point of actual candidate application.

Requisition Intake Meeting Form, and Sign-off

- Recruiter schedules an intake meeting with Hiring Manager to review requirements and gather additional information
- Recruiter schedules a second meeting that includes Sourcing Team Project Lead
- If a need for Sourcing has been identified for this search, the Sourcing Team Lead assists in gathering additional key data and then sends summary of candidate portrait to Recruiter and Hiring Manager for sign-off by Hiring Manager

Sourcing Team Activation

- Upon Hiring Manager's sign-off, Recruiter activates Sourcing Team to commence activities
- Sourcing Team begins to identify suspects/prospects and convert suspects/prospects to candidates

Sourcing Team Mobilization

- Sourcing Team constructs a list of viable profiles
- Sourcing Team enters profiles from various Sourcing channels into its Customer Relationship Management (CRM) system for tracking and reporting
- Sourcing Team documents all outreach via email/phone, text (SMS) and direct social media contact

Candidate Conversion

- Sourcing Team usually screens or pre-qualifies those profiles/prospects who have been converted into candidates
- Sourcing Team submits prequalified and packaged candidates to Recruiter

Nota Bene – If the Sourcing Team is an external third party, then who performs this step, the Sourcing Team or an internal recruiter, depends on the terms of the Service-Level Agreement (SLA) with the client (Recruiter or Hiring Manager).

Recruiter Tracking

- The Sourcing Team turns over candidate management to Recruiter for the duration of the process
- The Recruiter fully vets the candidate
- The Recruiter inputs all candidate information into the organization's Applicant Tracking System (ATS)
- The Recruiter submits candidate information to the Hiring Manager for review and initial consideration
- The Recruiter handles the responsibility of communications to the candidate, including disposition of their status in the ATS or other tracking mechanism

Milestones:
- *Identify 50 - 200 unqualified leads per requisition being supported*
- *Attempt to reach at least half of the leads via email, and if possible social media outreach*
- *Non-responsive leads ranked into a call sheet and followed up with until at least half of those have been pre-screened via telephone or email*
- *Obtain interest (referred to as "closing") for about 15 qualified prospects to send to recruiter*
- *Present 5 qualified prospects to recruiter for the posting being supported.*

Section 1. Working with Hiring Managers

Steven Covey, one of the widest read business authors in the modern era, wrote a book called The Seven Habits of Highly Effective People where he contends that activity should be prioritized around four quadrants:

1. Highest priority assigned to activities both urgent and important
2. Second priority assigned to those important, but not urgent
3. Third priority goes to those which are urgent, but not important
4. Everything else is a fourth priority

Recruiters find themselves in trouble when they let urgency override importance. In recruiting, many urgent tasks steal from what is important, that is to say what is in the best interest of the organization not just of one individual customer (hiring manager). For example, by submitting fewer and better candidates rather than focusing on "sending more candidates", hiring managers would have more time to conduct thorough interviews, and better understand the talent marketplace.

The Central Building Block: INTAKE MEETINGS

During the intake meeting, the hiring manager and recruiter discuss the requirements of the open requisition. The intake meeting also establishes the level of Sourcing strategy and the Sourcing plan itself. In larger organizations, the Sourcer will also attend the meeting.

Most likely, the recruiter has already been provided with the basic requisition listing generated by an internal system. The purpose of the intake meeting is to set expectations, discuss the mechanics of filling the position and produce keywords. The intake meeting is the requirements gathering phase of the process sometimes called the "requisition intake" meeting (also kickoff or briefing). The reason an intake meeting is crucial is that the entire ensuing recruiting campaign is based on the work accomplished in this meeting. If the intake meeting is not well done, then cascading errors will occur that will result often in failure.

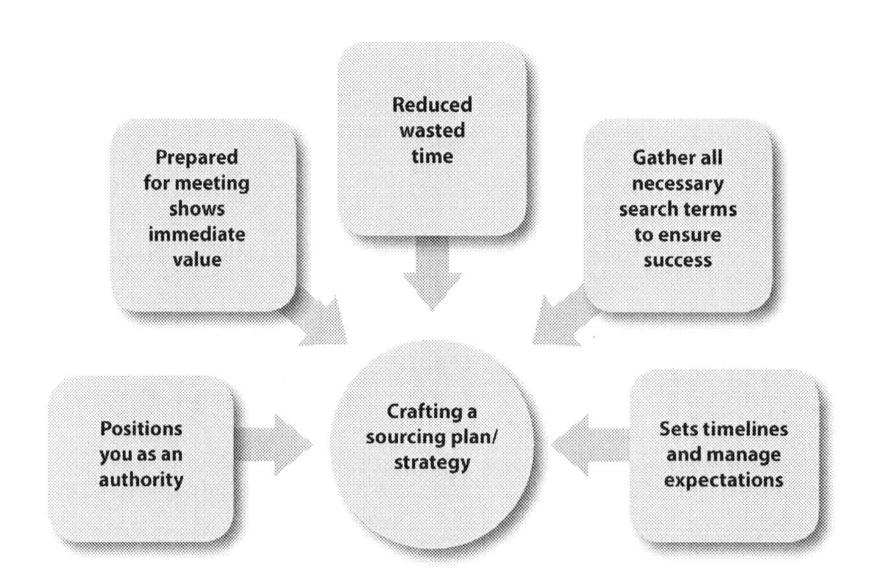

Figure 12 Intake Meeting

Most times, intake meetings are not properly conducted. Even when they are done, they are not done correctly. When undertaken, nine-out-of-ten times, an ineffective campaign can trace its failure to errors in this meeting. This juncture is the appropriate time for the hiring and recruiting teams to delve deeply into the job functions and responsibilities of the requisition, with a Sourcer present and exercising their keenest active listening skills throughout. Communication breaks down here if the right information is not drawn out from the hiring manager, or if the recruiter does not comprehend what the hiring manager wants. If that breakdown occurs, even in the best-case scenario, the danger is that recruiters will search for the wrong people in the right places or the right people in the wrong places.

When hiring managers are not happy with recruiters' efforts, the causes often reside in the recruiters' mindset. It is a mistake for recruiters to enter the meeting thinking "I already know this job" or "I have already worked with this hiring manager, so I know what he wants". Having an established relationship with the hiring manager can obviously create shortcuts and expedite the meeting, but still try to observe all formalities of the meeting.

Section 2. Keywords

The intake meeting will result in information that recruiters use to develop keywords. The actual skeleton of the meeting is discussed later in this section, but keywords are discussed here first, so you know what is your goal as you prepare and participate in the meeting.

The development of keywords may involve on-the-spot brainstorming, but it actually requires more time and critical thinking than one quick brain-racking session. Keyword development is more than just identifying skills; it is really about finding the language that your candidate speaks, and that requires continued vigilance as you pursue leads.

Look for words that describe the environment or ecosystem in which potential prospects operate such as systems, tools, and technology they use. Sometimes, these terms are simple buzzwords; other times, they are model numbers of specific software editions. Recruiters do not have to understand the complete inner workings of those applications, but they should be aware of the rare, difficult, and abstruse terms related to their candidates role and function. Also identify ancillary technology. For example, if a recruiter seeks to fill a position that will use Hibernate technology, then it makes sense to look for associated terms like JBoss, JavaE, BigData, J2S2, or Eclipse.

Whereas recruiters have the tendency to take a broader perspective of the open requisition when they write the job posting, employees by contrast typically take a ground-level view of the work they perform every day. The difference in these two perspectives can lead to a disconnection between the job posting and resume. It is best to consider phrases that relate directly to performing the job itself on a daily basis like "I'm an engineer working with ______." Just fill in the blank with other keywords to discover new sets of resumes.

Check your existing list of keywords. Probably there are words that represent technology. Others may relate to skill-sets. What should also be included are very telling words that represent actions, i.e. verbs. However, it is a good idea to add verbal phrases such as "write* lines of code" if looking for a software developer. The wildcard function is added to expand the search for phrases that contain different spelling variations.

Also turn your attention to sets of terms related to the degree of a person's skill or qualification, which works particularly well in homogeneous databases where individuals input data from a finite number of choices, or people who work in extremely organized structures. For example, military personnel and government officials are assigned "grades" that indicate type of work and rank or level, which makes it simple to identify their context quickly.

A reliable place to find keywords is to look at the resumes of successful individuals in positions similar to the open requisition and turn their content into keywords. For example, the hiring manager's resume may be a good start, or the resume of an industry rock star that is unavailable. Similarly, after reviewing a few resumes, recruiters may start to see a pattern in the ones that catch their eye, in which case, they should breakdown the pattern for inspiration. This technique may produce educational degrees, certifications, licenses, or particular schools that stand out.

If relocation is not available, then it would be reasonable to include geographic search terms like names of cities and their suburbs, postal codes, telephone area codes, and even local organizations and associations. These pieces of information all reveal an individual's point of origin.

Best Searches Include...

Job Titles *– include a variety of known and related titles, commonly accepted variations, names of neighboring roles.*

Company Names *– don't be limited to just competitors! Which organizations hire the same kind of people even if rom a different industry? Did you remember to include company abbreviations, stock symbols, and nicknames, email domains?*

Jargon *– unique and abstruse skill related keywords, names or abbreviations of licenses and degrees or certifications. Be sure to trying various alternate spellings.*

Location Names *– include regions inside major cities, town names, and local nicknames for places around town, area codes, and postal codes.*

Do Your Homework

Avoid showing up to the meeting empty-handed or just with the requisition that was provided to you. First, it does not inspire credibility about your work, and it limits the conversation only to topics the hiring manager knows about when you are the recruiting specialist. Second, your preparation beforehand establishes your expertise and should guide the conversation around the talking points that will ultimately facilitate your work performance.

Company Research

Make sure you know identify companies likely to be known to the hiring manager. These employers may not necessarily be competitors; in fact, they may be companies that are not even in the same industry, but if they employ the same talent or produce the same types of employees after some training they should make it on to your list. You want to educate yourself on similar product categories, names, and brands because they will affect your search criteria. A favorite technique to do so is the related: command from Google. In the keyword box, type "related:COMPANYsite.com" Google will pull up a list of companies that have statistically similar content, and organizations that describe themselves in much the same way. Visit the following resources for practical lists of companies:

ZoomInfo

The company search is free and allows you to look up similar organizations by industry phrases such as "Food and beverages" as well as keywords. The value this website offers is that it searches for competitors based on statistical analysis of the company's Web content, not on their SIC code or other rigid nomenclatures. The keywords a company uses to describe itself can change overnight but in contrast industry codes take many years to change.

Jigsaw

An online "business contact marketplace" with over 1.2 million members, JigSaw allows users to buy, sell, or trade contact information comparable to that contained on a business card. This data service uses a crowd-Sourcing, cloud model where users contribute contacts and contact information.

Quick Guide! JigSaw (www.data.com)

Backed by Salesforce.com and located at data.com, this free source of company information presents detailed search capabilities based on geographic criteria, type and size of company, industry, and even a few interesting fields such as area codes. Beyond just a list of company names this site also identifies subsidiaries, divisions and parent companies, and is a great place to validate job titles.

Because of this user provided real-time information, JigSaw data is self-correcting by design. Contacts are accurate and fresh because users gain points by updating contact information, and are penalized for uploading false or outdated contacts.

Conducting a search for contacts is easy. There are a multitude of criteria to search with, including: Company Name, Job Title, Department, Level, Industry Sector, Company Size, Metropolitan Area, and Area or Zip Codes. Once a contact is found, purchasing it will reveal the contact's full name, complete title, phone number and business email.

Before purchasing a contact, take a moment to confirm its freshness. You can see when the contact was last updated by clicking on the "View Entire History" link. Outdated contacts may still be useful, but it is best to check before you purchase the contact. You may also want to take a look at the reputation of the user who added the contact. Although the system is designed so that people can anonymously sell or buy contacts, users are held to a reputation metric based on the reliability of the contacts they have provided in the past.

One other item to consider is how many times a contact has been purchased. You may not want to buy contacts that have already been "passed around" quite a bit, or on the other hand, you may only want to purchase popular contacts. Finally, keep in mind that once you purchase a contact, all versions of that contact are now yours to keep. For example, if other users upload the same contact or update it at a later time, you will always have access to that new information.

LinkedIn™

LinkedIn™ provides easy access to company information under a section labeled "Companies". Most employers have a page, and within that archive, there is a listing for Affiliated Companies including not just subsidiaries but under a section called People Also Viewed, a list of companies other researchers like you identify as being similar to this one. And, a section called Insights takes you to a page listing facts about the company such as common job titles, demographics, recent moves and promotions, and people in your network who work there.

Google

Inference by proximity is a method that helps identify groups of things such as companies and job titles. Searching for the name of three or more closely similar companies will often result in pages listing competitors.

Indeed.com and SimplyHired.com

Vertical search engines like these two are designed to integrate many sources of content in a particular field, such as job postings, into one location. Pretend to be a candidate like the one you seek, and type in search terms as if you were looking for a job in your field. What you find will be a revealing list of titles, companies and locations.

Your company research should produce a preliminary list of eligible job titles. The size and style of an organization determines what kind of titles it uses, but there is a common pool of titles that most employers seem to use. At the same time, the duties and responsibilities can vary despite similar titles, and they can be nearly identical despite different titles. For example, a pro-grammar could also be a developer, a software engineer, or referred to with the acronym SDET or STE. You may consider some of these titles as pretty standard, but the hiring manager who may be more closely connected to the world than you, may disagree, which is fine. It is better to have the conversation early so more precise results are provided later.

A Preliminary List of Keywords

This list is a launch pad for discussion and future work. Discussing it at the meeting will let you know where to stay the course and where you need correction.

The Intake Meeting

What to bring and what to take from your meeting with the hiring manager.

What to Take to the Meeting

After you have conducted your preliminary search and gathered the first batch of search terms, it is time to meet with the hiring manager.

A Sample Intake Form

This form addresses everything that you anticipate you will need. You can bring it pre-filled, but it is not something that you send to hiring managers in advance of your meeting for them to fill out and have ready for you, which would be too presumptuous. Instead, you will use this form as a conversational guide.

☞ *CROSS REFERENCE BOOKMARK: SEE APPENDIX FOR EXAMPLE INTAKE FORM*

Sample Resumes

If you have filled a similar position, bring a few resumes from that search. Bringing in sample resumes can lead to important substantive discoveries. The hiring manager can then tell you what is attractive or what is disliked. Moreover, you can discern where you are disconnected and the reasons for it. For example, a hiring manager may emphasize that familiarity with Maximo is a requirement, but none of your resumes have this tool listed. You strongly believe your resumes are representative of the ideal candidate, but your resumes reflect experience with Tivoli. Examining this dissonance will reveal that Tivoli bought out Maximo and that either name can be used to identify the right pool of candidates.

What to Have before You Leave the Meeting...

When recruiters think they are ready to close the meeting with the hiring manager, they should possess the following information.

Validated Keywords

Recruiters need to ensure that hiring managers have reviewed the proposed initial keywords to ensure their efforts are focused in the right direction, and there are no surprises later. Completely understanding the requirements demands that the recruiter understands exactly what the hiring manager wants. The recruiter may be very intuitive but is not a mind reader. The recruiter must be willing to dig deeply here and the interaction may take on the characteristics of a formal interview, an inquisition of sorts. This discussion also includes validating keywords that should be excluded. For instance, review companies that are not relevant; titles, skills, and other jargon that are undesired; and vendors, partners, and companies that are off-limits. At the same time, confirm that employees who have left vendors, partners, and associated companies can be included.

A Portrait of the Ideal Candidate

It is not enough to validate keywords or receive recommendations where to look for candidates. Recruiters should have a clear profile or image of the ideal candidate in mind. Actually, recruiters should have two portraits – one of the candidates who possess the nice-to-have or wish list qualifications that will drive her resume to the top of the pile and one of the candidates who possess the must-have qualifications that will keep her resume in the pile.

Critical Answers

Recruiters should know the answers to the following questions before leaving the intake meeting:

- Is there anybody that I should definitely reach out to? There is a strong likelihood that the hiring manager has come in contact with ideal candidates through the normal course of business or professional networking.

- Is there someone I should definitely avoid? These individuals might be people who have already passed on the position previously or those with whom the hiring manager has had a negative work experience.
- What if I find a candidate who possesses every wish list qualification but one? Which one qualification would eliminate the person as a prospect? The answer to this question will shape where hiring managers are willing to compromise and where they will stay firm.
- What have been the challenges to filling this position in the past? This question is important to ask because it clues recruiters in to previous failures that they know not to repeat.
- Is relocation available? Is there any wiggle room in the salary? How do you structure compensation? You do not need every detail of these practical concerns, just a good idea because these answers will affect your search.
- If I find the perfect candidate today, are you ready to make an offer today? The answer to this question will reveal if the company is mobilized or if there is a challenge that might derail the recruitment effort despite your best efforts.
- What must this person do in order to receive an excellent performance review at the end of the first year? What should they have accomplished? Knowing these answers helps you develop better keywords and evaluate qualifications.
- If I could ask a prospect just one question, what would it be? This answer reveals the one essential component the hiring manager is looking for.
- Do I have the bios and profiles of the hiring manager and the interview team? With them, you can discover important structural patterns in the organization's hiring. The social theory of similarity dictates that people are instinctively drawn to people they think are similar to them, which, when applied to recruiting, indicates an organization values. Equipped with this knowledge, you can intuit the resumes that reflect these values.

How to Wrap Up the Meeting

Once you are sure that you have all the information that can be gathered in this sitting, it is fitting to end the interaction with a discussion of practical matters.

Review Your Search Techniques and Process

An explanation of your techniques and process lets the hiring manager know what you will do with all the information that you just gathered. This way, the hiring manager knows how you will spend your time and can let you know at what steps he or she would like to comment, provide input, or have reporting.

Review the SLA

Depending on how you perceive the atmosphere, the wrap-up is a good time to confirm the hiring manager's commitment to your SLA. Inviting their comment on the SLA at this point can avoid confusion and conflict at a subsequent point in time. You may just want to provide a very simple statement of work that establishes your standards of practice and manages their expectations of your services.

☞ *CROSS REFERENCE BOOKMARK: DETAILED SLA EXAMPLE IN APPENDIX*

Bring out Your Calendar

Start to construct a preliminary timeline with the hiring manager in the room. Determine the dates of goals and the reporting schedule. Also, customize the timeline according to the hiring manager's schedule. You do not want to interrupt the hiring manager in the middle of peak business or when they are on vacation.

> *It is a good practice to schedule resume review meetings with the hiring authority in advance of sending them resumes. This way the hiring manager has guaranteed availability for this critical step before their calendar is filled with other tasks.*

What to Do after the Meeting

Your meeting is finished but you are not done yet. A few more steps will ensure clear communication and help level set expectations.

Validate the Requisition

Now that you have had your meeting with the hiring manager, make sure what you seek exists. This is the "trust but verify" step of the Sourcing plan. Log in to your favorite job board and pretend that you're a candidate seeking those kinds of jobs and see what comes up. Log in to a job board and search as a recruiter and see what resumes come up with those key words. Just simply do a first pass, not to find anybody in particular right now but just to gain a sense of the volume of what's really out there. Is there enough talent – as it is currently defined – for you to find? Are there any glaring challenges with the location of the job? Do you need to go back and achieve more clarity on some criteria?

Complete an Executive Summary

Prepare a short document that summarizes the content of the meeting. It may also be a good idea to send a few sample resumes based on what was discussed to serve as a preliminary reference point. Also, any issues uncovered when the requisition was validated should be included here. This executive summary also helps minimize confusion and bad feelings down the road by setting expectations.

Section 3. Collaborating with Hiring Managers

Collaborating with hiring managers can be tricky. Just as the hiring manager has no direct authority over you, you do not possess any authority over the hiring manager. Therefore, it is important to manage the process using a "sideways" perspective of your fellow stakeholders, which first begins by understanding stakeholder roles.

Most hiring managers are not dedicated to just hiring; in other words, they have their own job functions related to the core business of your organization, which they must do well, or they would not be hiring managers. Even if you have limited recruiting experience, when you work alongside a hiring manager, you are the recruiting expert, the one who is wholly devoted to the hiring process.

Show Immediate Value

During the intake meeting, you must position yourself as someone who provides immediate value. Preparing yourself as discussed previously within this section should demonstrate your competence and your value in the process. If you arrive unprepared and ask questions such as "Where do you recommend that I find candidates?" or "What job titles are you looking for?" you are unfairly placing recruiting functions on the hiring manager's shoulders.

The intake meeting is also where you can educate the hiring manager about your process, reset unrealistic expectations, and reach consensus about recruiting strategies. Sometimes, you will sit down with top executives, which can intimidate less experienced recruiters. In this situation, remember that you are still the expert and do not allow pomp and circumstance to scare you away from performing your tasks or undertaking your process as usual. In your collaboration, you are a partner and not a servant, and your role is to support the whole company's hiring efforts and not just this particular person's objectives, unless the person with whom you are meeting is the CEO.

There are some hiring managers whose experience is so extensive and skilled that their comments can teach you aspects of business that everyone should know. In this case, listen well and keep the conversation on track towards your hiring goal. What can be particularly useful information to you then is an understanding of the hiring manager's experience working with recruiters. At some point, you should ask about the hiring manager's successful and less successful outcomes working with recruiters.

Understand the Job

When the open requisition is first brought to your attention, you may know nothing about the job or its department. Since you are servicing the company's objectives as a whole, you must know where this position fits in the organization and how it contributes to the success of the company. Plus, your knowledge about the position can become selling points when speaking with candidates.

Four Common Types of Difficult Hiring Managers

1. Overly Demanding.

These managers often demand ten years' experience for a tool that only existed for five. Their must-have list is really a wish list, but they do not see it that way. In the end, what they seek is not really found in candidate pools.

2. "I'm too busy."

These managers are so caught up in their own day-to-day duties that they embrace you as the expert and want to leave all decisions up to you. They do not want to review resumes, give feedback, interview people, or make the offer. They just want you to give them a body. These managers are also notorious for sitting on candidate profiles for weeks, stalling the process and diminishing credibility. While this collaboration style is easy in some respects, it leaves room for an imprecise hire, which means that your interpretation of a perfect hire does not meet theirs. If you find yourself in this situation, you must convey to the manager that there are two options: Exert more energy in the hiring process and spend less effort managing the hire later or spend less energy on the hiring process and exert more energy managing the hire later. Once a hiring manager understands this notion, then he or she will usually pay more attention to your process.

3. "I'll know it when I see it."

These managers expend the most resources in the recruiting process while they candidate "shop" at their leisure. Usually, managers should leave intuition for the interview, after candidates have been vetted through a process. To introduce this kind of gut-based search early in the process is to invite inefficiency and waste. If you are working with this type of manager, it is important to explain the market for the position. Furthermore, the hiring manager must understand that if "dream candidates" exist, those candidate may already be appreciated by their current employers and not be on the market. Alternatively, the package you offer may not capture their attention.

4. "I gotta guy."

Referrals are wonderful, and through natural networking, it may very well be true that the hiring manager knows a perfect candidate. However, problems occur when hiring managers want to skip steps in the process for the sake of their buddies or want to use the hiring process for personal advantage. Bona fide candidates should understand the reasoning behind the recruiting process and be willing to undergo formal review. If you must work with this type of manager, explain the purpose of each step of the process and suggest steps to ensure impartiality.

Taking Charge of Bumpy Conversations

While the recruiting process is collaboration with stakeholders, hiring managers are clients in a sense, and the friction that occurs in service settings also happens between recruiters and hiring managers. For example, you may be servicing 30 hiring managers at a time, so you have not been able to hand-hold one particular hiring manager who demands a lot of attention, and he wants to complain. Another example may be that you made a mistake, which costs the hiring manager a solid candidate, and she wants accountability. Each situation presents thorny issues, so let's discuss your best possible responses.

Issue: Heated language.
Best possible response: Remain calm.

No matter how much venting, yelling, or even name-calling occurs, adopt a neutral, listening posture. The other party wants to be heard, so listen. When you do speak, acknowledge that you are hearing them, and keep the contents of your words focused on addressing job-related comments and avoid anything that can be construed as a personal attack, even if the other person showed no such restraint.

Issue: You made a mistake.
Best possible response: Admit your mistake. Apologize. Correct it.

Hardly anyone likes to have every mistake revealed. Regardless, if you messed up, acknowledge your error and deal with the consequences. Dealing with the consequences means you must update your manager with what the landscape looks like in light of your error and what you are doing to avoid repeating the mistake. You may be demoralized at this point, but you cannot give up. You must persist in the process despite the fact that your performance has been called into question. It almost goes without saying that you must make every effort to deliver a skilled performance from that point forward.

What to Provide

Excuses do not help, but notes and details such as explanations, evidence, and case studies go a long way to heal hiring manager relationships.

Explanations

Some managers do not want a response from you. Rather, they just want you to listen. In these cases, do not insist on having the last word. Just acknowledge their message and let them know that you will consider it in your future collaborations or projects. If the hiring manager wants a response from you, then choose your words wisely and avoid inflammatory language. The truth is very handy even when it does not favor you. Sometimes you can undo a bad act, but you can't diminish the reach of its consequences. If you made an error in judgment, providing an explanation of your reasoning can often allow others to see your viewpoint and understand your actions. Perhaps others would have made the same judgment if they were placed in your shoes. Whatever you say, do not use more words than necessary.

Empirical Evidence

Quelling hiring mangers anxieties can be accomplished very effectively if you present empirical evidence justifying your decisions. Again, creating a "numbers case" for you should not be necessary for every decision, just the weighty ones. As a pre-emptive strike against discord, present raw facts and figures in your reporting, along with an invitation for comment. If hiring managers are kept in the information loop, they will see your challenges and have the opportunity to contribute to working solutions. Note that providing empirical evidence means you must document your work. This upkeep requires more effort on your part, but you will produce a better ultimate result.

The Numbers Case

> ***Quick Case:*** *On average, hiring managers interview five candidates before making a hiring decision.*

Visuals often say more than words alone. What follows is an explanation of a diagram or sketch that may assist in your dialogue with hiring authorities. Averages throughout the world are that five candidates are interviewed before a hiring manager feels comfortable arriving at a hiring decision. That number varies of course, but like with other important decisions people like to have options.

Your job is to provide those options. If you send only one candidate, they would not have much of a choice. In rare instances, recruiters are able to present an average of two candidates for each one hired. Admirable as that is, a Sourcing and recruitment strategy should be prepared with the objective of giving hiring managers a selection of at least three-to-five candidates.

Working backwards from the baseline goal of five interviewed candidates, you can arrive at the average number of leads needed per hire.

For example, you might explain to hiring managers that you must generate about 160 leads per hire. From this initial suspect pool, you would usually connect with 25 percent of the individuals with the others being unreachable due to bounced emails, disconnected phone numbers, or other sundry reasons. Among the 40 people you connect with, you are generally able to prequalify and garner the interest of half. The other half drops off because of disinterest or through elimination based on the hiring manager's criteria. Finally, hiring managers typically review four candidate resumes before selecting one to interview.

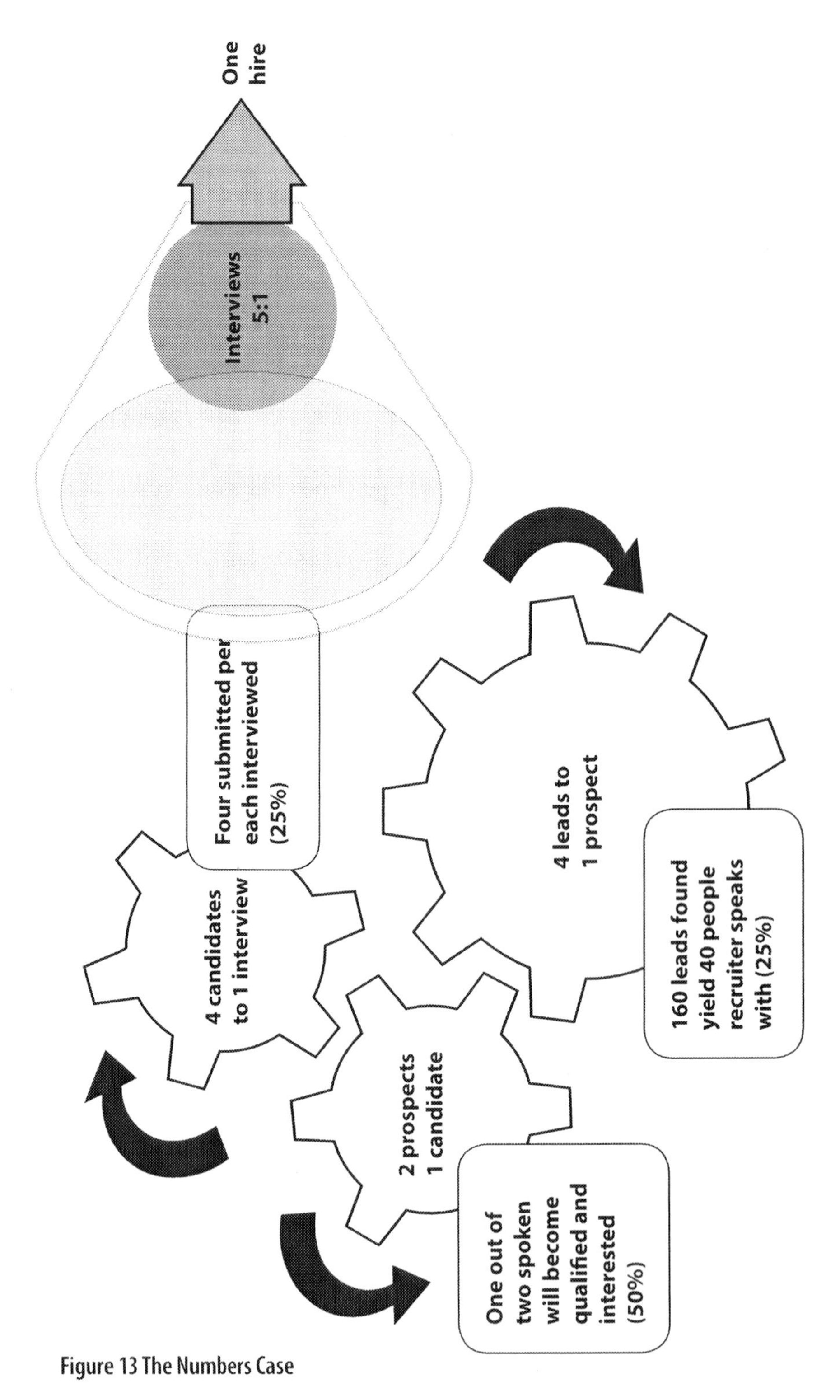

Figure 13 The Numbers Case

Making Everyone Happy...

It's impossible. Yet, you can avoid unpleasant surprises, which means that you must return to the earlier sections on preparation and the intake meeting. It cannot be emphasized enough: These two steps in the process are essential in establishing the rhythm and expectations of the entire crew of participants.

Quick Guide! Request Prioritization

As with recruiting, not all requests made of Sourcers will be of equal importance to the business at large. The following is a list of sample factors that can be used to determine the priority of a Sourcing request:

1) Business imperative
2) Number of associated job openings
3) Completeness of Sourcing order form received
4) Likelihood for the requirement to be filled externally
5) Other available outside Sourcing support
6) Customer's track record in adherence to SLA timelines and partnership guidelines
7) Leadership determination of business priorities

Part II: FIND

Chapter 4
Search Methodologies

Section 1. The FIVE: Find Attract Engage Manage Lead

Let's backtrack a little to return to fundamentals. In general, the recruitment world, revolves around five key concepts:

1. Find
2. Attract
3. Engage
4. Manage
5. Lead

While acknowledging all five concepts above, this Talent Sourcing and Recruitment Handbook focuses on the first three. Chapter Three herein addresses the first concept, **Find**, and examines the Internet as the most important instrument recruiters use to **find** talent.

Section 2. It's Not Why Use the Internet, It's How to...

Right off the bat, the twenty first century warrants stating that any recruiter who does not use the Internet has a rapidly deteriorating shelf life if they have not already been rendered obsolete. The proliferation of portable computing devices such as notebook computers, smart phones, tablets, e-readers, Internet enabled mp3 players and gaming consoles, in addition to traditional desktop computers makes access to the Internet not just commonplace but instantaneous and almost always an arm's reach away. At the other end of each of these devices is a user, to you a potential prospect.

The purpose of Chapter Three is not to describe the Internet's accessibility to end-users but to advance your Internet competence to find the right end-user possessing the highly specialized characteristics that can **grow, refresh, and renew your talent ranks.** In the same way that not everyone who knows the alphabet can write a Nobel Prize winning piece of literature, not every recruiter who knows how to turn on a computer can find the right, best candidate from the world's talent pool for an open requisition in ten minutes. Any recruiter whose skills cannot accomplish this task should continue reading on.

The Baseball Analogy

In 2002, the Oakland Athletics baseball team finished in first place in the MLB American League West despite having the third lowest combined team salaries in major league baseball. What's curious is that the Oakland Athletics won as many games in the regular season as the New York Yankees, a team that spent more than three times more cash on its combined team salaries. How did such a phenomenon occur? Were the Oakland Athletics merely lucky? Most baseball analysts attribute Oakland's success to the team manager's use of performance-based data, termed sabermetrics. Simply, the team manager and Oakland's front office applied different rules of interpretation to the same data that was available to each of the other 29 teams in the league to produce an effective team that achieved important industry benchmarks.

This example of the Oakland A's demonstrates the value of interpretation and the use of thinking time over mental and robotic adherence to convention. The management motto, "Think outside the box", becomes a survival truth when it comes to electronic recruiting. In fact, the entire discipline has moved beyond any definable "box" to match the immense and amorphous changes in the workforce brought about by the digital age.

In baseball, the number of participants to which data mining applies is substantially limited. In recruiting, the number of participants is exponentially greater. Because the field of prospects is potentially so large, the Internet turns from a treasure trove of information to an overwhelming headache inducing maze. For this reason, the importance of filtering using high-level methods of human interpretation cannot be emphasized enough. Use meaningful thinking time to develop elementary and creative data points and performance metrics unique to your open requisition so that you can avoid the situation where the Internet is a bottomless pit.

Taming the World "Wild" Web

Since Tim Berners-Lee posted the first public website in 1991, the World Wide Web has propelled the globe into a new digital era. What many computer users fail to grasp is that there is a difference between the web and the Internet, which is important here because the electronic tools described herein utilize the faculties of the Internet beyond the mere Web.

The **Internet** is a vast collection of inter-connected computer networks from all over the world. These networks communicate with each other using a set of standards called **Transmission Control Protocol/ Internet Protocol** or TCP/IP. The World Wide Web (www or Web) is the part of the Internet that can be accessed with software applications called **Web browsers** such as Internet Explorer, Firefox, Chrome or Safari. A browser is simply an application that allows us to "see" the graphical applications that live on other computers.

The "Web" consists of an ever-shifting collection of documents called **Web pages**, numbering in the billions and growing in excess of modern computer's capabilities of tracking them. Today, a Web page can be created with many different graphical tools, hypertext markup languages, programming languages, and server applications—it's no longer just good ole' **HTML**. HTML (Hypertext Markup Language) is the commonly used, World Wide Web consortium-approved method of marking code to enable browser display of a Web page's words and images. Now, for example, there is XML (extensible HTML), WML (wireless HTML), ASP (Microsoft Front Page and Active Server Pages), CFI (Cold Fusion), and JSP (Java Server Pages), and hundreds of other file types. In fact, Microsoft Word and Microsoft Excel documents are also frequently found inside websites.

Each Web page has a unique address akin to the physical address of a business or residential location, called a **universal resource locator** (URL), which allows other pages to point to them; these pointers are the **hyperlinks**. Again, hyperlinks connect pages to one another. Not all pages are directly connected to each other, but many are connected indirectly through webs of hyperlinks much like the silk threads in a spider web.

The Web, however, is not the Internet itself. Besides what is known as the Web today, there are other active Internet Protocols such as Email, File Transfer Protocol (FTP), Internet Relay Chat (IRC), Chat, or Instant Messaging and even older ones still in use like Telnet, Gopher, and Usenet, all of which talk with each other using TCP/IP. These days, the relationships among these separate parts are blurred to the extent that they appear to be one seamless part of the entire Internet accessible from any computer or mobile device.

The distinction between the Web and the Internet comes into play during a recruiter's search. Because every Web page has a unique URL (physical address), it is possible to find just about every person who has any kind of online presence. Web pages are stored in computers across the Internet. These computers are sometimes referred to as **servers**, or **hosts**. **Websites** are just like folders on your computer, and Web pages are just like files in your folders. A server or host may contain more than one website, and each website may contain many pages. The main website or folder has a name that frequently begins with *"http://"* or sometimes *"https://"*. For example, 4sct.com is a website. Inside the main "folder", the website, there are other folders that contain multiple pages, each with a unique name. This is what makes it possible to find every public Web page.

The main website's address is termed a **domain**, and it must be registered with a **registrar**, which acts like a post office that regulates traffic and mail delivery to physical addresses, by assigning domain names to a website, ensuring that no duplicate domains are ever created. The most popular registrars include Go Daddy (godaddy.com) or Enom (enom.com). Domain names indicate where a website is located and what kind of a website it is. Different types of websites are available, each with a special "top-level" domain that helps identify the nature of the website. **Top-level domains** are the codes to the right of the last dot on a website address.

For a complete listing of top-level domains and authorized registrars, consult the International Corporation for Assigned Names and Numbers (icann.org/registries/listing.html). Here is a list of the most common top-level domains and their significance:

.com	Companies, businesses, corporations (public and private)
.net	Unrestricted, intended for ISPs and networks
.edu	Colleges, universities, and schools
.mil	U.S. military use only
.org	Non-profit and professional organizations
.gov	Government agencies
.biz	Businesses, unrestricted
.info	Any kind of website, unrestricted
.name	For registration by individuals
.pro	Accountants, lawyers, physicians and other professionals
.jobs	Corporate career sites

The above top-level domains are worldwide. There are also country-specific domains that consist of two-letter country codes and denote a website that originates from that country. The full listing of country-specific, top-level domains can be found here: iana.org/cctld/cctld-whois.htm.

☞ *CROSS REFERENCE BOOKMARK: REFER TO CHAPTER9, SECTION 4*

Individual folders inside a website are separated by a forward slash (the / character residing left of the shift key on most keyboards), and the Web page itself is indicated by a final extension such as .html, .htm, .doc, .txt, .asp, .pdf, and so on.

Congratulations! Armed with a good understanding of the World Wide Web, you are now ready to go online and begin finding people.

Section 3. Logical Operators

Occam's Razor

"Entia non sunt multiplicanda praeter necessitatem"

Occam's (or Ockham's) razor is a principle attributed to the 14th century logician and Franciscan friar William of Ockham, who was devoted to the scientific method. The principle explains that simplicity is best, and adding more components without first eliminating some, serves to confuse and complicate.

Logicians, mathematicians, and scientists will cringe at the following definition, but, simply put, **logical operators** within the context of this book are commands you can issue to a search engine to aid in defining the relationship between two things, and specifying how you want them included among results. The most common one of these is a **logical disjunction**, a fancy phrase referring to the use of the OR Boolean operation. That term is used here not because of some whimsy, but because it more accurately portrays how keyword searches operate in a database than does the oft-misused term "Boolean". By definition, a Boolean argument can only have two outcomes, true or false. When searching databases, however, you are not asking a true or false question; rather you are expressing a preference for inclusion or exclusion of various specified terms. Basically, instead of inaccurately referring to a type of search as a "Boolean search string", the following discussion more precisely calls them "searches using/with logical operators".

Three Premises of Searches with Logical Operators

1. Precision

The most common mistake in conducting a database search is starting with keywords that are too specific and produce little results. It is actually better to start with a broad definition of search terms that bring back too many results at the beginning and then narrow the results from that starting point.

2. Simplicity

Simplicity will always outperform complexity. The simplest solution is always the best one because it is least prone to errors, miscommunication, and misunderstanding. Long search queries with lots of nested statements are seldom more useful than a couple of intelligently selected keywords.

"Any intelligent fool can make things bigger and more complex... It takes a touch of genius - and a lot of courage to move in the opposite direction." – Albert Einstein

3. Efficiency

Search engines are merely databases. A database is a structured set of data held in a computer and accessible in various ways. Not all databases have the same rules of operation, but there are some commonalities. A few universal search techniques make it possible for you to more efficiently search any database, regardless of how large or complex.

Order of Operations

In algebraic math, mathematical equations are evaluated from left to right. Likewise, most search engines process your search request from left to right. Therefore, it is important to enter the most important, required, and unique terms first from left to right.

Mathematical Order of Operations

Rule 1: *First perform any calculations inside parentheses.*

Rule 2: *Next perform all multiplications and divisions, working from left to right.*

Rule 3: *Lastly, perform all additions and subtractions, working from left to right.*

A homogenous database is basically a database that has all of the same kind of information in it. For example, both a well known ATS Kenexa 2X BrassRing® and LinkedIn™ possess homogeneous databases. All of the documents conform to similar criteria because they all take the shape of a resume. With homogenous databases, the order of operations does not matter because there is a precise, finite amount of data, and eventually all necessary information will be found within that exact finite amount.

The challenge in using search engines is that there is no finite amount of data because search engines constantly evolve and grow organically. Their database landscape changes so frequently that the database is never fixed and always left "open". With open search engines like Google and Bing, it matters very much that users follow the left-to-right rule because it will dramatically influence the results obtained. Therefore, when in doubt, it is best to assume a left-to-right processing order.

Three Boolean Operators: AND, OR, and NOT

There are only three **Boolean** operators in a search: AND, OR and NOT. Notice the capitalization – most search engines are not case sensitive, yet will only recognize these three as commands when spelled with all caps. That's it! You now know Boolean!

The term "Boolean" originates from the book An Investigation of the Laws of Thought by George Boole, an English mathematician and logician from the 1800's whose research focus was in algebra and differential equations. He minted the term Boolean algebra to explain logic in math using "true/false" values.

You can also use quotation marks and parentheses as operators. Parentheses should always be used when you apply the OR operator and quotation marks should always surround compound words and phrases of two or more words. Almost every search engine recognizes the use of both.

Just like the orders of operation in math, use AND before OR and save NOT for last. In addition, use NOT sparingly and then only when you are certain a term should be excluded or you risk unintentionally eliminating perfectly good results.

The following is a quick review of the three kinds of Boolean operations:

Conjunction

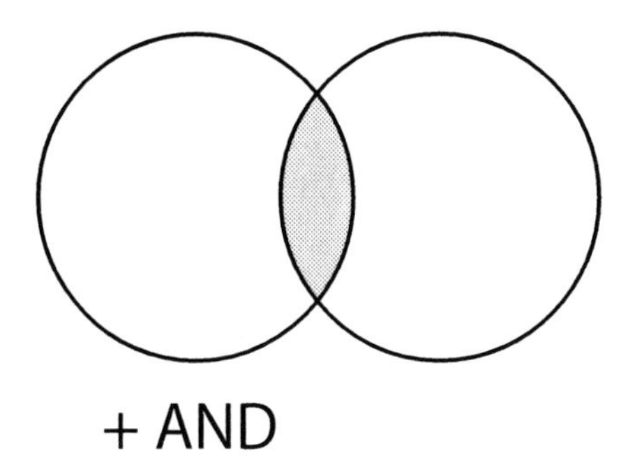

Use this command, and both keywords to the left and right must be present in every search result. The AND operation is a logical conjunction and the mathematical equivalent of addition. In some search engines such as Google and Bing the plus symbol (+) can be used in its place as shorthand, to save time and keystrokes. Requiring both words to be included in every result means the search will bring back the fewest results among the three operators.

Because most Web search engines such as Google and Bing assume that a space between words is equivalent to utilizing the AND operator it is not really necessary for you to type it in your search. However, many proprietary systems do require that you specifically enter the AND command to signify a search must return both words. It is therefore a recommended practice that you apply the AND operator everywhere even if it is not required until you learn to distinguish were it must be applied and where it is inferred by a space between words.

Disjunction

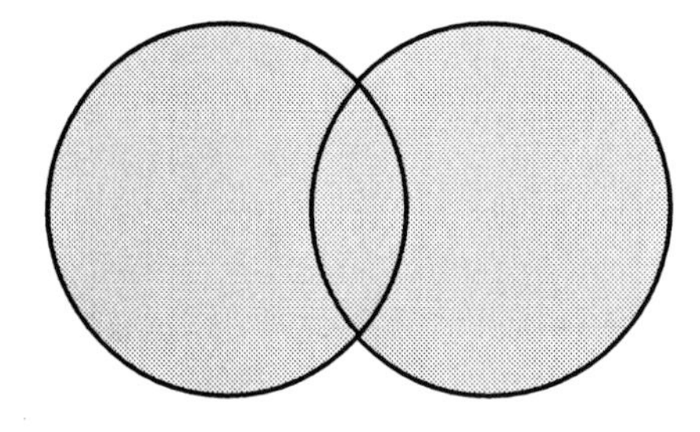

| OR

In searching with logical disjunctions a keyword must be present to the left and right of the OR operator. Results returned will include pages containing either or both of the keywords. The OR operation is a logical disjunction and the mathematical equivalent of multiplication. It will return the largest set of results, so use this only to expand your search results, and apply it sparingly. In some search engines such as

Google and Bing, the pipe or vertical line symbol (|) can be used in its place as shorthand to save time and keystrokes (A|B). On most regular QWERTY type keyboards this character is found above the "enter" or "return" key and below the "backspace" key.

Negation

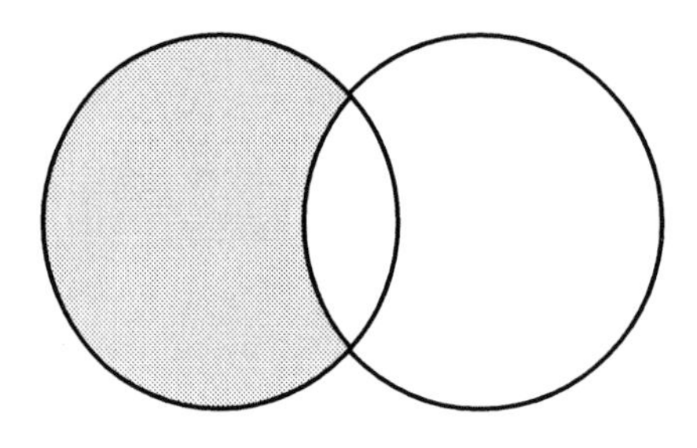

- NOT

Use this command, and your search must include the keyword to the left while excluding the one to the right. The NOT operation is a logical negation and the mathematical equivalent of subtraction. Using it will narrow and somewhat constrain the focus of your results. In some search engines such as Google and Bing, the minus symbol (-) can be used in its place as shorthand to save time and keystrokes. Take care when using the NOT command as it can eliminate good results when unnecessarily used. Also note that word processing programs with automatic spell checking tend to replace the minus symbol with the em dash (—). The correct symbol for use in search is the arithmetic operator representing the minus sign represented in Unicode as U+2212 as and in Ascii code as −, not the hyphen, en dash, or em dash, figure dash, horizontal bar, underscore, or maqaf characters.

Parentheses

( )

Use parentheses to indicate a subset or group of searches. Just like with mathematical orders or operations, search engines will process whatever is in parentheses first which is why it is recommended you always use them when employing OR. Parentheses can be misunderstood by a search engine, bringing you back erroneous results if you forget to include one of the two, or if you use square [ ], curly { }, or angle < > brackets.

Recommended Practice: *Always enclose statements using the OR operator inside a parenthesis like this: (A OR B).*

Quotation Marks

" "

Use neutral, straight or vertical **quotation marks** (also called **inverted commas** or **speech marks**) when looking for words that must appear together and in a particular order. Quotation marks join two or more words into one phrase. However, like with parenthesis they too can be misunderstood by search engines if you mistakenly leave out the beginning or ending quote, or use an incorrect character. A common mistake is to unintentionally mistype a single quote (‘) instead of the double quote (“) by not pressing the Shift button. Also, pay close attention when copying searches from a word processing application because search engines will not understand the typographically correct left-handed and right-handed quotation marks colloquially referred to as curly or squiggly marks such as the ones used in Microsoft WordTM. It is a recommended practice to type your parenthesis directly into the search engine query box, or use a plain text editor that will not autocorrect straight quotes into distinct opening and closing marks.

Search Engine Rules to Remember

Here are some basic rules you should keep in mind when working with search engines:

- Search engines do not give you access to all pages on the Web, only the ones they themselves have found and indexed. Typically, this means that search engines find pages that have been linked from other pages somewhere else. It is estimated that only about 30 percent of the publically visible content on the World Wide Web is indexed by contemporary search engines.
- Each search engine searches the Web and indexes pages in different ways, so different search engines will sometimes have overlapping results, but because of distinctive indexing and cataloguing methods one search engine will have a set of results different from another. This factor is particularly true for the deeper content that Sourcers and recruiters seek. Hence, you should become fluent in searching with different search engines lest you be dependent on one that may change its ways or become obsolete.
- The number of pages a search engine has indexed, known as the size of its index, is not the only consideration in search engine selection. Because volume does not always equate with quality you should evaluate different search engines on a regular basis. Among other factors relevant to your particular needs you should also compare search engines based on the number of results, the relevance of found content, how fast you can search through those pages and how easy it is to use advanced commands. Take the time to learn about the different search engines and determine which best fit your needs. Remember that if you do not find what you are looking for with one search engine it is possible what you seek has been indexed by another database. Great Sourcers never give up until they are certain the information doesn't exist.

> ***Web pages are public:*** *If you can visit them with your browser, and you haven't entered a password of some kind, then you are seeing something that is publicly available to everyone. You are not doing anything wrong, illegal or unethical, even if the content seems like it should be confidential or private.*

Given the preceding rules, it is important that you search more than one search engine to find candidates. Most people have one go-to search engine, but proficiency using at least three of them avoids the penalties of complacency. A solid research process uses at least Google, Bing and one other mainstream search engine such as Blekko, Gigablast, Exalead or IceRocket, plus a selection of specialized indexes. Each of these search engines allows you to search for the URL, title, and text of a page, and each has indexed the Web fairly extensively.

Although most basic commands are the same, each search engine can be searched in slightly different ways, so the commands may vary from one to the other. Knowledge of the advanced searching capabilities of these search engines is critical in successfully using the Internet to generate leads. Fortunately, most search engines have tutorials, or "Help" files, that illustrate the commands and options supported. A link to the "Help" file should appear on the front page, or sometimes under the "advanced search" option once you have conducted your initial search. Read these tutorials and familiarize yourself with a search engine's inner workings to increase your potency.

Section 4. Warning! Do Not Waste Your Time on the Internet

Resumes do not encapsulate humans. Rather, the broad range of human activity has been catalogued and evidenced by absolutely every page on the Web. Information about potential candidates can be found everywhere. Never forget that the Internet must be used efficiently to be an effective candidate search tool or else you run the risk of whiling away your life in a Sisyphean tragedy, recreating identical searches over and over only to come across the same candidates, or endlessly surfing the Internet finding candidates who receive dozens of calls from other ineffectual recruiters using similarly tired methods.

"A man should look for what is, and not for what he thinks should be." – Albert Einstein

A sensible approach begins with a primary search string that adopts the following characteristics:

- Validate your search keywords before you begin
- Be very selective, use only the essential keywords
- Apply the pendulum approach of iterative search
- Keep things simple

Keywords Are the Answer

The fundamental building block of any electronic recruiting search is the **keyword**. Keywords unlock the action in an Internet-based search. Do not waste time searching with inadequate keywords. Pick words unique to the industry to guarantee accuracy. Words like "accountant" or "engineer" are insufficient, because there are too many kinds of accountants and engineers, so your results will be unmanageable. More than eight keywords may confuse the search engine or return too few results, just as using less than four, may return far too many.

> ***Keep It Simple:*** *Start with four to eight keywords.*

To identify the appropriate keywords, use the following process:

The "Need" Question

Ask yourself what *needs* to be on the resume in terms of keywords before you start the search. Think of words with definitions that are concrete and inarguable. These are words that absolutely must be on a resume for that prospect even to begin to appear qualified (usually skill sets). For example, when searching for a UNIX Systems Administrator, the word "Unix" could be one that must be on their resume. Though useful as a search term, rarely do titles like Systems Administrator "need" to be on the resume. This rule is especially true in the technology sphere, where titles tend to vary greatly from company to company: One company's Systems Administrator is another company's SysAdmin, UNIX Administrator, Network Administrator, or even Senior Technical Specialist.

If in doubt look it up:

- *Abbreviations: Find out what abbreviations stand for at Acronyma.com and Abbreviations.com*
- *Concepts: Look up concepts related to your core keywords using OneLook.com, Reverse Dictionary, Thematic Search Engines like Yippy.com and Quintura.com, and the define: command on Google*
- *Technical Terms: Get simple explanations to complex concepts at HowStuffWorks.com and Techterms.com*

It probably doesn't matter to the hiring manager if your candidate was a Technical Specialist at his previous job so long as they worked in an administrator's role with UNIX servers. What are the skill sets this person will need to have on their resume? There should be few words, if any, that actually fit the "need" since many descriptions are concepts and not keywords. Do not catch yourself eliminating the "need" words in order to widen your search, because you will not be able to use those resumes anyway. After all, what good is a systems administrator without UNIX if the primary requirement for this position is that they administer UNIX systems? Your "need" words should be the first keywords in every search string you create, with other keywords being variable.

Do not be put off by more obscure, (abstruse) or rare technical terms that are probably only understood by people in that particular discipline.

Those often make excellent keywords because they point only to people with the desired skillset. For example, the abbreviation ATS may be interpreted as "Applicant Tracking System" if you are familiar with recruitment applications, but in fact, there are thousands of other definitions for ATS. Spelled out, the words Applicant Tracking System are much more likely to identify people in the recruitment/ HRIS sector.

Not all significant terms are esoteric; they may be simple or common words that become specialized when they are put together because they relate directly to the way in which a job is performed. Action phrases can be particularly useful. Take for example the words "write" and "code". When used separately in different places of a document they are not uniquely indicative. However, when put together, they create an action phrase such as "I write code" that very likely indicates a programmer and would only appear together on Web pages where programmers discuss their work in a phrase such as "wrote 900 lines of code".

Add Titles

Once you begin to see results, couple your "need" words with various versions of titles so that your outcome should be those individuals who have been in that role at some time or another. At this point, you can separate the wheat from the chaff. For example, you could use the following titles: "systems administrator", "network engineer", "systems engineer", or "network administrator" along with your "need" word UNIX.

☞ *CROSS REFERENCE BOOKMARK: REFER TO EXAMPLE JOB TITLE STUDY IN THE APPENDIX*

Use a variety of commonly accepted, standard job titles. Related job functions and responsibilities are also useful identifiers. In the Appendix of this book you will find an example study that illustrate how varied job titles can be.

Use Wildcards

Remember to use the wildcard function (*) to gather the various forms of different words. For example, use "pharm*" to gather every resume that contains any variation of "pharm", "pharma", or "pharmaceutical" and so on. Not all search engines support wildcards, and some have different ways of handling them, so be sure to read each search engine's "Help" file. For example, Google does not support wildcards for word stemming such as "pharm*" but will search for common synonyms to a concept such as pharmaceuticals.

☞ *CROSS REFERENCE BOOKMARK: REFER TO QUICK GUIDE: GOOGLE SOURCING OPERATORS USE SYNONYMS OR SIMILAR KEYWORDS*

If a search is too narrow, it may help to add a few similar keywords or synonyms inside an "OR" statement. Using the UNIX example above, you could search for other kinds of UNIX, which are similar. For example, it may be applicable to search for: UNIX OR LINUX OR Solaris OR HP/US OR AIX.

☞ *CROSS REFERENCE BOOKMARK: REFER TO CHAPTER 3, SECTION 2*

Make Associations

In identifying keywords, start with simple terms from the requirements of your search, associate other terms using lateral thinking and begin making some logical leaps. Logical leaps are what take you from finding a page online to another loosely associated subject or concept relevant to your search. Along the way, you will pick up other keywords to find what you need. For example a search for polymer chemist could begin by revealing a page designed to teach aspiring college students the different career paths they may undertake with a chemistry degree, but on that page is a list of resources about polymer chemistry. Among them is mention of the Division of Polymer Chemistry within the American Chemical Society located at polyacs.org. You now have not only a new keyword, but also an organization with members likely to be qualified for your open requirement.

Quick Guide! The KEY to Keywords

Do not limit yourself to just technical terms and jargon. There are various types of keywords you can use to search for candidate resumes, profiles and bios. Here are a few ideas:

- **Unique** terms only your candidate would know
- **Abstruse** rare, technically obscure terms
- **Significant** words used together only by professionals in that job function
- **Action** verbs used by people when explaining what they do Eg. "I ____ ____ for ___"
- What does the hiring manager have on **their resume**?

- Job Titles used by competitors, companies hiring similar talent, or similar organizations
- Skill related keywords and jargon
- Names of tools, products, specialized function or roles
- Names of educational degrees or certifications, their associated abbreviations and schools that grant them
- "Wash out" terms that should definitely **NOT** be on the profiles of identified prospects

Searching with the Pendulum Approach

If your keywords are too general, your results will not be accurate. If they are too specific, your results will be sparse. In both cases, the results mean you will have wasted your time. The best approach is one delivering between 40 and 120 results. After making an initial search attempt to gauge results, vary your keywords until you have the best possible combination, and try not to exceed 250 results. From there, you then limit your selection based on additional factors such as geographic constrains or more keywords. This is called an iterative search model.

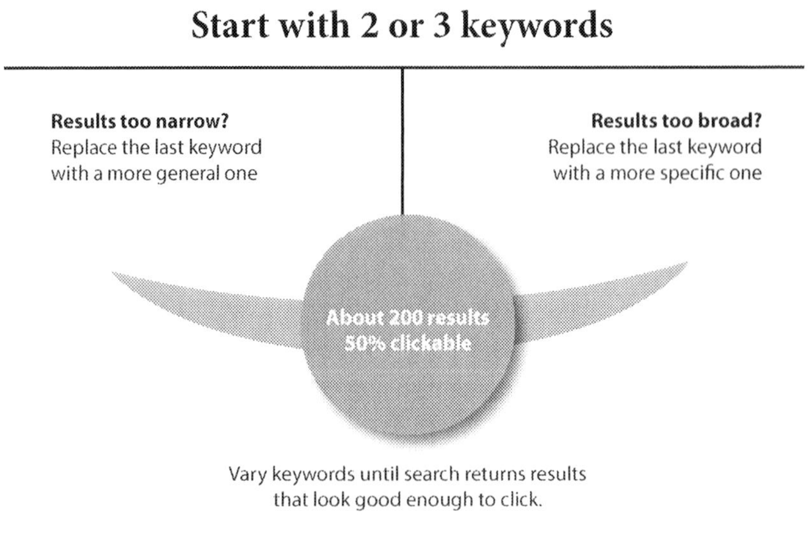

Start with 2 or 3 keywords

Results too narrow?
Replace the last keyword
with a more general one

Results too broad?
Replace the last keyword
with a more specific one

About 200 results
50% clickable

Vary keywords until search returns results
that look good enough to click.

Figure 14 Pendulum or Iterative Search Approach

Such an iterative approach to search is the most effective way to narrow down results from among the overwhelmingly vast set of data in the open web. Your first attempt at a search only sets the stage but will seldom produce the exact results desired. Following the iterative model you then search within that first set of data using more specific terms, swinging a virtual pendulum between two few and too many results until landing in a balanced state. In a few short minutes of experimentation this confirms your search is viable before wasting time clicking on results.

Check the Numbers

Once you have collected your keywords, but before starting your search, attempt a couple of different experimental search strings and gauge how many results you have before you actually start the search in earnest. Start by visiting the largest resume database to which you subscribe and testing out this method. Quickly skim the summary of candidates to make sure you are on the right track. Now apply the pendulum; throw in a search string that results in a narrow set of results, then throw in a wider string to judge your results. By using this approach when you initiate your search, you have a feel for your search as well as an idea of which approach you will need to take first.

If you have results in the high hundreds, or even thousands, your search is too broad and you will waste valuable time clicking on dead ends. If you do have results in the hundreds and your requirements are local, you could try narrowing them down by using geographic delimiters such as area codes, zip codes, city names, or states. If you are conducting a nationwide search then the geographic delimiters will not make sense. In that case, you could focus your results by replacing broad keywords with ones that are unique to the kinds of positions for which you are recruiting.

Start Narrow then Widen as You Go

This seems like common sense, yet you can still catch a recruiter attempting to search through 200,000 results on the first search attempt. Of course, there are exceptions when that kind of search is useful, but most of the time narrow search results will increase online effectiveness. Determine your search success by measuring what percentage of the pages the search returns is useful to you. Aim for at least 50 percent, meaning you would click through to view in detail at least one of every two results. This way, you may only have 10 results; but contacting five candidates right away is not a bad start.

Chapter 5
Fundamental Search Concepts

Section 1. Why Use More than One Search Engine?

The answer is simple: Because not all search engines are created equal.

Most expert researchers agree that while the Internet is increasingly hard to measure, one thing will always remain certain: No search engine will ever catalog all of the pages on the Internet. It simply grows too quickly. Search engines work by indexing data on the pages they find. When you search with a search engine, you aren't searching the Internet. Instead, you are searching that search engine's particular index of the pages it has been able to find from the public Web.

"To the man who only has a hammer, everything he encounters begins to look like a nail."
- Abraham Maslow

Each search engine goes about finding pages in a different way, and thus generates a completely different index than all the other search engines. The results you have from one search engine are seldom the same as those you obtain from others. Google boasted it had indexed 1 trillion unique URLs by 2008, but there is no way to measure or accurately determine the exact number of pages in the parade. Many search engines purposefully exclude Web pages from their front page in an effort to differentiate and customize their product to the consumer.

In a still oft-cited 2005 study by InfoSpace, Inc., researchers found that 11.4 percent of search engine results are shared across two major search engines, 2.6 percent are shared between three search engines and 1.1 percent are shared between the top three (Google, Bing, and Ask). In other words, 84.9 percent of results are unique to only one of those three search engines. Yahoo was previously included among top search engines, but since Bing began powering Yahoo searches in 2009, Yahoo results duplicate Bing results and will continue to do so until at least 2019.

Each search engine is configured to read only a specific number of lines of text before moving on to other documents. For example, one search engine may only scan the first 250 lines of text, while another will look through the first 500 and yet another is set up to read through 1,000 lines before stopping. Because the keyword you seek could be located in line 251, or 501 you may get different search results even if both search engines have found the same page.

Over 200 other factors affect how different search engines decide to index content they find. Among them are the number and quality of links pointing to and from a page, the number of times the page has been viewed, how often your search terms occur on the page, how close together the search terms appear, in which part of the page the words appear, the format of the page itself, other components that may be present such as images or video, and all kinds of rules regarding spam. How search engines handle unscrupulous webmasters trying to trick them so their pages get listed at the top of results significantly affects the

content visible to you. It is estimated that search engines must contend with over one million spam pages generated each hour. To you this means the page you seek could be buried in spam thus much harder to find, unless the search engine has handled the offending content effectively.

The above discussion clearly demonstrates that if you are using only one search engine, you are missing out on a vast amount of information. This is made worse by the fact that as recruiters and researchers we are interested in unpopular pages and deeper information than what average users are seeking. It is such unpopular information which most often contains leads and resumes and that kind of data is less likely to be found, indexed and ranked by more than one search engine. You can test this idea yourself by entering some keywords at http://ranking.thumbshots.com.

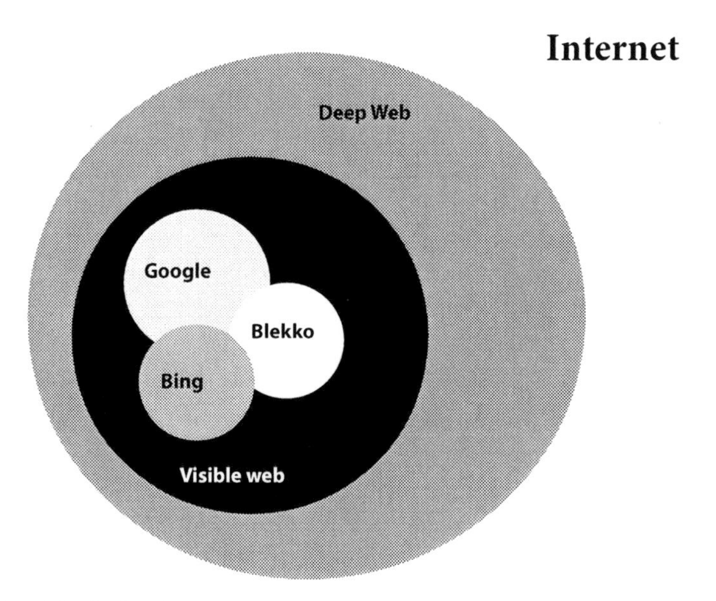

Figure 15 Search Engine Overlap

When selecting a search engine there are several things to keep in mind. These factors will help you determine where to search first.

Size

In this case, "size" relates to the number of pages a particular search engine claims to have listed in its index. At the time of this publication, Google claims to have the most pages indexed. But is Google easy to use? That question leads to the next points.

Functionality

Having the most pages indexed is quite an accomplishment and gives a search engine bragging rights. However, it's not the only thing that matters. Search functionality allows you to gain the most out of a search engine. For the casual user, simple searches are sufficient, but for recruiters it is important to find out if a search engine supports full Boolean searching or only allows limited search functionality, and what if any special syntax or commands are supported. Limited search functionality means that it will not allow you to use basic AND or OR statements as part of your search string. The more functionality a search engine has, the more advanced commands it supports. We will cover these commands later in this chapter. Remember to read the search engine's Help section!

☞ *CROSS REFERENCE BOOKMARK: SEE QUICK COMMAND! IN SECTION 3 OF THIS CHAPTER*

Relevancy

Some search engines are very adept at "guessing" what you really mean when you enter your keywords. Others simply bring back any page containing some of your keywords and may not return relevant results. User-friendly search engines such as Google, Yahoo, and Bing are continually refining ways to bring back relevant results, but they all use a different approach. Their help files should explain how they define relevancy. For example, some search engines may consider different types of popularity – such as websites with lots of other websites pointing to them – most important in determining relevance. Other search engines may take into account the "concept" behind a word, or may even cluster results around concepts and let you refine your search by clicking on those clusters.

Machines capable of understanding context, subtext and human intent exist today only in science fiction. Future generations of researchers will no doubt experience computers capable of appreciating natural language patterns. Perhaps then web search engines will be able to recognize the meaning behind queries. Until then practical semantic search applications incorporated into next-generation search engines like Bing.com are limited to the use of standardized ontologies or taxonomies (vocabularies) like schema.org or analyzing descriptive metadata, bits of information similar to what you may find in a library's card catalog, already present in the source code of pages.

Speed

No matter how big a search engine is, if it takes a long time to bring you results, or if it is difficult to navigate through the results, it will impede your efficiency. The bigger, more popular search engines today tell you how quickly they arrived at those results, so mind this information in the course of your search.

Search Engine vs. Directory

Many people confuse search engines with directories. All the listings in a directory are reviewed and manually added by a live person, whereas a search engine's information is indexed using automated software. You may find a directory easier to use for finding simple and highly relevant information, but they have a much smaller catalog of information. Search engines catalog far more content therefore are more useful for finding deeply buried information. Search engines are the first choices for complex recruitment searches, and for finding very fresh information.

Each search engine has unique quirks and special syntax. Although they are all becoming very user-friendly and simple to employ, you can benefit more from them if you know how to take advantage of special commands and features.

Section 2. The Sourcing Edge: The Art of Resume Sourcing

Spending time Sourcing for candidates on the Internet is just as important as posting a job. Sourcing is probably more valuable than posting, because it is proactive and gives the recruiter more control over the selection of candidates. In this marketplace, you can easily spend more time sorting through unqualified resumes of those who have submitted a resume to your posting than you will after a quick Internet search.

Sourcing is a skill that is not easy to master, though. Why? Mastery is challenging because no search is ever the same. You could have several recruiters search the same database and have completely different results. There is no set formula for successful Sourcing.

Understanding that, we have listed a few tried-and-true Sourcing basics to help in your searching:

Understand exactly for what you are searching. This guideline usually goes without saying, but it is usually the first thing to trip up your Sourcing efforts, so be careful. Get clear definitions from the hiring manager for all the terms with which you intend to search.

It's all in the keywords. Ask the wrong thing from a database and you will have the wrong results. Whether through search engines like Google and Bing, or in resume databases like Monster® and LinkedIn™, it's all about the keywords. If you are clicking through one resume after another and not finding what you need, then you are simply not using keywords that are specific and targeted enough.

Translate the job description to a resume. Because keywords are crucial when Sourcing, understanding what kind of keywords will be on the resumes you need is vital. Too many times the job description uses highly detailed keywords that your candidates would not bother with on their online profile, or even their resume. Do not let one keyword throw off your entire search. Consider the words a candidate would choose to use on their own resume, and every-day terms they would likely use when describing their job during casual conversations. Those keywords often prove to be more accurate than the jargon prescribed by hiring managers in formal job descriptions. Confirm with the hiring manager if those more casual words are present in the resumes they have been seeing. Avoid using too many keywords as this may eliminate good resumes from your search results. Keep in mind that not all of the keywords may appear on one single person's resume so use synonyms, and try several combinations of keywords.

Start small. Use a narrow search string to identify no more than 50 resumes; more than that is a waste of time. If you have to click through more than eight resumes to identify one that may possibly fit your needs then your search string should be altered. An ideal string is one in which every other search result is worth reading further. By focusing on a strong search you do not waste time clicking through unqualified resumes. Broaden your search as you go to make sure you have identified every possible candidate match.

Double-check your search string. It is easy to make a grammatical or syntactical mistake! If you are surprised at your lack of search results, it could very well be because there is a spelling error in your keyword or an unintentionally mistyped command such as not closing the quotation marks, or using lower case in your Boolean operators.

Consider it a work in progress. Mold and shape your search by pulling out good keywords identified from those resumes that were a match. These words may not even be skill sets. For example, in a search string for a technical project manager you might include words like "led team" or "lead staff" because of patterns you previously identify in qualified resumes. Always gather keywords from resumes you read so you can modify your search criteria as you learn from experience.

Do not stop short. Too often, recruiters only try a couple of searches and then stop after contacting only a few candidates. Make sure you use a variety of search methods to pull candidates. It's a numbers game, so keep going until you have at least 50 prospects before you call it quits.

Be patient. Sourcing takes a lot of time and attention to detail. Do not start a search at the end of the day or you may forget where you left off. It's helpful to block out an hour or two during your day when you only do research and Sourcing—no phone calls or visitors so you stay focused. Do not expect instant results right away. It takes time and experience to be strong at Sourcing and it does not come instantaneously. With practice your goal should be to have at least seven suspects to review after about ten minutes of intensive searching.

Keep track, document everything. Avoid duplicating steps by keeping a running list of which search strings you have used and which sources you have explored. You can do this easily with a spreadsheet or plain text document like the Sample Research Form.

Remember, Sourcing successfully is not an exact science. It takes time and attention to detail to thoroughly research online. As you learn about various places to go and source, keep these tips in mind.

Quick Form! Sample Research Form

One simple tool that Sourcers use is a research form that documents your entire search. Compilations of research forms can be used in later searches so that you do not re-invent the wheel. Once you have completed your research form and assembled a search string, be sure to keep track of where you copy and paste it into a search engine by using the following example form.

Download an example Research Form in Microsoft ExcelTM format containing worksheets for the twelve steps, the intake meeting, tracking methods and a convenient search string generator at: http://theSourcinginstitute.com/template

Sourcing Template Example

Source[1]	Keywords[2]	URL/Link[3]	# Results[4]	Qualified[5]	#Interviewed[6]
Eg. MonsterT	CPA, FAS109	www. monster. com/ egresults	40	6	2
Paid Job Board 2					
Free Job Board 1					
Free Job Board 2					
Databases					
Communities					
Associations	transfer pricing	Aicpa.org	16	12	4
Alumni Groups					
Social Network 1					
Social Network 2					
Search Engine 1					
Search Engine 2					
Niche Sites					

This example form includes recommended columns for 1) types of sources, 2) the keywords used to conduct the search through that source, 3) the URL or address of the search results page, 4) number of unique search results obtained from that URL, 5) number of qualified prospects generated from those unique search results, with those keywords, and finally 6) the number of qualified prospects who were interviewed. Add as many rows for each type of source as needed.

Quick Commands! Major Search Engine Syntax

The following chart lists search engine functions and terms, with notes on the correct syntax to use on Google and Bing, two of the major search engines. As you narrow your search, you will need to add more specific keywords and commands.

COMMAND	Google.com	Bing.com
AND	resume Java	resume Java
OR	(UNIX OR Linux)	(UNIX OR Linux)
NOT	resume -jobs	resume -jobs
"word phrase"	"software engineer"	"software engineer"
website	site:company.com	site:company.com
Page Title	intitle:resume	intitle:resume
Page Address	inurl:resume	inurl:resume

Nota Bene: *Do not use a space after the colon character when employing site:, intitle:, and inurl: commands.*

Terms should be typed in order of importance from left to right. As with the aforementioned pendulum, swing from results that are too-narrow and too-broad by changing each term one at a time working backwards from the least important term on the right of your search criteria. To make fine adjustments modify the OR terms first, followed by the ANDs and finally append more specific keywords related to the skillset, location (city, state, postal code) and the commands from the table.

Section 3. Building Search Strings

Building a top-notch search string is critical to obtaining successful results. The term "Boolean Search" is avoided here in favor of logical operators, a more precise description. There are three important logic operators you will need to use frequently when Sourcing. They are conjunctions, disjunctions and negations.

For the purposes of this book, logical **conjunctions** are operations that return search results only if all of your requested terms appear in each listed result. Many search engines including Google and Bing assume that a space between keywords in your query means you are asking for **all** of the listed terms to be included. If you are not certain that is the case then your search expression should include the Boolean term **AND** between every word.

A logical **disjunction** is a statement that is true when **at least one** of the listed alternatives is true. Use disjunctions when you have a list of key terms that are all equivalent. Keywords must be separated by the Boolean term **OR**. Any or all of the terms will be present in results. To ensure the search engine understands your request when using disjunctions it is best to encapsulate your equivalent terms inside a **parenthesis**.

☞ *CROSS REFERENCE BOOKMARK: REFER TO THREE BOOLEAN OPERATORS IN CHAPTER 4*

Logical **negations** are statements requesting the absence of a particular key term or search word. The statement is true only when the word being negated is not found in the pages resulting from your search. Although they appear very complicated, search strings are actually rather simple. Putting together a well thought-out search string directly in different search engines will result in efficacious returns.

To keep it simple, remember that there are two crucial elements to every search attempt that rarely change.

Identifying the Resume

A Web page is made up of several elements on which to search. The URL or Internet address of a page, the page title, links to or from a page, and text or images in a page are all elements on which you can search. One goal is to find home pages or Web pages that are host to resumes or give resume-related information. To do so, tell the search engine to give you those pages that are like resumes. At the beginning, think of all the terms one might find on a resume, such as "resume", "CV" or "Curriculum Vitae", or "Bio". Also, think of other terms that appear on resumes such as "Objective", "Education", "Experience", and "Licensure" (for certain occupations). By specifying that you want those pages that have the word "resume" in the URL, or text, or title of the page, you are increasing your chances of getting a resume. Initially, part of your first search could look like this:

(resume OR CV OR Vitae OR bio OR homepage)

Of course, using this part of the search string alone would generate millions of results, so continue to the next key element to your string.

Job Specifications

Here is where your keywords matter. As you learned previously, it's all about the keywords. You need to take the key terms from the job itself and put them in the form of a Boolean search string. For instance, if you are looking for an embedded software engineer in the wireless telecommunications industry, with a wireless keyword like CDMA and some brand names, you could compose a string such as the following:

CDMA AND embedded AND (Motorola OR Ericsson OR Nokia)

Note that in Google, the "AND" Boolean is unnecessary; however, in other search engines such as your ATS, it may be, so learn how to use it until you are comfortable leaving it out. Your search string should now look like this:

resume CDMA AND embedded AND (Motorola OR Ericsson OR Nokia)

Now all you need to do is eliminate some of the pages you do not want, for example, job postings and other employment-related documents. One way to do so quickly is to use a synonym search as in Step #1 above, but in the opposite or negative sense. Ask Google to NOT return results with words related to "jobs" using the minus sign ("-") like this:

resume CDMA AND embedded AND (Motorola OR Ericsson OR Nokia) -jobs -job

Once you have an initial search string created, you can continue to mold and form it to fit your particular needs and mix it up to have a wide variety of good results. Most search engines will want to see this string in different forms, but the concepts are the same. We will review some other special commands later. Remember, if you build it right, the results will come.

Section 4. Search Engine Rules to Remember

Here are some rules to remember about search engines:

Rule #1:

Search engines **do not give you access to all pages on the web**, only the ones they themselves have found and indexed. Typically, search engines find pages that have been linked from other pages somewhere else. Each search engine searches the Web and indexes pages in different ways, so different search engines will sometimes have overlapping results, but because of distinctive indexing methods one search engine will have a set of results different from the other.

Rule #2:

The number of pages a search engine has indexed is not the only consideration in search engine selection. As you evaluate different search engines, also consider **how fast** you can search through those pages, **how easy** it is to use advanced commands, and **how relevant are the results**. Take the time to learn about the different search engines and determine what best fits your needs. Remember that if you do not find what you are looking for with one search engine, it doesn't mean the information doesn't exist.

Rule #3:

In light of preceding rules it is important that you **search more than one**

search engine to find candidates. Most people have one go-to search engine, but proficiency using at least three avoids the penalties of complacency. A solid process uses at least Google, Bing and one other search engine such as Blekko. Each of these three search engines allows you to search for the URL, title, and text of a page, and each has indexed the Web fairly extensively.

Rule #4:

Although **most basic commands are the same**, each search engine can be searched in slightly different ways, so the commands may be a little different. Knowledge of the advanced searching capabilities of these search engines is critical in successfully using the Internet to generate leads.

Rule #5:

Read the help file. Fortunately, most search engines have tutorials, or "Help" files accessible on their front page or by searching for "advanced search" help. Read these tutorials and familiarize yourself with a search engine's inner workings to increase your potency.

Rule #6:

Web pages are public. If you can visit them with your browser, and you haven't entered a password of some kind, then you are seeing something that is publicly available to everyone. You are not doing anything wrong, illegal or unethical, even if the content seems like it should be private.

Section 5. Simplicity is Best

Keep the search simple and save time; it is really that simple. Here is an example job requirement for an embedded systems engineer with the following skillset:

- Algorithms, C and C++ Coding Skills
- DSP (Digital Signal Processing)
- Natural Language or other high-level language experience
- Cross-platform development
- Hardware design experience
- Mechanical engineering background

Your search, for example, could be:

C AND DSP AND embedded AND engineer

This string works well when searching internal applicant tracking systems, Monster® and LinkedIn™. Start with the most important keyword(s). Sticking to this job requirement, for example, your "need" words are (best determined in discussions with the hiring manager): DSP, digital/embedded and C (related to programming embedded systems).

When searching Google, Bing and most major search engines, you will want to add biographical keywords like: resume, CV, "about me" and remove AND.

For example:

DSP pivotal embedded C "about me"

Then add the OR statements to further narrow your search like this:

For ATSs, Monster.com and LinkedIn™:

C AND DSP AND embedded AND engineer AND ("natural language" OR "hardware design")

For most major search engines, like Google and Bing:

C DSP embedded engineer ("natural language" OR "hardware design") "about me"

Note that while the words to the left and right of AND do not have to be in parentheses, it is best to enclose your OR statements in parentheses. Some search engines will be able to understand if there are no parentheses, but using them all the time reduces the risk of confusing the search engine. Try not to complicate your search by using more than four ANDs when searching ATSs, Monster.com and LinkedIn™ or eight keywords when searching search engines.

Example Search

On a resume database or ATS, begin with

C AND DSP AND embedded AND ("hardware engineer" OR design)

Note that if using a search engine where results are not guaranteed to be resumes, you will need to add some keywords to focus results and eliminate job postings. You could also leave out the ANDs. For example, the above search when used in a search engine could be:

C DSP embedded ("hardware engineer" OR design) resume -intitle:job

Too many results return from this search? Attempt to narrow the search by adding a new term such as *algorithm*:

C AND DSP AND embedded AND ("hardware engineer" OR design) algorithm

Note: Do not forget to add resume and -intitle:job when using Web search.

Better, but still too many? Try adding another keyword:

C AND DSP AND embedded AND "hardware engineer" AND (algorithm OR "natural language")

Note: On Google, this string would be C DSP embedded "hardware engineer" (algorithm OR "natural language") intitle:resume -intitle:job

Do not be limited by three or four attempts. If you aren't able to narrow your search, keep tweaking the terms until you arrive at what you need. Take one or two minutes to adjust your search string before you start clicking on the results. Seek to return from 40 to 120 results within a resume database like your ATS, LinkedIn™ or Monster™. On the open Web as with Google or Bing, your goal is from 150-250 results, and where at least half of the results are something you would click on.

The successful Internet Sourcer knows that it's not only where you search, but also how you search that really matters. You could be searching the same database or source as someone else but come up with completely different results. In fact, it would be rare that you would come up with the same results. The only cases where you will come up with the same results are in highly niche, skill-set searches — but let's face it, how many times do you have to search for a scientist with experience using a Sciex API 3000 machine?

> ***Use Your Head:*** *Your hiring managers will stress that your candidates must know "such and such". But, usually by the very nature of the position those requirements would be a given. For example, say a hiring manager wants to hire an accountant who must have general ledger experience. Would you use "general ledger" in your search string at all times? No, because by the very nature of being an experienced accountant, a candidate would have this knowledge. If you're unsure of these kinds of embedded competencies, ask the hiring manager. Although you may intuitively know these things, you may catch yourself breaking the rules.*

Develop your own style of searching. Once you have taken to heart the three basic tenets of Internet Search: **Keywords, Pendulum** and **Simplicity**, then you can begin to perfect your online research. The objective is to spend two to ten minutes online and have enough results to begin recruiting.

Section 6. Domain Searching

Although certain sites may be non-public, they are still accessible from the Internet and are part of the public domain, but their addresses may not be published or advertised extensively. Finding a little-known domain registered to a company from which you want to recruit is like finding a secret treasure. Just because a page isn't being directly linked to from the home page of a website doesn't mean that page is inaccessible. If you cannot enter the front door of the site, then use side doors via the advanced function on a search engine.

Many times, companies will have pages right on their website that are not linked to any of their main pages. Search engines will continue to index those pages because they find links to them from other places, so they may be able to pull them up for you. All you need to do is enter a specialized command such as "site:" in Google and add the words you expect to find on your page. For example, we can ask Google to search for a job title within the Symantec server in order to find names of potential executive candidates, like so:

site:symantec.com vp

Once you have a name, it is easy to gather more information on this individual by using a metasearch engine as previously discussed. It's amazing how often companies provide information on their key employees right on their site.

Here are some important facts about Hosts and Domains:

What is a host or a domain? A domain is the root of the website address, such as www.symantec.com, while a top-level domain is the extension at the right of the last dot, in this case, ".doc". Examples of top-level domains are .com and .edu.

Whois.net. From whois.net/, enter the name of a target company, for example Symantec, and see all the websites with that company name in the root address. Some may be active, some may be on hold, others may just be registered but with nothing coming up. Any one of these could contain information about the company, its employees, customers and so on, which may not be listed from their primary location at symantec.com. Advanced search will let you search domains from the left of your keyword (as in "starts with") or to the right of your keyword.

WhoIs Source. The Domain Explorer at domaintools.com/ allows you to enter a company name and see names of domains already registered to that company. Results are different, and sometimes more revealing, than with Whois.net. For example, a search for Symantec as the registrar shows 249 domains with the word Symantec in them.

ARIN. From arin.net/tools/whois_help.html, you can access the American Registry for Internet Numbers; search by company or registrant name to find blocks of IP addresses registered to them.

Chapter 6
Search Engines

Section 1. Google.com in a Nutshell...

- Indexes over twenty different document types including Adobe PDF, Microsoft Office (.doc, .xls, .ppt) and others like .rtf, .txt, .ps, etc. Refer to the Appendix for a full list
- Eliminates "page not found" errors with cached pages
- Lets you find similar pages or pages that link to a particular Web page
- Can search pages you have previously visited
- Added advantage of Verbatim tool to search for the exact words you enter into the search field

Type in your keywords at google.com and hit "Enter". Google looks for Web pages that match and automatically adds the "AND" Boolean between the words you enter, so it only returns those pages that include all of your search terms in the page. It does ignore punctuation, special characters such as: @# percent^*()=[]\, stop words like http and .com as well as certain single digits and letters. Google also has a spell checker that corrects the spelling of most common words.

Choose keywords that are unique and most likely to appear on Web pages for the best, most relevant results. To restrict a search further, just include more terms. Google also prefers pages in which related query terms are near each other. This means that results will be ranked higher if more than one instance or variant of your selected keywords are found close together. For example, a page mentioning Java, J2EE and J2ME in close proximity will likely appear higher among your search results than one where

Java is all alone in a paragraph, J2EE is further down the page, and J2ME is at the end of the document.

Google Cache retrieves archived results from pages that have been removed since the last time their spider went through the site. Typically, the Cache goes about six months into the past, which reduces "404 Page Not Found" errors and helps you find content that has since been removed. If you come across a page that is no longer there, you may see "Page Not Found" or 404 errors. In those cases, Google may still have a copy of the page in its archive. You can use the cache: operator by appending it to the website address or URL as follows and if Google has an older version of that page, it will display it:

cache:www.hire4ce.com

This is useful when conducting peer regression search discussed in Chapter 6, because you can identify people who were listed in About Us pages that no longer appear online.

Here are a few operators that can help with your searches on Google:

Operators	How to use them
link:	Use this operator to find pages that link to a specific page within a website. For example: link:theSourcinginstitute.com The above will find pages that link to The Sourcing Institute home page. You can also specify a page within a site like this: link: theSourcinginstitute.com/blogs/
related:	Use this operator to find pages similar to a website. For example, to find pages similar to www.theSourcinginstitute.com, search for: related: theSourcinginstitute.com
site:	This operator will find information about a topic from a particular website. For example, to find information about tax accountants from KPMG, do a search like this: "tax accountant" site: kpmg.com

Google uses a special syntax for finding only documents written in a particular format. The *filetype:* command allows you to specify that the search return only documents in that format. Resumes are frequently written in MS Word (doc), Rich Text (rtf), and sometimes Plain Text (txt), but the most common file type among resumes posted on public websites is Adobe (pdf).

Searching for a document type will bring back these files instead of regular HTML pages. When used in conjunction with keywords that would be found on a resume, this command can help focus a search. For example:

(filetype:doc OR filetype:pdf OR filetype:rtf OR filetype:txt) (resume OR CV OR "curriculum vitae" OR present) "Cisco Certified Architect"

Not all resumes are named "Resume" so to locate those kinds of documents you can use a combination of words commonly found in resumes like this:

(filetype:doc OR filetype:pdf OR filetype:rtf OR filetype:txt) (work OR project OR experience OR certifications) "Novell Engineer"

Other kinds of documents like Excel and PowerPoint can also reveal some leads, so try doing searches such as:

RHCE Linux *@redhat.com (filetype:ppt OR filetype:xls OR filetype:doc OR filetype:pdf OR filetype:rtf OR filetype:txt)

It is unusual to find job postings created in some of the above document formats, so the above searches are very useful in eliminating many of the useless pages resulting from a typical search.

Be careful when you use the *filetype:* operator in a Google search, such as filetype:xml galway

> "Google searches for files with the .xml extension, not for files of file type XML. Not all URLs or pages have the .html file extension. Some pages (like http://www.google.com) have no extension at all, and some have an extension that doesn't match their file type. Limiting your search to a specific file type will return pages with that file extension, and may return fewer relevant results." – From Google Search Help Page

Search Pages You've Visited with Google Web History

If you are signed in to your Gmail account, Google will store information related to search queries you conducted including the keywords, time and date, and which results you visited. Google Web History is on by default when you create a Google account, and uses that history to personalize other services across its product line.

With Google Web History, you can search only the pages you've visited in the past, and even search your previous searches. This technique is useful when trying to remember a particularly effective search you stumbled on while doing something else, and didn't have a chance to note. You can also find trends on your own search activity, such as which sites you visit most frequently, and top searches that return your best results. As an added benefit, Google will autocomplete the search box with queries you have conducted before, saving you a bit of time and effort.

Verbatim Tool

As Google becomes more sophisticated, they make an attempt at guessing what you mean when you enter a query, and may bring back results that include its interpretation of what you may want. You can turn off this "guessing" by using Verbatim, and Google will search using the exact words you entered, as spelled, and not attempt to bring back synonyms or related terms. To activate this feature:

- Click on **"More"** at the top of the search results page
- Click Verbatim
- Type your search terms into the search box and type **Enter**

Useful Google Downloads

Google offers some very useful free tools you can download to help you manage information.

- With the **Google Toolbar** (toolbar.google.com), you can perform Google searches from any site, eliminate annoying pop-ups, and turn on highlighting of search results
- With the **Google Desktop Search** (desktop.google.com), you can rapidly scan all the files and emails on your computer, just as easily as searching the Internet

- The **Google Translate Tools** (google.com/language_tools) let you enter a website written in another language and translate it to English, or vice versa

Specialty Searches

Google Specialty Searches allow you to search through specific collections of information.

- **Scholar**.google.com (academic research papers)
- Google.com/**blogsearch** (real time blog post search)
- Google.com/**patents** (USPTO database search)

Quick Guide: Google Sourcing Operators

Here are some logical operators and field search syntax you can use on Google.

Wildcards:	**Extends results when current results too narrow.**
* (the asterisk, SHIFT 8) Ex: "software * engineer"	Acts as a "fill in the blank" search for any word/ words. Multiple asterisks separated by spaces represent that many words. Finds software database design engineer or software test engineer, but not the term "software engineer", itself.
Number range:	**Find ranges of numbers from low to high.**
.. (two dots, not three) Ex: "product manager" intitle:resume 30002..31999 Ex: "CCIE * 2010..17999"	Finds product managers in zip codes for GA: 30002 (Avondale Estates) 31999 (Columbus) Finds people with Cisco Certified Internetworking Expert certification numbers between 2010 and 17999. Tip: Visit Zipmath.com and use their Zip Codes in Radius search to find zip code value ranges for desired geography
Title and URL:	**Finds pages with specific words contained in the document name | address**
intitle:resume inurl:resume + KEYWORD Ex: (intitle:resume OR inurl:resume) CPA "tax attorney" -job	Finds the word "Resume" in the document name Finds the word "Resume" in the address of the page Finds a document name or page address that includes CPA or tax attorney, but not the word job. Tip: Using both to find more resumes! (intitle: resume OR inurl:resume)

File type:	Finds content in specified format
filetype:pdf + KEYWORD	Finds Adobe PDF files Other useful formats: doc .ppt .xls .txt .rtf .tiff .jpg
Website:	**Searches Google for any content originating in that website/ domain**
site:temple.edu site:.gov + KEYWORD	Returns any pages found by Google anywhere within the Temple.edu website Returns any pages found on any .gov websites (works with any Top Level Domain)
Alerts:	**Receive search results via email daily | weekly**
google.com/alerts	Enter search string and subscribe to ongoing search results via email address or RSS

Google Custom Search Engine (google.com/cse)

With Google, you can build your own personal version of a search engine called a CSE (Custom Search Engine that indexes only the websites you specify and ignoring all the rest. Keep in mind that any search engine you create could be found and utilized by anyone who receives or finds the link. However, they will not be able to modify it or even learn how it works unless you specifically invite them to do so via the administration panel within Google CSE.

Custom Search Engines can be open or closed. An open CSE looks at the entire Google index but applies a collection of synonyms and other types of refinements of your choosing that are specialized to the content that you're trying to find. Closed CSE's are ones where the only search results included are those from a specified list of URLs that you provide.

Create Your Own CSE

To create a Google CSE, you must have a Gmail account (free). Log into your Gmail account and then head to google.com/cse. A blue button should say: "make you own search engine". If you've already created one or have been invited to contribute to one, you may see a link below the button that says "manage your existing search engines". Following that link, you can edit or manage anything that you either created or are sharing, or you can click on the blue button and you will be taken to where you begin creating your own search engine.

You cannot start a 'custom search engine' without specifying at least one website, so you will need to have a few URLs ready before you can begin. Having a handful of keywords and their synonyms would be also helpful, but not required at this point.

Choose the standard edition, which is free. Site search is for commercial purposes, such as when you have your own website and is an entirely different type of CSE. Check that you read and agreed to the terms, hit the "Next" button and you will be taken to the page where your search engine will have been created. You can always come back change settings such as layout or other customizations, but for now simply push forward. The next page is just the script that you would need to copy and paste if you want to embed the CSE on your website, so skip that as you do not currently need it. Jump to the basics and let the fun begin. Under search engine keywords, enter words that reflect the type of search that you're doing, i.e., what you are looking for.

The only other choice here is whether you search just the sites that you specify (a closed CSE) or the entire Web (an open CSE) with emphasis only on your selected sites. For your first CSE, begin with just the selected sites. For example, if you want to look only within the associations of professionals and conferences of professionals that you're seeking then just search that content. The results will be far fewer, but more focused. If you search the entire Web then you're going to need to do a lot of filtering because you're going to be dealing with the same kind of junk that you deal with in an open Google search. With an open CSE, refinements and synonyms become extremely important.

Before leaving this page enable image search so you can do headshot searches, then save your changes. It may appear as if nothing happens, but Google will reset itself so your work is saved.

Synonyms

One of the advantages of creating your own custom search engine is that you can define any group of words as synonyms. This becomes a custom vocabulary or taxonomy, which eliminates having to type in every different variation for a job title. When you search for that synonym, your CSE will also include all the other related job titles you listed under it. For example, you could have a synonym for accountant that would also look for CPA, financial analyst, tax manager, and so on. Synonyms could also be lists of geographic locations such as city names or area codes. Variations of company names are also a useful way to employ synonyms.

Refinements

The difference between refinements and synonyms can be muddled. A refinement is a collection of sites. You could apply a refinement to any search in your CSE that would limit the search to only a particular subsection of websites, or alternatively, you could append search commands just as you would in a regular search.

Section 2. Bing.com in a Nutshell...

- Indexes different document types such as: htm, pdf, doc, xls, ppt, txt, and xml
- Supports a high number of search commands and keywords
- Suggests helpful related searches
- Has the ability to conduct Social Search
- Performs semantic and conceptual searching
- Geographic search function with loc: command
- Customize search results with your own settings

Bing.com crawls the Internet on its own, separately from any other search engine index, and has built up its own very large independent index. Thus, there is little overlap with other search engine results, making it a mandatory stop in your search routine. With each one of these search giants competing against each other and crawling independently from each other, it is becoming more and more important for real seekers to use several search engines in order to find those valuable clusters of data buried in deep corners of the

Web. If you are comfortable with Google, then Bing will be very familiar. Almost all of the special commands are the same, with very few exceptions.

Search Basics

Your search results depend upon which keywords you use. You do not need to worry about case sensitivity and common words such as "a", "an", and "and the". However, you must capitalize the NOT and OR operators. Bing automatically adds AND between your keywords, so it's not necessary to type this between your search terms. Use unique words that you would expect to find in the Web pages for which you are searching. Place the most important keywords at the beginning of your search query. Bing can handle up to 150 characters, including spaces, in the search box, but keep in mind that only the first 10 search terms are used to receive search results.

At the top of the Bing search results, you will find linked tabs organizing your results into categories related to your search. Bing will also deliver variations of your search query on your search results page labeled Related searches for your preceding search query. If you are including a date in your search, type the name of the month and not the number.

Similar to Verbatim on Google, Bing supports the use of the + symbol. Preceding a word with a plus symbol forces Bing to search for that word exactly as spelled, and turns off searching for associated words. With it you can force Bing to search for terms that are regularly ignored.

Term grouping and Boolean operators are supported in the following order:

1. Content in parentheses () solved first
2. Followed by content in quotation marks ""
3. Then followed by the **NOT** or - operator
4. Leaving **AND** or **&** second to last
5. And finally, the **OR** and | operator

Because OR is the operator with lowest precedence, enclose OR terms in parentheses when combined with other operators in a search, or they will be solved for last and may return inaccurate results.

Social Results

Bing can return results from your Facebook friends and others from social networks like Twitter, Quora and Foursquare who might know something about what you're searching for. In the top right corner of the screen, sign in and connect to your Facebook account to see any results from your Facebook friends and other networks. Social search results will appear on the right side of the page under the headings: From Friends and From Social Networks. If you want to turn off social search results, simply click on the top right corner of the screen where your name appears and click Sign out.

Customize Your Search

In the cog shaped icon at the top right of your screen next to your name, you will see a Preferences icon. Click on it and it will open up the General Settings page where you can activate these features:

- **SafeSearch:** Turn off adult content. Beyond being prudent, this step also eliminates a great deal of spam or other junk results that slip in due to shady SEO Webmaster tactics.
- **Search suggestions:** As you start typing a search, the search suggestions pane automatically shows you suggestions based on what you've entered. Here is where you can turn this on or off.
- **Location** brings back search results related to your local area.

The Web settings page allows you to customize how you want your search results to appear and to which language you want to limit your search results. There, you can also turn on Search History, just as with Google, or clear your history and view your searches.

Added Bonus: Bing Rewards

Sign up for Bing Rewards and earn credits by searching. Points can add up quickly if you are conducing some heavy Sourcing. Not only will you be doing your job but at the same time earning credits towards rewards like Xbox LIVE and Hulu Plus subscriptions, Redbox movie rentals, gift cards, or donations to charities of your choice.

Advanced Field Search Syntax

Keyword	Definition	Example
contains:	Keeps results focused on sites that have links to the file types that you specify.	To search for websites containing links to Microsoft Windows Media Audio (.wma) files, type **music contains:wma.**
ext:	Returns only Web pages with the filename extension that you specify.	To find reports created only in DOCX format, type your subject, followed by **ext:docx.**
filetype:	Returns only Web pages created in the file type that you specify.	To find reports created in PDF format, type your subject, followed by **filetype: pdf.**
inanchor: or inbody: or intitle:	These keywords return Web pages that contain the specified term in the metadata, such as the anchor, body, or title of the site, respectively. Specify only one term per keyword. You can string multiple keyword entries as needed.	To find webpages containing "msn" in the anchor, and the terms "spaces" and "magog" in the body, type **inanchor:msn inbody:spaces inbody:magog.**
language:	Returns Web pages for a specific language. Specify the language code directly after the language: keyword. You can also access this function using the Search Builder Language function.	To see webpages only in English about antiques, type **"antiques" language:en.**
link:	Returns Web pages that link to that particular website	link:www.theSourcinginst itute.com returns Web pages that contain hyperlinks to this website

loc: or location:	Returns web pages from a specific country or region. Specify the country or region code directly after the loc: keyword. To focus on two or more languages, use a logical **OR** to group the languages.	To see Web pages about sculpture from the U.S. or Great Britain, type **sculpture (loc:US OR loc:GB).** For a list of language codes that you can use with Bing, see Country, region, and language codes at http://onlinehelp.microsof t.com/en-us/bing/ff808526 .aspx.
prefer:	Adds emphasis to a search term or another operator to help focus the search results.	To find results about football but that primarily pertain to the organization, type **football prefer:organization**.
site:	Returns Web pages that belong to the specified site. To focus on two or more domains, use a logical **OR** to group the domains. You can use **site:** to search for Web domains, top level domains, and directories that are not more than two levels deep. You can also search for web pages that contain a specific search word on a site.	To see Web pages about heart disease from the BBC or CNN websites, type **"heart disease" (site:bbc.co.uk OR site:cnn.com)**. To find Web pages about the PC version of Halo on the Microsoft website, type **site: www.microsoft.com/gam es/pc halo**.
feed:	Finds RSS or Atom feeds on a website for the terms in your search.	To find RSS or Atom feeds about football, type **feed:football.**
hasfeed:	Finds Web pages that contain an RSS or Atom feed on a website for the terms in your search.	To find Web pages on *The New York Times* website that contain RSS or Atom feeds, type **site: www.nytimes. com hasfeed:football.**
url:	Checks whether the listed domain or Web address is in the Bing index.	To verify that the Microsoft domain is in the index, type **url:microsoft.com.**

URL Search

Many of the other field search commands with which you are already familiar are supported. The "site: command" allows you to narrow down a search for results within a particular URL or, of course, can also be used to eliminate any results from said URL. The link: command will return results of pages linking to a particular URL. For example, this search query will return Web pages linking to drupal.org

link:drupal.org

Use of the "filetype:" syntax on Bing is identical to that of Google, but there is one command that Google does not use. The "contains:" command limits results to only pages that have a link to a particular type of document. This command is different than searching for the document itself. Instead, it searches for the pages that host that kind of document. A commonly used string will limit results to only pages that contain links to MS Word or

PDF documents, thereby eliminating many commercial pages, career sites and job postings which very seldom have attachments.

Next, try adding this string to your regular keywords:

resume (contains:doc OR contains:rtf OR contains:txt OR contains:pdf)

For example:

"c++" win32 Seattle resume (contains:doc OR contains:rtf OR contains:ps OR contains:txt OR contains:pdf)

You will find that many of the resulting 1,000 or so pages are the home pages of individuals who link to their resume in a variety of formats.

The "Inbody:" Command

One other command that Bing handles exceptionally well is the "inbody:" command, which specifies that results must contain that particular keyword only in the plain text body of the document, and not in any other location.

One of the most common sets of characters present in resumes is a year. With the exception of 2000, which is all too commonly used as a model number, among other things, there is almost inevitably a year somewhere on a resume. It could be a graduation date, or simply a date of employment. However, searching for numbers like 2010 will bring back everything from dates to titles and all kinds of useless data in between. With the "inbody:" command, you can limit your results to only text present inside the body of a document. Combining that with some simple keywords, yields very effective results. For example, try:

"software engineer" "C++" (inbody:2010 OR inbody:2011 OR inbody:2012)

Because not all resume documents will spell out that they are a "resume", this method tends to uncover some rare finds. If your search results are too large – in the thousands – consider adding some of the basic "AND NOTs" worth retaining like:

"C#" developer resume (inbody:project OR inbody:2013) -job

Another particularly useful word to look for in the body of a document that will most likely indicate a resume is the word "present". Combine a variety of years along with the word present and the possibilities are very high that you will find a resume. Use it like this:

"software engineer" C++ inbody:present (inbody:1997 OR inbody:1998 OR inbody1999) -jobs -careers

Now all you have to do is add more skill keywords and you are on your way to finding untapped resumes.

For example, change the Cisco domain for any other company, or you could even use several companies in this way: (*link:cisco.com OR link:lucent.com*) Java resume. You can also use the "link:" command to look for MS Word Documents or PDF documents containing links to employers. Begin with:

Java resume

then, on the third box down where it says "any of these words", enter the following:

link:cisco.com link:lucent.com

Select Microsoft Word (.doc) and click the search button. You should now have a list of Word Documents that are most likely resumes of people who worked at Cisco or Lucent.

In addition, you can use the "File Format" search to look for blogs. Enter a few keywords such as:

J2EE VMWare

in the first box under "all of these words" and then select RSS/XML (.xml) from the File Format list. You should now have a list of blogs discussing J2EE and VMWare.

Geographic Search

Bing allows your search to include only results from a particular geographic area using a Location command ("loc:"). For example, a search using the field command "loc:GB" will attempt to limit results to U.K.-based sites. This command uses standard two-letter country abbreviation codes from ISO-9000. While it does not work for U.S. states, the command can be very useful in filtering out results from countries outside of the U.S., or when conducting a search in Canada, filtering out U.S.-based content.

Further, once you have begun a geographic search, you can focus on results using only a particular language. For example, to receive only results in English, use "language:en".

Section 3. Blekko.com in a Nutshell...

- Spam free, fully customizable social search engine
- Integrates social components with websites like Facebook
- Builds upon the searches of other users
- Does NOT support logical disjunctions (_ OR _)

Blekko's claim to fame is they "slash out web-spam, content farms and malware". According to the search engine, it achieves this goal by "having a smaller crawl of 3 billion pages that

focuses on quality websites". It created what are called slashtags, essentially user generated commands that organize websites around topics to improve results. Blekko founders created a manifesto, which they call the "web search bill of rights", to express their values:

Web Search Bill of Rights (from blekko.com):

- Search shall be open
- Search results shall involve people
- Ranking data shall not be kept secret
- Web data shall be readily available

- There is no one-size-fits-all for search
- Advanced search shall be accessible
- Search engine tools shall be open to all
- Search & community go hand-in-hand
- Spam does not belong in search results
- Privacy of searchers shall not be violated

Blekko is a boutique search engine that has gained popularity because it possesses features unavailable elsewhere, and it intuitively eliminates spam or less credible results. Perhaps its greatest strength is the ability to add a set of websites to create an ad-hoc custom search engine quickly. Blekko custom search engines are defined by their use of "slashtags", which allow users to personalize clusters of searches or use custom search engines. Their creator can designate these custom search engines either public or private. When made private, assigned users with editing privileges can collaborate.

Blekko.com and slashtags are available to you without requiring a log in. You may just use other peoples' slashtags, without having created any of your own. For example, if your username

is john-smith and you click on your username in the top corner of Blekko.com, then it will bring up a list of slashtags that you have created. If you see a slashtag in the list that you want to share with someone that is not logged in, click on it and observe what loads in the Blekko Search box. Copy the text in the Search box and send it to the user with whom you would like to share your slashtag. This text will look something like this, if your username is john-smith and your slashtag is named Private Wealth Managers:

/view /john-smith/private-wealth-managers

Now your colleague can simply go to blekko.com and copy and paste the above text into the Search field and it will bring up search results for the slashtag Private Wealth Managers that John Smith created without requiring a login.

If you do create a free account, two advantages to logging in are: 1) You can create custom slashtags and 2) You can search among your likes and your friends' likes when you connect your account to Facebook with the /likes private slashtag. This feature is pretty attractive on a personal level because it allows you to find what others you know recommend, have mentioned, or may know about themselves. When logged in, Blekko pulls information from

Facebook about the sites that you and your friends have liked and makes that data searchable and visible in your search results.

There are 3 types of slashtags, topical, user, and built-in. Topical slashtags are created by Blekko itself and maintained by experts. They are similar to a Directory. A full listing of such tags is located at blekko.com/tag/show#tab3.

Blekko also creates built-in slashtags, but they function more like search operators or modifiers, rather than collections of websites. They perform functions such as date-delimited search, or call up types of content like /blogs or /people for individuals' profiles.

The third category of slashtag includes those created by users, like you, and other members of the Blekko community. Think of them as collections of favorite websites you can search separately or in conjunction with built-in slashtags.

To create your own slashtag or ad-hoc custom search engine, you must be logged in to Blekko. Once you are logged in, pull up any search results page and select "Create a slashtag", or simply type /add into the search box. You will need to provide a name for your slashtag, but do not worry about remembering it because you can always look yourself up later and find all the slashtags you've created. Proceed to "Keywords about your slashtag" where you enter terms that describe the type of content you would like this slashtag to find. For example, if you were looking for private wealth managers, you would describe their titles, and also describe the kinds of pages your search should return. For example:

"Private banking", money, investment, "fund managers"

You will want to enclose phrases of two or more words within quotation marks to denote that those words belong together, otherwise Blekko may interpret *private* and *banking* separately, which is not necessarily the same as *private banking.*

Next, enter a list of websites from which to return results. If you do not know where to begin, you can find other slashtags to build upon, or search for websites utilizing keywords. If you have a list of websites in a spreadsheet or other document, just copy the list into a notepad (or Mac text edit) file, one line per domain, and you can import the entire list as a .txt file.

Once you have selected or imported all the websites you want to collect into your slashtag, decide if this search is for your own private use or if you wish to share it openly with others. Either way, you can invite other Blekko users to have administrative rights to your slashtag by entering their user names.

You are now ready to use your own slashtag in searching Blekko.

Even if you choose not to create your own slashtags, you can use those created by others, or the ones built-in by Blekko itself. But that's not all that's useful. Go back to the Blekko homepage and check out People Search. That's a slashtag that was created by Blekko. Users create most slashtags, but if you go in the directory, you will see that there are some that are fundamental to the search engine, and this is one of them.

For example, try "tax partner /people-search"". Notice that it brings back only profiles of people. It's actually looking through the people pages of a lot of indifferent websites. If you are ever curious as to what a particular slashtag does, all you have to do is add the word 'view' to a slashtag; view. In this case, it will indicate that Blekko looks at 33 websites and list those sites. That way, you can determine exactly what the slashtag is looking for.

Blekko does not support Boolean operators, such as AND, OR, NOT, and parentheses. AND is implicit in all searches, and NOT is expressed using a minus sign, such as CPA tax partner –jobs. There is no way to express an OR in your searches; instead use multiple searches. The search engine also do not support using * as a wildcard in the search box.

Advanced Slashtags

A full list located at: blekko.com/tag/show.

- **/likes** search only your Facebook friends' likes
- **/edu** searches universities & colleges... so what does **/gov** do?
- **/blog** searches Typepad, Wordpress, Tumblr, etc. while /forum finds on-line discussions
- **/images** and **/video** search only... yup, you guessed it
- **/operators** searches available commands
- **/people** delivers nothing but profiles!
- **/date** searches a slice of time which you can sort by freshness or with **/dr** sort by relevance
- **/date=** "Nov 3, 2011" or **/date**=2012 and also **/date**="Nov 3, 2010-Nov 2, 2011"
- **/similar** returns more pages like one that is specified and **/links** brings back sites that link to a specified site
- **/rss** transform a search into an instant RSS feed when added to a tag

Section 4. Exalead.com in a Nutshell...

Features

- Proximity search operators NEXT and NEAR
- Phonetic and approximate spelling commands
- Easy one-click language and file type filtering

Although the search industry changes daily, there have not been many major changes in the last several years that affect the way recruiters use search engines. While Exalead, another boutique search engine, has been around since 2004, the new and improved version now has much to offer recruiters. Like the old AltaVista, Exalead focuses on the use of advanced syntax that allows searchers a very high degree of control.

One of the best commands AltaVista employed in the past, before it was made obsolete via absorption by Yahoo, was the NEAR command. This command allowed a search to include words that were close together, helping us find pages where the words "mechanical" and "engineer" appeared close enough to indicate that the page may contain information about a mechanical engineer without the necessity of finding the two words exactly adjacent. Exalead brings back proximity functionality of the NEAR operator for words that are close to each other, and builds upon that with the use of the NEXT command for adjacent words allowing us to construct a search like this:

"embedded systems" NEXT engineer

Under the search box, you will find Related Searches, which provide you with different kinds of searches related to "engineer" and "embedded systems".

You will also find the following aids on the right-side of the screen:

- **Site type:** allows you to search only blog or forum sites
- **Filetype:** allows you to refine your search by document type of your choice
- **Related terms:** links could be very helpful for narrowing down your search results

One more advantage to using Exalead is the ability to search for words that may have been misspelled, or where you are uncertain of their pronunciation. By using the "soundslike" and "spellslike" commands you can find all variations of systems which could include sistems, sistemas, or systemmes, and so on. Your search is much more flexible and can include a multitude of variations of your keywords with little effort, expanding your results and minimizing your frustration.

soundslike:systems spellslike:embedded NEXT engineer

If you replace NEXT with NEAR, your search will include a slightly broader set of results, as the phrase "embedded systems" and the word "engineer" must only be within close proximity, not necessarily adjacent.

Exalead also supports searching based on the date pages were created or modified. With the simple use of date commands like "before:" or "after:" you can limit your results to fresh pages only, or historical pages only. Both the "before:" and "after:" commands accept the international accepted date format of YYYY/MM/DD. This format is particularly useful with Peer Regression search.

Familiar commands supported by Exalead include intitle, inurl, filetype, language, and link (followed by a colon).

Quick Chart! Exalead Commands

Command	What does it do?	Examples:
+	Search for a group of exact words and requires them to be all spelled exactly as typed.	+The Sourcing Institute
OPT	Adds optional items that if found will elevate the relevance of that page among search results, but are not required to be included in the results.	"embedded systems" OPT "digital signal"
NEXT	Requires words or phrases to be adjacent.	"embedded systems" NEXT engineer
NEAR		
soundslike:shakespeare		soundslike:

spellslike:		spellslike:exlaead
language:		movie star language:en
link:	Find results that link to a particular website	ink:www.theSourcinginstit ute.com
before:	Find results before a particular time	"embedded systems" intitle:resume before:2009/01/01-job
after:	Find results after a particular time	movie star after:2004/05/21 "embedded systems" intitle:resume after:2009/01/01-job

Section 5. Gigablast.com in a Nutshell...

- Query refinement through Gigablast allows you to drill down on your search
- The only engine where you can search an IP range
- Turn your search results into XML feeds
- Search your own custom list of domains

You will have a blast with Gigablast. A more recent newcomer to the scene, Gigablast is making an impact with some interesting features. One thing you will notice right away is that if you come up with a search that has few results, you will be given the option to expand your results to "partial matches", thereby enabling you to find things you may have missed by making your search too narrow. They call this feature "Super Recall", and it comes in handy. You can turn the feature off by prefacing all your search words with the "+" symbol.

Although it does not refine quite like other search engines, it does allow you to drill down using keywords it extracts from your search results. Once you have your search just the way you want it, you can tell Gigablast to publish your search results as an XML RSS feed that goes straight to your favorite RSS Reader.

The Gigablast Advanced Search functionality is very comprehensive, allowing you to build complex searches easily. However, perhaps the single greatest feature of the Advanced Search is the ability to enter a list of sites you want to search, and search only within those sites. For example, you could list all the schools your company recruits from, or search through a list of communities such as Geocities, CompuServe, and Tripod. You could also enter a list of local ISPs and search through all their member's homepages simultaneously.

For example, from Gigablast.com go to the Advanced Search function. Enter your "must have" keywords such as ajax php mysql in the all of these words box. In the any of these words box, enter your resume keywords such as project. Finally, in the Restrict to these sites box, enter a list of blog communities such as blogspot.com typepad.com weblog.com blog.com spaces.live.com. Do not worry about commas; just separate the site names with spaces and it will work just fine.

To prove how much fun you will have with Gigablast, try the following search that should yield pages of potential candidates, many of whom have project experience posted in their blogs.

Refer back to the "Private Wealth Managers" example from the Google CSE, which produced a nice list of website addresses. Grab a few title sites and paste them into the "Advanced Search" bar on Gigablast. You could paste up to 50 websites. For your purposes here, however, use as many as will produce one hundred results per page. Say "no" to site clustering so that sites are not clumped together. These efforts alone should customize your results. Next, enter a phrase like "private wealth" and click search. Gigablast will only search through the content on those specific sites that you have listed.

You could embed your list elsewhere on the search engine, and you can also change the job title. For example, you could switch from "private wealth manager" to "fund manager", and you could alter your search to produce multiple angles of search attack. In fact, logical disjunctions would be appropriate here. Note that everything else that applies to the most popular search engines also applies to Gigablast. Piles of names will begin to emerge. You could also try natural phrase searches such as "from left to right" or "clockwise". The main selling point of Gigablast is that it actually creates the energy that it uses to search, which makes it a kind of "carbon neutral" search engine, an interesting feature for users who like to support green, sustainable measures.

Gigablast does not just limit your results to a nice list of websites; you can return back to the website juncture and narrow other search factors. For example, you could add multiple phrases, change the language, and even restrict your search to pages that link to a particular URL. In addition, you could link back to a particular association from just your list of websites. Gigablast's features let users extrapolate different searches as they continue digging through results. Just paste several sites that you already know you want to search and voila, you have just created an ad hoc, custom search engine. Notice that there are no refinements or synonyms, but at the same time, it is very user-friendly. Gigablast requires no special accounts or passwords, and you can copy code for it and embed it into your website.

Keyword	Definition	Example
type:	Returns only Web pages created in the file type that you specify.	To find reports created in PDF format, type your subject, followed by **type:pdf**. For MS Word use **type:doc**. Others supported are xls, ppt, ps and text
url:	Returns pages containing that exact URL	To find mentions of a specific website within other websites
suburl:	Returns pages containing that word somewhere in the address or domain	Use suburl:edu to find only .edu websites, or suburl:about to find the word about in the URL of results brought back
link:	Returns pages with links to a specified website	Can be used as a negative as in *-link:dell.com aspire* to return pages containing the word *aspire* but not linking to dell.com
title:	Returns pages with specified words in the title	Functions like the intitle: command on Google and Bing

Section 6. Metasearch Engines in a Nutshell...

If metasearch engines allow you to search multiple search engines at once, why would you ever want to search only one at a time? Because you can only use the advanced commands of an underlying search engine on only a few metasearch engines. Typically, metasearch engines allow only simple searches with basic Booleans such as AND or OR. For this reason, it is not recommended that you use them for deep research.

Instead, adjust your expectations for metasearch engines. They are a terrific resource for getting quick hits on simple searches. For example, if you need more information about certain individuals in order to make a decision or you need to find their contact information, you can simply put the person's name into a metasearch engine to launch several search engines at once and wait to see the name come up elsewhere on the web. Here is a listing of some of the best metasearch engines out there:

Mamma.com – The mother of all search engines is also known for having purchased the desktop metasearch tool Copernic. Mamma will scan Open Directory, LookSmart, Business.com, About.com, Ask.com, Google, Live.com, Entireweb, Gigablast, FindWhat, Kanoodle, and Ah-ha.

Boounce.com – Installs a tool bar into your Web browser that features other search engines so you can run the same search using different engines without having to re-enter your search string. This ad-on also eliminates duplicate results.

Dogpile.com – An Infospace service like WebCrawler, this metasearch engine can also search news services and stock information.

DuckDuckGo.com – The number one reason to use this search engine is its privacy policy, which declares that it does not store or share your information. DuckDuckGo will retain your interest because it avoids spam and clutter. Use the !bang feature to find instant results from your most frequently visited sites or within a specific site without further semantic commands.

Sperse.com – Provides the option to run specialized searches for content mainstream search engines do not typically index.

MetaCrawler.com – This speedy crawler can search audio/MP3 files, newsgroups, auctions and images among other information.

Millionshort.com – Eliminates the top 1 million popular sites to reveal harder-to-find content.

WebCrawler.com – Instantly provides Google and Yahoo search results.

Zuula.com – Enables users to switch back and forth from multiple search engines and offers customizable search engine tabs.

Section 7. Search Engine Alerts in a Nutshell...

Some search engines like Google and Yahoo do not publish easily visible RSS feeds of their search results. With those search engines, you must instead use the "Alerts" feature, which will send you an email containing new search results as they are found by the search engine crawler, or will permit you to subscribe to a feed of results.

> ***Refine Requirement:*** *It is a recommended practice that you refine your search query until you are certain it brings back desired results before you save it as an alert.*

Google Alerts (google.com/alerts). From this page, enter your search string as you would in the regular search engine interface; then select Web or Blog and choose the frequency with which you would like to receive updates. For example, if you select "as it happens" you will receive an email any time there is an update to the index that includes your keywords. If you choose "Daily", then the alert will wait until the end of the day and send you any new results it has found, if any. Likewise, by selecting "Weekly", you will receive a summary at the end of every 7-day period that includes new results from the past seven days. You can also choose to receive alerts about news items like press releases or magazine and newspaper articles that include your keywords. The "News" search is particularly useful for tracking mergers and acquisitions, layoffs, and other competitive intelligence about a company. Useful keywords for this type of search are the company name or ticker symbol.

Yahoo Alerts (alerts.yahoo.com). Similar to Google Alerts, Yahoo Alerts will email you as the Yahoo search engine finds new items, which is to say it returns Bing results. From the above URL, select "News;" then check the "Keyword News" box and click on the "Set Up Alerts" button. You will be taken to a page where you can add the keywords you would like your search to include, as well as those you would like to not include. Keep in mind that if you enter words under the "include" box, then all those words must be present in the results. There is no OR functionality in either of these two search boxes. After entering your search terms, click on the "Set Up Alerts" button once more and you will be asked to confirm the alert by clicking the "Done" button. Once you do, you are taken to your Alerts management page where you can edit or turn off selected alerts.

Both RSS and Alerts can take time to configure, but once they are running will save you considerable amounts of time. The initial effort pays for itself with rewarding results that are continuously delivered directly to either your RSS Reader or your inbox, with little need for maintenance. Consider saving RSS Feeds and Alerts of searches for the typical types of candidate you are always seeking, and also information about competitors, layoffs, mergers and acquisitions.

Chapter 7
Passive Candidates

Section 1. The Passive/Active Continuum

Certain buzzwords have been floating around recruiting circles for quite some time, such as "passive candidates" and "active candidates". What makes a passive candidate desirable? What makes an active candidate less desirable? To understand these concepts, let's first examine what makes an individual passive or active.

Imagine a straight line. On the left end of the line is the extreme passive candidate. On the right end of the line is the extreme active candidate. The line represents the amount of time or effort per week an individual spends searching for a new job. A truly **passive candidate** spends zero amount of time each week on their job search. They are not looking at job postings or Sunday classifieds, nor have they posted a resume or profile in a career database. However, if contacted them about the right opportunity, they may be interested in pursuing it.

As you move to the right of the continuum, you see candidates who are more active in their job search. These individuals are active candidates because they devote time and energy to their job search. Maybe they post a resume confidentially to see what comes their way or spend an hour or so looking at job postings while sitting at their desk over lunch hour. They could also be checking with their trusted industry contacts to see if there are any appealing openings at other companies.

Visualizing this continuum is important because a variety of your recruitment methods involve targeting different folks on this continuum depending on the amount of effort a candidate must expend. Placing an ad in your Sunday paper will target the most active candidates. Why? The amount of effort it takes to read through the Sunday classifieds, make note of an interesting job, and then respond by fax or email is somewhat high. Likewise, the proactive recruitment method of "direct Sourcing", or searching the Web, will generally target the less active, candidates. Somewhere in the middle lies Sourcing from resume databases such as those found on Monster and CareerBuilder.com.

What makes a passive candidate desirable and an "active" candidate less desirable? There is a popular notion that "active" job seekers are disgruntled, unhappy job hoppers and therefore undesirable — though this is probably overstated especially after all the recent economic shakeouts. The reality is that "active" candidates are less desirable because the competition for them is stiff. Recruiters tend to spend quite a bit of time on the right side of the continuum targeting only "active" candidates with job postings and advertising. Passive candidates are more work because the recruiter has to validate their interest and assess their skills without knowing anything about them.

Imagine a pond. The pond is where your active candidates are, and they generally bite quickly on your fishing line. But there are many other lines around you and competition is fierce. Now, imagine the ocean. The ocean is where your passive candidates are. While they can be slow to bite on your line, the competition is significantly diminished, and conversely the size of the fish – or the quality of your candidate – is considerably increased. A majority of recruiters are fishing in the pond, and even more narrowly in "popular" areas of the pond. Fishing in the ocean, or at least in larger lakes and less popular locations, increases the number of potential candidates and sometimes, their quality, or "size".

List your various recruitment methods and services. Now, from a job seeker's perspective, place your list on your passive/active continuum line. If you draw a triangle underneath the middle of the line so that it resembles a teeter-totter (remember those?), ask yourself if your methods are more heavily weighted on one end versus the other?

The key is balance. Balancing proactive or outbound recruitment methods such as Sourcing with reactive recruitment methods that create inbound candidate traffic such as that from job postings will cast your fishing line in all the right places. Balanced recruiting results in overall higher quality of candidates, and a broader selection from which to choose.

Section 2. Fishing for Passive Candidates

Many people respond to the passive/active continuum analogy with questions: "How do I complement my active candidate Sourcing with some passive candidate Sourcing?" or, "How do I throw my fishing line into the ocean of passive candidates?" These are great questions and hopefully the beginning of a journey that will take you from traditional recruiting methods to more of an investigative, creative marketing recruiting approach.

The Internet can be a wonderfully exasperating source of passive candidates who are hanging out but difficult to track down. Tracking these candidates down involves a certain amount of "private investigator" work. You need to find out where they go, where they interact, and what associations they may belong to.

The best way to explain this kind of investigative work is to put it in your own terms, by asking, "Where would you search the Internet if you were looking for high-level technical recruiting candidates or human resource managers?" Hopefully this is somewhat easy for you, because as an HR individual you have your favorite sites and would know where to go to find people like yourself.

Listen in on those who seem to know a lot about the topic being discussed. Many times people will identify themselves in a forum as well as note their title and organization. The key is to listen and not post your position, which can be very disruptive to any forum or conversation.

You also know that recruiters often post the jobs for which they are recruiting, so you may want to try going to a job board, searching under the industry/position of the background you are seeking, and taking note of the names that are attached to those job postings. Finally, you may want to go to those sites that assist recruiters and HR individuals in their jobs, such as Staffing.org (*staffing.org*), HR World (*hrworld.com*), or SHRM (*shrm.org*). At these sites, you may want to look for a forum, guest book, or alumni section. At this point, you have *not* contacted any of these individuals; you have simply noted names, titles, companies and where you discovered them.

Section 3. Finding Top Level Executives

Executives generally have a heightened public presence. Senior executives have accomplished more that may have been reported by trade journals or the subject of press releases. They may also work for a publicly traded company that must disclose key personnel by law. Thus, top-level executives are generally easy to identify using online resources. The following are a few of the best starting points when researching executive talent.

Yahoo Finance

Yahoo's Finance section provides you with statistics about public companies for a quick snapshot of publicly traded companies Simply enter a ticker symbol, or look it up by company name. For example, under the Insider Trading section find information on the major shareholders and stakeholders and how many shares they recently bought and sold. In another section you can see messages in a discussion group about the organization. Some of these messages originate from company employees who post anonymously or use confidential handles.

CompanyPay.com

This site ranks the top 24,000 executives based on how much they make, and lists their total compensation along with their name and company. You can search by company name and obtain a snapshot of their senior leadership. Another great source of executive bios, their compensation and Insider Trading is Reuters.com. From the "Stocks" section enter a company name or trading symbol then select Officers & Directors under Stocks in the left-hand menu.

JigSaw.com

In addition to being a source of leads, JigSaw also provides detailed company profiles. You can search for both private and publicly traded organization and obtain details about their employees, along with other vital company information.

Zoominfo.com

By using natural language processing and artificial intelligence technology, Zoominfo reads nearly every news article, press release, company website, and SEC filing published on the Web. Then it extracts specific information about people and companies (name, title, company information, previous employment and education) and organizes all that information into profiles for each contact, combining multiple mentions of the individual into a single record. Every day they scan millions of records. You can search people and companies for free. For more in-depth searching and the use of their JobCast referral tool, upgrade to a PowerSearch account. Zoominfo's database of people and companies currently consists of over 34 million people from every organizational level and 2.7 million companies from nearly every industry and is growing quickly.

Hoovers.com

Not only can you find names of executives using this site, but you can also research an industry, find a company's competitors, find the latest news on an organization, and research company culture, benefits, and what type of employer an organization is. Hoovers is truly a one-stop research shopping area. It is just one of many ways to find executive level individuals, but probably one of the least expensive while being extraordinarily comprehensive in research resources.

The best approach when working on executive-level positions is a three step process utilizing sites like Hoovers, Ziggs, JigSaw and ZoomInfo:

> **Research your current organization.** While you may already know all your organization's competitors, it cannot hurt to double check. How was your growth last year? How does that growth stack up against your competitors? Take notes on how you compare to them, so that you can hit those "hot spots" with passive candidates. Click on your competitors—and your competitors' competitors—in order to retrieve an exhaustive list of the companies that would be considered a background match for your candidates.
>
> **Research your competitors' officers.** As you click through company profiles, list those people who are in your target position. Make sure you note their full name, title, company, and location. If a full list of officers is not available, click through to the company home page. Many times a company will list their officers' bios on their individual sites as well, either in a Press section or in the About Us area.
>
> **Contact a list of possible candidate by email.** Executives on these lists are truly passive candidates, so it's very important that

they be handled with kid gloves. A phone call may be disruptive to their day as well as hazardous to their current position if it is misunderstood or overheard by superiors, so emailing is frequently a better route to go. Now you may be thinking, "Names are great and all, but how do I get their email address to contact them passively by email?" One effective way is to try to see if you can find an email address on the company website that displays the format in which email addresses are managed. It might, for example, be joe.smith@4sct.com, jsmith@4sct.com, or j_smith@4sct.com. You know the full name of the individual, so usually it is a matter of simply finding the email format.

Section 4. The Sourcing Edge - Peer Regression Analysis

Nobody grows up in a vacuum, personally or professionally. At some point, most individuals have either influenced or been influenced by others. On a personal level, these people are friends and family. On a professional level, these people are educators, coworkers, employers, subordinates, mentors, mentees, or collaborators. Sourcers use **Peer Regression Analysis** (PRA), borrowing loosely from statistical and economic regression analysis, to track down and isolate these influencers or effectors and responders in order to extrapolate a short list of passive candidates.

PRA frequently uncovers individuals who are not very visible. For instance, individuals discovered using PRA methodologies are unlikely to be found using the searches described earlier in this section because those searches utilize the shallow versus deep Web. While these individuals' low public profile necessitates increased effort and Web penetration to find them, their invisibility makes them an untapped market and a boon to hiring organizations.

PRA begins by identifying a **PRA Target**, a person who should be at the top of a candidate list but who is most likely unattainable. The Target may be "the one who got away", an ex-employee, or some other industry luminary who is considered popular or expert. Upon selecting a target, a Sourcer can begin PRA to identify the Target's effectors and responders. PRA methodologies draw largely upon a social scientific principle

commonly known as **Similarity** or **Attraction Theory**, which posits that individuals seek out or are drawn to others they perceive as similar to themselves, including in terms of world view, thought processes, or personal achievement; essentially, it is the notion that "like attracts like".

Commonalities are the basis for Attraction Theory, and they comprise the heart of PRA. From a ten-foot overhead view, some commonalities are glaringly apparent: Same industry, same title, same revenue benchmarks, and same college. Other commonalities are not so apparent unless viewed from fifty feet overhead: Same worldview, same value system, same work ethic, and same hobbies. By identifying macro commonalities, previously hidden influences manifest themselves. Although a neophyte might be engrossed by obvious commonalities, an experienced Sourcer will also chase less apparent commonalities for two main reasons. First, these commonalities often reveal whether the candidate will be a good fit within the organization, i.e. whether or not the candidate's personality matches the corporate culture, which leads to greater opportunities for the candidate to contribute and longer executive retention. Second, these commonalities can have a forward looking recruiting impact in that they often lead to other individuals with different skill-sets and work experience but who might be appropriate for an organization's talent pipeline.

One PRA methodology that bears much fruit and maintains a high degree of repeatability is an **image-based regression**. An image-based regression uses images on the Web to identify the Target's effectors, responders, and other associates and is described below. Note that the fundamental concepts of image-based regression also translate to other subjects (e.g. video, Facebook postings, Tweets).

Image Search. The first step is to enter the Target's name into a search engine using the Image Search function. Next, click on photos that possess the appearance of recording some achievement or a business context. Look for the people alongside your target. Most business photos have captions that include not just the names of their subjects but also the relationships among them. Begin to tag these individuals, noting as you go along the individuals your Sourcing radar detects as solid leads. From these tags will spring the names for your rudimentary candidate list.

Search Terms. Just as in previous sections, it is important that you refine your keywords to maximize the potency of your search. In addition to using the appropriate syntax described earlier in this chapter, Sourcers must adjust their keywords to reflect vocabulary naturally used in connection with images or **natural phrasing.** For example, try constructing a search string like this:

"shally steckerl" ("l. to r." OR "l to r" OR "left to right" OR "r. to l." OR "r to l" OR "right to left" OR "back row" OR "clockwise from")

All the keywords in the search string are commonly used in image or photo captions. These words also automatically harvest formal group photos, reducing the number of unnecessary results.

Be clever in your use of natural phrasing. For example, expand your search using the following string:

"shally stecker" ("my team" OR "our team" OR team)

The "team" approach often produces a complete company roster, which is valuable information that can be tucked away for later use.

Using a proximity syntax search function on Exalead might look like this:

worked NEAR "shally steckerl"

Once you have tagged a few names, place a series of names in the search field. Note that two may be too prolific and five may be too restricting. An ideal name-based search will have three to four names.

"sam breadon" "bill veeck" "august busch" "william dewitt"

A name-based search is not confined to an Image Search but is often generated by the names derived from one.

TinEye.com. This "reverse image search engine" uses image identification technology to produce search results. TinEye boasts an indexed catalog of over two billion images. No keywords are necessary. Upload your own image, or give it the URL of an online image, and find out where else that image is being used. For example, take your target's executive headshot and upload it into TinEye to find other professional events or forums where they were an invited speaker, moderator or highlighted attendee. Other websites to integrate into your image regression include photo sharing sites such as Flickr.com, PhotoBucket.com, SmugMug.com, and the mobile phone sensation Instagram.com.

Document-Based Search. By now, you should be able to conduct a competent image-based regression on major search engines and TinEye, so it is time to apply the same principles of an image-based regression to a different medium. A **document-based regression** is based on the same concepts and many of the same keywords as an image-based regression, but uses publicly shared documents and files as its medium instead of a photograph. To begin, visit online document repositories such as **Docstoc.com, Scribd.com, Slideshare.net** and **TooDoc**.com. What you are looking for is anything written or uploaded by your target so you apply your PRA techniques to find out whom else is writing about or uploading documents on the same topic or in the same industry.

> ***Cloud Doc Search:*** *Check out this convenient custom search engine! http://shally.me/rtcloudcse Simply type in some keywords, select the CloudDocs label and search the top 9 sites.*

When used in the context of forecasting and headcount planning PRA can revolutionize the operations of an organization via the construction of talent pipelines. Prudent organizational behavior avoids "on demand" hiring. Long-term corporate planning requires steady, meaningful communication between staffing leadership and separate internal business units so that staffing leadership can mobilize for growth based on current or future capital investments or product mandates. Top global companies recognize the value of developing pipelines encompassing the top one percent of talent to fill anticipated open requisitions for coming years. When companies actively support PRA endeavors, Sourcing expenditures turn from sunk or day-to-day costs into discrete capital investments.

Senior executives do not instantly become visionaries upon attainment of a title. Visionaries must have been managers or directors at some point. PRA, aligned with a forward-looking talent strategy, makes it possible for a future ideal candidate to enter the organization earlier and start making big waves sooner, all the while undergoing training, professional development, and other grooming for future senior leadership roles.

Chapter 8
Referrals and Social Networks

Section 1. The Power of Referrals

Rare is the person who doubts the power of referrals. Many recruiters would gratefully employ referrals to fill their job vacancies and do so in fact. Further, the referral process is the number one obstacle to the job seeker who is at large with a limited social network and waiting for a job posting to appear.

Gone are the days when an employee would talk about a job opening at an old-fashioned cocktail party and meet someone looking for a job that happens to be a suitable candidate. In this age, entry into the referral market requires an online presence, and it is taken for granted that any individual will have an e-mail account. Further, it is not surprising that an individual will belong to a social network such as Facebook, Twitter, Cafemom, or Meetup.com for purely personal reasons. However, it is different for recruiters. When recruiters made their career choice, they gave up the luxury of maintaining membership in these networks for purely personal or social reasons. Membership is a must!

Major Benefits of Online Social Networks

The single most powerful advantage of online social networking is finding new connections you didn't know you already had. Presumably, someone you know, a first-degree connection, generates referrals arising from online social networks. Because you already know someone who knows them, you can feel more comfortable that they are a quality prospect or, at the least that you can do some checking up on them. Also, because of that mutual connection, you can more easily overcome cumbersome barriers of etiquette and begin a relationship with a little more trust and warmth than with a total stranger.

It takes time and energy to build a network, either in person or online. Social networking is becoming involved, and putting your name out at every opportunity is less important than being yourself and making a contribution. Do not be afraid to connect, stay connected, share, participate, be vulnerable, and open yourself to the world. These actions will prove invaluable in your business development.

What Your Social Media Activity Should Include

- Rekindling old connections
- Maximizing value in your weak connections
- Building business relationships with clients or hiring managers
- Finding and meeting prospective jobseekers
- Growing a referral network
- Heightening your corporate and personal brand
- Making new connections and growing your sphere of influence
- Opening doors to future career opportunities;
- Increased pay or promotions
- Increasing visibility which improves influence and effectiveness internally with your organization as well as externally
- Educating yourself and asking questions about other organizations
- Conducting competitive intelligence on companies, industries or individuals
- Making fewer cold calls and being better prepared for them
- Leveraging contacts you already have

Connections can have many unexpected positive results. Always remember that online social networking enables you to find prospects that may not be familiar with your company or business and creates an opportunity to connect with them and sell them on your opportunities. They may be unfamiliar with your organization, or they may not have even been looking for something, and you emerge at just the right time and with an opportunity that might be advantageous to them.

Section 2. Common Issues of Online Social Networking

Privacy

Despite popular perception, online networking is safe and users can ensure their safety by remaining vigilant about what information they share. The major social networks are mindful of your privacy and have developed comprehensive privacy policies. Make sure you read these policies and if you do not agree with the policy, then do not join the network. It is also a good habit to review those policies regularly so you are aware of any changes in them and can immediately cease activities on those networks that adopt practices with which you are uncomfortable.

Remember, the more you share, the more you are exposed, but the more you share, the more likely you will benefit from the network. Only you can assess the risk presented by increasing your exposure and whether the benefit of using the network outweighs the risk. The reciprocity between online networks and users is based on trust. People who are very guarded about their privacy may not achieve great results from using these networks.

It is worth mentioning that you can minimize the risk of someone hacking into your account and absconding with your contacts by selecting advanced passwords.

Barriers of Entry

Finding the time to devote to registering and setting up an account is often difficult. Entering your information into an online social network can take anywhere from a few minutes to a few hours, depending on what rewards you seek to reap. Again, the more you share about yourself, the easier it will be to make connections, but then you must invest a solid chunk of your precious time. If you only upload a few contacts, you will likely receive very little benefit since these systems only search for connections through people you already know. You need to know at least one person with a large network or else you are very limited in whom you can reach. Search for people you know who may already be in the network and ask them for a connection, particularly if they are well connected themselves.

The most challenging barrier is persuading people from your "in person" real life network to sign up. You know they have lots of connections, and they would be willing to help you, but they are not already signed up. If you do persuade them to sign up, you can both benefit from each other's connections, but of course that may lead to a situation where you feel obligated to help them more than you would otherwise.

Maintenance

A large network is wonderful if it exists for your convenience alone, but mutuality of benefit is what keeps these networks operational. If you possess a large network, you can reach a point where you are barraged with requests from contacts. The good news is that you can turn on or off e-mails about your accounts or from your network, and with some networks, you can even change your settings to accept requests only from specific levels. The other side of turning off the communication is that you lose out on reminders that help you to remember to groom your network.

Evaluating new "friends" or connections is difficult. You may receive requests from people you have never met or do not remember, and writing a response is potentially awkward and embarrassing. Just like when meeting someone in person you cannot place, you may have to bite the bullet and explicitly ask "Have we met?" It is also an increasingly popular practice to simply ignore or decline the request.

Do not add contacts indiscriminately. Be just a little picky. Remember, you are a reflection of your networks, and you owe it to your friends, connections, and contacts to act a little bit like a gatekeeper to reduce their exposure. Wouldn't you want them to do the same for you? Plus, people know you not only by who you are but also by those with whom you choose to associate.

Integration with Software and Between Networks

It is easy to feel pulled in many different directions and that you are logging in and out of too many websites or flipping through too many screens all day long. Some networks like LinkedIn™ have useful Toolbars that integrate with Outlook and make it easier to keep your network fresh. With most of the networks, you can export your contacts. Take this step regularly so that if for some reason your account is lost, you can still retain your connections' contact information. You can also take that information with you to import it into another network. Unfortunately, it's impossible to synchronize across networks. You may find some of the same people in several networks, but the best strategy is to choose your favorite three or five and stick to them or else you will be spending all your time maintaining networks.

Losing Touch with the "Real"

Email is very cold and unemotional. Relying on email and similar messaging to connect with people can wash out the emotional side of building relationships. Remember to pick up the phone and call your contacts every once in a while. This way, they are more likely to forward your requests, and ask you for requests, making your network stronger.

Free Now, Pay Later?

Many online social networks either do not charge fees or offer different tiers of service at different price points. Networks that do not currently charge fees may decide to impose membership fees later. Even if you have a limited budget, do not dismiss fee-based subscriptions out of hand. These companies are working hard to provide a product that is worth the fee, and many networks' value will increase accordingly.

Section 3. Two Major Concerns of Referral-Based Recruiting

Social networking can be very rewarding; however, it can be hit or miss just as meeting people in person. The same downsides to in-person networking apply to social networking: The expense of time and energy to build a network as well as the possibility that the right person just may not cross your path. The problem with generalized social recruiting is that it depends more on luck than talent.

A successful referral campaign possesses two key characteristics: The quality of the network, and personalization.

> **Quality of network:** Targeting the right audience for a campaign and ensuring that the message is relevant to them are key factors in the success of referral campaigns. Belonging to a variety of specialized networks becomes critical at this juncture. Generalized networks such as Facebook do not deliver a network of high quality unless you create a special "Friends List" containing pertinent connections. Fostering strong relationships ahead of time with linchpins in your network ensures that you will receive strong recommendations from them as they refer your message to their own connections.

Personalization: Email messages work best when they come from your own inbox, are sent one at a time, and you use your contacts' names when addressing them. Send the message only to known contacts with which you have had communication in the past. Personal messages to known contacts will bypass spam filters. Because they come from your own inbox directly to the recipient's and not through some third party server, the identity of those who cannot or do not want to help, or those who choose not to use the online tool, is protected.

When the shoe is on the other foot, and a trusted member of your network solicits you for a referral, be sure to respond in a timely and courteous fashion. Doing so will bolster your social reputation and credibility and make it more likely that others will respond to your inquiries.

Quick Summary! Pros and Cons of Referral Networking

Many tools in a recruiter's toolbox have both positive effects and drawbacks. Knowing where the pitfalls are helps recruiters prepare for them in advance, making the tool more effective or eliminating some of the constraints.

+ Pros	- Cons
Time to hire – Referrals can produce hire results very quickly.	**Responding to everyone** – After reaching out to people personally and individually, they expect a personal response. You cannot leave your referrers in the dark about the process or they will not help you again. Courteous responses take time and effort!
Cost of hire – The cost of referral hires is limited to the recruiter's time plus any referral bonus.	**Size of network** –Referral campaigns work best when there are at least 100 contacts. Not having enough recipients can severely curtail results, making the effort ineffective. While there may be no such thing as "too many" contacts, however, there certainly are diminishing returns when campaigns go out to networks that are very large, particularly when considering the effort required in managing such large campaigns.
Future networking opportunities – In addition to actual hires, referral campaigns produce contacts that could someday become future hires or lead to others.	**Targeting the audience** – An incorrectly targeted audience could backfire. For example, negative publicity via blogs or other media, being publicly accused of spamming, or risk upsetting sensitive networking contacts. Careful consideration must go into planning who should receive the requests. In contrast, a small but correctly targeted audience will yield excellent results.
Increased good will and reputation – By trusting your network to help and putting some money on the table, you make new friends and can increase your reputation.	**Technical difficulties** – In order to personalize and send large batches of emails, a user would have to be familiar with the technical aspects of email merge or have access to an application with similar functions.
High response rates – Employee and non-employee referral programs will have much higher response rates than traditional email initial contact and advertising campaigns.	**Misinterpretations of the message** – Some people can misunderstand the "referral" as some sort of a bribe, not quite understanding the intent of the message. Also, contacts from staffing firms may interpret the referral as a request for fee-based services.

Are Rewards Important?

Misinterpretations of the message – Some people can misunderstand the "referral" as some sort of a bribe, not quite understanding the intent of the message. Also, contacts from staffing firms may interpret the referral as a request for fee-based services.

Referral hiring may not be for everyone, particularly "external" contacts or non-employees. Recruiters can wear out their welcome by constantly asking for help in filling positions and offering little or nothing in return. It may be easy to call in a few favors and obtain some hires initially, but without any incentive besides good will, expect results to diminish over time and referral requests to elicit no response. When the closest resources are tapped out, any new referral hires will only come from points in the network beyond the relative acquaintance of "friend of a friend" contacts.

Because the referral path for a favor-based campaign includes a "friend of a friend" and not a close contact with a vested interest in helping you, your contacts may lack motivation to make a referral in the absence of a reward. A little social lubrication in the form of a cash reward or other concrete incentive, whether for profit or charity, may allow you to tap into your friend of a friend's networks as well as your own. A rewards-based system can also help you bypass the limits of the Dunbar Number or at least buttress a chain link between networks.

In brief, Dunbar is an anthropologist at the University College of London, who wrote a paper on "Co-Evolution Of Neocortex Size, Group Size And Language In Humans" in which he hypothesizes:

> *... there is a cognitive limit to the number of individuals with whom any one person can maintain stable relationships, that this limit is a direct function of relative neocortex size, and that this in turn limits group size ... the limit imposed by neocortical processing capacity is simply on the number of individuals with whom a stable inter-personal relationship can be maintained.*

Essentially, in his paper, Dunbar suggests that it is impossible to have more than 150 "close friends" in any given community. His theory is at the heart of many discussions regarding the effective depth of a social network.

If Dunbar's hypothesis is correct, then a rewards system can motivate contacts and enable deep penetration into a network. Perhaps the biggest obstacle is that your organization needs to be prepared to offer a reward to non-employees. This paradigm shift could prove a bit difficult for companies that do not offer rewards as part of their employee referral programs already. With that obstacle removed and an adequate budget, referral networking can clearly benefit a company's recruiting efforts, both directly in filling open requisitions and indirectly in building a passive talent pipeline composed of individuals seeking to cash in.

It's easy to ask someone for help in finding a candidate, but the seriousness of the request is elevated when we back a request with some funds. Typically, employee rewards range from $500 to $10,000, depending on the level of the position, the difficulty in hiring, and the recruitment budget. Putting their money where their mouth is, recruiters can engage their network to help them in exchange for a little something in return. This technique establishes that the request is not frivolous, but rather that it means business, putting some skin in the game. It adds a "business transaction" level to the request for a favor. A reward is also important in motivating communities. Groups and associations are much more likely to help spread the word if they can benefit their community members by obtaining that reward.

Chapter 9
Searching Communities

Section 1. The California Analogy

In the 1960s, The Irvine Company developed an area of Orange County, California, into a planned suburban city known as Irvine, California. Essentially, Irvine is a super-planned community with more than 230,000 residents, a full array of concierge-like city services, and a highly visible presence of nationally branded retail businesses. Only fifty miles away from Irvine, is the beachfront town of Venice, California. The history of Venice goes back more than a century and evinces very little urban planning for most of that time. Had city officials paid more vigilant attention to Venice, then perhaps Venice would not have been nicknamed "Slum by the Sea" in the 1950s. Today, however, Venice is a thriving beach town where chain restaurants are not allowed and the vicissitudes of its past are embraced as character and uniqueness.

Clichéd, trite, yet true, America is a free country. Its citizens have a right to mobility, and where a person seeks to reside is a reflection of the mind inside. Apply this perspective to online real estate, and it becomes easier to understand why some people avoid popular social networks and choose to live their virtual lives elsewhere. So, when you think of online communities, think of the most popular social networks as if they were online cities like Irvine and the virtual communities discussed herein as towns like Venice – organic, unique, and dependent on their residents for character, culture, and maintenance.

Section 2. The Blogosphere

Web logs are online diaries, more commonly known as **blogs**. Due to the inherent nature of blogs, blogging is a very democratic activity. Blogs enable their owners, **bloggers**, to carve out their own online fiefdom where they establish the boundaries of their own turf.

Applying the mathematical concept of "absolute value", each blogger inherently possesses the same absolute value as another. Where bloggers vary is in the content that they post. Very few bloggers have the skill set, personality, and appeal to be true blogging generalists. Most bloggers have a distinct take on a specified subject.

The blog space, or **blogosphere**, can be a wealth of information to recruiters, for not only are you likely to uncover the same information as you would on a resume, you are also likely to become more familiar with the blogger and the blogger's community. PRA definitely applies to the blogosphere, for blogs are heavily linked and interconnected. By finding one blogger, it is very easy to find other like-minded individuals discussing similar topics who link to other blogs, and very often they are experts in your target skill set.

Some blog features are universal:

- Content is generated by the blogger
- Content typically deals with one area of interest with blog entries containing links to websites, images, and commentary
- Numerous blog services make it easy for individuals to begin blogging without any knowledge of HTML or programming skills
- Blog entries are arranged in a chronological fashion with the most recent postings appearing first
- As blog services become more sophisticated, more user features have become available that allow either bloggers to divide posts by subjects or blog readers to change the blog's settings so that posts are divided by subject, both of which are growing trends
- Bloggers are capable of inviting commentary from blog readers and leave comments for others to read

Popular Blog Hosts

While hundreds of websites offer free blog hosting, you may find that most people rely on a small selection of highly popular hosts. Use this list either to select a blog host for your own "Recruiter's Blog" or to search among those hosts for experts who blog on your subjects of interest to you. Bloggers sometimes have links to their profiles or additional information about themselves, so look for those links on their blogs.

Here are the three popular blog hosts in the United States:

- **Blogger.com.** One of the oldest and largest blog communities, Blogger was established in 1999 and is now part of Google.
- **TypePad.com.** Frequently the choice of professional bloggers, this full featured and hosted solution is extremely customizable, comes with oodles of preconfigured themes, and offers exceptional customer support.
- **WordPress.com** (and wordpress.org). Wordpress.com is different from Wordpress.org in that the .org version provides free open source blogging software and users host their blog themselves, while the .com version is a full-service blog hosting site.

Here are the two most popular **micro blogging** hosts in the United States:

- **Twitter.com.** Twitter posts are famously limited to 140 characters. The concise nature of Twitter makes it a snap to receive updates posted by Twitter users. Twitter has also spawned its own jargon using hash tags ("#") and contributed to the increased general awareness of memes.
- **Tumblr.com.** Tumblr places a premium on a clean presentation. Tumblr is very popular with users under 25 and has a higher retention rate than Twitter, so recruiters should familiarize themselves with this site as these young people grow in their careers.

To search the content of these blogs using a major search engine all you need to do is utilize the following commands:

site:blogger.com

inurl:blogger.com

Section 3. Finding Blogs

Since blogs are basically nothing more than Web pages, there are many ways to find them. For example, you can look for telltale signs such as the tools or software used to create them, or the names of blog components such as "comments", "posted", "trackback", "tags", "RSS feed", "Archives" and "permalinks".

Refer to the list of blog sites below for more ideas on combining several blog hosts in one search. You can easily find blogs using the "site: command" on search engines to scan through the blog host. For example, to find people discussing J2EE on LiveJournal, go to *google.com* or *bing.com* and enter:

site:livejournal.com J2EE

Try replacing livejournal.com with other popular blog host domains such as tyepepad.com, blogdrive.com, blogspot.com (Blogger), multiply.com, mindsay.com, spaces.Live.com or xanga.com. You can also combine several into one query like this:

(*site:livejournal.com OR site:blogspot.com OR site:multiply.com*)

Another way is to use the "inurl:" command. If you search for "inurl:blog OR inurl:weblog", you will find pages that are most likely blogs because they have the word "blog" or "weblog" in their address or URL. For example, from *google.com* enter:

(inurl:blog OR inurl:weblog) J2EE VMWare

This string doesn't just apply to technical skills. You could easily search for keywords related to attorneys, accountants, doctors, nurses, or any other profession. The beautiful thing about blogs is that even someone with the most basic computer skills can be a blogger.

Yet another way to find blogs is by searching for blog components. Some blog authors choose to have the ability to link to individual blog articles or posts permanently. To provide this function, blogging software uses something called a "permanlink". When someone posts a blog item, the software assigns that item a permanent link, or permalink, which is effectively an "internal link" (called an anchor in HTML). Anchor links contain a hash mark (the pound symbol: #), followed by the bookmarked text. In some search engines you can search for pages that have an anchor. As an example, from Google, you would use the command "inanchor:permalink" and combine it with other keywords such as blog or weblog, along with skill-specific search terms such as the following:

java (blog OR weblog) inanchor:permalink

You can use the same technique to search for blogs with comments. The

HTML code for comments in an anchor is "#comments". You could do the same search as above using comments instead of permalink. Similarly, you could search for trackback, which is a blog feature that lists links to other blogs referencing the topic posted by the blogger. Not all blogs will have trackback, comments, or permalinks, but many may at least

have one of those features. Here is an example of a combined search using all three of these blog features:

java (blog OR weblog) (inanchor:trackback OR inanchor:permalink OR inanchor:comments)

Another fairly comprehensive search that would take advantage of searching for those components would be something like the following:

Java "Software Engineer" (comments OR "RSS Feed" OR archives OR posted OR tags OR trackback OR blog)

There is one more way to find candidates who blog: Go directly to the source of the blog and search the host website using a specialized search engine.

Quick List! Other Blog Hosts

These blog hosts are still popular around the world despite the relative market dominance of TypePad and WordPress.

- 20six.co.uk
- Blog-City.com
- BlogHarbor.com
- LiveJournal.com
- Mindsay.com
- SixApart.com
- Squarespace.com
- Xanga.com

Blog Search Engines

Most of the blog hosting companies offer the ability to search through their blogs to find specific topics. Not all blog owners opt to include themselves in search engine results, so to crack this potential source, it may become necessary to search directly through blog hosts. Because you are searching a specific corner of the Web, you do not have to use many keywords. One or two keywords describing the primary skills you seek in a candidate should suffice. Here is a list of the largest and most useful specialized blog search engines that scan popular blog hosts, and keep track of updated blogs:

- Blogarama.com
- BlogDigger.com
- BlogLines.com
- Blogsearchengine.com
- Blogstreet.com
- DayPop.com
- Feedster.com
- Gigablast.com
- Google.com/blogsearch
- IceRocket.com
- LiveJournal.com
- Technorati.com

When conducting a search via these specialized search engines, be sure to keep it simple. Use natural phrase search terms like "I work for" in conjunction with company names, or do simple job title searches. Using too many keywords in searches at the above sites will return very few results. Remember that you are searching through individual blogs so your search is already narrow enough. As you search for candidates with your desired skills, make a note of blog communities to which they belong. You will begin to identify patterns and blog communities they frequent.

Section 4. RSS

RSS is an acronym most lately known as "Really Simple Syndication" and consists of two families of open communication standards: Rich Site Summary and RDF Site Summary. RSS is an XML (extensible markup language) format for news and content that allows a website owner to syndicate content to other websites easily. When a site publishes an RSS Feed that means that the website's headlines are being pushed to other websites wishing to receive them. In this way, the syndicated website's content is automatically published on subscriber sites. Sometimes these RSS messages being sent out also include a summary of the blog post, or even the post in its entirety. You can subscribe to feeds and thus be able to read posts from all your favorite blogs right from one location without having to log on or visit each of the sites separately. In addition, many search engines publish RSS feeds, allowing you to effectively subscribe to search results.

For example, to create an RSS feed from search engine results, you can do the following:

From IceRocket, select either "Blogs" or "Web" then conduct your search. In the results page, you will see a button where you can select the RSS Reader you use (see below), or simply right click on the RSS link and copy the shortcut, then paste it into your favorite reader.

Think of RSS as the "TiVo" of the Web. You can use RSS Feeds to stay informed and receive headlines from websites you would normally have to visit individually. In order to receive RSS Feeds you must use either an RSS Reader software application or subscribe to an online reader service. Both are very simple to configure and use. Some examples of RSS Readers for your PC include:

NewsGator.com A "news aggregator" application that runs in Microsoft Outlook. It allows you to subscribe to various syndicated news feeds (such as Weblogs or news sites) and have news from these sites be delivered right into your Outlook folders. You can also subscribe to the online version of NewsGator for free.

NewzSpider.com A free, easy-to-use aggregator that installs on your computer and allows you to collect new blog posts from all your favorite sources into one single program.

SYFACiL.com A RSS Reader, bookmark manager, and file upload manager that supports multiple browsers on your PC. It also offers an Internet Explorer Toolbar with additional functionality.

Bloglines.com Besides being a blog host, Bloglines is also an easy-to-use service for subscribing to news feeds, which also lets you publish a blog easily from your feeds. Available in several languages, it supports browsing from a mobile device and is completely free.

My.Yahoo.com My Yahoo allows for personalization and centralization of your entire Yahoo services. You can add any RSS feed or traditional news feed from any website to your My Yahoo page. It's not as full-featured as some other news aggregators, but is a convenient option for Yahoo users and makes for a nifty stating page. Completely free, but you must have a Yahoo account.

Other RSS Readers RSS readers are easy-to-use. Most of them provide a feature that allows you to copy the URL of the website containing the RSS feed to which you want to subscribe, then paste that URL into some type of "Add Subscription" box inside the reader. Once you click "Add" the feed will be added to your list. It's also easy to create folders and organize all your feeds. Some add a feature that lets you make public and share any of your folders or collections of feeds so others can read the same subscriptions as you.

Besides being a way to receive updates when your favorite bloggers update their blogs, this is also useful in helping you find blogs. You could, for example, search for pages containing the word blog somewhere in the text, and RSS elsewhere in the URL. Within Live.com you can use the command "hasfeed:" to find only sites that publish RSS Feeds. For example if you are looking for information about layoffs, a search for hasfeed:layoffs will reveal blogs and sites that publish RSS Feeds about the topic of layoffs.

Section 5. Where Can I Find Virtual Communities

There are several virtual communities found on the Internet. The original "virtual communities" consist of websites where people could "host" or use free Web space to put up their personal information. Among the largest of these are:

- Geocities.com by Yahoo
- Tripod.com by Lycos
- Angelfire.com by Lycos
- MySpace.com from News Corp

How Do I Find Candidates Inside Virtual Communities?

Most virtual communities have built-in search engines available directly on their sites. These search engines utilize simple Boolean search terms to find candidates for you. Because these are personal pages and not corporate pages, you can use the word "resume" as well as the skill sets of the targeted candidate to search and get good results. Location keywords may also be a good idea, if applicable. Remember that some search engines require that AND and OR be typed in uppercase. Try the following search string in the search box at some of the above virtual communities:

resume AND "software engineer"

Similar to the above free Web hosts, many ISPs (Internet Service Providers) make some Web space available to subscribers. Though there are thousands of ISPs throughout the world, searching through the top providers can be an excellent source of untapped leads. Use the site: command to search through people with pages hosted by their ISPs. Start with big hosts such as:

- Charter (site:webpages.charter.net)
- Comcast (site:home.comcast.net)
- CompuServe (site:compuserve.com)
- EarthLink (site:home.earthlink.net)
- AT&T (site:home.att.yahoo.com)
- Bellsouth (site:bellsouth.net)
- CenturyLink (site: qwest.centurylink.com)
- Freeservers (site:freeservers.com)
- Roadrunner - Time Warner Cable (site:rr.com)

Virtual communities such as those listed above do not usually have site-specific search engine, so must be searched using an independent search engine. For example, to search through members of the CompuServe community, you should use Google in this way:

site:compuserve.com "software engineer"

By replacing compuserve.com with one of the free Web hosts from the previous section (e.g., tripod.com), you will find software engineers with homepages in the Tripod community. Since you should not be limiting yourself to using only one search engine, let's review an example of the same kind of search using Yahoo. The "site:" command works just the same in Yahoo as it does on Google. For example, from yahoo.com enter:

site:tripod.com "Software Engineer"

This search reveals a large population of software engineers with a virtual presence in that community.

Discussion Groups

Just as in real-life or "in person" communities, people gather together online to meet or discuss their interests. The three most popular online groups are Google, Yahoo and MSN. They each have their own rules, but generally you must sign up to a group in order to participate in it. There is no cost associated with online groups, so the only investment is your time. Some groups allow you to see their content and discussions without registering as a member, but you may not be able to see the addresses of other members or interact with them unless you subscribe to the group.

Groups.Google.com. In 2001 this popular search engine company purchased the Usenet archives managed by Deja News Research Service on Deja.com. The revolutionary Deja.com service allowed the general public to search Usenet discussions and was, until 1995, the only domain of technically savvy people with News Readers and access to Usenet servers. Google has evolved the Usenet concept into modern day online discussion groups where users can easily post and answer questions in a specific discussion or search through millions of discussions to find a topic of interest to them. As a result it has gained in both popularity and population size.

With a few simple commands, it's possible to find experts responding to questions about a vast number of subjects. Such experts can potentially lead you to your target candidates or even sometimes become candidates themselves. Groups are not limited to those with technical interests. You can find discussion groups on broad topics such as media and pharmaceutical and on much narrower topics such as a particular specialization or geography.

To find groups based on specific keywords in their name or description, simply use the "group:" command. To locate people interested in the Java programming language, for example, conduct a search for group:*java*. The * symbol tells Google Groups to look for any combination of words preceding or following the word Java. Results will include groups like comp.lang.java.advocacy and it.comp.java.

Finding particular keywords in the subject of a group is also useful. For this search, simply utilize the "insubject:" command followed by your search words. For example, the command

"insubject:resume" will locate thousands of resumes posted to a wide array of groups.

Another useful technique is to search for particular keywords in the email address of the person who originated the posting. If you want to find group messages written by people from Pfizer, for example, search for "author:pfizer.com".

Groups.Yahoo.com. Similar to Google Groups, Yahoo Groups also allow people to discuss particular topics, but it also has a few additional features like the ability to share files, view a list of members, create databases and even have a group calendar. If a list of members is available, that is a great place to start building a list of potential contacts. Though not everyone will have a full profile in their Yahoo account, most of them do list their email address and frequently their Instant Messenger address.

Many Yahoo Groups allow anyone to read their messages, but only those who join the group can post messages or utilize any of the other features. While many groups allow anyone to join, in order to prevent abuse some require prospective members to explain why they should be allowed to join the group, or provide some kind of evidence that they belong in the group. Yahoo offers a simple search interface where you can enter a few keywords like Java and Unix to find groups matching those interests. Once you find a group, it's important to familiarize yourself with any group rules before you begin actively recruiting in the group. You can always ask the group owner or moderator, listed in the home page of the group, about the ground rules.

Groups.MSN.com. Unlike Google, the community pages of MSN Groups are loaded with features. Similar to Yahoo Groups, a community can share any number of files, keep a group calendar, and even have a photo gallery. Many of the features are viewable to unregistered users, but by joining the group you may gain access to a contact database, internal meeting minutes and other protected documents. To find MSN Groups simply visit live.com and search using the "site:" command. For example, at the time of this book's publication, this search "C# site:groups.msn.com" on Live.com resulted in over 200 pages and numerous groups interested in "Dot Net".

In addition to the online groups listed about, there are two more types of "discussion groups" which utilize the Internet to communicate: Electronic Mailing List and Forums. They are discussed below.

Mailing Lists and Forums

Before the rise in popularity of online groups like those discussed in the previous section, there existed two other kinds of online communities that shared a very similar philosophy. The oldest, originating mainly as electronic distribution lists for people who want to receive emails directed to an entire group, is an Electronic Mailing List. Similar to paper-based mailing lists, subscribers opted to receive announcements or messages meant for the entire group, and often no one else. Today, Mailing Lists are the choice for groups preferring to remain private and not post their messages to the public domain, as is the case with the groups previously discussed.

Mailing Lists are frequently managed by automated programs called Listservs, and have well-established rules of etiquette. Members who join can send a message to one single email address and that message is then forwarded to all active subscribers. Anyone can then reply to the original sender privately, or to the entire list. Recruiters join these electronic mailing lists so they can find potential experts who may be replying to questions by sending messages to the whole list.

Some lists are open for anyone to join, while others have membership requirements. Moderators will usually approve membership requests, and in some cases, group messages go through the moderator before being sent to everyone in order to prevent abuse or violations of the group rules.

A vast catalog of Mailing Lists can be found at lsoft.com/lists/listref.html and also freelists.org/. You can also search CataList and FreeLists by interest keywords to find lists specializing in your candidate's industries or specialties. Although these electronic mailing lists are typically private, some do choose to archive past messages online so they can be referred to or searched in the future. Searching for the words "mailing list archive" along with some skill specific terms may reveal a few such archives.

Once electronic Bulletin Board Services (BBS) grew in popularity, the Mailing Lists concept combined with the idea behind a private BBS and spawned a new kind of group that behaved like a combination of an exclusive Mailing List and a password protected online group. These groups are called Forums, and they have a few key differences when compared to other types of groups presented here.

Forums take place entirely online and messages are not distributed to individuals' inboxes. In addition, users will need to register to access Forums and sometimes even pay a small subscription fee. The advantage is that unlike mailing lists the messages are kept private and users can choose to maintain anonymity. Even though some people do choose privacy, it is still possible to find ways to contact experts posting answers in forums. Many of them include their email address when they create a new forum message, and most modern sites have the ability to see user profiles, which can include home page URLs and Instant Messenger addresses.

As with all of the other groups mentioned so far, people go to Forums to discuss specific topics and do not appreciate off-topic messages. Therefore, a recruiter must be sure to use discretion and would do well not to post messages to the group without first having a clear understanding of the group's culture.

Associations and Conferences

Associations can be a hybrid in that many have online groups, mailing list or forums, but they also have in-person meetings, events or conferences. Both the online presence as well as the in-person events of associations can yield highly targeted candidate leads or provide an avenue for referrals. According to Job-Hunt.org, seven-out-of-ten people in the U.S. belong to at least one association, and 25 percent are members of four or more. So, local and national associations, and societies are great places to make connections. Here are some suggestions on where to find associations relevant to your target candidates:

- **WEDDLE's** (*weddles.com/associations/index.htm*). A very extensive list of professional associations and societies organized by industry or specialty.
- **IPL** (*ipl.org/div/aon/*). The Internet Public Library lists prominent non-profit organizations and associations with a Web presence.
- **Job-Hunt.org** (*job-hunt.org/associations.shtml*). Associations by job type and some additional resources.
- **Job Bank USA** (*jobbankusa.com/indassoc/mainindex.html*) Select by industry or browse alphabetically.

In addition, the Concept Marketing Group (marketingsource.com/assoctestdrive/details) sells a list containing over 35,000 associations. You can purchase it online, in print or on CD starting from $165.

Finally, you can also search for keywords like Association and Directory or List along with your keywords describing your desired candidate specialty and will probably find related associations.

Once you know the name and Web address of an association related to your target candidates, take a moment to do a simple "site:" search through its website to see if you can easily identify some points of contact. For example, , if you wanted to find Management Accountants, you could use any of the major search engines and the following command:

site:imanet.org (he OR she)

Adding a simple "he" or "she" statement to your search will bring you results of pages where individuals are addressed using subjective personal pronouns. People who are being addressed in

the third person are typically those who appear on bios, or pages describing people such as staff, speakers, members, and association officials. You can also search the association site for words like: Member, attendee, roster, list, staff, director, vice president, president, panel, speaker, presenter, and so on.

Usenet (now Google Groups)

Usenet began as a global discussion system over one of the oldest Internet protocols, Network News Transfer Protocol (NNTP). Your computer probably still has a default newsreader. Google acquired Usenet and kept it going at *http://groups.google.com*. It is now called Google Groups, and as its name indicates, it is broken down into groups organized by specific subject and subtopics. People who have interest in a topic will simply join in the online conversation or start one of their own. Messages are linked together in "threads" so you can follow the conversation from start to finish. Some groups are very specific. For example, there are groups for every kind of computer language.

As you can imagine, this area of the Web could be an excellent place to listen in and find out more about the positions for which you are recruiting as well as the people who may be able to fill them. A word of caution: Do not solicit directly from groups unless the group rules specifically allow your doing so. Proper etiquette requires that you participate in the group before creating a new conversation or publishing an announcement. Even when it is permissible to do so, if you solicit directly, you risk angering group members who may respond by flaming or mail bombing you. For more information on proper netiquette go to *http://www.cs.indiana.edu/docproject/zen/zen-1.0_6.html*.

The best way to proceed is to search all groups with keywords that define your potential candidates. Some newsgroups are even dedicated to job postings or to resumes. These groups include misc.jobs.resumes and misc.jobs.offered. It is often easiest to search by state (e.g., ca.jobs, co.jobs, or ny.jobs) or industry (e.g., bionet.jobs.wanted, or comp.jobs), since that is usually how the newsgroups are broken up.

There are some simple ways to quickly search through the vast library of Google Groups. From *http://groups.google.com*, you could enter the command "*group:*" along with a keyword describing the type of skills you are seeking. When using the "group:" command, you can use wildcards to help you capture more information. Using the asterisk (⊠) on both sides of your keywords allows you to find all groups with names containing your keyword, as in

group:*PHP*

This search reveals all the posts from groups such as comp.lang.php or mailing.www.php-dev. There are several such groups, but now you have a very good starting point for finding people who ask and answer questions about PHP. You can then use additional keywords—company names, products, projects, or specific tools—to narrow down your search.

Another useful shortcut is the "insubject: command", which directs the search engine to find results with the keywords that appear only in the subject line of the message. Many people post their resume to groups with the word "resume" in the message. Try this search:

insubject:resume

Combining the above command with specific keywords will help you uncover resumes that may not be posted elsewhere.

Chapter 10
Applying Sourcing to International Recruiting

One of the most salient running themes throughout world history is the search for new markets and trade routes. A more recent theme is the addition of services to goods in the global marketplace, meaning products exchanged internationally are increasingly not limited to tangible goods produced in a factory but include products developed in services-based industries. Sure, kings and queens of past dispatched expeditions to little-known corners of the earth to find artists and authorities, but today, it is entirely plausible that even small businesses and individual contributors can procure talent from around the globe.

Difficulty in procuring talent from a global pool arises when a substantial segment of the talent pool is pervaded by an externality such as unique, non-native culture or language. Consequently, recruiters and Sourcers must adjust their processes to reflect the corresponding shifts in practices and perspectives to find the candidates with the appropriate underlying skill set.

International recruiting is further complicated because, when they cross country borders, recruiters cannot merely focus on the recruitment process, per se, but must also be cognizant of the effects of those efforts on the home country (e.g. company perception or national laws and policies). Thus, international recruiting is really a two-front process. Additionally, hiring and human resource managers must concern themselves with three cultures brought about by international recruiting: The native culture, the adopted culture, and the resulting blended culture. Truly, international recruiting creates a ripple effect that reverberates throughout an entire organization.

Establishing a global recruitment practice requires more care and sensitized handling than simply sending recruiters overseas. In this chapter, the critical factors affecting the launch of a global recruitment practice and how to tailor previously discussed search methodologies for an international campaign are explored, beginning with the assessment of your organization's current level of preparedness.

Section 1. Assess Your Current Structure

You may be an American, and you may be a cowboy, but you cannot just come guns-a-blazin' onto an international workforce market. If you do, you risk making the recruiting process about you – the recruiter – and your cultural illiteracy, rather than about the candidate and the candidate's ability to contribute to your organization. Without the proper due diligence, you run the risk of failing to meet your immediate objective and damaging the organization's credibility and reputation in the process, thereby increasing the risk that your next requirement in the region will fail too.

Before you even set foot on another terrain, though, you must examine what you have at home. If your organization's basic infrastructure is not properly evaluated and prepared to handle the influx of new international recruits, your campaign will be fruitless.

Consider the following factors critical to an international recruiting campaign.

Local Reputation

Your organization may be a brand giant in your home economy, but it may be little known or little regarded abroad. Perhaps a local provider occupies the entire field that your employer wishes to enter. If so, then your recruiting department must also act as brand managers and marketers, spreading your corporate message. Engaging a local public relations firm can greatly heighten your brand image, but first consult your own marketing department to see if there are any campaigns you could co-author or if there are any marketing dollars which could be used for a joint outreach effort in your target region. Then ask yourself this question: If your organization's brand is a well-known, is that recognition limited to its product or service? Or does the brand name carry over to a strong business reputation, as well? Brand recognition is different from business reputation, and it is entirely plausible that members of a community like your organization's product or service, but do not respect its business practices.

Current Presence in the Region

Explore the operations that tie your organization to the target region. You may already have an existing office there. Any kind of local or regional presence, whether it's for order fulfillment or field sales or operations can provide very important local insights as well as a reputable location for your interviews. Physical presence, even only part-time, goes a long way towards establishing credibility.

Vendor Contacts

Local vendors are your potential allies, and they can serve as your advance team. They can even cover gaps in your current global readiness. An internal investigation should reveal current vendor contacts, and the Sourcers on your team may be able to provide you with a shortlist of proposed new vendor contacts. Here are a few types of firms that should be on your vendor list: Temporary or administrative staffing, contract and contingency staffing, executive search, business process Outsourcing, direct marketing, public relations and political consulting, immigration law, travel, relocation, and real estate. By establishing a trusting relationship with vendors, you can have the same great service internationally that you expect domestically even if the volume of your business at those locations is far less than in the U.S.

Employment Packages

You may offer a respectable employment package filled with great benefits in your company's home country, but that same package may not induce candidates in your target region. Be prepared to evaluate and institute changes in the employment package that affect compensation, health benefits, and vacation days, to name just a few areas. Familiarity with local customs and practices proves particularly insightful in this regard. Come to the table knowing what you will be asked and are therefore prepared rather than embarrassed or left wanting later.

Onboarding Plan

Once a hiring manager selects a candidate, that individual must undergo training and other onboarding before settling into a business unit. While usually the purview of other parts of the HR team, training and onboarding are processes about which recruiters should be knowledgeable. Your existing leaders and managers are most likely to have three separate interactions with a successful candidate: First, the interview; second, training; and last, supervision. These interactions are loaded with responsibility and are not limited to the international recruiting process. What is unique to international recruiting is the opportunity to establish and grow new markets as well as engage in true business development first-hand. Many junior or established executives will accept roles away from home as a way to progress swiftly within their organizations. Accordingly, recruiters can accomplish two objectives with one effort: They can meet immediate recruiting needs and build a pipeline for future senior executive positions.

Section 2. The Sourcing Edge: Identifying the Talent Landscape

Identifying the talent landscape abroad requires an additional step in the recruiting process in which recruiters acquire basic knowledge of the targeted geographical region. Usually, knowledge of this kind is naturally absorbed and accumulated by living within the region. For example, just as most American recruiters would automatically know not to schedule an interview on the fourth Thursday of November (American Thanksgiving), a South Korean recruiter would automatically know not to schedule an interview on the fifteenth day of the eighth month of the lunar calendar (Korean Chuseok or Harvest Festival). Many Americans have not even heard of the lunar calendar, which underscores the point that American recruiters need extra, specialized information before entering workforce markets abroad.

At this point in an international recruiting campaign, recruiters' time may be best spent collaborating with business units and hiring managers instead of undertaking extensive Internet research. Thus, it pays to bring in Sourcers earlier in the process so that they can apply their research techniques to debrief you on the following types of pertinent information:

- Demographic information such as population sizes, major cities and metropolitan areas, and major universities.
- Identification of regional socio-political activities and potential upheavals.
- Summaries of applicable international treaties and laws, including visa information, and a list of experts who consult on these matters.
- Infrastructure assessment.

- Economic indicators like major industries, top employers, the size of the labor force, and unemployment rates.
- Workforce practices such as average hours worked per week, average daily schedule (including average lunch break), and average paid vacation time.
- Miscellaneous local variables that impact recruitment campaigns such as national and religious holidays, major weather patterns, times zones, and location of airports and transportation hubs.
- Travel advisories.
- Profiles of competitors with local operations, along with their products, revenues, and vendors.
- Common job portals where jobs are advertised to employment websites, popular blogs, and online media publications.
- Groups relevant to your company's industry such as standard professional organizations, associations, conferences, and discussion lists.
- Major information gatekeepers and spokespeople, well-known professors, bloggers, or other prominent individuals, who can help introduce your recruitment brand to the local market.
- Historical information affecting local stereotypes and stereotypes of Americans.
- Customs and etiquette.

Section 3. Intercultural Issues and the Key to Success

A society may look and act in recognizable ways very similar to cultures from your company's home country, but the biggest mistake you will make is to be misled by that relative familiarity. No matter how similar another country's culture is to your own, do not assume that recruiting in that part of the world is just the same as recruiting in your home country. The real secret to a successful international recruitment practice lies in the recognition of cross-cultural nuances, which seep into such quotidian activities such as basic phone conversations and personal introductions.

Figure 16 Global Village

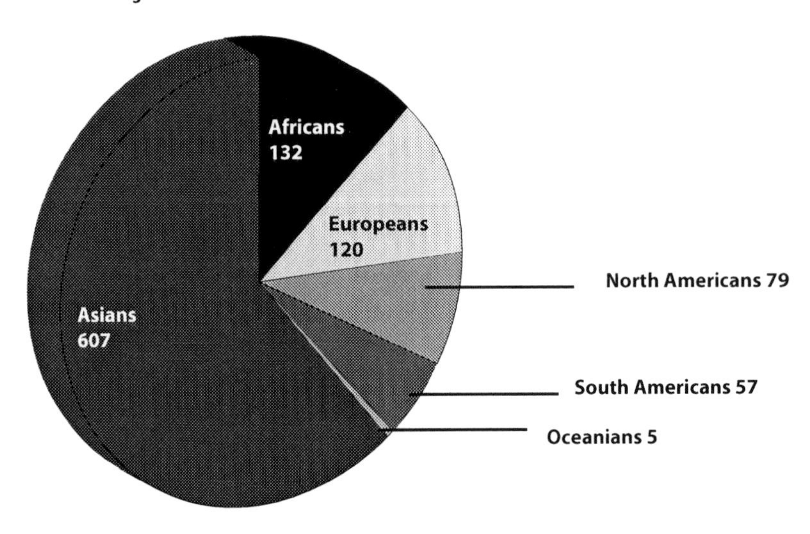

Figure 17 Distribution of Religion

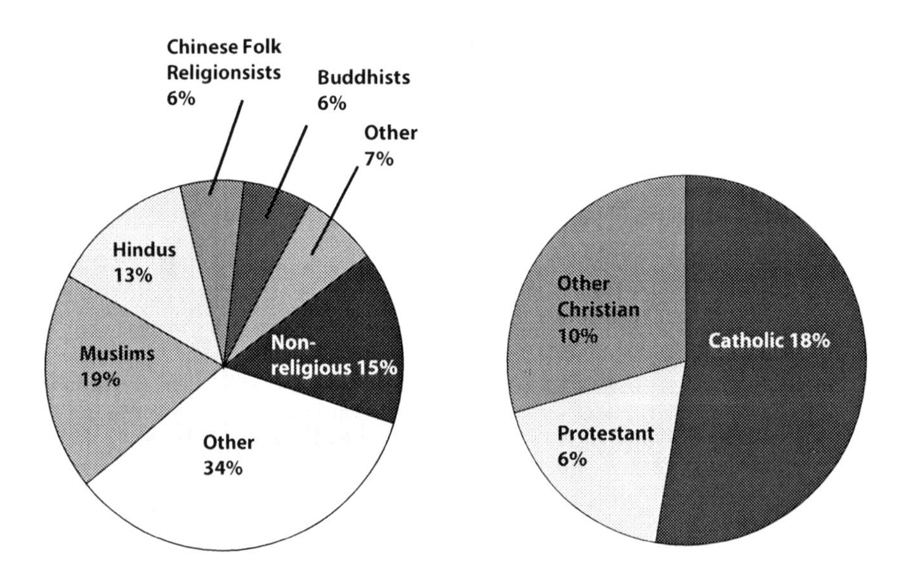

The Cultural Sensitivity Imperative

An analogy may help illustrate how different people are and how important cultural sensitivity is. The *Bureau of the Census, The World Almanac and Book of Facts* says if the world were a village of 1,000 people 607 of the people in the village would be Asian.

Of people with religious beliefs in that village there would be:

If the same analogy were applied to the United States, the numbers and percentages would skew very differently. For example, only fifty-six people out of a thousand would be Asian, 6% and 769 would call themselves either Catholic or Christian. These numbers indicate that basic cultural tent-poles and references will vary widely from region to region.

Here is a list of example practices by country that represent a departure from American customs:

- **Australia:** Australians respect people with strong opinions, even if they do not agree, so state your point directly.
- **China:** Chinese find "no" difficult to say. They may say "maybe" or "we'll see" in order to save face.
- **Colombia:** Do not be offended if you are called a "gringo". Colombians use this term to refer to people from the United States, and it is not meant to be insulting, as it may be in other cultures.
- **France:** The French do not tell or like to hear jokes. They prefer intelligent and satirical wit. Funny stories of real life situations are appreciated.
- **Greece:** Expect Greeks to ask personal questions, such as "Are you married?" or "Do you have children?" This habit is not considered rude, but an attempt to know you personally.
- **India:** When an Indian answers, "I will try", he or she generally means "no". This is considered a polite "no".
- **Japan:** Do not expect a Japanese person to say "no". "Maybe" generally means "no".
- **The Netherlands:** Do not call the Netherlands "Holland". Holland is a region within the Netherlands.
- **Russia:** Never refer to a Russian as "comrade".

No one is immune from the occasional cross-cultural gaffe. Former President George W. Bush and his family were at a parade in Norway when the Longhorns marching band from the University of Texas passed by. Undoubtedly spurred by affection for Texas and the institution Bush's daughter attended, the President and his family held out their hands in the Longhorn salute, index and pinky finger raised. Unfortunately, that same hand gesture has a different meaning in Norway, so instead of seeing the hand sign as a tribute to his home state, many Norwegians perceived it as a salute to Satan, an absurd result that could have been easily avoided.

While it is possible to recover from these embarrassing incidents, a social faux pas usually leaves a question in the balance – why didn't they know beforehand? Regrettably, the answer, namely sheer ignorance, usually undermines their credibility. The main idea here is that your international endeavors should not bear the distraction and damage from avoidable culturally based errors because you have a strong working knowledge and understanding of your market's culture and people.

Establishing a Hub

Each region or country you add to your recruitment goals may require a separate strategy that takes into consideration local customs and idiosyncrasies. Therefore recruiting is best done by locality and by region. A hub is a particular location from where you can centralize your activities abroad. Based on your findings about the talent landscape you should be able to select which countries will host your new International recruitment hubs.

In a similar way that a Target catalyzes a Peer Regression Analysis, the best place to start establishing your new hub is with the local gatekeepers identified in your preliminary Internet research.

In other words, set meetings with well-known professors, association leaders, local members of your country's diplomatic corps, and chamber of commerce leaders to confirm the inferences you've drawn from your preliminary reports and to identify new leads and considerations.

Ask them questions such as:

- What are the top schools? Are they private or public?
- What is their selection process when admitting students?
- What are the top employers in the area?
- What associations or conferences are in the area?
- What is your company's reputation with locals?
- What challenges have other companies faced when recruiting locally?
- What pitfalls should be avoided when talking with locals?

Be sure to offer to be a resource to them, and leave plenty of your business cards with you. Ask if you can add them to your mailing list for when you send out job opening announcements. Also ask if they would be kind enough to forward your job postings to their contacts. You can even extend any reward program to them or employ them as consultants.

Find your company's local HR representative, or if there is none, the equivalent of a local Labor Department and ask about rules regarding what information can be solicited from prospects during initial phone conversations. If "direct recruiting" is not acceptable, you can use the safer alternative: "I'm new to the area and I want to make an introduction". Also ask your local HR or Labor Department contact about any interview questions, which may be considered inappropriate or illegal. For example, in many countries, it is acceptable to ask about parental status and even religious beliefs, but in some it may be inappropriate to ask about educational background.

Along the lines of initial contact, the use of mobile phones worldwide has skyrocketed and in some countries they have almost replaced traditional landlines. In fact, you may want to consider looking into using SMS or "texting" when communicating with prospects because in quite a few countries, text messaging is used more frequently than placing regular voice calls. Free texting applications like WhatsApp or Kakao are used more routinely outside the United States.

To begin using your new hub, have your Sourcers continue to look for local leads and consider hiring a local marketing company for assistance in sending out initial contact emails or regular mail to local talent. Once you have generated some interest, it is time to plan a trip for your recruiters and hiring managers. After you have gained experience with a few recruitment campaigns, you can rely less on vendors and do more of the outreach directly.

Standard Communication Techniques Do Not Cross Borders

Many common business practices are globally accepted because cash is cash whether in euros, pounds, yen, or rupees, but recruiting is one of those functions that may be defined very differently in other countries simply because people are people.

One example of a recruitment strategy that may not translate very well is cold calling. Many cultures consider direct solicitation to be somewhat rude, and they are frequently unsure how to react or respond to direct approaches. In some countries, direct contact with a competitor's employee at work may even be illegal. Be sure to explore what kind of direct contact is acceptable to locals. The resources provided by the Society for Human Resource Management (SHRM) shed light about t different employment laws from other countries and can be found at shrm.org.

If phone recruiting is not a viable option for you then you must also learn the customs associated with face-to-face meetings, which will affect everything from your schedule to your posture and conversation topics. Note that Americans are stereotyped as over sharers, and conveying personal information during meetings or online may be viewed as either discomforting or suspect.

Section 4. The Sourcing Edge: International Sourcing Techniques

Your Sourcers can research and identify the landscape, help design your strategy, and funnel ongoing information and leads to your recruiters for their local recruiting campaigns. However, Sourcing is most beneficial when it is a worldwide function separated only by Internet channel. For example, one Sourcing channel could be international job boards while others could be social networks, university alumni, leads databases, and so on. Address each channel separately, one at a time, until you identify how best to reach and communicate with local talent.

Top Level Domain Searches

The Internet Assigned Numbers Authority (IANA), the organization in charge of assigning names, has created approximately 248 country-code **Top Level Domains** (ccTLDs) using the International Standard for Organization (ISO) two-letter country code protocol. The purpose of establishing these TLDs for each country is to identify that a particular domain is registered in that country. You are already familiar with other TLDs such as .com, .net, and .org which are much more widely used, but sometimes webmasters want to make clear the geographic origin of a website, so they will choose to register their site under a country domain. For example, the largest ccTLD in use today, as measured by the number of websites hosted under that domain, is that of the United Kingdom. Web domains ending with .uk are registered in the United Kingdom.

Though the physical presence of a company, or even their servers, could be anywhere in the world, companies choosing to use .uk do so to indicate they are a UK based website. Searching for websites that end in .uk could reveal leads and resumes from people who may very likely live in the UK. It is important to note, however, that it is possible for an individual to publish their resume in a .uk website yet live in another country or even in the U.S. It is also very possible that people who live in the United Kingdom may publish their resumes on a .com website. As a result, TLD searches are not guaranteed to produce leads from a particular country, and this is by no means the only technique you will need, but it is one of the easiest to apply.

To search for websites from a particular country all you have to do is add the "site:" command to your keyword searches on most major search engines. Use it to limit search results to only those appearing within the TLD of a particular country. All four of the top search engines (Google, Bing, Yahoo and Ask) support the "site:" command as do many of the smaller engines.

For example, if you were searching for Software Engineers in the UK you could start with something like the following:

"software engineer" resume site:uk

The "site:" command also works as an OR statement. For example, if you are seeking leads from both the UK and Ireland, you can use it as follows:

"software engineer" resume (site:uk OR site:ie)

A list of all worldwide ccTLDs can be found on the IANA website (iana.org/domains/root/db/). The following is a selection representing some of the most popularly searched domains:

Australia	**.au**	**India**	**.in**
Austria	**.at**	**Ireland**	**.ie**
Canada	**.ca**	**Netherlands**	**.nl**
China	**.cn**	**Spain**	**.es**
European Union	**.eu**	**South Africa**	**.za**
Finland	**.fi**	**Sweden**	**.se**
France	**.fr**	**Switzerland**	**.ch**
Germany	**.de**	**UK – all**	**.uk**

Country Searches in the Major Engines

Most top search engines have versions dedicated to certain countries. The greatest advantage of using the "local" version of the global search engine is that you may be able to conduct a search for pages hosted in that country, even if they are not hosted on domains that end with that country's TLD. In addition, these top search engines support language specific searching so use keywords containing localized skills language and idiomatic natural phrasing to search for pages written in your target country's native language.

- **Bing** (http://bing.com/account/worldwide). This page takes you to the dedicated Bing pages in regions like Africa, the Americas, Asia, Australia, Europe, and the Middle East.
- **Yahoo** (*e*verything.yahoo.com/world/en-US). Search Yahoo in regions like the Americas, Asia Pacific and Europe, or in different languages.
- **Google** Interestingly enough, at the time of publication, Google does not list all of its domains by country code. Instead, enter "google" and the country code to find out.

Local Search Engines

Many countries have local search engines that were created and hosted in that country. These local search engines often have a unique local focus. As a result, they may find and index pages overlooked by the big global search engines. You can also use these native search engines to find pages originating from that country but buried so deep in the Web they are hard to uncover despite being located on more traditional TLDs like .com and .net. What follows is not intended as a comprehensive list, rather a sampling of some of the largest and most popular country-specific search engines:

- Australia: sensis.com.au
- Austria: austronaut.at
- Canada (French): La Toile du Québec (toile.qc.ca/)
- China: Baidu.com, Sina (http://cha.sina.com.cn/), Sohu (http://page.search.sohu.com/)
- EU: Euroseek.com
- France: Francité.com, Nomade.fr, Voilà.fr
- Germany: wseeker.com
- Greece: search.forthnet.gr, phantis.com

- India: Sify (http://search.sify.com/fsindex.php), Zatka (http://zatka.com/search.php)
- Italy: abcitaly.it, arianna.libero.it
- Latin America: latinguia.com/search
- Romania: h2.ro
- Russia: yandex.ru. Rambler.ru, Tela.dux.ru
- South Africa: Aarvdark.co.za, ananzi.co.za
- Spain: ozu.es
- Switzerland (French): Search.ch

Localization and Language

Another key method used to find people from other countries is to search for resumes in their language. Just because a document is called a resume in English (the word is adopted from the French word résumé) does not mean people who speak other languages will use the same word. The words Curriculum Vitae, for example, are commonly used instead of resume. However, many languages have their own words to describe this document. Contact a native speaker of your target country's language and have them spell the word for you in their native tongue; then use that keyword instead of the words resume or résumé in your local searches. Here are some examples of how résumé translates in other languages:

- Arabic: سيرة ذاتية, خِصة
- Arabic (Other): سـ يرة ية ذاتـ, خِصة
- Chinese (Simplified): 回复
- German: Lebenslauf
- Greek: επαναλάβετε
- Holland: samenvatting
- Japanese: 概要
- Korean: 이력서
- Polish: Zyciorys
- Portuguese: Resumo
- Russian (Cyrillic): Резюме

- Russian (Other): Ðåçþìå
- Spanish (Europe): Currículo
- Spanish (Other, Latin America): Resumen
- Swedish: återuppta

Consider the impact that language has on a search. A simple search on Google using the German word for resume, *Lebenslauf*, and looking for pages containing C++ and written in *German* (search for: language:de Lebenslauf C++) yields over 13,000 results. If we replace *Lebenslauf* with *Curriculum Vita* (language:de "Curriculum Vita" C++), we find over 1,600. However, looking for pages written in English and also containing the C++ and *Lebenslauf* yields a paltry 860 results. Using the TLD for Germany and searching with the word *Lebenslauf* (site:de Lebenslauf C++) yields over 8,700 pages, but if we use *Curriculum Vita*, instead, we find only 2,000.

What is most amazing about this comparison is that there is very little overlap in those results. So, the best search would combine both a search for the appropriate local word as well as other variations plus looking for both pages written in that language or hosted by domains in that TLD. For example, try something like the:

(site:de OR language:de) (Lebenslauf OR "Curriculum Vita") C++

Adding job titles, skills keywords or competitor names to the above will focus your search.

Translation

As you conduct your searches, particularly if you are using the localization technique above, you will find pages written in foreign languages that you may not understand. Do not despair. The Internet provides a solution, however imperfect, to the instant translation of text. So, if you find a page but cannot read it, copy the text and head to the websites below where you can paste the text into a box for instant translation:

- BabelFish.co
- BabelXL.com
- Bing.com/translate
- Frengly.com
- Translate.google.com

Because words have many meanings – for example, consider that the word resume could also be used to express "picking up where you left off" and thus may not translate correctly using an online translation service, you may also want to utilize an old fashioned Language Dictionary. A few dictionaries that can translate words from English to other languages, or vice versa, are available online:

- German – *vokabeltrainer.pons.de/cgi-bin/wb/wb.pl*
- French and Spanish – *elmundo.es/diccionarios*
- Japanese – *http://dictionary.goo.ne.jp/ej*
- Russian – *rustran.com*
- Polish – *poltran.com*
- Arabic – *almisbar.com/salam_trans.html*

International Social Networks

Though easily overlooked as a source of international candidate, social networking sites can easily reveal leads from all over the world. In fact, 81 percent of Facebook and over half of LinkedIn™ users are located outside the United States. You may already know that from the People tab, you can limit your search to people "Located in or near" any one of at least 200 countries. Merely select a country and search for people with the desired job titles or from target companies.

But using the "Located in or near" search is quite limiting, particularly if your search needs to encompass more than one country. There is one more way to take advantage of LinkedIn's large database of people. Instead of choosing a Location, try using the "keywords:" search instead. By entering the names of several countries separated by the OR command, you can do a multinational search. For example, enter "Belgium OR France OR Netherlands" and LinkedIn™ will search for profiles containing those words either in the Location field, or in Education, or even in any other part of a user's profile. The only downside to this technique is that occasionally, you run into people who are not from or live in the country in which you are searching. Their profile may have come up in your search because they mention that country as a place they have visited or where they once studied, instead.

A recent report by Mashable.com reports the social networks below as dominant in their region:

- China – QZone (http://qzone.qq.com)

- Russia – Odnoklassniki (Odnoklassniki.ru)
- Iran – Cloob (http://cloob.com)
- Latvia – Draugiem (draugiem.lv)
- Europe – Vkonkakte (http://vk.com)

If a particular region is not listed above, then the most popular social network for that region is Facebook!

PART III: Attract & Engage

Now that you have completed Find, it is time to move forward to Attract and Engage. Whether you are converting inbound respondents or conducting outbound outreach, you must at some point engage prospects, candidate and applications in conversation. Part III of this book focuses on communicating with candidates.

Chapter 11 Employment Advertising

Up to this point, the heavy lifting has been done unilaterally on your part. Now that you have an advanced understanding of the first component of THE FIVE, Find, it is time to move onto the second and third components: Attract and Engage. The most innocuous and simple way to attract and engage a candidate in the job hunt is through your job posting.

No one is a mind reader. You may be in possession of the best job opportunity a candidate could hope for, but you will not attract the best candidates if you do not provide the right information in the job posting. The best job posting captures the candidate's attention immediately in the title. Even if the job posting title and summary captures the candidate's attention, that individual must then willfully choose to click on and open your job posting. Any faulty turn can repel the very person you need. Similarly, an effective job posting will automatically weed out undesirable/unfeasible candidates from the beginning of the process.

Section 1. Job Posting Basics

So how do you find more of the right kind of people to apply for your jobs? First, let's review some of the basics of job posting:

Post Early

As soon as you are charged with a new requirement, post it! Then take the time to organize, search resumes, conduct your research, and contact your leads. Did you know that the "most read" day on job posting sites is Wednesday? Research by major job boards has demonstrated that a majority of job seekers turn to them mid-week. Apparently, candidates arrive on Monday and are instantly overwhelmed with work. On Mondays, the possibility of working somewhere else germinates. By Tuesday, they are ready to consider "looking around" but do not act until Wednesday and most likely during work hours! Wednesday is the day when Computerjobs.com, Monster.com and other sites register a disproportionate majority of hits on their sites. So, if you plan to post your jobs on a schedule, it is not be a bad idea to make that a Tuesday so that mid-week job shoppers see it as a fresh posting.

Keep Job Titles Simple

Using standard occupational terms — not unique company departmental titles – makes it easy for people to "translate" their current position and decide if they would be a fit for the position. The job may have some other internal title for HR or departmental purposes, but if candidates do not understand the title they may skip over the job. Your job titles will set your ad apart by clearly explaining the position. Furthermore, when a job board search engine returns a list of positions organized by title, the job seeker must decide which position to open based solely on the information in the titles. Not until the job seeker clicks on the posting itself do they encounter the actual full description.

Include Skill, Hook and Location in Title

The first thing a job searcher sees is the title of your job posting. If that does not catch their attention, they will not even bother to click on your job and read the important details. To make sure you achieve the best results from your job posting, the title should clearly state the primary skill required for that job, the most attractive feature of the job posting, and a clear definition of the job location. Even though the most popular career sites offer a separate column for location, you should repeat the location again in the title to reinforce it. This technique serves two other purposes as well: First, if the job is passed around to someone else, the location will be in the subject line of the email. Having the location in the subject line of the email helps you keep track of candidates in the event that multiple positions with the same title are located around the globe. Second, when a candidate does a search by location, your job will be ranked higher because the location keywords are in the name of the job itself.

Examples: Which job title do you think would be clicked on first?

Production Support Implementation Engineer

and

WinNT UNIX Systems Administrator, mature start-up, north Phoenix?

How about the difference between these two?

Sales Executive

and

Major Account Executive, flex hours, top pay, San Diego beach

Repeat Location in Summary

People will assume your job posting is located at corporate headquarters unless you clearly state a location. In the title you should have already included the city or state; here is your chance to elaborate on that detail. Do not just put in the name of the city again – use the neighborhood, subdivision, highway exits, or any details that let people easily identify what the commute would be like or if the location is conveniently located. Travel time, distance, proximity to schools or daycare, and accessibility to rapid transit are important descriptive factors that may affect a candidate's decision to apply for the position. In addition, certain geographical locations attract or repel different people. Remember, candidates who are not interested in the job for themselves may send job postings to their friends who are not "actively" searching but will be drawn to a compelling description.

Identify Yourself

A line about who you are is always welcome. If you specialize in a certain area such as sales, software, hardware or retail, say so – it builds credibility. And, there is nothing wrong with having more than one specialty, so in one job posting, you could term yourself a "sales recruiter", and in another, an "engineering recruiter". Even if you have a formal application process, it makes your job stand out if you sign it with your name and specialty, as opposed to simply "human resources". Candidates like to know they are dealing with a real person and real jobs, not with a generic "resume collector".

Section 2. Useful Information to Include in Job Advertisements

Other information which is useful to include is whether you sponsor visas, accept college students, offer training or career development, aid with relocation, provide attractive stock options, or reimburse tuition or certification, to name a few. If you state clearly that the position requires a specific degree, for example, you will receive fewer irrelevant resumes, potentially reducing the amount of time you spend filtering inappropriate resumes. A company URL and links to specific products, press releases, testimonials, or a benefits page are quick credibility builders. Candidates who are initially only slightly interested in your posting will become more trusting and likely to pursue the job further.

Remember Good News Spreads

The best job posts are short and informational because that encourages people to pass them around. When a job seeker reads a job posting that catches their attention, but then turns out not to be a good fit, they will often pass it along to their friends and peers who are also looking for work. Being concise works for you here because the sender is not asking the recipient to commit a long time reading the forwarded message. Because some of this informal referral pool may be even less aggressive about searching for jobs, you end up reaching an audience that isn't readily accessible from your company's career page or the job boards.

Sell the Sizzle

The really good candidates can afford to be picky. To attract them, your posting must have some sizzle. Briefly describe the company. Why is it so exciting to work here? What makes it special? Why should anyone come to work for you? What new product or technology will candidates learn? Are there any special benefits or perks? What is unique about the location? If you have low turnover rates or a high level of employee referrals then flaunt that. Are you growing? How are you different than other companies, or what makes you an "employer of choice"?

View Job Posting as Advertising

A job posting sells your company. Even if the reader does not apply, they will receive a strong message from you, which should be the same core message presented in all your marketing material. A job posting should read like a snazzy, compact marketing brochure. What is the image you want people to have of your company, even when they do not apply? If your job posting doesn't sell the "sizzle" and represent the core values of your company, how are job seekers going to feel comfortable applying? If you do not sell to the job seeker as they glance through the job posting, the only people who will respond to the job posting are the people who probably failed to even read it in the first place.

Express Corporate Culture

Saddled along with the imperative to view the job posting as advertising is the opportunity to share and brand your organization's unique corporate culture with candidates. In a memoir, Jack Welch, famed former CEO of General Electric, explains that one of the critical factors in the successful merger of two organizations is whether the separate entities share a similar corporate culture. Interpolating this notion to individual employees, it stands to reason that the candidate with a compatible corporate culture is more likely to respond when a job posting expresses similar values and practices. Moreover, that same candidate is more likely to transition into the company with greater ease and personal satisfaction, leading to greater retention. There exists one caveat here: Misery may love company, but expressing corporate culture is most advantageous when it reflects good-to-best business and workforce practices and is reinforced by happy employees.

Chapter 12
An Integrated Approach to Outreach

Section 1. Initiating Contact Through Email

Once you have a finalized list of prospects, it may be tempting to call individuals directly, particularly if there is someone about whom you are particularly excited. However, initiating contact via telephone may not be the most appropriate course of action. Metaphorically, the stars must be aligned for an initial phone conversation to produce a positive result. First, you must actually connect with the individual directly. Then, the individual must have both the right frame of mind to entertain your pitch and the time to hear it. Concurrently, you must present your message accurately and in an engaging fashion. Finally, the individual must be instantly intrigued enough to agree to speak again. The risk that any one among many factors may go awry is significant.

Instead of a telephone call as your first attempt, consider using email to initially reach out to prospects. Email is the quickest, most unobtrusive, and prudent way to approach your targets, particularly among today's extremely mobile population. Possibly the biggest advantage to using email is its potential to plant a seed in the prospect's mind.

A cold phone call is flattering, but it is way too easy for the recipient to hang up the phone before you can convey your message. In an email you can present your entire content in the written manner of your choosing, which matters because the more care and craft you use to write your email, the more likely that the message will interest your reader. Further, unlike a phone call, an email requires no immediate response, so the reader has time to digest your job opportunity. In effect, the idea of your job opportunity can germinate in the reader's mind. Then, a reader will respond to your email only when motivated by genuine curiosity rather than mere politeness. After all, there is no obligation to respond to the email at all.

Subject Lines

Even the most hypnotic and persuasive writing is a useless attempt at communication if the intended recipient does not open your message. Your subject line should prompt readers' curiosity so that your message is opened. Like headlines in the news, subject lines are the first part of your message someone reads and often the only part of your message they ever see.

You have precious seconds to convince someone to open your message. Having a literature degree or being a Nobel Laureate will not help unless you first capture their attention with an effectively compelling subject line. Pique their curiosity enough, and they will open neigh even read your message; pique their curiosity insufficiently, and they will delete it without even a moment of hesitation or guilt.

In print media there is a well established fact that 80 percent of readers scan the headlines yet only 20 percent of them read on to the body of the article. Headlines in media are designed to turn pages so readers have an opportunity to be attracted by advertisements as they flip through. In an email, subject lines have the equivalent effect.

ABC's of Compelling Subject Lines

Action: What are you asking them to do? If you do not ask them to do something, that is exactly what they will do. Are you eliciting a response? Can you be more interactive? Can you be more compelling? Examples of action could be as straight forward as "please reply".

Benefit: What's in it for them? You are the one initiating contact, so do not make the interaction about you or your company. Why should they bother opening the message? How will they benefit?

***Answer WIIFM:** "What's In It For Me" from the prospect's perspective*

Clarity: With conviction comes clarity. Are you being concise? Are you convincing in as few words as possible? Are you removing skepticism, or does it "sound too good to be true" when people read the posting?

Subject lines are to emails like theater trailers are to blockbuster movies. Wit, pun, clean humor, relevance, personalization and honest directness all work very well in subject lines, so long as you do not directly solicit them to consider an employment opportunity. In other words "Great job, apply now" does not work as a passive outreach subject line. Something else that will not work well is the use of ALL CAPS, the Internet equivalent of yelling, a practice that alarms corporate spam filters. Aggressive junk mail filters that do not already know your address will also frown upon special characters in your subject line such as the exclamation mark (!) hash or pound symbol (#), the "at" symbol (@) and the asterisk (*). Using punctuation is not necessary in headlines and the same goes for subject lines, but if you absolutely must punctuate or use a question mark it will not count against you like those other characters.

Bad subject lines make small networks.

The Resume Posting Experiment

A Senior Java Developer in the midst of a job search confidentially posted his resume on a major job board and allowed this book's author to study his responses to observe email campaigns from a job seeker's perspective. The results were surprising.

By way of background, this person has over seven years' experience in IT, including over three years in the development of object-oriented applications using Java, C++ and myriad other technologies. He also has a Master's degree in Computer Science and stated that he was willing to relocate.

He provided only his first name and email address for people to contact him. On the first day of his posting, he received 13 emails. The second day, he received 12; the third day, seven; the fourth day, six; and the fifth day and thereafter, a sporadic one to two emails per day. In total, within 40 days of posting his resume, he had received 58 emails.

> ***Recommended Practice*** *Utilize two variations of subject lines but with the same email body so you can test which of the two versions garners a higher percentage of responses. This is referred to as A/B testing.*

Of the 58 emails, only nine came directly from companies and only one star response emerged. A Seattle-based tech company sent a personalized email from the hiring manager describing the department, position, and the hiring manager's excitement about the company's direction. Executive search firms sent the other 49 emails. Additionally, just eight of the 58 emails stated the responsibilities and specific details of a position that correlated to his background. The other 50 emails were obviously canned messages with superficial and careless content:

Hi. I am looking for strong Java developers to work in Boston. Are you willing to relocate?

If so, call me at...

Or

I NEED JAVA PEOPLE! If you have those skills, please call me at...

Two automated emails from a large Silicon Valley software firm even thanked him for applying to their company when he clearly had not. You can guess which company received a response from the Developer.

Not every job seeker's experience is the same, but what happened to the Developer underscores the theme of this chapter: Send a good message and receive a good response.

Section 2. Do's and Don'ts of Initial Email

The following elements are essential elements to include and avoid in initial emails with candidates, whether passive or active.

Basic Courtesy

Etiquette evolves with technology, but will always continue to exist. Whatever standards develop, there will always be some form of communication convention. Recruiters must find a way to connect professionally, maintaining decorum yet remaining approachable.

DO...

Introduce yourself. It is important to identify yourself and establish your credibility. You need not provide your resume, only enough information that provides some context.

Respect the recipients' time. Be sure to give recipients time to respond and mention that you are initiating contact this way out of respect to their time and privacy. If after two or three days, you have not heard back, and you know they are a good prospect, give a call – one call, not several; you do not want to seem pushy. Likewise, do not send repeated emails or you risk coming across like a spammer.

Say "thank you" and provide an out. Use such messages as: "Thank you so much for your time. Please call me at your convenience so we can talk. I am sorry if I interrupted your day

and will not contact you further if you prefer". Then, be sure to leave your phone number.

DO NOT...

Be sycophantic. If you are overly servile or obsequious in your tone, you risk alienating sensible individuals and attracting those whose egos are over or under-sized, which can lead to human resource problems down the line.

Use overly informal greetings. Avoid "hi" in your initial email, and stick with the conventional "Dear" in your salutation.

Personalization

You are communicating with **them**, so make **your** outreach about **them**. If your approach is general or directed at no one in particular, expect no one in particular to respond.

DO...

Use the prospect's name. Referring to an individual by name makes your email more personal and less spam-like. If you are utilizing a mail merge application, include a field for the recipient's name. Confirm you have typed their name correctly. Misspelled names show a lack of effort and interest on your part. Your recipient is likely to be even more disenchanted when they have unusual first names like Shally, Reagan or Bukola.

Establish that you are a human. It is harder to delete an email, when you know that an actual human being is on the other end of the exchange. It is also more alluring to respond when it appears the sender knows you and your good work. Establishing a human component is as simple as sharing how you came across the candidate's name, which also goes a long toward establishing good will with the candidate.

For example, "I noticed you had some interesting answers to the JSP question posted on the Bulletin Boards..." Another example is, "I see from your Monster posting that you have had some excellent experience in recruiting for telecommunications account managers..."

State your reason for contacting them. If you provide no good reason for contacting them, they have no good reason to reply. If your goal is merely to begin a dialogue, then there are acceptable ways to preface yourself: "You seem to know quite a bit about Internet recruiting. I wondered if you could spare a couple moments of your time so I could pick your brain" or "As an expert in your industry, I wondered if we could talk...".

Mention if the prospect was referred. Not only is it more likely that a prospect will respond if you have a mutual acquaintance, but you can boost your credibility too, because the prospect can confirm who you are with your mutual connection.

DO NOT...

Use too much personal information. Individuals may overexpose themselves online, or you may have uncovered all sorts of personal information in your search, but there is no need to make references to anyone's private life.

Content

Marketing expert Elmer Wheeler explained it is the sizzle that sells the steak. Heed his words and take care not to give away the farm by driving away your prospects with details that could turn their interest from positive to negative.

DO...

Provide the right details. Use your best judgment in deciding what information is necessary for readers to make an educated response. If it's appropriate to provide the actual job description, then do not skimp on the writing here. Use the job descriptions as described in Chapter Three.

Include a call to action. End your email with some type of instruction for your readers so that they know exactly what they are supposed to do with your message.

Adopt a professional tone. Your language level should adhere to standard business styles. You can always later adjust your tone to match the rapport you develop with your prospects. Adopting a professional tone includes good grammar and no spelling errors. Just as you dislike English usage problems in a candidate's resume, so too can your recipients be bothered by errors in your messages to them.

Keep it plain. The problem with using HTML or other graphics in your initial message is that overly slick visual elements can de-personalize your message or look opportunistic. This is not an institutional opportunity for mass corporate branding. A tasteful logo that you use for all emails is appropriate, but anything larger may be distracting and can actually alert spam filters to block your message.

Mind the length of your message. A long email risks losing a readers' attention. Include what you need but no more.

DO NOT...

Over-hype your company or your hiring needs. A "soft sell" can be very effective. Ideally, the facts will speak for themselves. Leave the hype to the company website.

Insert unnecessary information. Not all information is required from the get-go, and too much information can confuse, mislead, take up too much space, and show your poor judgment.

Quick Template! Example Initial Contact Email

SUBJECT: Bold favor to ask you, please read

Dear [their name],

I work for [COMPANY] and was doing some research when I came across some info about you online. I noticed you worked at [COMPANY] a while back and thought you may be someone who might be able to help me if I asked nicely.

I was hoping you might be able to suggest whom I could talk to about [ROLE] positions that we have open. I'm particularly interested in having our recruiters talk with [TITLE] who you know may have also worked at [COMPANY]. I have recently just started at [COMPANY] so my network of senior contacts is pretty small at the moment. As you know, senior individuals prefer to use their professional network to find senior positions.

Hope you can help at least point me in the right direction?
Sincerely,

Shally Steckerl

Section 3. Sending Mass Emails

Any email addressed to multiple recipients can be characterized as a **mass email**. Internet users send mass emails when they wish to disseminate the same information to a large audience, primarily for their own personal convenience and not necessarily that of the recipients. This technique is not necessarily a bad practice, but it can become so without careful consideration. You want to avoid your messages being designated as **spam**. And typically, spam is distinguished by an indiscriminate recipient list and a canned message that lacks content on a personal level.

Well crafted mass emails possesses the following features:

A compilation of pertinent information. Always use the right contact information to include specific names and email addresses as well as employers and titles. Gathering contact information can require substantial legwork, so allot the right amount of time to this activity.

A concrete goal. Avoid nebulous "fishing expeditions". Professional emails to outside parties are not places to take random polls or to gauge possible reactions to pending business decisions. There are other forums and mechanisms to obtain that kind of information. Having a discrete goal will ensure that you do not waste precious resources including your one-time chance to establish a relationship with your recipients.

Construct a timeline. You must afford time for events to shake out properly. If you were pressed for time, it would be unfair to shift the time burden onto your recipients by expecting them to respond more quickly than customary. More importantly, knowing how your recruiting timeline feeds into the timeline of your organization's objectives produces corporate harmony.

Recipients organized by purpose. Filter names into different groups such as passive or active candidates or request for referrals only.

Recipient groups organized by priority. An email campaign may require a series of mailings, each to a new set of recipients. Therefore, prioritize your different recipient groups so that they correlate to your timeline and place the group that will produce the best leads at the top.

Content tailored to the different recipient groups. You can create a template easily or save a previously drafted message for future use. Take your stock draft and customize content for each recipient group. For example, if you are soliciting referrals, then add information about a possible referral bonus. If you are approaching passive candidates, then modify your greeting to acknowledge their status. While it may prove unfruitful to personalize content when the number in the group is large, addressing salient commonalities demonstrates a degree of care in preparing your message.

Utilization of a mail merge program. You can use the blind carbon copy (BCC) field if you plan to send the same email to several addresses, and do not want the recipients to be aware of each other. However, it is often more effective to use a program with merge fields, which allow you to personalize a mass email to a large number of individuals. These programs like SendBlaster or GroupMail use software more powerful than the simple BCC. They use databases or contact management software to generate messages that can be sent individually or personalized.

A clear call to action. Your message is not merely to inform, it is to elicit a particular reply. Without an overly demanding tone, convey your request. Specify how and to whom the recipient is to respond.

Recommended Practice: *Include the call to action at least twice, once after the introduction paragraph, and again at the end of the message.*

Individualized responses. Once you have obtained a response to your mass emailing, it's important to reply quickly and individually. For example, if your mass emailing consisted of asking a list of people to send you their resume and you got some responses, then acknowledge your receipt to each one and thank them for taking the time to write back to you. You can use the same message for all your replies, as long as you personalize it and reply directly to them. This way, any suspicions or doubts they had of your being a possible spammer will be removed.

A clear process flow for viable leads. Know that once you send out your email, you will have activated a sequence of events. Put your proverbial ducks in a row so that you have to stop and regroup as little as possible.

Section 4. Email Inbox

Since you will be sending many emails, you should expect to be receiving plenty of replies. Consider that in many industry sectors job seekers far prefer to utilize their professional network to make personal contacts as they explore new career opportunities rather than applying online, so do not be surprised if using these techniques results in emails response rates that exceed 30 percent. Today's job seeker is Web savvy, armed with knowledge of the Internet and likes to use the "Send" button frequently.

Managing and Organizing

In reactive recruitment environments where you may find yourself treading water with an overwhelming response to your job posting, it helps to know how to control the flow. Email enables candidates and applicants to market themselves in high volume like never before. Stamps, expensive paper and envelopes were once the only barriers preventing the job seekers from burying your desk in mountains of mail. With such barriers removed, good candidates are left camouflaged in your inbox, hidden among hundreds of "other" candidates, unsolicited junk and irrelevant email. Many of the best candidate emails may appear camouflaged like subtle networking requests with their job seeking interest unapparent.

Some mail you will definitely want to keep, even if it's a bit of "resume spam" because it can be useful in the future, but other mail belongs in the recycle bin. Of course, there are all those messages that require action. Good resumes and ideal applicants could be lost to inbox bloat.

Most email providers employ robust, top of the line enterprise grade spam filters, which capture a vast majority of the real junk, but there is still much allowed through. A system that helps organize and prioritize allows you to select real opportunities from the marginal more rapidly.

Folders, colors, views and rules are what the spam doctor prescribes.

Folders

Use folders to organize all incoming mail into these three: 1) Action Required (your to-do list), 2) Delegate (what you can hand off or anything that has you waiting on someone else) and 3) Archive. Delete everything else.

Colors

Most email programs allow you to assign color formatting to messages from specific senders. For example you could apply a gray label to anything you suspect of being junk, a red one for internal messages from colleagues or anything marked urgent, blue for friends and family, yellow for news, green for new business and so on. This strategy makes it easier to distinguish messages as they arrive.

Views

Make a date with your favorite beverage and set aside a period in the mid-morning and perhaps one in the mid-afternoon, to review email using views. You can scan a high volume of messages when you organize them by thread or conversation topic- or simply if you sort by subject line.

This technique groups related messages together so you can archive or delete entire threads at once without combing through the mess. Sorting by sender lets you do the same with groups of messages from one person, organization or email domain. The "sent to" view sorts all of what's left into emails sent to you only, to you and others, to a group, or where you were cc'd (carbon copied). If you are alone in the To: field, that message is likely of a higher priority than others where you are one of many copied. Perhaps you can safely archive most messages where you were copied to be kept informed but where your direct involvement is not needed. Glance through the remainder and you will easily be able to pick out messages from services like lists, groups, networks such as LinkedIn™, and so on.

Recommended Practice: *Sort your emails by sender, subject and "sent to" to scan through a bloated inbox quickly.*

Rules

Spam will never cease, but you can take back some control with rules. There are a vast number of activities you can manage with rules, limited only by your imagination. Here are a few ways to utilize them:

- Create alerts that show up on your desktop
- Create tasks and TO DOs or reminders for specific messages, senders, subjects, emails with certain keywords
- Craft automatic replies (auto responders)
- Distinguish internal from external email
- Expire or move email after a certain number of days
- Filter all the items from a mailing list, group or source like LinkedIn™, Plaxo, newsletters, etc.
- Filter junk email that makes it into your mailbox
- Flag items for future activities
- Forward specific senders or topics to your mobile phone or to an assistant
- Handle messages forwarded from another user's mailbox
- Mark specific emails as read
- Search for phrases in messages
- Sort messages by email account
- Turn emails into tasks, contacts or calendar items

Recommended Practice: *Look under the Help menu of your email program for items relating to "Organization" or "Rules" to learn more about this topic.*

Quick Tip! What to Do with "Flames"

A flame is an online criticism of your message and varies from relatively neutral admonitions to strongly worded, highly antagonistic insults. Nearly everyone who has used email to initiate conversation has experienced a flame. So long as your messages are unobtrusive, subtle, and informational — and not direct solicitations – the likelihood of "getting flamed" is low and will continually diminish from trial and error. If the flame has merit, learn from the criticism and adjust the content or tone of your email accordingly.

It is critical to remain silent when you receive a flame. If you reply to a flame, you are only making matters worse. Even if compelled to apologize, you should remain silent. It does not matter if your response is apologetic, the mere fact that you replied to a person's inflammatory comments can escalate a simple "venting" situation into an ego battle that neither party wins. The alternative and better course is to delete a "flame" message and move on.

Section 5. Results to Expect from Email

The most critical factor in achieving a high response rate is the relevance of your targets. Sending a mailing to a general audience will net a smaller percentage of positive responses than a mailing to a specialized or specific audience. For example, let's say you are seeking Sarbanes-Oxley auditors for a position in Chicago, and you email 100 accountants you know nationwide. The response ratio will be smaller in that case than if you were to send the same message to a 100 certified public accountants. Similarly, the response rate will increase if you deliver your message to 100 "Big Five" auditors in Chicago.

Once you have a targeted audience and your message has been polished to the point where it is as effective as it can be, you can expect to obtain results somewhere along the following lines:

5 percent: Not available yet.	Of the people you contact, 5 percent may not be currently available but would be willing to stay in touch for future opportunities. Although this response is not a direct success, it may lead to something in the future. Call this your "future interest" pipeline.
5 percent: I have a friend.	These are gatekeepers who pass your message along to their friends.
5 percent: Take me off the list!	Another 5 percent of your recipients will ask that you remove their names from your mailing list or that you cease any further contact. Do not take this type of response as a personal rejection. Promptly make a note of this request in your contact management tool to avoid contacting them again and being called a spammer as a result. Create a list of people NOT to contact via email, and find out whether your ATS or CRM system has an email opt-out checkbox that will mark a record so no emails are sent to specific names.
10 percent: Returned undelivered.	There will always be a segment of recipients whose email addresses have expired. Roughly 10 percent of the working population changes jobs every year, and others switch email providers or protocols. This segment may also include improperly formatted addresses or spelling mistakes. When a message bounces back, check the address for accuracy and resend.
15 percent: Sure, let's talk.	This outcome is a direct hit and the ideal response. Whether they send a resume, ask for clarification, or express simple interest, these individuals have graduated to actual candidate status. As your message improves, your target audience narrows, and your reputation grows, and this slice of the pie is where you should expect change.

60 percent: Silence.	At the beginning of any mass email campaign, it is reasonable to expect that a majority of your messages will end up in the recipient's trash bin. Very few people will take the time to respond if they are not interested. This portion of the list represents your room for growth. Perfect your pitch, sharpen your list, and build your reputation – and you will move individuals from this group into the "Sure, let's talk" described.

Do not feel personally dismissed or rejected if you do not receive as much active interest as you would like. A low percentage rate does not necessarily mean failure. Unsolicited commercial emailers keep plugging away despite massive rejection because they expect only a 1-3 percent response rate. Masterful recruiters, in contrast, eventually attain a response rate between 45 and 80 percent. In the end, the rate or ratio does not matter so long as there is some quantity of responses that provides good leads.

Quick Sample! Closing the Conversation

If there is no longer mutual interest, close out the conversation and use a message similar to the following to elicit referrals:

> Recruiting is such an important goal for us that I would be remiss if I didn't share that we have committed to some very aggressive goals over the next few quarters. I would be grateful if you could think back to some of the best people you have ever worked with, and let me know who they are. They do not have to be people who are looking for work, but rather those you would love to work with again, or possibly even hire onto your team if you could. As I did with you, I can locate them and call them confidentially without mentioning your name and see if they may be receptive to talking about other opportunities with us. If you can think of anyone, please reply back and let me know.
>
> Thank you and please do stay in touch!

The message above is appropriate when the reason for closing the conversation is the candidate's choice.

Another Quick Sample! Follow Up Email

Following up on a previous lead requires fewer resources than developing an entirely new set of contacts. Use the following sample message to follow up with candidates who were not interested initially.

SUBJECT: 4SCT would like to get back in touch with you

Dear Robin,

When we spoke for the first time several months ago, you had indicated that the timing was not right for you to consider career opportunities in Software Engineering at 4SCT. I wanted to check-in with you and schedule a convenient time for a follow-up conversation.

[COMPANY PITCH]

I look forward to catching up with you. Please take a minute to visit my online calendar [link to your online calendar here] and schedule a time that is convenient for you. Please also forward a current copy of your resume/CV so that we can better discuss the team that best aligns with your skills and experience.

Signature

Author's Note: Intercultural Lessons Learned the Hard Way

Intercultural recruiting is discussed in-depth in the International Recruiting section of Chapter Three and revisited here to share information learned by trial and error. While engaging in Sourcing and recruiting campaigns throughout the world, many recruiters have seen situations, which make for interesting case studies. Here are some examples of those lessons learned:

Russia, Romania, and Ukraine: Spam in these countries is written almost exclusively in English, so if your email subject line is in English, your message will most likely be deleted. The better course is to ask a native language speaker to write your subject line, and then you can write the content of your message in English with little problem. Additionally, it may be very easy to find Eastern European prospects on the Internet, but take care when explaining how you found them. Eastern European cultures are more guarded than that of the American, and you may come across as suspicious if you do not express yourself well.

China: Most online resumes are written in English, but a significant number are not, so it is good to search for them in both languages. In addition, Chinese candidates deliberate and take time to make a decision and often prefer to have the last word in a conversation or meeting. Cultural understanding is critical in gaining trust. Rank is valued, so arranging meetings with business leaders goes a very long way in gaining a candidate's interest.

South Africa: Direct email response rates are relatively low, unless the emails come from an academic contact, so professors should be strong recruitment allies. Prospects respond better via introductions from gatekeepers like professors, co-workers, and group leaders. That said, do not give up on direct contact.

Australia: Direct phone calls work best, and prospects are very approachable, but the use of agencies is also quite common. Chances are, prospects will be flattered if a company calls but you may have to explain yourself a bit more.

Germany: Searches in German yield much better results than in English. Direct recruiting tends to be viewed negatively, particularly when calling someone's place of employment directly. Email responses are relatively high. Germans are comfortable with asking and answering direct personal questions during initial phone interviews.

Latin America: Face-to-face meetings are highly preferred, and social chatter is favored, particularly during the first part of the conversation. Introductions and referrals work best, but direct contact is certainly acceptable. Be careful when writing emails, which tend to be perceived less casually and viewed as "official business".

Intercultural Communication Resources

The following are additional resources that can help you understand local culture and bridge differences in preparation for your email campaign:

Portals to the World (*www.loc.gov/rr/international/portals.html*) This site is maintained by the U.S. Library of Congress and contains selective links providing authoritative, in-depth information about nations and areas of the world. They are arranged by country or area with the links for each sorted into a wide range of broad categories.

Country Profiles from the BBC (*http://news.bbc.co.uk/2/hi/country_profiles/default.stm*) These full profiles provide an instant guide to history, politics and economics of countries and territories, as well as background on key institutions. They also include audio or video clips from the BBC archives which are a great way to "get to know" local customs. Since the BBC is a British company, this site is worth checking for a non-American viewpoint.

Geert Hofstede's Dimensions Analysis (*www.cyborlink.com*) As with Jungian personality dimensions, Hofstede's analysis can assist you in better understanding the intercultural differences within regions and between counties.

One-Stop-Shop Country Overviews (*www.atlapedia.com*) A user friendly interface that leads to interesting overviews of each country together with physical and political maps.

Section 6. Instant Messengers

Online messaging continues to spike in popularity since the inception of ICQ (I seek you) in 1996. With more people using their computers during the course of their daily work routines, it's no surprise. Instant Messengers are computer applications that allow people to communicate using text messages sent directly from one computer to another via a separate part of the Internet called Internet Relay Chat or IRC. AOL Time Warner was issued a patent for instant messaging, and although they have not announced plans to enforce the patent, each competing service has had to develop their own technology.

As a result, hundreds of "chat" clients exist, each with their own quirks and protocols.

Going all the way back to the original free IRC channels and applications when first invented in 1988, there are thousands of IRC networks worldwide. People use IRC to communicate directly with each other. For more information about IRC, or to download the most popular client, or see an example of the variety of networks, visit mirc.com. There is also a dedicated IRC search engine searchirc.com/ that monitors about 2,500 IRC networks.

Instant Messenger Applications

Chatting is a conversation that happens in plain text, but because it is so interactive, it has more in common with a telephone call than with email exchanges. Although there are hundreds of IRC Channels, four stand out as the most popular and widely available on employee's desks:

AIM.com, AOL Instant Messenger, AOL's chat client quickly became the largest chat provider. Once it became compatible with Lotus Sametime, many corporations adopted AOL Instant Messenger (AIM) as the standard for their employees. The new AIM for Business offers security features that make corporations feel comfortable about allowing their employees to use AIM.

Yahoo Messenger *www.messenger.yahoo.com/* Yahoo introduced a number of extra features, which make their chat client extremely popular. Among those is the ability to use webcams for video chatting. Other features include being able to place "calls" using a microphone, leave voicemails, and track all kinds of online information, such as a Yahoo email account and stock portfolios.

Windows Live Messenger *http://get.live.com/messenger/overview* The Live Messenger client produced by Microsoft also introduced advanced features like file sharing and search engine integration, together with other collaborative features, making this client very attractive and one of the most popular today.

Skype: A kind of "social networking meets instant messaging" application that also allows users to place calls to each other using Voice Over Internet Protocol (VoIP), join public Skype casts or chats, and even make calls to ordinary phone lines.

There are also two newer applications that are rapidly gaining in popularity as social media becomes mainstream. They are:

Google Talk: Gmail users can use Google Talk while they are reading their Gmail, but an application is also available that marries instant messaging with email and phone calls, similar to Skype.

Facebook Chat: Now with separate phone applications, people can send Facebook messages, texts and chats through their mobile devices while connected to wireless Internet signals, thereby saving their mobile carrier provided SMS credits.

Why do recruiters need to know about these clients? Because if you are trying to reach candidates who spend all or a large part of their day on the computer, you may be able to contact them more quickly via instant message than by phone, or even email. One of the advantages to instant messaging is that people who spend all day on the phone can type even while they are listening to a conference call, waiting on hold, or even multitask while having a conversation.

The only challenge is that most users choose to install only one or at most two chat clients, so you will not be able to connect with someone if you are not using the same chat client as they are. Some instant messaging applications attempt to connect with all of the services from one platform, but these applications can be unstable and are frequently being blocked by some of the three main providers. As a result, you may find it necessary to install all three of the above messenger clients anyway, and possibly even an IRC client like mIRC.

Some applications that attempt to combine all of the chat protocols include:

- **Trillian** (www.ceruleanstudios.com): The free version allows users to connect with all other chat clients from one simple application. For $25.00, the Pro version includes video chat as well as connectivity to Jabber, Novell GroupWise and Rendezvous.
- **Meebo** (www.meebo.com): Users who are unable to use chat clients at work due to IRC or other restrictions can use Meebo and log into their

chat accounts from a website.

- **Gaim** (http://gaim.sourceforge.net/): A multi-chat client application for Linux.
- **Fire** (http://fire.sourceforge.net/): A multi-chat client application for Mac.
- **Miranda IM** (http://miranda-im.org): A very small and fast multi-chat client that is less resource intensive.
- **Adiumx** (http://adiumx.com): is a multi-chat client application for Mac.
- **IMO** (http://imo.im): is a multi-chat client that works well behind firewalls, and supports the user logging into IRC, Jabber, MSN, Skype, Facebook, GTalk, Yahoo, AIM and ICQ. Something similar for PCs would be **Pidgin.im**

Beyond the ability to be able to communicate instantly with candidates, chat clients also reveal information about people. Users frequently create online profiles that include data about their job and interests, their blogs or other websites, and even additional ways to communicate with them, including their email address. This information may be viewable if you know an individual's instant messenger "handle".

For example, at *http://members.yahoo.com*, you can search for members by specific interest. Once you find someone, or in the event a candidate gives you their handle, be sure to follow basic etiquette guidelines for online chat. A useful guide to instant messaging etiquette can be found at *www.blacktable.com/imhandbook.htm.*

Section 7. Text Messaging and SMS

Using a candidate's cell phone SMS (**Short Message Service**) is another way to utilize instant messaging that can set you apart from other recruiters. This feature is available with most phones, and is quickly becoming standard. In fact, in European countries, text messaging is used very heavily, in many occasions more so that voice messaging. To create a text message, all you need is your own SMS-enabled cell phone and your candidate's cell phone number. Each phone will have a different way to use SMS. One way is to discover how your phone does so is to browse to the Messages window, select "Text messages", and then "Create message".

At that point, you can enter a short sentence or two and send them to your candidate's cell phone number for instantaneous receipt. You can, for example, send your phone number and a simple message such as, "Would like to speak with you. Please call me at ____________". They can either respond back via another text message or simply hit the "Send" button, and their phone will automatically dial the number you entered in the message. Experiment by sending messages to the phones of your friends or co-workers.

Email to SMS

You can send messages directly from your email program to SMS enabled phones. It's important to note that you can only send plain text – no images – and that messages are limited to 160 alphanumeric characters including the subject line. If you exceed that limit, the phone will receive the message cut up into pieces of up to 160 characters each.

For example, a message containing 200 characters will generate two SMS messages: The first one with the last 40 characters, and second one with the first 160 characters. Therefore, try to keep your messages under 160 characters so this situation doesn't happen. To send an email to a phone subscriber's SMS inbox use the following:

AT&T: 10digitMobileNumber@mobile.att.net
Cingular: 10digitMobileNumber@cingularme.com
Nextel: 10digitMobileNumber@messaging.nextel.com
Sprint: 10digitMobileNumber@messaging.sprintpcs.com
T-Mobile: 10digitMobileNumber@tmomail.com
Verizon: 10digitMobileNumber@vtext.com

If you do not know what provider your prospect uses for their cell phone service you could put your contact's regular email address in the TO: field and then put all six of the SMS address "options" in the BCC: field. For example:

To:shally@4sct.com

Bcc: 7705551212@mobile.att.net, 7705551212@mobile.att.net, 7705551212@cingularme.com, 7705551212@messaging.nextel.com, 7705551212@messaging.sprintpcs.com, 7705551212@tmomail.com 7705551212@vtext.com

If you want to try out SMS without buying a texting plan for your mobile phone check out free SMS services available with Google Voice and Yahoo Mail accounts. From them you can send and receive SMS messages directly from the Web interface without even having a mobile number.

☞ *CROSS REFERENCE BOOKMARK: SEE THE APPENDIX FOR A LIST OF SMS ABBREVIATIONS*

Quick Comment! Use "Check-Ins" to Source Prospects

Federal law mandates all cell phone carriers to provide the latitude and longitude of all users, with accuracy between 50 and 300 meters. This law exists so that people who call 911 using their cell phones can receive emergency services. Obviously, cell phone carriers must comply with the law, but their compliance also means they now have the technology to provide a new set of services, for profit, based on users' locations. Many applications have popularized the use of these location-based services. For example, applications like Foursquare, Yelp, Twitter or Facebook let users generate a "status update" or "check-in" that reports users' geographic coordinates.

Check-ins are modern-day "smoke signals" that are used for three main reasons: First, to inform people they are somewhere special; second, to let people know where they can join the user; and third, to learn about locations or receive special coupons, discounts, and other freebies available only to those who "check in". The most popular check-in locations, in order, are restaurants, coffee shops, bars/clubs, users' own homes, retail stores, and event venues, and most people choose places that are close to either their work or home. For recruiters, Sourcing through location-based services is a new way to discover prospects. Basically, if you know a company's address, you can search check-ins to discover where people from that company go to congregate during lunch or Happy Hours.

Websites like CheckInMania.com make it very easy to obtain this information. Using that or a similar website, here is a way to source prospects:

- Enter the address of your target company or branch location.
- Find and click on local coffee shops, restaurants, or watering hole.
- Identify who checked in via Foursquare or Twitter.

- Identify those who check in more than once at the same location or repeatedly in areas surrounding the target location.
- Click on profiles through CheckInMania.com.
- Look for Facebook or Twitter icons on profiles.
- Click on other related icons to discover information about individuals. For example, clicking on a Facebook icon will lead you to users' last names, schools, interests, and other information found in the "About Me" section. Clicking on a Twitter bio may provide links to blogs or LinkedIn™ profiles.
- If a location-based search leads to a Twitter user, reading the user's tweets can reveal important job information that you can use to identify prospects. For instance, followers, people followed, and any exchanges can reveal other individuals with similar interests and experience as the user. Also, read the tweets to find out if the user tweets co-workers, peers, supervisors, subordinates, or customers.

Humans tend toward predictable behavior in most cases, yet the possibilities are endless when it comes to finding people based on their everyday patterns. Digital anthropology has unique implications for recruiters; previously hard-to-discover information and people are now easier to find. Of course, Sourcing with location-based tools has the potential of mystifying prospects, so it is always good to clue them in on how they were found.

Chapter 13
Calling Candidates

Section 1. Passive Candidate Cold Calling Techniques

At some point, recruiters or Sourcers must call passive candidates. This group of candidates is touchy because they have no previous relationship with you and may be surprised that you know things about them when they know nothing about you. The following is a discussion of time-tested, completely intuitive, and absolutely ethical communication techniques that are persuasive enough to remove skepticism from cold calls.

Introduction to Cold Calling

A **cold call** is a business-to-business call because you are calling another professional to explore a possible opportunity. A recruiter's cold call is different from a sales, telemarketing or customer service call. In those instances, a successful transaction or exchange results in deepening a customer relationship. It is important to remember that the act of recruiting is not the act of selling; rather, it is about connecting people with employment opportunities. Nobody is selling or buying anything, and no money is exchanged. For recruiters, cold calling is the act of talking to candidates and ascertaining if they are or should be looking for another job.

A **connect** occurs when recruiters are able to speak directly with the intended candidate. Connects do not occur when recruiters leave a voicemail, talk with an operator, and definitely not when recruiters speak with the intended candidate's manager. In other words, a "connect" is when you dial the phone number of a candidate and you speak directly with the intended person. A close occurs when both you and the candidate have made a commitment to take the next step. A close is a positive outcome when you continue to like the candidate's background after you have had a conversation, and the candidate commits to taking the next step.

While both connects and closes are positive outcomes, a connect does not automatically result in a close. Further, it should take about ten-to-fifteen minutes to transition from a connect to a close. Less than a minute is rare; and anything reaching or passing an hour is just too long and probably not worth your time. Fifteen minutes is plenty of time to know whether you want to move this person to the next step.

Preparation

Before picking up the phone to call a potential candidate, you should be informed about the people and the companies you are calling and current events related to your own business. It is also a good idea to find some point of intersection between you and the candidate. However, it is inappropriate to contact a candidate's family and friends at any time during the recruiting process.

Immediately before beginning a **cold calling block**, a passive candidate phone campaign, call two strangers with no agenda and no specific purpose to shake off the cobwebs and put yourself in the right frame of mind. Plus, these people may be valuable additions to your network although it does not really matter.

> ***"Try a thing you haven't done three times. Once, to get over the fear of doing it. Twice, to learn how to do it. And a third time, to figure out whether you like it or not."***
> ***—Virgil Garnett Thomson***

The next step in engaging passive candidates is to make a telephone call to a complete stranger who is not expecting your call. The topic of cold calling can often be fairly controversial, especially amongst recruiters that learned their trade more recently and have depended on email as a primary method of initiating contact. To dispense with an enduring myth, cold calling is a simple, business-to-business communication. In recruiting, it is one professional reaching out to another in order to explore if there may be any interest in a particular opportunity. You are **not** selling or telemarketing.

There are a few other myths when it comes to cold calling, some of them true, some of them simply excuses that lazy recruiters make up so they do not have to pick up the phone. After all, isn't the telephone the heaviest piece of plastic you will ever have to lift off your desk?

Know This Before You Dial

Be informed about the people and companies you will be calling before you begin dialing. From a young age, you were probably told not to talk to strangers, yet here you are doing just that. It can be daunting, so ease up by making the person that you're calling less of a stranger. For example, any connection or expression of similar interests will go a long way towards establishing rapport.

By showing interest in an individual and what they have accomplished you can break the conversational ice more rapidly than through high pressure sales tactics or intentional misdirection. Be congenial by appropriately weaving in

observations about your prospect's world that you have discovered through social media. Here are a few pieces of the puzzle you should always be prepared to discuss with passive candidates:

Why Join the Company?

"If you cannot explain it simply, you do not understand it well enough." – Albert Einstein

Remember you are talking with people, and people have fears whether they disclose them or not. Knowledge is a straightforward way to remove the obstacle of fear from your conversation with prospects; and revealing a few key facts before typical objections arise is the simplest way to avoid knee-jerk rejection. Fear of change has a sneaky way of paralyzing decision making. Put them at ease, and their objections will be surmountable. Leave their fears unanswered, and their objections will accumulate. Why should anyone be interested in the opportunity for which you are recruiting? The answer lies at three levels:

THIS Company (Big Picture)

Why is your company/client the best employer for them to work with?

They may or may not be looking for a new opportunity, but it is safe to assume that if you are after them, then their skills must be in demand and others may well be after them. If not now, then soon enough. Yes, you may be the first one they spoke with about new opportunities, but you awoke their interest so it is very likely you will not be the last. If you have any hope of getting them to leave their job for your opportunity before they start shopping elsewhere, your company/client had better be a compelling employer.

THIS Team (Work Environment):

People leave people, not companies. During exit interviews, one of the most commonly cited reasons for leaving is because the employee feels underappreciated, undervalued, underutilized or is simply no longer inspired. Perhaps it's the role itself or perhaps it is their manager, but they are much more likely to be interested in your opportunity if you emphasize how this new team will be right for them. Is this the group or department that obtains all the cool toys? Do many of the promotions in the organization originate from this department? Are there any perks this team brings to the table that others do not? Perhaps this team leader, manager or director is a thought leader and mentor known for developing their staff. Are they easy to work with? Are they nurturing?

THIS Role (Critical to Success):

More tactical than the other two, this level connects your individual prospect directly with your company or client's success. Employers do not pay someone's wages for a job that is not necessary. Why is this position important to the company? Why are they spending their money on it? How is this job critical to the success of the company? Every position within an organization contributes to the whole. Trace the steps, obtain input on how this position matters and where it makes a difference. This insight will be far more motivating than "salary and benefits" alone.

Initial Conversation Topics

Social, professional, and extracurricular activities are a bridge to connect with a candidate during a phone call. Find some common ground to use as a springboard to launch the conversation. Talking about prohibited activities either identifies one of you as a criminal or promotes suspicion and distrust.

Connecting with Candidates

The goal of connecting with candidates is to create a bridge that will help seal trust and establish rapport so that the unease of speaking with a stranger is minimized. Trying to become friends is simply unprofessional and destroys credibility, and discussing current events is just off-topic and irrelevant.

Physical Awareness

You should stand up and smile during a call because humans subconsciously recognize this emotionally positive and attentive action and will perceive you as friendlier and more professional. Bad habits include sitting in your favorite chair, drinking a refreshing beverage, and standing up and yelling into the phone receiver.

Persuasive Strategies

When talking to candidates, one best practice is to demonstrate they are likely to be more valued by the hiring manager in the opportunity for which you're recruiting than they are in their current position. A common reason that employees leave their jobs is that they feel as if they or their work don't matter. It just never happens that employees leave their jobs because they are overrated.

A classic rookie mistake is to disrespect the candidate's current employer, so do not do so, ever.

When you compare the candidate's current company to your company, only highlight strengths of your company to keep the conversation upbeat. Highlighting negative features of their current company puts a depressing tone into the conversation. And, commenting on negative features while highlighting strengths of your company is also not recommended because it pollutes the conversation with negativity. Finally, talking salaries places too much emphasis on money too early and attracts candidates with a greedy streak.

Language Practice

While scripts are generally frowned upon because they take away from the natural rhythm of a conversation, it is important to practice certain phrases to ensure you use language that moves the interaction forward instead of turning off the candidate.

Found You Online

When you explain how you found someone's information be sure to say, "I found you online", instead of "I found you on the Internet". Even if the candidate is not normally paranoid, using the word "Internet" tends to scare people.

May Be Stronger

When speaking with a candidate you should say "I want to talk to you about an opportunity that may be/might be stronger" instead of "...that is stronger". The word "is" comes across as stronger because of its definiteness, whereas "may be" or "might be" feels less aggressive.

I'm Not Looking

If a candidate's response is "I'm not looking" or "How did you get my name?" you can infer that there is a trust issue. It is probably because you didn't establish sufficient rapport early enough.

No Doesn't Always Mean No

Listen carefully and you will notice that sometimes people say "no" just to be rid of you, because at that moment, it is easier than paying attention. They could have answered your call while in a meeting, on their way to somewhere or something important, while driving, about to enter an elevator, sitting near their boss, or simply when they were in a bad mood that day. Brush past this initial objection by ignoring it and acknowledging they are busy. Say something like this: "I can tell you're very busy at the moment, but this call is important, would you prefer I call you tomorrow morning or is this evening better?"

Section 2. Persuasive Conversational Styles

If you spoke with 100 people, you would communicate well with a given percentage of them because of compatible conversational styles. If you learn and adopt attributes of other conversational styles, then it logically follows that you will connect with a higher percentage of people. And, if you are able to connect with more people, then you increase your pool of potential prospects and professional contacts. Therefore, your goal in learning about conversational styles is to increase your network via improved cold calling techniques.

The Four Primary Conversational Styles

Conversational styles relate to how we expect others to communicate with us as well as how we communicate with others. While many people demonstrate attributes of other styles, everyone has one primary and one secondary style. There exist only four different conversational styles. In any conversation, you have about 90 seconds to identify the other party's style and match it. To do so, you have to encourage them to speak long enough to establish their conversational style. Then, if you understand your own conversational style, you can adapt it to their style and treat them as they want to be treated.

Analytical

The Analytical conversational style may come across as emotionally distant because facts are placed ahead of feelings. If your style is Expressive or Amiable, take care not to let that distract you from your objective. Keep in mind Analytical candidates are just not sharing their feelings, but they do have them. Particularly, when under stress, they will tend to overanalyze and delay decision making. An Analytical conversational style is driven by activity so keep things moving along; give them focus and direction at a soft and steady pace but do not be pushy. The Analytical motto is "do it right or not at all".

Speaker Attributes:

- Cautious, Curious, Formal
- Talks in terms of "I think"
- Excellent with logic and data, wants to know how
- Enjoys details and precise speaking, likes to plan
- Asks questions
- Likes having time to decide
- A "poker face" so hardest to read

Your Approach:

- Provide facts, figures, and percentages in a list or bullet points. Avoid expressing yourself in terms of feelings.

- Have citations or sources for data when necessary.
- Ask if they need more information or time.
- Avoid saying "I think it's a good idea..." with no data to back yourself up.
- Allot time to accommodate slower tempo while they analyze and think through decisions.
- Avoid pressing them for a decision or you may repel them.
- Ask if they need more to time to contemplate what you have presented. Just acknowledging that they might need time to consider what you say makes a huge difference.

Helpful phrases:

- "Based on what you've told me...."
- "I know you need some time to think about it...."

Amiable

The Amiable conversational style describes people who are partial to co-operation and loyalty. Their focus is on the why and whom. They will seek to feel included, and want your approval. Their motto is "we're great!"

Speaker Attributes:

- Collaborative, Supportive, Encouraging, Patient, Relaxed
- Talks in terms of "I feel"
- Enjoys team accomplishment
- Likes to establish trust and invoke mutual care
- Very good at finishing volumes of work
- Can take on the majority of a project as long they are not the focal point
- Comfortable abiding by rules, following instructions, and maintaining guidelines
- Avoids conflict or hurting other's feelings

Your Approach:

- Highlight cooperative aspects of the position.
- Focus on tradition, emphasize the team approach.
- Do not confront, dictate or be autocratic.

- Adopt a positive tone and avoid negative word choices.
- As with Analytical types, allow for enough time in the conversation to accommodate their slow-to-medium tempo and ask if they need more time for decision-making.

Helpful Phrases:

- "What I think is ___, do you agree?"
- "Here is how you will be safe/secure...."
- "What was your experience like working with/in/alongside...?"

Expressive

The Expressive conversational style describes people who seek attention or are motivated by applause or accolade. Their motto is "let's all do it!"

Speaker Attributes:

- Enthusiastic, Dynamic, Demonstrative, Persuasive
- Talks in terms of "I want"
- Multi-tasker who enjoys checking things off on a TO DO list
- Possesses excellent people skills, interested in "who else"
- Likes to be creative and challenged, prefers optimism
- Wants to be entertained or entertaining
- Will make volumes of work look effortless so long as they are having fun

Your Approach:

- Engage in "small talk", do not go right to business.
- Focus on the future, use stories and illustrations.
- Maintain a brisk pace to match their faster tempo.
- Avoid long pauses and redundant information.
- Emphasize multiplicity in job aspects.
- Use lively language and energetic tone.
- Show personal interest, compliment them.

Helpful Phrases:

- "What other information can I get for you?"

- "Here is what I think, what's your opinion?
- "You know what's best for you. I'm just here to present an option."
- "Here is how you will stand out."
- "So, Jessie, I think [feeling 1], [feeling 2], [feeling 3], what do you think?" These are not emotional feelings per se. Instead, you couch a fact in feeling language.

Driver

The Driver conversational style describes people who are comfortable with tension and may even try to create it. They are motivated by the end result and will seek to be in control of the conversation. If stressed, they tend to overlook details or appear not to have heard them. Their motto is "just do it".

Speaker Attributes:

- Taskmaster, Demanding, Competitive, Strong-willed
- Talks in terms of "I will"
- Enjoys organizing, leading, running projects, and deadlines
- Accustomed to being the focal point
- Great at systems, rules, and "big picture" tasks
- Excellent at delegating, needs to know what and when
- Annoyed by trivialities
- Fast tempo, results driven, takes charge
- A "poker face" so hard to read

Your Approach:

- Arrive at your point, focus on the present not the long term.
- Provide factual highlights not details.
- Give them options, end conversation segments with a question.
- Ask questions using plain language to solicit feedback, speak in terms of concrete results.
- Do not ask unimportant or irrelevant questions.
- Do not give too much detail or be too personal.

Helpful phrases:

- "Here is what I think, what's your opinion?"
- "So, Jessie, I think [fact1], [fact2], [fact3], what do you think?" The set of facts here should have a logic flow that leads to the conclusion you want the candidate to have.
- "What would you like from me in order to...."
- "Here is how you will win."

Many variations of these styles have been given other names such as colors or bird symbols. Other authors have modified these styles for implementation into an assortment of professional disciplines. The phrases above have drawn on these references and been tailored to help Sourcers and recruiters initiate contact with passive candidates. The references include:

- The work of Marie Amey-Taylor, EdD
- Material published by Wilson & Wilson Assoc.
- "Relationships Strategies" by T. Alessandra
- "Four Conventional Conversation Styles" by Merril & Reid
- "What Color is Your Personality? Red. Orange. Yellow. Green" by Carol Ritberger
- "Secrets of Face to Face Communication" by Peter Urs Bende
- "Persuasion Engineering" by Richard Bandler and John La Valle

Section 3. Anatomy of a Cold Call

Establishing rapport has more to do with confidence and conviction than it does with force. You cannot "make" people believe something, but you can guide them into understanding. Locate the Cold Calling Flowchart in the Appendix and utilize the outline below as you follow the flowchart during your cold calls. Rely on these aids until the technique becomes intuitive.

1) **Establish Curiosity:** When a prospect answers the phone, recognize their conversational style, and use the techniques from this chapter to establish rapport. Respectfully pique their interest without giving them reason to hang up on you. Ask if they have a moment, then patiently wait for an answer. If you interrupt them before they answer not only are you being disrespectful but you have also defeated the purpose of asking the question in the first place, losing all credibility.

2) **Objection:** "How did you get my number" is the only true objection, and one that simply means they do not trust you or are uncomfortable with how you have come across in your approach. Go back to practicing the conversational styles. When responding to the "Do you have a moment to talk with me" question, any answer from the prospect that asks who you are or why you are calling as an affirmative and means you have permission to move right into Breaking Tension.
3) **Breaking Tension:** Address the "pink elephant" and pre-empt their ability to object to the awkwardness of the call, by acknowledging that the call is, in fact, awkward.
4) **Introduction:** Clearly state why you are calling and what you do, without using titles, department names or anything that would need to be explained further. Simplicity is the key here. Every piece of information you give them that requires clarification brings with it opportunities for the call to be derailed. The only thing that belongs in the introduction is why **they** should stay on the line with **you**.
5) **Objection:** "I'm not looking." You already addressed this point, but sometimes it does come up again so move to the center of the flowchart for a solution on how to get back on track.
6) **Qualify Motivation:** Turn the tables and have the prospect tell you why they should be looking for better opportunities. This technique places you in the seat of evaluator, and them in the position of being evaluated.
7) **Profile:** This step involves your standard pre-screening process.
8) **Evaluate:** At this point, you must make the decision: do you want to present them to your hiring manager?
9) **Take away:** If they hesitate when you ask them about a good time to call, pull the carpet out from under them with this technique and immediately discover their hidden objection.
10) **Referrals:** If they are not interested, or you screen them out, consider inviting them to be a networking connection and become a resource for you in the future.

Section 4. The Cold Call Workout

Many people don't like to go to the gym, preferring instead to exercise at the beach or somewhere with a view. When that's not possible however, and they need to work out, the only option is to shut themselves up in a big sweaty room with a bunch of others. Many recruiters have a similar aversion to cold calling, so using a gym is the perfect way to explain how you can become proficient at cold calling.

When you're using a gym and miss a few months, you cannot just hop back on the treadmill and run a seven minute mile. After a long absence, it's best to ease back into the practice to avoid injury. And, that measured pace is also appropriate when you're just starting out on your use of a gym.

First Evolution

Make a list of the candidates to call. If they are Sourcing leads, prioritize them based on the amount of information you have and how many of the position's criteria that information indicates they meet. For example, leads with a title and employer, as well as one or more details that identify them as high potential leads should be called first.

From your inbox or job board the process is a bit different. Start with the most recent, and work backwards. Set aside a block of time for cold calling every other day or so, depending on how many calls you have to make.

These blocks of time should be long enough – say for example two hours – to reach a significant number of prospects. Pick up the handset and dial numbers back to back, leaving voicemails and making brief notes, without ever putting it down. Whether you connect or not, just keep calling for the entire period. As it is with going to the gym, after using this approach for a few weeks, your cold calling will become routine. At least you are showing up consistently, even if you are not completely happy with results. Congratulations, this is the hardest obstacle to overcome.

Second Evolution

Now that you know how many connects you are likely to make in an average call block, the next step is to use that information as a goal for every calling period. Then, keep calling until you have made that number of connects. For example, if on your typical calling block you dialed 50 people and connected with 10, your new goal for a calling block is to connect with 10 people.

Third Evolution

After a few weeks of consistently meeting your connect goal, you can also commit to a specific number of closes per calling block. Keep in mind that a close is any positive outcome, meaning a conversation that leads your prospect to take an action that moves them forward in the recruiting process, such as sending in a resume, filling out an application, completing a screening call, and so on.

A Note about Taking Notes:

It should take you around 15 minutes to qualify a lead and close. If your prospect turns out to be more resource than candidate, schedule a time to continue your conversation later so you can finish your cold calling block. Do not waste time between calls typing extensive notes. Instead scribble highlights on a notepad during your call block, so that once it is over you can enter adequate tracking information in your CRM or ATS.

Section 5. Asking for Referrals

Even though you may have disqualified a prospect or they weren't interested in your opening, you have invested your time in making a call so do not waste the opportunity and leave empty handed. *"David, before I let you go, could you suggest anyone that might be qualified for this type of role? Not necessarily someone who is looking for opportunities right now but someone you would hire if you were looking to fill this position?"* You could also say, *"So David, before I let you go, can you tell me who you replaced at [previous job] or who replaced you? Where are they now?"* Reassure them you are not going to call the other person and say you were given permission to call them, but that you will instead treat their referral as confidential just as you would with any other information they provided.

A recruiter named Mark Jennings developed one of the best techniques for obtaining a referral. He called it the "mental rolodex". It's based on the theory that when you ask a person if they know someone, their brain often becomes jumbled up and they draw a blank. But if you give them specifics about the opening's requirements, their mind uses that information to key suggestions. *"So David, before I let you go, could you do me a favor? Do you know anybody who graduated from MIT and works in Atlanta? Do you know anybody that works at Genentech in Boston? Do you know any CPAs in the Seattle area?"*

Section 6. Outreach Cadence

The frequency of your outreach process depends on the type of role and sense of urgency for this position. For example, with executive or scientific position, the lifecycle is longer, so reaching out once a week may be appropriate. With temporary or contract IT roles, things move rapidly, so reaching out once a day may be acceptable. Regardless of the spacing, you should make at least a total of five separate outreach attempts.

For example:

1st Week: Tuesday, send first email. Wednesday leave first voicemail, followed by first social media outreach such as through LinkedIn™.

2nd Week: Second attempt at the same email, but with a different subject line, second voicemail, and second social media attempt, this time through Facebook.

3rd Week: Third attempt, this time a different subject and email body, a third voicemail, and a text message or chat message.

4th Week: Send a fourth email, this time very brief. Call several times, but leave only one voicemail message. If you have a fourth way to reach them through social media, use it.

5th Week: The Last Ditch. (see below)

For roles with a much higher sense of urgency you could combine the email and voicemail into the same day; then wait a full day before a second attempt, followed by a third attempt on the third day. Then, wait two days or over the weekend before trying one more time. After two more days then try the Last Ditch.

The Last Ditch

The Last Ditch is the step in the contact process where you inform the candidate that you will no longer be contacting them. Most of the time, a candidate will return your call or email after the last ditch even if they do not let on that they have received it. Keep in the mind that the minimum number of times you should contact a candidate is five times before performing the last ditch. The best candidates are really busy, and if you give up after a couple of attempts, you'll just look like everyone else and not stand out as someone with whom the prospect should speak.

Leaving Voicemails

A professional, simple voicemail is upbeat, confident, and sounds interesting, but is brief and to-the-point. When leaving a voicemail be aware of that too much information can work against you, so simple is always better. In addition, voicemail can be circulated and even permanently recorded. Assertively state your name and leave a number where you can be reached. Adding other information such as your title or the purpose of the call is likely to result in a lack of response.

When You Hit a Road Block

It is just not possible for all the names on a list to be enthusiastic about your job opportunity no matter how plum it may be. When all else fails on a call, you should ask for a referral. Do not ask for a reference, a follow-up meeting, or a recommendation. Make sure to let them know that you are not going to mention their name unless it is okay with them. In addition, if you're in a position where you just spent some time with a candidate, and they are not going to work out at least try to source some competitive intelligence such as how many people are in the organization.

Section 7. Presenting Candidates

Basic Sourcer deployment results in a list of the names and contact information for suspects who match the requirements and qualifications developed during the intake meeting. This list represents individuals who have not been contacted or otherwise pre-screened. Armed with that information, you can take the steps to convert suspects into prospects, prospects into candidates, and finally candidates into applicants. In traditional recruiting models, recruiters handle these tasks. In cutting edge models, Sourcers or Sourcing pods are dispatched to accomplish them. If external Sourcing providers are used, then the SLA will dictate the level of service provided by the Sourcers.

Prescreening: From Suspect to Prospect

Promoting a suspect to prospect means you will initiate contact with the suspect. Contact can begin via email or a phone call. To initiate contact via email, you must invest considerable time and effort in writing your message. You must also determine whether you will send a mass email or individual messages. Please refer to the section on Sending Email.

This email campaign is different from a referral campaign because the recipients have distinguished themselves by matching the requirements; the number of recipients is probably fewer; and your goal is different. Here, your goal is to establish a two-way connection, not just to solicit information as you would in a referral campaign. Consequently, the nature of the message is more personal and the email's content must be more individualized. If you send a mass email, take advantage of email programs that offer a high level of customization. Sending emails requires patience because you must wait for recipients to respond on their own time. The good news is that if they do respond, then you know you have interested them in some small measure, and you have more assurance that a subsequent phone call will be welcome.

If you elect to initiate contact via the telephone, you are essentially cold calling suspects to establish a connection. In an

initial phone call, you should present your pitch with as much persuasion as possible. It does not have to be stated forcefully, but it should deliver essential information quickly to provide the listener with context. An example of a pitch is provided below.

Quick Sample: First Call

> *"Hi my name is Jamie, and I work for a Sample Company, a partner of Large Enterprise. We are currently helping them identify talent for some key opportunities in their Big Division. I came across your details on the website for the American Society of Executives. I reviewed your background and expertise with key hiring managers in the Big Division, and they asked me to reach out and see if you would be interested in knowing more about an opportunity. Do you have 15 minutes now or would you prefer to schedule another time when we can speak confidentially?"*

☞ ***CROSS REFERENCE BOOKMARK: REFER TO CHAPTER 12, SECTION 3 SCREENING: FROM PROSPECT TO CANDIDATE***

A prospect is someone with whom you established a two-way connection. Once a connection is established, you can move forward towards promoting the prospect to a candidate. A candidate is someone who meets requirements, continues to hold your attention, retains interest in the opportunity, and is being considered further but has not yet signed a formal application. Converting a prospect into a candidate calls for you to inquire more deeply into the candidate's qualifications. At the close of your initial prescreening conversation or soon after, schedule a time for another conversation when you can both talk more in-depth. Creating a form or questionnaire to follow during this phone conversation is instrumental because it will keep the conversation on track and act as a checklist for all information to cover. Weather called a "tech screen" (technical screening) or more formally referred to as a phone interview, this deeper review of qualifications should be applied consistently and fairly to all those competing for the same role, and conducted by properly prepared recruitment staff, hiring authorities or their delegates.

☞ *CROSS REFERENCE BOOKMARK: REFER TO APPENDIX FOR SAMPLE QUESTIONNAIRE*

Whenever the conversation takes place, there is a list of information that you have to go through. In addition to the questionnaire, you may have to probe beneath mere talk about qualifications for a sense of the prospect's behavioral characteristics. Looking at a prospect's behaviors reveals critical information that points to whether a prospect is a good personality fit. You can elicit this type of intelligence using precise, skillful phrasing. Below are some examples.

Quick Questions: Behavioral Add-Ons

- Can you tell me about a time when you...?
- What was your role?
- What did you do in that situation?
- What did you say?
- What were you thinking?
- How did you feel about it?
- Can you give me a specific example?
- What was the result of that action or step?
- How did you demonstrate initiative in that situation?

Answers to behavior-based questions contribute to your assessment of the quality of the potential candidate. If the potential candidate proceeds through the recruiting process and actually ends up in an interview with the hiring manager or an interview panel, chances are that the individual will be asked these kinds of questions again. This situation is an inefficiency that must be borne by the potential candidate to ensure progress in the process. Also, this redundancy means that you do not have to complete a comprehensive interview akin to the one performed by the hiring manager or interview panel. You want to ask enough questions to provide an initial sense of the person. Plus, you want to ask the same questions to all potential candidates to develop a baseline or reference point for all candidates.

Do NOT Ask These Questions

While some questions are inappropriate, others are outright illegal, so knowing what NOT to ask is just as important as knowing what to ask when talking with prospects. Questions that tend to reveal certain types of information about a legally protected class of workers are illegal, whether done intentionally or unintentionally. Avoid questions that address race, gender, religion, national origin, geographical information, marital status, age, physical and/or mental status, ethnic background, and sexual orientation. Also avoid asking prospects and candidates about anything that is not directly related to job performance. Information of the type listed below should be generally regarded as off-limits.

Off-limits Applicant Information

- Gender, maiden name, marital status, including a title like Miss
- Spouse's name (may reveal sexual orientation, ethnic background, national origin, or similar prohibited information)
- Spouse's employment
- Dependent status, if they have children, number of children
- Age or birth date
- Citizenship, national origin, birthplace or relatives' birthplace
- Religious denomination, cultural affiliation, or holidays observed
- Volunteer activities (unless the job requires direct community involvement)

- Physical features including height, weight, complexion, or skin color
- Mental condition
- Arrests that did not result in conviction
- Photos (except for acting, modeling and other performance or entertainment jobs where appearance is part of the job)

When certain pieces of information are essential to determine whether someone can carry out a job's duties, it is better to inform all prospects and candidates upfront about them. For example, instead of asking about a person's religious affiliation because you want to make sure that the potential candidate can work on weekends, just state that the job requires work availability on Saturdays.

☞ *CROSS REFERENCE BOOKMARK: REFER TO CHAPTER 15, HABIT #1*

Packaging: From Candidate to Applicant

At this point, the prescreening process is over, and you must move on to packaging remaining candidates, a matter of paperwork. The content included in a candidate package includes the results of all your previous efforts:

- Name and contact information (phone, email)
- Current employer, role, function and title
- Current location
- Resume or Curriculum Vitae
- Fact-based summary of your conversations, including direct quotes
- A paragraph describing your perceptions and thoughts as the recruitment expert conducting prescreening conversations with the candidate
- A brief paragraph highlighting how this candidate's qualifications directly relate to the position's requirements
- Other miscellaneous information important for later interviewers to know in order to prevent inefficiencies in the recruiting process
- Optional – It is a recommended practice that you include a summary highlighting the candidate's two most relevant accomplishments, preferably written by the candidate. This step obviously creates work for the candidate, but it allows them to express themselves directly to the hiring

authority, in their own words. Alternately you could simply paraphrase and include the two accomplishments yourself in your summary.

***Optional:** Include a summary highlighting the candidate's two most relevant accomplishments, preferably written by the candidate.*

You may also want to prepare packages for candidates who generated buzz in your recruiting pod, but whom you eventually excluded from your final list of validated candidates. Creating packages of such "close call" provides a wider range of options for and thus may be appreciated by the hiring manager.

Actually, transitioning a candidate into an applicant is now a matter for recruiters and hiring managers. Because you have already established a rapport, it makes sense for you to invite the candidate to apply or to inform the candidate that someone else will be in contact, but it also makes good sense for the recruiter to take over and you, the Sourcer, to focus your efforts on another campaign. At this point, any accepted candidate would be entered into an ATS by a recruiter.

Packaging candidates is no easy or simple task, but the results should be evident: Packaged candidates whose interest is already confirmed and piqued and whose quality has been ascertained and corroborated.

Packaged Candidate Hand Off

Delivering a bundle of packaged candidates to a recruiter and hiring manager signals the terminal point of Sourcing activities, but it is important that you tie up a few loose ends. You just exerted enormous energy to package the candidate efficaciously, and each candidate has become accustomed to swift attention. If the hiring manager and recruiters drag their feet now, they risk changing the tone of the search and losing top candidates. Thus, it is appropriate to educate the hiring manager on how you set expectations for the candidate so their efforts can address them.

It is also worthwhile to "strike while the iron's hot" and solicit feedback while it is fresh in stakeholders' minds. Soliciting comments can be done two ways. First, you can arrange for an interview feedback meeting to take place after the interview panel has met with the candidate. Try to put the meeting on the books once the interview has been set but before it actually takes place. Second, you can submit a survey for the other stakeholders to complete.

Chapter 14 Social Media Recruitment Building Blocks

Section 1. Fundamental Elements

Getting noticed online today has been compared to being heard while whistling next to a tornado, but with effort, planning, and experimentation you can stand out among the millions of status updates competing for attention. What follows are eight fundamental building blocks that will grow your signal, so it is widely detected through the noise.

1. KISS

Just as necessity is the mother of invention, simplicity is the mother of communication. Does your social recruitment message "Keep It Short and Simple" (KISS)? Or does it need to be deciphered with a secret decoder ring, a reference guide, or a team of attorneys? If the latter, do not be surprised when it fails to spread. Be concise, and stick to your point. Trim text to a core message, leaving no room for interpretation. Those forced to guess will either guess wrong or decide not to pass along your message.

Quick Hint! *Use second-person pronouns (you/your) liberally, and lightly sprinkle other possessive forms (our/ours).*

Superfluous embellishments, fancy or flowery language, and clever word play have their place in marketing, but apply great care that your pursuit for perfection entices more than it alienates. In social media, brevity should not come before clarity. What is your message? Why is it important? How does it affect the readers or someone they know personally? What should they do about it?

2. WIFM

Social media requires that you provide the same information as in recruitment emails and job postings: The answer to the question, "What's in it for me?" Failing to do so shortens your message's lifetime. Of course people are self-interested, so why not feed the ego when it will also benefit your cause? Relate to them by tying your story to what drives them. Answer these four key questions in your reader's mind:

- What? This is your core message (KISS).
- Why? State directly the reason your message is important to them?
- So what? Make your message about your audience.
- Now what? Inform you audience what the next step will be. Highlight your call to action for them!

3. Timing

If your message is drowned by noise, change the timing of your posts. Occasional repetition is okay, particularly for the benefit of those in other time zones. The best timing is when you can find balance between wide readership and narrow competition. Say you noticed the largest segment of your target audience checking their online sources around 3pm Eastern Time. You may be tempted to post at that time, but if it is a much more competitive time-slot, the probability that your message will be forwarded, reposted or even read at all could actually be lower due to the proliferation of other competing messages. In contrast, there may be relatively fewer people reading their online sources at other time periods, so your message may spread wider during slightly less busy times. Test various windows to see how your particular audience reacts.

4. Channels

Where you spread your message affects how widely it is cast. The three most popular and commonly accepted channels are Facebook, Twitter, and LinkedIn™, but it is very likely that an influential segment of your audience is listening to other less crowded channels as well. Find them.

5. Story

People care about people and seek connections, so pushing a horde of isolated facts will not serve your goals as well as crafting a story does. Not all content needs be tied to a single message, but weaving the same messages into various posts and approaches gives your target audience continuity and encourages them to return for more of the story. Dare to be different. Break the mold a bit. If your competitors use images, switch to video. Try your hand at humor. Find a hook that becomes your calling card.

6. Push

What will go viral or become noticed is unpredictable. To increase the probability that your message will spread widely, rely on your community. Recruit professional friends, colleagues, and others in your network to help you disseminate your message. Use every vehicle you can. For example, format a series of Tweets into a blog post. If you do not have your own blog, ask other bloggers to post it. Message your Twitter followers directly and ask them to re-tweet a post. Call out your colleagues using Facebook walls and ask them to share your content with their friends. Also publish your message through relevant LinkedIn™ Groups, use your entire LinkedIn™ network, and post it as a status update. Do not forget to tell your contacts what to do with your message, and briefly explain why they should assist. If you provide various formats for your message, members of your network can grab the one they prefer without having to translate from one media to another.

7. Teamwork

Social media is not a solo proposition. The best way to beat the noise is to become a choir. Many voices together are louder than that of any one individual. You will not be able to activate everyone in your community to help you broadcast each of your messages, but with enough connections you can distribute the workload. Develop a list of VIPs who have demonstrated a willingness to help you pass along a message from time to time. Keep track of this list so you do not overburden any particular person with too many requests. Make it very easy for them to help you. Find the win-win connection.

Take the position that you are providing content of potential interest to their network so any action is therefore mutually beneficial. Make sense to their audience, and you will recruit all the gatekeepers you need.

8. Keywords

Headlines tantalize. People skim news headlines the same way they skim online content – looking for words and phrases that pop and capture interest. Catchy headlines are not necessary. Focus instead on the keywords most often used in searches about that topic. Investigate basic keyword popularity with Google's Adwords tool: http://adwords.google.com at no cost. For maximum effect, invest in the keyword tools that experts use such as www.wordtracker.com and www.SpyFu.com where you can enter a competitor's URL and find out the keywords they use when they pay for search engine ads, which their top ad competitors are, and the organic keywords that rank high on search engines.

A clever social media recruitment strategy begins with a planned approach, grows through focused content, is delivered through selective media, and involves your community. Study your audience carefully because without them, your message is just noise. See the world with your target audiences' eyes: What do they like and dislike? Where do they go to obtain information? What else are they reading about there?

Communication is as much up to the sender as it is the receiver. No matter how well you think you are stating your message, if your intended audience does not "get it", then it is entirely up to you to shake up your content to corral them. The more your initial audience understands you, the more likely your message is to go viral.

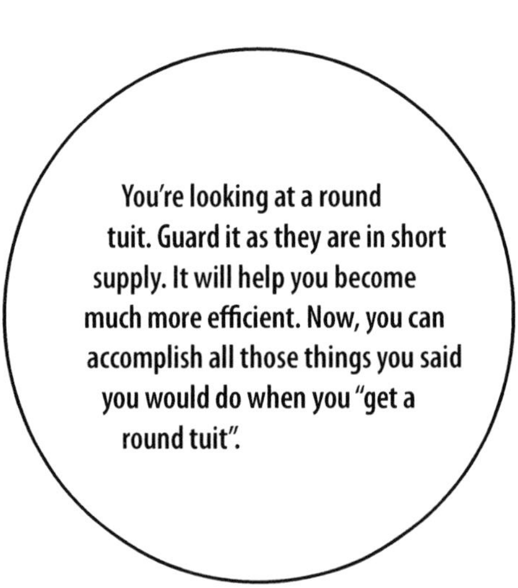

You're looking at a round tuit. Guard it as they are in short supply. It will help you become much more efficient. Now, you can accomplish all those things you said you would do when you "get a round tuit".

Figure 18 Round Tuit

Section 2. Writing Successful Recruitment Content

Blogging is demanding work and proving return on investment can lead to thorny circumstances, but it is a worthwhile long term recruitment marketing activity. The first step on your way to rocking the blogosphere instead of fizzling into oblivion is to fully commit. Plan out your work and approach your plan with discipline. Here are some tips to help you start:

Digital Curator

People want answers. Provide candidates a solution to their tiresome job, dead-end career, miserable boss, low pay, meager benefits, lack of meaning in their employment, or whatever else may ail them. If you want to share personal experiences or opinions and be entertaining that's fine, so long as your readers learn something from your experience. There is already too much content so instead of erratically adding to it, turn your focus to "digital curation" or thought leadership. Give your candidates a digest of relevant news and they will keep coming back.

Broadcast IS NOT Conversation

If you use your blog as an employment brand pulpit full of canned rhetoric, or a paltry platform from which you distribute job postings, do not be surprised at low traffic numbers. Social media is social, and blatant advertisements are not a conversation. People seek connection, not a sales job.

No Podium Piggy

Self-promotion is never as well perceived as making others look good. Share your spotlight generously by inviting colleagues to write an item or two, or contribute a regular column. Repost other blogs with your own added commentary. Conduct brief interviews of interesting people at work, conferences or other events. Ask readers for their opinions. Leadership is shining a light, not hogging it.

Sharp Point

Rambling is an unpardonable offense. Even brevity can be off-point. The less your readers care about your epigrammatic yet pointless outburst, the more likely they are to drop you from their RSS reader. Make that count twice for the title. Newspaper headlines turn pages, blog subject lines are clicked. As with emails, blogs that do not pique curiosity while removing skepticism stagnate.

BlahZZzz...

Be succinct. Dare to be brief. Expertise is not demonstrated in the length of a blog post. Short or long, content is judged by depth, persuasiveness, effectiveness, relevance or a combination of those attributes. As social media recovers from its Twitter hangover, long form articles are coming back in favor, but take care not to overdo it or risk ending up in the "read later" folder. Round Tuits are in short supply these days. Focus instead on the "why", and the "who cares", sprinkled with enough "how" and "now what" so there is room to experiment, and your readers can make a discovery of their own.

Share Bear

No matter how fabulous your posts are, if you they are hard to share they will not go as far. Sharing buttons are commonly integrated into most blogging platforms but if yours lacks one use AddThis.com for free. With it your readers can click to share your posts on Twitter, LinkedIn™, Tumblr, Stumbleupon, Delicio.us, etc.

Sharing buttons belong at the beginning of your post so they show up within the first few lines of RSS readers.

Ears Wired Shut

For every person who takes the time and trouble to leave you a comment, there were twenty who thought of doing so but didn't. It is very important to reward people who care enough to make the effort. You need not agree, simply acknowledge. It is courteous to reply. A short "thank you for your thoughts" encourages people to return and comment more often, next time likely with more depth. This will also recruit others to comment that had previously not followed through.

Eye Candy

Have you noticed the massive popularity of infographics? Videos, images, charts and graphics all make your post more "re-bloggable" and appealing. They also boost traffic. People's innate curiosity for images is a major driving force behind the growth of Facebook, Pinterest, Twitter and the like.

Target

Who is your audience? What do they want? Trying to be everything to everyone will not work unless you're already a celebrity. Narrow focus leads to loyal readers. Uniqueness counts twice as much when it is relevant. If you want to blog about another topic, start another blog.

Cadence

Perhaps the toughest part of narrowing your audience is the frequency with which you post. Writing is hard work, and when you focus your range of topics, it becomes even more difficult to keep coming up with new ideas within your central theme. Avoid the trap of self induced writers block by preparing several original posts in advance, staggering them out interspersed with reposts, quoting others' posts, sharing cool videos and images, and of course plenty of content curation.

Section 3. What's Your Purpose?

Social media can be used to help your Sourcing efforts immensely. Having a strong social media presence across a variety of platforms is an important part of lead generation, building your database, building your brand, engagement, and reaching new channels. What follows is a review of the various purposes with which you employ social media for recruitment.

Participation

Building and strengthening two-way communication with your target talent improves their impression of your brand. It saves money that you would have spent on traditional channels by proactively and continuously soliciting referrals from your online network and builds your reputation by staying top of mind with your target community.

Social media sites allow members access to other each as individuals and as a group via their built-in contact system, email, and even phone. They allow you to start and jump in on public and private conversations, as well as to make direct and reciprocal contact with specific individuals, groups, and communities of interest.

Branding

An increased online presence elevates your brand and grows your network. People who recognize you and/ or your employment brand are more likely to respond to your calls and emails. Be active and participate on Facebook pages, LinkedIn™ Groups, Twitter accounts, and blogs that belong to your prospects, your target audience at large, or your industry specialty/sector.

Traffic Building

Social media results in increased hits to your jobs and career pages and reduces the money spent on traditional advertising. Comment on other's blogs, groups, and pages, and link back to your jobs and career sections. Aim to have 15 new (incremental) "backlinks" pointing to your domain each week.

Online activity in social media channels results in favorable organic ranking increases among search engines queries about your company and your jobs. People who want to find you will find the page you want them to see, not that of a competitors or some other "social" property hijacking your name for their brand. Optimize all your content and social media profiles to make it easy for the search engines to index. Participate consistently in a variety of online social destinations that your target community frequents.

Competitive Intelligence

Another benefit of social media is your ability to garner competitive intelligence by gaining industry buzz on where the talent pool of the competition is headed, the types and availability of talent communities, and "who's who" in the sector. You can also utilize social media as a brand and competitor reputation meter.

By correctly identifying where your target audience hangs out online, you are able to make fewer mistakes and build your list of keywords by observing the natural language that people are using to describe their jobs, products, and companies.

Talent Pipeline Building

Build your talent pipeline by engaging with future prospects online. Social media is an effective way to pre-screen passive candidates. Build and maintain your pipeline in a CRM program so that you are able to reach out to prospects when you have a job for them.

Efficiency Improvements

Use social media to pre-close candidates before they fully engage. Save your recruiters time by eliminating telephone and email "tag"; let recruiters focus on engagement, and on the business side, while Sourcing focuses on the time-consuming tasks of search and identification.

Quality Enhancement

Avoid mainstream sources of talent and find experienced people directly from your client's competitors.

Access to New Channels

Access search engine, the deep Web, social networks and other Internet data channels that are not available through traditional recruitment efforts. Open yourself up to a wider community; by being a "friend of a friend", you can take advantage of the viral networking effect and build your referral networks.

Each social media site performs a different function and plays a different role in your recruitment efforts. There is no single site that you should engage with; instead, you need to use each site for its own unique functions to complement the other platforms that you are using, resulting in a robust, effective social media strategy.

Section 4. Social Media Marketing

Social media marketing for recruiters refers to the deliberate use of social media outlets to Find, Attract, and Engage prospects as well as to preserve a talent pipeline. The two most popular social media outlets for these purposes are Twitter and Facebook. The way these sites can be used to source content posted and hosted by others has been covered earlier in this text. The discussion here focuses on recruiters' direct use of the sites not as an audience but to post and host content.

Twitter

Many companies and organizations have a general Twitter presence or multiple presences, each of which is not necessarily linked to one individual. Twitter is mostly easy to comprehend, but the following are some factors to consider in your basic Twitter strategy.

Exchanging Tweets. If other users take the time to mention you, comment on or retweet (RT) your tweets, or just ask a question, tweet them back even if it's just say a simple "thank you". Do not leave people waiting indefinitely for a response. If you are busy or cannot otherwise answer a question, then delegate tweets to an appropriate team member so that call-outs do not fall through the cracks.

Canned messages. Because people will discover your Twitter presence at different times, they will ask you questions that you have already answered before. To address their questions without endlessly recreating your work, write a blog post elsewhere that presents Frequently Asked Questions (FAQ) and answers. Then, you can refer or link to that post when those questions pop up. In addition, for individuals in highly regulated industries, it is a good idea to obtain pre-written and pre-approved 140-character responses to common questions that will keep you in compliance and out of trouble. Copy and paste these responses from a template each time a similar question comes up. This way you can still engage in real time, but you are not trapped into answering a question on off-limit topics.

Limiting your audience. Not all tweets should be shared with the entire Twitter universe. Inserting "@reply" to the beginning of your tweet limits the reply to only followers who follow both you and the person to whom you "@reply". On the other hand, if you want everyone to see your response, add a #hashtag or other words before the @reply. If one exchange takes up too much attention or steers your content off track, offer to email the other user directly. Using phrases such as "email me if I can provide any more detail" or "happy to assist if you drop me a note via email" can keep your content focused as well as let others know you are willing to pay personal attention. If an exchange takes an ugly turn, immediately take the conversation to DM (Direct Messages are private messages between users). This strategy should include heated debates. You do not want to repel followers with an angry or defensive response.

Language level. Your tweets should have their own voice and use the same language you would in an in-person exchange or via chat or email. Emoticons and exclamation points are okay as is the use of first person. In fact, the use of first person emphasizes that there is an actual human behind the Twitter account.

Write Tweets that People Read and Re-Tweet

Twitter's growth has exposed a weakness in the recruiting world because Twitter makes it easy to ridicule, ignore, or ban spam robots that spew job posting RSS feeds. Instead, Twitter requires users to provide good, albeit brief, content. It is very tough to fake bad content in 140-characters or fewer. Moreover, follower count is a weak metric because this number does not measure actual influence. To gain insight on your tweet's influence and quality, it is better to look at your re-tweet data.

With any outgoing message, your goal is to compel your target audience to take notice – and to take action. In an email campaign, one way to achieve this goal is to have your email forwarded to someone else. A re-tweet is the twitter equivalent of a forwarded email, and it means your message works because someone is making the effort to pass it along. The more your messages are re-tweeted, the farther your reach, and if you want to influence a new audience of people and gain their interest in specific job opportunities, it helps to be re-tweeted by people who do not already follow you.

Many tweets are never noticed. To avoid sending your tweets into oblivion, here are a five more tips and suggestions to help you build your true reach through re-tweets:

1. **Be pithy.** You may think 140 characters is short enough already, yet high performing tweets are typically even shorter. Plus, with room for others' comments, you will be re-tweeted more often.
2. **Write frequently.** As with blogging, you will not build trust by showing up only once in a long while. The challenge is that inspired tweets do not come easy. Fortunately, sources of inspiration abound. Sit down with your social feeds for ten minutes a day to digest the most popular posts from among your Facebook, Twitter, and LinkedIn™. Make a list of tweets with your thoughts and comments as you read your feeds and then send these tweets to Buffer to be staggered and posted automatically out to your followers during times they are most likely to read them.
3. **Make it special.** Excellent traditional blog posts are unique, but excellent

tweets are the ones that are retweeted. When you re-tweet, do not just "retweet", but add something to the original to immediately upgrade the quality of your Tweets. It shows your followers that you are fully engaged with the content and not just a "thought repeater". Showing active engagement conveys your willingness to think critically, which builds credibility. If the message is already perfect, try adding a crisply relevant #comment or personal endorsement.

4. **Maintain balance.** Tweeting nothing but linked content is common and boring. Furthermore, only tweeting linked content alerts "spambots", so think of content to disseminate other than a shortened URL. Strike a balanced among links, questions, thoughts, comments, quotes, videos, or photos. Ask for feedback and solicit others' opinions. Diversifying your content encourages a breadth of engagement and can jump start conversation. Merely adding "...you?" at the end of your tweet should generate responses.
5. **Use tags wisely.** #Hashtags should be used sparingly and wisely, only when you are certain they add value. Well implemented, they improve the quality of your tweets, increase engagement, and widen access so you can be found. Overuse them and you become annoying, confusing, or frustrating to your followers. Focus on your tweet content then add one or two hashtags. If you join words, try using CamelCase to increase legibility, which means "Sourcingconference" should be "SourcingConference". Though technically not a #hashtag, a creative use of tagging is to @mention a well-known or established expert on your tweet's topic. This call-out can bring attention from their audience to your twitter stream.

A cautionary message: Before using #hashtag, it pays to research so you do not accidentally hijack others' established tags, which can make you look clueless or rude or even provoke nasty retaliation. To find out what and how tags are used, visit WhattheTrend.com, Twubs.com, Hashtags.org, and Tagal.us

Use Twitter to Build Your Pipeline and Influence People

Sourcing a solid list of candidates can lead to an embarrassment of riches. On the one hand, you have the relief of selecting from a pool of multiple strong candidates, but on the other, you cannot hire them all, even though you like them and you know more positions will open up in your organization in the future. This type of dilemma will occur more frequently as your Sourcing strategies sharpen. The best solution to this problem is to utilize social media marketing techniques, and doing so will help keep former candidates interested in your activities, avoid unnecessary repetition of Sourcing activities, and help ensure a talent pipeline for your organization. Thus, for recruiting purposes, social media marketing is also pipeline maintenance.

Below is a discussion of the most effective external website tools that can help keep prospects in your sphere of influence on Twitter.

- **Klout.com** and **Peerindex.com** - both supply metrics to measure your influence among your followers. Check out Klout's "True Reach" feature in particular to reveal the response your messages receive.
- **Followerwonk.com** - Find and follow your competitors' followers. Adapt and modify your content and hashtags to reflect what these other followers say matters to them.
- **Socialbro.com** - Identify demographic information about your followers that will help you participate in holidays relevant to them.
- **Bitly.com** - Learn what language or words you use that catalyze click-throughs, so you can increase engagement among your followers.
- **Manageflitter.com** - Clean up and perform maintenance on your Twitter account by removing followers or unfollowing others who post nothing but spam or have not been active in a very long time.
- **Bottlenose.com** - Manage your Twitter stream and discover which #hashtags, topics, and users mentioned you. Connects Twitter, Facebook, and LinkedIn™ accounts for the same user.
- **ifttt.com (If This Then That)** - Brilliantly automates "actions" or tasks that follow the simple logic of "if this happens then do that". Define the occasion when something specific happens ("this") and also the corresponding other action that should follow ("that"). Can automate actions on sites like Buffer, Delicious, Craiglist, RSS feeds, Flickr, Foursquare, Evernote, Gmail, Google Reader, Instagram, Instapaper, LinkedIn™, the telephone, Tumblr, Twitter, Vimeo, Wordpress, YouTube and others.
- **The Twitter mobile application of your choice** Several choices exist that offer similar Twitter services. The real tip here is to use different applications for different accounts. For example, use the native Twitter application for a personal account, and use Seesmic for your business accounts. This division helps ensure that content is not posted to the wrong ac-

count.

Here is additional information to consider in developing your strategy of influence.

- Add Google Analytics UTM codes to your tweets so you can track referring traffic from multiple sources regardless of how often users shorten your message.
- If tweeting from a professional event like a speech, conference, event, webinar or Twitter chat, let your followers know, and tell them to put you on "mute" for the day using an app like Proxlet, if they do not wish to follow the topic.
- A few common threads appear when the most 'retweetable' users in recruitment are examined: Content is far more correlative to the number of re-tweets than the popularity of the person who posted it; tweets containing exclusive news and information seem to have the most value and deepest reach; and tweets heavy with slang or abbreviations are often overlooked.
- Keep Twitter lists of publications (or companies, or competitors, or people) that matter most to your industry and community. When news breaks in or about your industry, you want to share it first, which builds authority.

LinkedIn™ in a Nutshell...

- Focuses particularly on business networking
- Excellent for professional branding and showing off your expertise in a particular discipline
- Utilizes profiles that look like resumes
- Attracts an excellent mix of people ranging from individual contributors to senior executives
- Makes it easy to search for industry experts, potential employees, hiring managers, deal-makers, people from specific geographies, or people with particular keywords in their profiles
- Sets trusted people apart via endorsements
- Claims 200 million members, including members of every Fortune 500 company (2012)

- Ensures your company profile page is complete and detailed, you have control of its content

In addition:

- Engagement levels are typically low, with little potential for your content to go viral. Engagement in the Answers section is higher than elsewhere on LinkedIn™.
- LinkedIn™ attempts to be an ATS and career site so they make little effort to drive traffic to your corporate domain. Work around this impediment by integrating your blogs via RSS feeds into the Groups you create on LinkedIn™ and ask your team members to include the feeds in their personal profiles to drive traffic to your domain.
- Take note that all content you generate within LinkedIn™ is going to be used by LinkedIn™ to attract others to LinkedIn™. This fact is good for your brand but bad for your SEO because LinkedIn™ competes with your own brand for search engine traffic.

LinkedIn™ has become the most effective social network for recruiters since its inception in 2004, and it has effectively dispelled the notion that membership is best suited for people with a technical background. A multitude of industries occupy LinkedIn™ space. Many people who would not otherwise join an online network for purely "social" reasons do join LinkedIn™ because of its perception as a digital age necessity to ensure employment. After all, more than half of all LinkedIn™ users opt to "learn about career opportunities", which is an open invitation to recruiters.

In using LinkedIn™, recruiters should seek to do the following:

- Find and meet prospective jobseekers
- Grow a referral network
- Conduct competitive intelligence research
- Build business relationships with clients or hiring managers
- Educate yourself and ask (or answer) questions about organizations, associations and competitors
- Heighten your corporate and personal brand

The best way to utilize LinkedIn™ is to complete your profile in full so you can be easily found, making sure that all your relevant employers, activities and associations are listed, and also making sure that you are sharing your network with others. Once you have established a network, you must dedicate some degree of effort, at least a couple of hours per week, to building out your network by connecting with others. Once you have a few hundred connections you should be able to search LinkedIn™ and achieve amazing results. The larger your network becomes, the deeper into LinkedIn™ you can reach, and the more contacts you will be able to see. The author of this book has maintained his position in the top 25 most connected users since 2004, and according to his profile he can see people in 147 industries and 420 geographic locations worldwide.

A search on LinkedIn™ is not the same as a search on a general search engine because most users do not fully complete their profile and have very few keywords on their page, which makes your usual search string ineffective. In place of a search as described earlier in Chapter Three, use variations of job titles, company names, industries, and geographic locations to begin finding prospects from the "People" tab.

LinkedIn™ supports full Boolean search in the Keywords, Title, and Company fields. Search for multiple Job Titles with the following string

("account manager" OR "account executive") president

Sometimes it is wise to uncheck the box called "Current titles only" and "Current companies only" because you may find that the people you seek worked at your target company in the past, and now in their new role, they may be in a company you didn't think of searching, and they may have a slightly different yet equivalent job title.

Once you find an individual you would like to contact simply call the company where they work directly. This way you avoid time delays associated with waiting for your connection to forward a request, and you will not be burdening your contacts with many requests. On the individual's profile you can see the name of their employer, along with their location, so just look up that company's number and give them a ring. If an introduction is more to your liking then simply click on "Get Introduced" and craft a well written but concise request to the first degree contact in your network who can connect you with your newly found lead.

One other alternative is to utilize LinkedIn's own internal messaging system called InMail, which allows you to send an email directly to a contact on LinkedIn™ without having to know their email address. On average, InMail messages are 70 percent effective. Considering that cold calling and other methods of initial contact have much lower response rates, InMail is a very good option. To send InMail, you must be a paid LinkedIn™ member.

There are several levels of membership from which to choose, and what each one offers changes from time to time. When deciding if you should invest in LinkedIn™, determine which license you are most likely to use to its fullest advantage, based on the number of InMails your team may need to send per month.

If you use Microsoft Outlook and are able to install small applications to your personal or work computer, LinkedIn™ offers a very useful feature called the LinkedIn™ Outlook Toolbar. With the toolbar, you can easily upload contacts from your Outlook directly into you LinkedIn™ network and see summary profiles of individuals who contact you via email. The Toolbar comes with a very powerful dashboard that helps you strengthen your network by reminding you about people you should invite, reach out to, or reconnect with. The Toolbar also has a function that allows you to create a new Outlook Contact from someone's email signature simply by highlighting the relevant text and clicking on the "Grab" button.

LinkedIn™ does have one major limitation in that it only includes people who have voluntarily opted-in to be part of a professional network for one reason or another. While it is estimated that as many as 75,000 new people join each week, it is important to remember that these are people who have an inclination or desire to network with others. As such, LinkedIn™ is a powerful networking and recruiting tool, but it will never be the single source of leads for savvy searchers.

Creating Your Own LinkedIn™ Group

LinkedIn™ Groups offer great value and help prevent some difficult situations. Here are 10 reasons every recruitment team should create one:

10. **They offer immense value to your target audience.** Groups can be focused and adjusted on-the-fly, responding to your community's needs in a timely way. You can switch the direction of a Group easily by posting a new discussion about a hot topic, thus gaining your audience's trust and attention, particularly if you offer valuable insights or information they do not find elsewhere. As a recruiter in a specialized area, you often have access to information about products and services, companies, or the direction your industry is taking. Offer this knowledge to your candidates; it's invaluable.

9. **Group Discussions:** An excellent way to engage your target community in a conversation. Because discussions elicit responses from your target

audience, you are engaging them in conversation. As a bonus, discussion posts are searchable (just like LinkedIn™ Answers), and they are all in one place. That ties your topics together in a common thread and further establishes your authority or expertise in your field. You can even have several different groups, one for each of your niches.

8. **You can message everyone in your group, even if they are not your direct connections.** Regardless of the size of your network, you are limited to contacting only those people already at first degree. However, with Groups, you can send a message to the entire Group, which can easily grow to be bigger than your first degree network.

7. **It's a great destination you can include in your signature file.** You should already have a profile link in your email signature file that encourages your message recipients to "connect with you on LinkedIn™". Adding a second link to "connect with other experts in your field" provides your readers with all the value listed here, but also gives them another reason for becoming part of your network.

6. **You can prequalify your members by obtaining detailed information about them.** Often listed in the member's own profile is information such as their employer, job title, geographic location, areas of expertise, their websites and sometimes even contact information. This allows you to focus your marketing using tight demographics.

5. **If the content is good enough, it can drive viral marketing (word of mouth).** If your group posts or messages are good enough, they are forwarded and passed around. That easily results in recruiting more members for your group, effectively growing your network reach.

4. **Groups are an easy way to build your brand in your target niche almost overnight**. Even if you already have an established brand, Groups allow you to gain credibility and brand yourself even more. They let people know that you have a depth of knowledge in a particular area that is of professional interest. That expertise is particularly advantageous in tough economic times when people have more questions than answers. By becoming a resource to your target community, you gain their trust. Though you may have to answer questions that seem unrelated to your practice area, you will also establish yourself as the "obvious expert" to whom they turn for an answer when a question arises that is directly matched with your knowledge and skill set.

3. **Groups are a group project.** While managing your personal profile is something you will not likely entrust to someone else, managing a group should be a team effort. You can assign any number of your team members to help you manage requests to join, post discussions, and read through responses. Doing so is a great way to involve your entire recruiting staff in a joint project that benefits the entire company. Plus, if any of your teammates leave, you can simply revoke their management privileges, while retaining them as a group member (or not). In this way, all your team contributes to building up the group, but no single employee can "take it with them" when (or if) they leave.
2. **People are more likely to accept a group invite than a personal networking connection.** Think about this – if you invite a complete stranger to "connect with you", it is quite personal. Inviting them to join your group, in contrast, is less direct and more often accepted. Say you were at a networking function, and invited someone of professional interest to come to your office for a chat. They may be a bit suspicious or hesitant, but they would likely be much more open to the idea of attending an event or function your company was hosting. Inviting them to join your group is less of a commitment than inviting them to become your personal connection, yet has the same net effect on your network.
1. **Best of all... LinkedIn™ Groups are free to create!** They cost nothing to start, and little effort to maintain, particularly if you engage your team and thus distribute the work load, yet the ROI is huge.

Facebook in a Nutshell...

- Seeks to make the world more open and connected
- Shares content by publishing news stories generated by users' status updates as well as shares content on the "Timeline" of each user
- Allows third party applications such as games and advertisements to interface with users
- Claims over 1 billion users, 81 percent of whom reside outside North America
- Started out as a school alumni network but has grown to include corporate alumni as well

Facebook is the world's most populated social network, which is an alluring prospect to a recruiter who seeks to be more open and connected. The historical rub of this social network is that most users have been conditioned by newsfeeds littered with pictures of other people's children and parties to have little or no professional expectations of the network. This conditioning eliminates the value of Facebook's massive user population.

> ***CyberSleuths Group on LinkedIn™:*** *If you are a recruiter with any kind of interest in Sourcing, you absolutely must join the author's LinkedIn™ Group. It's a no-cost way to network with your peers, share your news and candidate pipeline needs, discuss Sourcing tips, and find answers: linkedin.com/groups/CyberSleuths-742/about*

Recruiting in Facebook

The good news for recruiters is that there are many new Facebook applications geared towards exchanging professional information such as business cards and resumes. One such application is BranchOut. BranchOut was released in 2010 and has gained 30 million users and collected 500 million professional profiles in the short span of two years. BranchOut embraces a folksy grass roots approach to professional networking by promoting it through people who were friends before they were "contacts" and by using the same status update tools that advertise your birthday to advertise job openings. However, it would be an error to mistake BranchOut's folksiness for naiveté. One look at the Press and Investor sections of the website makes it clear that BranchOut is the subject of much legitimate buzz. Indeed, many industry observers view BranchOut as LinkedIn's most dangerous competitor.

BranchOut embraces the concept of using social recruiting to tap into the pool of passive candidates, which raises the question of whether the public at large can do recruiting on their own. It is reasonable to conclude, however, that Sourcers will maintain their job security thanks to their experience with and highly specialized knowledge of talent identification and engagement.

Facebook Pages

In general, all individuals on Facebook have a personal timeline, which is intended for non-commercial use only. Anyone who wants to establish a branded presence on Facebook, including for commercial or official use, must create a Facebook Page and becomes its administrator or "admin". The following discussion, therefore, relates to Facebook Pages and not to personal timelines. Keep in mind that the initial admin can select other

Facebook users as admins of a Page, but all admins must also have a personal timeline. Depending on what they hope to achieve through Facebook, recruiters can create their own Page, become admins for their organization's recruiting Page, or do both.

Within recruiting circles, much fuss has been made over social recruiting applications that utilize Facebook connections to produce job prospects. Despite the fact that many investors have poured money into these applications, the actual effectiveness of social recruiting when compared to other recruiting models remains hazy. So, until social recruiting shakes out further and produces more meaningful, empirically driven success stories, it is highly recommended that you view Facebook more as a recruitment marketing channel and less as a means to find prospects. In other words, recruiters can source or research prospects on Facebook, but they should not expect that publishing a job post on Facebook itself will lead to an influx of strong candidates.

As a recruiting marketing channel, however, Facebook is able to help drive the kind of interaction that promotes access, engagement, transparency, branding, and reach. Whether you maintain your own page or are an admin for another page, the following principles will help you achieve a productive presence on Facebook.

Be Real

People want to relate to other people, not with "constructs" or mindless entities, so in your communications, be yourself. You are your brand. Be honest about who you are, what you care about, and what you do. If you skip the canned branding rhetoric and just express your passion for your industry and your role, the branding will come naturally. If you write on behalf of your organization, humanize the voice so readers are certain that there is a person on the other side.

Share. Do not sell

Sell techniques often appear one-sided and continue only until the potential buyer makes a decision, at which time all contact terminates. When you use Facebook, don't sell your company or a job opening, but instead share information that encourages a response so that a conversation can begin. Because you share and not sell, there is also less chance that the interaction will terminate, especially if your content quality is high.

For example, share insider news, PR announcements relating to your company's core business, company sponsored volunteer events, or snapshots of various places, positions, and people within your organization. Maybe you do not want to divulge the whole recipe, but you can also reveal a bit of your company's "secret sauce". Basically, so long as there exists a through-line or purpose that somehow relates to a professional task even if only loosely, any topic with a tendency to educate, entertain, or engage is suitable for your Page.

Write Well

Accept that your writing will not always be perfect, but strive to be genuine and clear as you can. Additionally, use a consistent voice that falls in line with your marketing mission. Avoid misspellings, grammar and punctuation errors, and hasty abbreviations.

Commit

Once you create your Page, keep breathing life into it. You do not have to write every day, but maintain a consistent level of updates and engagement. Page maintenance should actually occupy a consistent space in your weekly schedule.

Invite Interaction

A fundamental premise of your recruitment marketing is the notion that other people's opinions matter. Another premise is that one interaction will lead to more interactions with more participants. Therefore, it is worth confirming which of your Facebook connections will reciprocate or mirror your efforts to engage. You can either test engagement implicitly or expressly agree to mutually support each other's Pages through a barter or cross-promotion strategy regarding content placement. The connections to enlist first using these methods are business partners, colleagues, teammates, and anyone else in your sphere of influence.

Facebook also provides features that promote interaction. For instance, there is a tab on the left side of your homepage labeled "Questions". By utilizing this tab, you can send a message that asks a question to Page members. These questions comprise an ad hoc poll or survey, which you can use to gauge your network's thoughts and cares about specific subjects. Here are some sample questions you could ask:

- "Hello! I'm trying to connect with more people in the [X] sector; does anyone know where they hang out online?"
- "What kinds of posts do you want to see MORE of on this Page?" Or you can ask the opposite – what they want to see less of on the Page.
- "What do you think of our benefits/career site/employee referral program/job ads/recent press release, etc.?"

Interact as a Reader Yourself

From your Facebook Page, click the "Home" button found at the top right of the screen. On your homepage, you will find news from other Pages that you have "liked" before. It looks like a Personal Newsfeed because it functions similarly. Browse postings and like, comment on, or share them as you see fit. It is a good idea to like and comment on only material that is aligned with your own message strategies because your interactions are published to other users' newsfeeds and thus can support or detract from your branding efforts.

Part of your recruiting strategy should be to check whether prospects have their own Facebook pages. If so, you should like their Page at a time when it will gain their attention. Make sure your Page is cleaned up before doing so, because these individuals are likely to check out your Page, and you want to put your best foot forward.

Reach People Offline

Your Facebook Page must wait for other Facebook users to visit in order to be useful. Consequently, you must drive traffic to your Page, including using other media to do so. When you connect with prospects and industry folk on other platforms like Monster or LinkedIn™, inform them of your Facebook Page. Likewise, post links to the Page wherever else you have an Internet presence, include the Page in organizational literature, and also consider placing it in your email signature.

Track Metrics

The feature on your Facebook Page's homepage that measures useful data much like Google Analytics is called Insights. It is really worthwhile to learn how to use this feature and the metrics it supplies. Your goal in tracking certain data points is to determine what drives traffic to and interaction on your site. Thus, it is also important to document efforts and strategize initial Page activities to create a baseline for future comparisons.

Section 5. Content Ideas

The strength of your social media marketing resides mostly in the quality of your content. To begin planning your content strategy, you must first develop a social media marketing calendar. By using a calendar to set your marketing agenda, you ensure that your marketing efforts coincide with both broader organizational goals and social, cultural norms. Your vetted calendar should show the following information:

- Federal holidays
- Socially and culturally important dates and seasons (e.g. the Super Bowl, school holidays)
- Dates and deadlines for important organizational goals and benchmarks
- Important dates in your organization's industry (e.g. conferences, conventions)
- Important dates within your job function (e.g. recruiting events, conferences)
- Important dates tied to international locations or localized markets, if any

Once you have a calendar, establish two different schedules:

ONE – The regular schedule of social media marketing posts among your different platforms.

TWO – An ad hoc schedule to implement when there is a special announcement or event that you want to promote heavily. There is no need to plan every detail. Instead, establishing the framework of an ad hoc schedule is essentially a time-holder to make sure that you are on pace, instead of lagging behind.

Now that you have a marketing calendar and a posting schedule, you should have a clearer picture of how much original content you need to produce. Something to consider is whether you want to serialize your content so that one larger piece is broken into smaller segments for publication at different times. Also, you can strategize how to use similar content among different platforms.

Quick Comment! Cross-Pollination!

You may use countless outlets during the course of your social media marketing efforts, but your readers will usually have a clear affinity for just a few social media platforms. Thus, it makes sense to "cross-pollinate" multiple social media with the same content to broaden your audience instead of relying on a limited number of channels. Fortunately, these different platforms can be used easily in conjunction with one another. Coordinating your cross-media marketing efforts not only expands your audience but also helps you preserves resources.

If you have three different channels, you should not have to start from scratch for each channel. You can stage your efforts to occur in a multi-layered approach, thereby reinforcing previously introduced ideas and increasing the chances of meaningful thought penetration.

Twitter, Facebook, & LinkedIn™

These three sites are the most important platforms for your social media marketing, and they happen to work quite well together. Below are some examples of what you could do if you wanted to cross-pollinate similar content among the three sites.

- When your Facebook page or LinkedIn™ group hosts a discussion or other event, integrate your Twitter presence by announcing it to your followers. By the way, your tone should reflect that your announcement is merely an "FYI" and not a plea for others to join.
- Generate a "Tip of the Day" and rotate it through your Twitter, Facebook, and LinkedIn™ profiles. Not at the same time – but on different days and times. Each audience is separate, and not everyone will see the same content or in the same way.
- Ask a question about something meaningful to you - asking for advice works very well on Facebook, but expect engagement in all three channels. Collect the responses, write a blog post, and then tweet the link while mentioning your contributors.

Content Ideas

When you have the marketing calendar and posting schedule in hand, you must determine what kinds of content you want to produce and publish. In no way is the following list comprehensive. Content ideas are limitless. What follows is intended to spark your imagination so you can customize these ideas to your business objectives.

- **Open jobs.** Disseminating a job posting is not exactly what you want to do. Instead, you can post a link to a job posting as an FYI. You can also share insider information about the open position that encourages prospects to check out your Page.
- **Industry news and information.** Important news in your industry will become well-known in your circles, so unless you have a scoop on big news, stick to new insights or new information only you can contribute. For instance, you could share an anecdote or empirical data about a recent business experience that others can comment upon.
- **Blog Posts.** If you maintain a blog elsewhere, you can repackage the content of your blog posts to fit the format of other media outlets. Sometimes, all that is needed is a new headline. Track your use of recycled posts so you know when to introduce fresh content.
- **Items with high entertainment value.** People like entertainment wherever they find it. Sometimes, just telling jokes, riddles, or puzzles can capture your readers' attention long enough to build good will towards your brand, even if your post was brief.
- **Images.** Photos often require no explanation and offer visual variety. Videos are also effective in the same way and allow others to be "there" with you. Images are often the most likely posts to go viral, so expend some effort discerning what images to use.
- **#FollowFriday.** Do a #FollowFriday topic or special theme. Use this hashtag to shine light on your most engaged community members from Twitter and your other networks, which groups people together who have something in common but do not run in similar circles.

Section 8. Other Social Media Destinations

YouTube.com

Video is a powerful channel through which to inform your audience. Response and viral effect is high for short videos that are distinct, real, informative, and entertaining. Use YouTube to quickly engage and respond to your target talent communities.

In the event of a reputation management crisis, YouTube performs well as a channel through which to do damage control or repair reputation.

Branding on YouTube is second only to Facebook when people are researching your employment brand. However, to be successful, you must have frequent messaging that aligns directly with your recruitment branding.

Videos rank also high on search engines, so focusing on SEO is important. Create your own YouTube channel for excellent exposure and SEO for your brand.

While YouTube's ability to generate traffic to your career site is growing, it still remains a minimal source of referrals. Most people who search and watch video from their portable device remain inside the YouTube environment, jumping from one video to another, seldom following links to pages. Annotations and chat inside the video can grow engagement and clickthroughs are rising but at this time YouTube is not a great source of visits to your jobs/career page.

Flickr

Extremely high search engine indexing makes Flickr a great way to receive free advertising and SEO. Linking from photos has huge results, especially as "social search" becomes more prevalent. Flickr is a good way to share visually appealing content with target audiences, and it has a moderate degree of viral effect. It is highly integrated with many other social media destinations, easy to use from mobile apps, and quality images do receive many views. Despite these many benefits, however, there will not be much traffic generated back to your sites.

Digg

Digg is a great tool for branding and exposure. The goal is to make your story and stories about your employment brand interesting enough to be picked up and repeated by well known bloggers. Alternately, your posts could be of such mass appeal as to become popular and receive lots of votes. Even if your story doesn't become popular, it is still going to be indexed quickly and show up on search engine results. Digg has high viral potential and traffic generation power when you hit it right, but otherwise can be rather dormant. Individual posts have the potential to send thousands of clicks and visitors to your company pages. Note that with little interaction, it is not an engagement channel, but it can drive people to other destinations in which you participate and that do have higher interaction levels.

StumbleUpon

StumbleUpon is a high traffic generator. When your stream is discovered, it goes viral very quickly. Keeping a diverse portfolio of interesting stories related to your brand, product, company, and industry will increase the possibility of going viral.

If you can boost a story to the top of its "tag" page, the large user base will make sure you have tons of exposure, so it's a great place to keep an active profile and drive SEO. If your content will not go viral, try the paid campaigns that can raise awareness of your employment brand among very specifically targeted demographics. Be prepared to pay an average of five cents per click. StumbleUpon is mainly about content discovery, so engagement remains very low.

Tumblr

Tumblr is an excellent engagement vehicle, due to the ease of asking and answering questions, combined with very simple and easy-to-use commenting systems. There is high viral potential, thanks to an extremely user-friendly sharing platform that is well-connected to many of the other major curating and content-sharing platforms, such as Instapaper, Flickr, Facebook, and Twitter. It is highly popular among the Y Generation, who use it to express their opinions, and in some circles, it is the alternative to Twitter.

Because it is so simple and user-friendly, it is one of the best blog platforms, despite the fact that it tends to be used more like Twitter than like a blog. With a wide variety of ready-made apps and bolt-ons, you can very rapidly build something highly polished and appealing.

Tumblr is an excellent link building tool, but not a destination that will generate much traffic back to your site. Using images, animated gifs, and videos tends to generate higher clickthroughs.

Quick Chart! Which Social Media Destination Should You Use?

Goal	Facebook	Twitter	LinkedIn	YouTube	Digg	Reddit	Stumble	Flickr	Tumbler	Blogs
Engagement										
Branding										
Traffic Building										
SEO										
Influence										

Quick Reference: What to Post	Both	Twitter	Facebook
Engagement	No fluff, stay relevant, interesting, informative, thought provoking, controversial or funny	Every other tweet should be interactive: @replies or @mentions, "via" and RT, questions, comments	Ask people for their thoughts and opinions, curate content, place targeted ads
Frequency	Post links no more than 50% - 75% of the time	Max 1 tweet per hour, stick to news updates or blog posts	Max 5 wall posts per day, no need to respond to everything
Language	Post about blogs you read or write, events, questions, opinions	Professional language is more re-tweetable, complete sentences not required, shorthand ok when easily interpreted by everyone	Conversational language drives engagement, comments visible much longer, ask questions
Length	Concise and clear	Keep to 120-130 characters so there is room for others to re-tweet you and comment	Max 5 lines of text, 4 is better, links and photos excluded
Images	Best photos tell a story on their own	Be picky and share only pictures that mean something without captions	More is better, interesting pictures get many views, write captions

Part IV: Achieve

Chapter 15
Determining Success and Positive Outcomes

In the most basic recruiting process, there are two main stakeholders, the hiring manager and the recruiter, and obviously, they both want the same thing – to fill an open requisition – and are on the same team. In the end, the shared goal is usually accomplished, but if one or neither of the stakeholders is happy with the result, was achieving the goal really a success?

There is a common impression among recruiters that hiring managers are difficult and picky. The essence behind this notion is basically true but should not be construed negatively. Hiring managers are difficult only because their perspective is influenced by their subject matter specialization; just as they are not qualified to do your work, you are not qualified to do theirs. Thus, you do not know the minutiae of their duties and responsibilities, which also can make them picky. Plus, recruiters do not have to work alongside the candidate, and the hiring managers do. They want someone who will not only perform the job requirements but also be an interpersonal fit.

At the end of the day, however, you can only control your own actions, which is the topic of the following chapter.

Author's Note - Case Study in Time-to-Fill

A few years back, I was retained by a pharmaceutical company (Pharm-Co.) to provide my Sourcing services. Pharmco was in desperate need of a mid-level executive to oversee regional merchandising and discounts management. I worked directly with the hiring manager, a senior level executive. In the course of my initial conversation with him, he revealed that the position had been open for nearly a year, and the work remained incomplete for the duration. It was disturbing to hear him tell his story because the consequences were significant: The cost of leaving the requisition open for so long was over $10 million per month. The position was fully funded, so it was not a budgetary concern. Instead, his internal recruiting team simply did not understand the value of his open requisition and had not serviced his department. Clearly, this situation was harming the company, and the damage caused by it could have been avoided through increased mutual education and communication between the hiring manager and recruiter.

Section 1. Assessing Your Performance

Most organizations require all employees to undergo some sort of performance review. Commonly, this performance review is an annual process that will affect your compensation. Other times, this review is part of a restructuring or expansion plan. These reviews are a critical component of a well-functioning organization. While there are endless ethical, philosophical, and accounting implications to the evaluation of human capital, the discussion contained herein adopts a pragmatic approach

designed to lead you to an observable and practicable method of self and organizational assessment with specific regard to your recruiting activities.

Section 2. Using Jargon

The exercise of assessment holds great possibility for fussiness. To minimize room for error, be careful with your vocabulary, for the terms you choose matter, particularly when it comes to accounting. Further, whenever you present data, be sure to include definitions in a simple key or as footnotes to avoid confusion. In the definitions below, different functions are ascribed to different individuals. Note that the edges of each position can be blurred depending on the size and policies of the organizations. Adapt these denotations to your corporate customers and be consistent.

Internal client – An internal client is another department within your organization that uses your services. Often, the hiring manager belongs to an internal client. For example, at a Fortune 500 company, the recruiting arm would consider the legal department an internal client, and the hiring manager would be a senior level attorney to whom the new hire may report. Smaller scale organizations may not call co-workers internal clients, per se, but the concept is the same – you and internal clients have the same ultimate boss.

Hiring Manager – The individual who actually makes the hiring decision. This person may belong to an internal client group. It is common for the hiring manager to interview a candidate. Most likely, the hiring manager will work alongside the new hire on a day-to-day basis. Hiring manager may be someone who is not an expert in recruiting or human resource matters. It is very common for hiring managers to work directly with Sourcers.

Recruiter – An individual whose primary job function is to identify and vet prospective candidates for employment. Corresponding job duties include running background checks, calling references, conducting initial interviews, presenting and negotiating offers, and managing third party resources such as Sourcers and independent recruiters.

Requisition – In general business terms, a requisition is any formal request for resources. In the recruiting world, a requisition is a formal request for a position that has specified responsibilities and duties and is backed by a budget. An "open requisition" is an unfilled request.

Sourcer – An individual who uses extensive and deep Web research to produce a highly specialized list of hard-to-find passive candidates from specific competitors, organizations, or associations. Sourcers deliver names and contact information to recruiters and hiring managers. A Sourcer generally has limited contact with candidates and does not participate in the Engage step of recruitment.

Time-to-Fill – The time it takes to fill an open requisition.

Requisition Open Date – The date when a request for hire is formally approved, usually tied to budgetary concerns or project timelines.

Requisition Close Date – The date when a hiring request is obsolete, either because the position is filled or the request is withdrawn.

Start Date – The date when a new hire begins work.

Section 3. Comparing Apples-to-Apples

The purpose of collecting and analyzing data is to demonstrate that your methodologies possess proven value instead of just being "a good idea". A baseline is a set of historical data used for comparison. The purpose in establishing a baseline is to identify achievement, areas for improvement, and other factors that correlate and contribute to productivity. For example, a simple baseline for recruiters could be the number of positions they filled in 2012. Then, recruiters can compare positions filled in subsequent years to the baseline. Baselines can be made by stringing together as many data points, disparate units of information, as you like. A more complex baseline for recruiters may include the number of positions filled on a quarterly basis or based on senior executive or diversity hiring. Comparisons are most revealing when the same data points are used in repeated reviews and multiple baselines are used.

Establishing a baseline is easier in an existing organization than in a new one for the simple reason that new organizations have no historical data with which to mine. Newly minted businesses generally have to balance hiring goals and start-up capital. Whatever your starting point, begin tracking data right away and set a future date when it is appropriate to sit down and review what you've collected. If you organization does not track data for some reason, then do so on your own, using data generated by your own activities.

Metrics take two or more data points to produce a distinct value of measurement. The goal of any metrics system is the quantification of performance that can be examined, tested, and projected. Developing metrics is generally more sophisticated than simply tracking data, for it usually requires a calculation. Without some sort of metrics, it becomes very difficult for a recruiter to define organization-wide success. The terminology of data interpretation can be confusing, but what really matters is that you use whatever terms you select on a consistent basis. Although many companies use specialists for advanced data research, utilizing good metrics does not have to require more than elementary school arithmetic.

Section 4. Crunching the Numbers

You can assemble data points in any number of ways. Adapt an approach that creates sensible meaning given the nature of your own work. As a starting off point, here are some suggestions for measurements to track your success:

> **Sum of offers accepted.** Add up the total amounts of compensation accepted by candidates each month, quarter, and year. These amounts should include base salary, signing bonuses, and other additional compensation. This amount can then be tracked as a moving average, and gives you a good snapshot of how much impact you have had on your organization. You can provide feedback to your customers by separating the offers made for each department or client group that you support.
>
> **Number of hires.** Track how many people you hire per department or client group each month, quarter, and year. Develop a quick snapshot of how you are doing in comparison to last month or last quarter by simply dividing the above sum of offers accepted by the total number of hires. For example, if you made three million dollars in offers and hired 35 people the same quarter last year, you had a salary per hire ratio of $85,714. If you made two million in offers and hired 21 people this quarter, then you know that this quarter, your salary per hire ratio is $95,238. A comparison of the two figures tells you that although you hired fewer people this quarter than the same quarter last year, you have a higher salary ratio, so your hires should be more impactful, and your performance has improved.
>
> The logic behind the arithmetic here may not seem obvious, so let's run through it. Employees frequently view promotion and the promise of a higher salary as a reward for their having done good work previously. This perspective is true in many senses, but it is not wholly accurate, for it limits the employer's side. The employer, and thus the recruiter, assigns salaries based on *expected contribution*, and following this train of logic, higher salaries should be associated with greater contributions.
>
> Positions with higher salaries tend to be "complex hires" for recruiters because they require more care and research to find

the right combination of education, expertise, and experience, which in turn demands that the recruiter be more skilled. With complex hires, the number of hires becomes less important because the cluster at the top tends to be smaller than the cluster lower in organizational hierarchy. The metric described herein captures this logic because it correlates recruiter's work with contribution, or impact, on the organization.

One last note: Be sure to account for cost of living increases, and consider the average salary for that client group before you commit to any specific reporting or improvement figures.

Cost-per-hire. This metric consists of dividing the total number of offers accepted by the total recruitment costs. This measurement can be a bit misleading because sometimes, there are hidden costs such as attending conferences or the cost of your website. In addition, turnover costs such as replacing bad hires and retraining new hires, opportunity costs, productivity losses, and other business expenses may not be fully considered by this metric. Using cost-per-hire to evaluate historical performance may be appropriate as long as your business leaders understand that there are many factors that are unaccounted for, including quality of hire.

Time-to-fill. This commonly accepted recruitment metric is interpreted in a wildly different fashion from organization-to-organization. Before you calculate your time to fill, it is important to establish a few guidelines.

The first controversial measurement is the beginning of the recruitment cycle. Some organizations start counting from the time the requisition is approved, others from the time that it is open to internal applicants, and others begin counting from the point the job posting is public, while still others will not begin counting days until the job posting has been closed and no further applications will be received. Be sure to pick one of those starting points and always be consistent, otherwise this metric will make absolutely no sense.

The other end of the time-to-fill equation is a candidate's start date. While there is little debate about what the "start date" is, some companies consider time-to-fill to end when a candidate has accepted the offer in writing, while most others end the measurement when the candidate shows up for their first day of work.

Customer satisfaction. Your customer will typically be the hiring manager, but you may also have other customers such as fellow recruiters or the HR department. Design a quick customer satisfaction survey that you can send to your customers once a year or at a contract's close to track which areas have improved and which need additional work. It is impossible to encapsulate all facets of performance using sheer numbers, so a customer satisfaction or follow-up survey is important because it can capture the intangible components of your interactions. Request anecdotal information, for personal stories provide atmosphere and a human touch.

Quality of hire. This measurement follows how many of the hired candidates complete their first six months of employment. Some organizations also measure how many reach the two-year mark or stay on for four years. Theoretically, the longer a candidate stays with the company, especially if they have moved up in the ranks, the better they were in terms of quality of hire.

Recruitment costs. This metric is not necessarily your recruitment budget but should closely reflect it, since it is the total amount of money spent per month, quarter, and year on recruitment activities. Make sure you include such items as your recruiter and support staff salaries, utilities (e.g., Internet connection, phone bill), referral fees, placement fees, office supplies, tools, subscriptions and memberships, job postings, and other recruitment advertising costs. When you examine recruitment costs, be sure to brainstorm all the angles. If effective strategies are in place, then correlating these costs to success elsewhere elevates recruitment activity beyond a sunk cost. For example, connecting the cost of Sourcing strategies with previously stated methods should reveal its effectiveness.

Quick Comment! Why Data Matters to You Personally

In most companies, recruiting is a stand-alone unit, and not even the top brass may fully grasp the potential of an effective recruiting arm. Additionally, when recruiting is not an organization's core business, it may be cast off as a sunk cost, a necessary cost of doing business with no expectation of a return on the investment, much like an office lease or electric bill. This perspective can affect how the decision-makers view your department budget and your salary. So, when it comes to dollars and "sense", you must be completely defensible. If you can collect data and utilize a system of metrics, it becomes easier to demonstrate the value of your work, which can help you develop a better budget, advocate a new work strategy, negotiate a better salary, or even find a new position elsewhere.

During periods of assessment, it is critical to consider your entire mutual sphere of influence. To point your thinking in the right direction, consider the adage that "a rising tide lifts all ships". Simply put, if a company's recruiting arm is effective, then the overall productivity and performance of the company should either align with or exceed company goals. Likewise, if the top brass is riding that rising tide, it should also be apparent how the recruiting team contributed to the success they are enjoying.

Section 5. Productivity Tracking

You can improve productivity with a simple measure such as tracking your activities on a spreadsheet, assigning them a multiplier, and adding them up to determine their total contribution to your success. The following is a short list of the types of activities you could track on such a spreadsheet:

Activities

- **Find:**
    - o Resumes
        - From ATS
        - From Google/Web
        - From LinkedIn™
    - o Web Search
        - Search A

- **Attract:**
  - o Post Jobs
  - o Social Media
- **Engage:**
  - o Emailing New Prospects
  - o e-Screening Candidates
  - o Outbound Cold Calls
  - o Outbound Warm Calls
  - o Phone Screening Candidates
  - o Responding to Inbound Candidate Calls o Skype/Chat
- **Manage:**
  - o Participate in Training
  - o Packaging Candidates
  - o Responding to Hiring Managers
  - o Responding to Internal Emails
  - o Submitting Resumes for Review
  - o Updating candidate data in ATS
- **Lead:**
  - o Attend Meetings
  - o Review Candidate Feedback with hiring team

Here is an example of a scale to measure the value of each activity. You will want to modify this for your own personal work habits. Assign each of your activities on the spreadsheet a value from the scale to use as the multiplier.

Productivity Multiplier Rating Scale

+5 Highly productive, directly results in a hire

+4 Productive, assists or supports a hire

+3 Productive, supports team hire

+2 Personal development, job enrichment

+1 Business development, team/company enrichment

0 Neutral - neither productive nor unproductive

-1 Operational requirement, necessary

-2 Operational requirement, distraction

-3 Mental health break

-4 Trivial, counterproductive

-5 Bottleneck, causes work stoppage

Quick Chart! Sample Productivity Tracking Spreadsheet

ACTIVITY	JANUARY							
Day	**1**	**2**	**3**	**..**	**31**	**Minutes**	**Scale**	**Productivity**
Find: Resumes: ATS	25	25	50			50	5	250
Find: Resumes: Web	25	25	50			50	5	250
Engage: Social Media	45	15				60	3	180
Outbound warm calls	30	30				60	5	300
Manage: Package Candidates	10	10				20	4	80
Manage: Hiring Manager Calls	20	10				30	4	120
Engage: Email Campaigns	15	25				40	3	120
Post Jobs	25	25				25	2	50
Find: Deep Web Search	30	30				30	2	60
Engage: Skype/Chat: Personal	10	5				15	-2	-30
Training	60	0				60	3	180
Team Meeting	0	30				30	1	30
Subtotal Minutes	495	0	0	0	0	495	A VG	132.50
Subtotal Hours	8:15	0:00	0:00	0:00	0:00			

Figure 19 Productivity Tracking Chart

Ensuring Success: Forecasting & Building a Talent Pipeline

Most organizations expect hiring to be turned on and off as needed like a light switch. During times of growth, requisitions are opened once the need becomes urgent, which is usually too late, and to respond, additional recruiters are rapidly hired either on contract or as full-time employees. New recruiters with little company experience and virtually no knowledge of corporate culture are then expected immediately to turn around and hire the next wave of talent and do so quickly. Even organizations enjoying solid partnerships with contingent staffing vendors expect to deliver such quick ramp-ups and turn-around times that it becomes practically impossible for vendors to provide the careful evaluation necessary to present the highest quality available.

> ***Quick Tip:*** *Hiring top talent is the single most critical aspect in attaining growth with staying power.*

Maintaining a high quality of hire while building and retaining a solid employment brand enables organizations to respond effectively to fast-changing talent demands. It's simply not feasible to turn recruiting on and off "on demand" and achieve optimum results. "Just in time" hiring, in contrast, is a companywide strategy built around creating a scalable pipeline that allows the flow of talent into recruitment processes to ebb and flow, suitably matching demand.

Behind this seemingly intricate dance, the most critical piece is the care and maintenance of a candidate network so that sufficient contacts within the prospective talent pool are kept warm and can be reached at the right time. As long as the talent recruitment function maintains strategic relationships with company leadership, hiring managers and the candidate network, hiring "just in time" is possible.

With appropriate forecasting of an increased demand for talent, a recruitment organization can quickly scale up by engaging an already expectant pool of talent, instead of starting over from scratch each time needs change.

Chapter 16
Personal Work Habits

Professional development and training varies from one organization to the next and usually focuses on subject matter expertise. It is frequently presumed that employees bring their own administrative skill sets with them that conform to corporate norms. Thus, lapses in basic work competencies are usually not addressed until after they have already caused a problem and are exposed in front of an audience. Often, organizations can avoid regrettable consequences with the application of common sense, yet experience shows that common sense is not so common. This book embraces a holistic approach to recruiting, and the purpose of this chapter is to discuss the elemental habits that should be a part of your work behavior so you do not jeopardize time, money, or livelihood, the stakes involved in each habit discussed. With such stakes, these activities rise above mundane levels and bear great potential to add valuable substance to your performance.

Ten habits follow, and their title descriptions apply to all jobs, but their subsequent discussion focuses on their role in recruiter's careers. Remember that the habits described below are portable across organizations and even industries.

Habit #1 – Comply with the Law

From a legal perspective, recruiting work generally falls under the umbrella of labor and employment law. Just as food sellers must follow health codes and contractors must follow building, plumbing, and fire codes, so recruiters must comply with federal and local laws designed to protect the rights of the American workforce. Additionally, legal liability can attach itself in other miscellaneous ways. Following is a brief discussion of the various ways that recruiters and their employers can be held liable for misconduct in their recruiting activities.

Federal Level

The U.S. Equal Employment Opportunity Commission (EEOC) is a federal agency charged with enforcing the following federal laws (http://www.eeoc.gov):

- Title VII of the Civil Rights Act of 1964 (Title VII)
- The Pregnancy Discrimination Act
- The Equal Pay Act of 1963 (EPA)
- Age Discrimination in Employment Act of 1967 (ADEA)
- Title I of the Americans with Disabilities Act of 1990 (ADA)
- Sections 102 and 103 of the Civil Rights Act of 1991
- Sections 501 and 505 of the Rehabilitation Act of 1973
- Genetic Information Nondiscrimination Act of 2008 (GINA)

These laws make it illegal to "discriminate against a job applicant or an employee because of the person's race, color, religion, sex (including pregnancy), national origin, age (40 or older), disability or genetic information" (www.eeoc.gov/eeoc/index.cfm).

Note that the above-mentioned laws do not apply to all employers. For federal law to apply to your workplace, your employer must meet certain requirements regarding "type of employer, number of employees, and type of discrimination alleged". (http://eeoc.gov/employers/index.cfm) For example, businesses and private employers must have at least 15 employees who have worked more than 20 weeks before some laws apply. In contrast, employment agencies that regularly refer candidates to employers are covered regardless of their size. If your employer is subject to enforcement by the EEOC, it behooves you to review your recruiting methods with an in-house attorney or to submit a request to your manager for an outside legal review.

As of the date of publication, the following were listed on the EEOC website under "Prohibited Employment Policies/Practices" (www.eeoc.gov/laws/practices/index.cfm).

Recruitment

"It is also illegal for an employer to recruit new employees in a way that discriminates against them because of their race, color, religion, sex (including pregnancy), national origin, age (40 or older), disability or genetic information.

For example, an employer's reliance on word-of-mouth recruitment by its mostly Hispanic workforce may violate the law if the result is that almost all new hires are Hispanic.

Application & Hiring

"It is illegal for an employer to discriminate against a job applicant because of his or her race, color, religion, sex (including pregnancy), national origin, age (40 or older), disability or genetic information. For example, an employer may not refuse to give employment applications to people of a certain race.

An employer may not base hiring decisions on stereotypes and assumptions about a person's race, color, religion, sex (including pregnancy), national origin, age (40 or older), disability or genetic information.

If an employer requires job applicants to take a test, the test must be necessary and related to the job and the employer may not exclude people of a particular race, color, religion, sex (including pregnancy), national origin, or individuals with disabilities. In addition, the employer may not use a test that excludes applicants age 40 or older if the test is not based on a reasonable factor other than age.

If a job applicant with a disability needs an accommodation (such as a sign language interpreter) to apply for a job, the employer is required to provide the accommodation, so long as "the accommodation does not cause the employer significant difficulty or expense."

Job Referrals

"It is illegal for an employer, employment agency or union to take into account a person's race, color, religion, sex (including pregnancy), national origin, age (40 or older), disability or genetic information when making decisions about job referrals."

Where violations of federal law are found, the EEOC may seek a variety of remedies as outlined by the law that was broken, including job placement/reinstatement, back pay, value of missed benefits, compensatory damages, punitive damages, attorneys' fees, court costs, and liquidated damages.

Other Applicable Laws Fair Employment Practices Agencies (FEPAs)

The federal government is not the only authority on employment practices. Many local authorities (state, county, city, and town) have also passed laws that they enforce and with which your work must comply. The EEOC calls these local agencies "FEPAs". To determine the local laws that apply to you, begin with a visit to your state's official website. Note that if your organization conducts business outside its home state, then other local laws may apply.

Civil Actions – Tort Law

Individuals, including corporations, sometimes commit civil wrongs or torts for which an aggrieved party can seek a legal remedy. Basically, under tort law, a plaintiff brings a claim in a civil court alleging that the defendant committed some action that amounts to a violation of recognized public policy. Common business related tort claims include interference with a business relationship, interference with a contract relationship, unfair competition and even slander. The tort claim that a plaintiff pursues depends on which court is involved and the location where the plaintiff seeks redress.

Civil Action – Contract Law

Signatories to a contract agree to abide by the terms set forth in the contract. When there is a breach or nonperformance of an agreed upon term, one party may bring a court action against the other party. If you have an employment agreement or an independent contractor agreement with an organization, then ensure that your conduct conforms to the terms of the agreement even if a non-conforming action is otherwise legal.

Whistleblower Laws

In the year 2012 the U.S. Congress passed legislation strengthening federal whistleblowing protection for employees who report specified illegal or harmful acts by their employers. Essentially, employers are forbidden from retaliating against whistleblowers and may be required to reinstate employees and pay back wages among other penalties if they do. While the facts of these cases rely mostly on the acts of human resource departments and managers, recruiters can be drawn into such matters because they were the individuals who initially screened an employee.

Finally, the above guidelines are intended to provide only a general overview of the field of labor and employment law and to encourage you to ensure that all your professional activities conform to the law. They are not intended to provide comprehensive legal information about recruiting activities. If you have questions, you should seek the guidance and advice of an attorney or research the answers on your own.

One last interesting note on the topic: If you work for or with a publicly traded company, you can easily determine if there are any legal actions that involve your company by reading the company's annual report, whose publication is required by law. (http://sec.gov) That document will immediately reveal the issues, practices, and policies of the company as well as any lawsuits to which it may be party.

Habit #2 – Carry out Your Responsibilities

As a recruiter, you deal with requisitions and their job functions, duties, and responsibilities on an hourly basis. Therefore, it seems self-evident to say that you should know your own, but gray areas arise when there are many cooks in the famous kitchen or when the opposite situation occurs and you are left to your own devices to handle the universe of human resource management. It is then appropriate to remember that employers can exercise control over your job assignments and the methodologies you use. Unlike with independent contractors, employees must use the means dictated by their employers to carry out their duties and responsibilities, even if employees disagree with them. So long as your employer acts lawfully and pays you wages, you are obligated to perform your work assignments as directed by your employer.

Wise managers will avoid micro-managing employees or steering employees away from the duties most closely related to their stated titles and functions. However, if you have the latitude to establish your own practices and code of conduct, do so with a clear purpose – have reasons for your actions and know how to articulate them.

Frequent issues that arise in recruiting relate to the topic of nonperformance. Recruiters can do everything right, yet fail to meet the objective of completing a hire because their work is affected by other stakeholders in the process. For example, a recruiter can present several strong applicants to a hiring manager and then lose the candidates' interest because the hiring manager did not make a timely decision. In this situation, it is unfair to characterize the recruiter's efforts as ineffectual or criticize them for nonperformance.

Because these types of situations can occur with some regularity, it is very important that recruiters understand what is within their control and to take steps to measure their work as described earlier in this text.

☞ *CROSS REFERENCE BOOKMARK: REFER TO CHAPTER 14*

Habit #3 – Be a Good Steward

In 1989, Warren Buffett, CEO of Berkshire Hathaway and perennial contender for the title of richest man in America, purchased a jet he named "The Indefensible" because the corporate spending for the plane was considered unjustified. Buffett's use of the plane was labeled a job perk. Nearly twenty years later, Buffett renamed his plane "The Indispensable" and stated that "[the company] was better off by me having a plane available to go and do deals or whatever it may be. We have done things I wouldn't have done if we hadn't had a plane. And I think it's...a big mistake to start demonizing anybody in this game." (www.ainonline.com) Rare is the job description that requires access to a private jet, but Buffett underscores the important point that sometimes resources should be used because the expenditure leads to greater opportunity for enterprise.

A steward is someone who has been charged with the care of property or resources that belong to another, and they are generally accountable for their care to someone else. For example, in a publicly traded company, the owners are the stockholders, and the obvious stewards are members of the board of directors and other key decision-makers who manage the company and are supposed to use its resources to create profit for the stockholders. When mismanagement occurs, stockholders and governments can exercise their rights under the law to hold these individuals accountable. However, it does not really matter if an organization is a publicly traded company or not. Unless you own your business, you are accountable to your organization for the resources left in your possession. Even if you own 100 percent of your business, you may still be accountable for the resources you use if you are servicing a contract with certain parties like a government entity. When you think of these resources, think of anything that your budget pays for, including your time on the clock.

When planning a recruiting budget, review your total expenses for the previous years and determine which expenses generated the most leads and which activities consumed the most time. Figure where dollars are best used, including where money spent on external third parties or additional infrastructure can actually save you money. Do not forget to factor in the work hours spent towards research. Then, you will have a better picture for budgetary purposes.

> ***Follow the money:*** *If you do not follow your own money, someone else will and you will have to explain it.*

Habit #4 – Manage Your Time

The subject of time management has become a cliché, but what does it actually involve? To manage your time most effectively, the number one activity you should undertake is utilizing and practicing the research methodologies outlined previously, which are already geared to save you time and most likely represent the bulk of your work.

Additionally, here are other actions that will help shave off valuable minutes every day.

Be organized. You are dealing with massive amounts of information that will make no sense unless you know their purpose. When sorting through data dumps, organization is vital. Use folders to organize your Internet Favorites, resources, job boards, candidates, requisitions, company information, research, and Sourcing forms. It is also a good idea to keep a notebook or journal in hard copy so that you can take note of good ideas you find while searching. By writing them down in your notebook you can come back to them later without interrupting your search. Use your research form to track all the synonyms and keywords you find, lists of competitors and their URLs, association sites, universities, niche job boards, and other targeting information so that you can quickly refer to it while conducting research.

Be persistent. The staggering amount of information available online can make it intimidating to conduct searches, especially if you enter a few keywords and the search engine comes back with hundreds of thousands of results. Half the battle is targeting the right kind of information. With dozens of requisitions demanding attention, it becomes easy to give up and move on to the next set of requirements—but do not. It takes a bit of time to set up search formulas, but once they are established, you should be able to obtain search results in under ten minutes.

Triage information: Data can cause clutter, and some people are data hoarders. Their data drives are akin to houses stuffed to the ceiling with old newspapers, magazines, and other junk. Do not be a packrat. When you have completed a project, ask yourself if this research will mean anything to you in a year without the context you have now. If the answer is no, delete the data. If yes, then save it in your archive folder, where you can find it later using today's sophisticated desktop and inbox search tools.

☞ *CROSS REFERENCE BOOKMARK: REFER TO CHAPTER 5*

Know when to ask for help. Do not wait for bad consequences to occur to ask for assistance. You should be your own hero by seeking out internal or third party resources in a timely fashion, which may include that you consider them during planning phases. In fact, it is a good idea during the initial phase of any new project to understand what other parties might be able to help you meet your deadlines. It cannot be repeated enough that Sourcers and Sourcing techniques are your best bet for results when time is your most critical factor. Inherent to Sourcing is the crucial element of efficient time use. Sourcers are trained to avoid becoming bogged down in time sucking Internet searches.

Carve out blocks of time in the day for recurring activities.

- 1 hour per day to return voicemails
- 1 hour per day to reply to non-urgent emails
- 1 hour per day to make cold calls and network to newly found leads
- 1 hour per week to send out some email campaigns to new leads
- 1 hour per week to conduct research on your competitors
- 2 hours per week to apply what you learn in this book and discover new skills
- 4 – 16 hours per week for Sourcing sets used to conduct Internet searches for new requisitions

25-Minute Sourcing Sets

In a sense, Sourcing is a performance-based activity like a recital for a musician or a sporting event for an athlete. Just as many people can swim but few do so like Michael Phelps, many people can surf the Web, but few raise Internet-based research to the level of Sourcing as described in this text. Sourcing completely engages time, focus, and thought, and the act of Sourcing should be free from distractions.

Sourcing sets are dedicated periods of time when Sourcers perform their research functions. For these professionals, Sourcing sets are "the main event", their time "in the ring". Sourcing sets have clear starting and ending times and are scheduled events. The key to their effectiveness is that Sourcing sets remain *uninterrupted.* In other words, sets are indivisible.

During a Sourcing set, phones are turned off; doors are closed; and Sourcers are left alone.

Here is what Sourcing set deployment looks like.

25 minutes (:00-:25) – SOURCING SET 1

10 minutes (:26-35) – BREAK

25 minutes (:36-60) – SOURCING SET 2

Basically, you break down your Sourcing activities in scheduled events, one hour at a time. Then, that hour is broken down into two Sourcing sets with a break in between sets. The 25-minute block is not just a guideline; it is an explicit instruction, and you should actually use a timer. A Sourcing set is 25 minutes for a very specific reason – 25 minutes is the equivalent of a mental sprint. It is long enough to accomplish work, yet short enough to keep your complete focus on a single goal.

You can schedule this hour to occur multiple times a day, in which case, Sourcing begins to feel like line changes in hockey or substitution patterns in basketball, except that you are a team of one. If you schedule Sourcing hours close to one another, be sure to include breaks in between Sourcing hours to keep your mind refreshed. The value of employing this technique is immediate: Larger goals break down into smaller ones; you will achieve a series of mini-accomplishments; you will move swiftly; you will feel renewed more frequently; and your time will produce more results.

Handling Interruptions

While you may take Sourcing very seriously, others may not understand the importance of your process and interrupt you anyway. Thus, it is up to you to enforce the boundaries of your activities.

When you encounter an interruption, there is a recommended response to preserve the effectiveness of your Sourcing set:

- **Clearly inform the other party that you are occupied:** "I'm sorry, but I'm in the middle of an activity."
- **Quickly negotiate how you will connect later:** "Do you need to speak to me in person? Or can you send me an email?"
- **Reschedule the interruption:** "Can I call you back during my next break?" Sourcing sets are only 25 minutes, so the other party most likely does not have to wait long for your attention.
- **Follow-up:** Actually call or connect with the person as agreed.

If your Sourcing set is actually set aside in favor of a distraction, do not count that block towards your souring hour. Instead, begin anew.

Self-Interruptions

As you progress down a search path, the Internet itself presents myriad distractions. Email or message alerts, advertisements, and even related but not essential articles can also derail your efforts. So interrupting yourself is just as dangerous as having somebody else interrupt you. So remember – no calls, no emails, no coffee breaks, no restroom breaks, and close the door if you have one. If you have no door, then seek out a meeting room, or just go to a coffee shop, anywhere that will ensure you will not be interrupted for your 25-minute set. You will be surprised, amazed, even shocked at how much better your results are.

Habit #5 – Prioritize Your Tasks

Educators know that visual aids have been proven to help all types of learners, even those who are not primarily visual learners. Applying this axiom, one of the simplest and most effective ways to create order from chaos is to create a visual aid for yourself that can be displayed prominently in your workspace, either digitally or in hard copy form. The most common types of visual aids are a rotating list of priorities, short and long term, checklists for repetitive or administrative tasks, and ongoing to-do lists. Make sure the content of your lists allows for interruptions and shifting priorities, so you can fit in other tasks as they arise. Also make sure your plan includes not just requisition-related activities but also professional development and other organizational priorities. Keep your focus by visually separating the contents of your lists into three sub-lists with the following labels: Essential, non-essential, and important but not business-critical. Some recruiters keep this plan in a notebook or planner while others prefer to use electronic task management systems such those with built-in office productivity tools.

- Handle what is Important first
- Deal with what you can second
- Archive anything that may be useful in a year
- Delete the rest

Pareto, an Italian economist, noticed that 80 percent of the wealth was owned by 20 percent of the population. That observation has since been applied to many other areas of business, including managing our day. If you make a list of all the categories of tasks you perform each day, you can discover which ones are among the 20 percent that contribute to 80 percent of your success. List them in a table and track how many minutes or hours you spend on each type of task each day. Add a column to rate how that task directly contributes to a hire. This technique is a rough approximation, so use a simple scale such as 3 for tasks that directly contribute to a hire, 2 for those that assist or support a hire and 1 for everything else. By multiplying the time by the rating you will discover which tasks are most productive. Delegate, eliminate or simplify low productivity tasks. Refer to the back section for a sample spreadsheet.

Prioritizing your tasks requires interdepartmental cooperation. Your tasks should align with organizational goals. Avoid future conflicts by ensuring everyone "gets a turn". Building a pipeline is critical here. If you are constantly putting out fires instead of foundation building, expect to be burned.

Habit #6 – Archive Your Work

Why re-invent the wheel every time you begin new initiatives or are asked to carry out a repeated responsibility? There is a reason employees with experience are valued more than novices, and the same is true for corporations. Building a reliable corporate memory contributes to efficacy and keeps your organization moving forward. In other words, knowing the benefits and lessons of collective trial and error should steer you down the most productive and profitable paths.

"A person who never made a mistake never tried anything new."
– Albert Einstein

Save your formulas. Once you determine the searches that work best for you, hang on to them. Keep them in research form, in your notebook, or as favorites in your browser. In Chapter Three, there is an example of a research form using Excel that will help you track all the searches you perform throughout the day. Make backup copies of your "search templates" and keep them up to date. Search strings that brought you success before should be used as a springboard for searches later—avoid reinventing your search strings when possible. In addition, create your own "crib sheet" with a list of prepared Boolean search string formulas ready for each type of search or search engine you use. Just cut and paste your position-specific keywords from the research form and you are off to a good start.

Create a document protocol. Use the "Save As" feature to save resumes to your folders. The same way you create Bookmark Folders, you should create folders on your hard drive for each position you search. That way, when you run into a great resume you can "Save As" into a folder for future use.

Implement a back-up and shared file system. If your organization has not instituted a company-wide system, then do so on your own using cloud-based programs like DropBox, Google Drive, JungleDisk, Cubby or Sugar Sync.

Quick Comment! Recordkeeping by Law

Archiving your work will not only save you time, but it will help you follow the law.

Note the following recordkeeping requirements as described by the Equal Employment Opportunity Commission (EEOC) (eeoc.gov/employers/recordkeeping.cfm).

EEOC Regulations require that employers keep all personnel or employment records for one year. If an employee is involuntarily terminated, his/her personnel records must be retained for one year from the date of termination.

Under ADEA recordkeeping requirements, employers must also keep all payroll records for three years. Additionally, employers must keep on file any employee benefit plan (such as pension and insurance plans) and any written seniority or merit system for the full period the plan or system is in effect and for at least one year after its termination.

Under Fair Labor Standards Act (FLSA) recordkeeping requirements applicable to the EPA, employers must keep payroll records for at least three years. In addition, employers must keep for at least two years all records (including wage rates, job evaluations, seniority and merit systems, and collective bargaining agreements) that explain the basis for paying different wages to employees of opposite sexes in the same establishment.

THESE REQUIREMENTS APPLY TO ALL EMPLOYERS COVERED BY FEDERAL ANTI-DISCRIMINATION LAWS, REGARDLESS OF WHETHER A CHARGE HAS BEEN FILED AGAINST THE EMPLOYER.

☞ ***CROSS REFERENCE BOOKMARK: REFER TO CHAPTER 15, HABIT #1***

Habit #7 – Respect People's Privacy

During the natural course of job performance, recruiters will become privy to sensitive, personal information about others. Obviously, some information must be shared with stakeholders in the hiring process, but even in the absence of a legal requirement to keep such information confidential, think twice or even thrice before disclosing the following about a candidate or employee to a third party:

- Reasons behind hiring decisions
- Compensation including salary history
- Contents of reference letters or conversations with references
- Personal information uncovered during background checks
- Reasons for an individual's separation from a former employer
- Contents of academic transcripts or other records
- Any information that may cast an individual in a negative light
- Family information
- Medical disclosures
- Information regarding any past or pending legal actions
- Miscellaneous personal disclosures, even if seemingly neutral

Even if the information you reveal is not negative about an individual, the fact that you revealed any information at all could be construed as suspect and chip away at your credibility as well as lead others to make mistaken inferences. When your candidates are future colleagues, it is particularly important to remember that your comments contribute to corporate culture and atmosphere. Plus, it must be the candidate's choice to share personal information with co-workers later. If you must share information, make sure disclosures are in line with your duties and responsibilities. Also, take care to safeguard your files to avoid inadvertent leaks of information. When people see your efforts to respect others, they will know that you respect them.

Habit #8 – Actively Increase Your Subject Matter Expertise

As with any job, the more experience you have, the more knowledgeable you will be about your profession, and attending professional development and training events will only help you gain subject matter expertise. If your organization does not offer an internal formal training program, seek a budget to train yourself using external options: Membership in a professional association, association conferences and events, subscriptions to newsletters and other industry journals, and coursework at local educational institutions. If your organization cannot provide a budget for outside training, bear the expense yourself and find out if it is eligible for a business expense deduction from taxable income. If you cannot afford the expense, actively undertake to educate and train yourself using free resources. Investing time and resources in your own brain will always pay a dividend. After all, an education cannot be taken away from you, and perhaps one day you too will enter the job market.

Increasing your subject matter expertise means gaining knowledge about all aspects of your industry and market, including your potential clients and competitors. Apply the research methodologies discussed in Chapter 3 to develop your business intelligence, and use your acquired business intelligence to cultivate strong working relationships with your hiring managers and deliver effective job performance.

Habit #9 – Keep Your Computer Skills Up-To-Date

Many software companies provide certification to demonstrate your computer proficiency and to keep you up-to-date. Take whatever certification programs your resources allow. In the meantime, here are some time-saving shortcuts that will boost your productivity during the workday.

Quick-keys. Quick-keys are the best way of going after what you want done fast. Most people are familiar with basic keystroke functions, and here are others used by Windows and Outlook.

Windows Control Key

Mac users *Replace the Control key with/Command key.*

Navigation

Alt+Tab: Switches between windows. Hold down Alt+Tab to show a list of open windows. While holding down Alt key, press Tab repeatedly to scan through all the windows. Release Alt to switch to the window selected. On Vista, use the key instead of Alt for a better view.

- Ctrl+A: Selects or highlights all of the text in a document or Web page
- Ctrl+End: Jump to bottom of an open document or web page
- Ctrl+F: Find - displays a dialog box – type a word and search for it the open document
- Ctrl+Home: Opposite of Ctrl+End, jumps to the beginning of the document/page
- Ctrl+M: Mail - opens the default Mail application
- Ctrl+W: Close current document
- Esc: Closes a dialog box without performing any other action

Formatting

- Ctrl+B: Bold - applies bold to highlighted characters
- Ctrl+C: Copy - copies highlighted text to the Clipboard
- Ctrl+I: Italics - applies italics to highlighted characters
- Ctrl+K: Clears – removes all formatting (bold, italics, etc.)
- Ctrl+P: Prints the document/page currently open
- Ctrl+S: Saves the current document

- Ctrl+U: Underline - applies underline to highlighted text
- Ctrl+V: Pastes the text placed in the clipboard when using Ctrl+C
- Ctrl+X: Cuts out highlighted text and places a copy on the clipboard
- Ctrl+Z: Undo last action

Outlook

- Alt+S: Saves and closes an email message, contact, calendar item, task or note
- Ctrl+Shift+C: Create new contact
- Ctrl+Shift+M: Create a new email message
- Ctrl+Shift+K: Create a new task
- Ctrl+Shift+U: Create a new task request (to assign)
- Ctrl+Shift+N: Create a new note
- Ctrl+Shift+A: Create a new appointment
- Ctrl+Shift+Q: Create new meeting request
- Ctrl+Shift+E: Create a new email folder
- Ctrl+R: Reply to currently highlighted or opened message
- Ctrl+F: forwards an email message, contact, calendar item, task or note
- Ctrl+1: Takes you to the inbox window (Ctrl+2 Calendar, Ctrl+3 Contacts, Ctrl+4 Tasks)

> ***Mac users*** *Replace Ctrl key with the Command key.*
> *Other OS X keyboard shortcuts listed here: http://support.apple.com/kb/HT1343*

View sites in text-only mode. To speed up your search on the Internet, turn off the images in your Web browser. On Google Chrome, you can disable images under its "Settings" menu, and on Google Opera you can do the same under its "Pages" menu. Note that turning off images will render certain websites unreadable. Also, in this day and age when Internet connections are much faster than even five years ago, disabling images may not be necessary to save your time. Check the speed of your connection to make this determination.

Increase your cache. Files you download are stored in a cache on your hard drive; so when you return to a site, it is unnecessary to download the files again— just access them from your cache. After a while, though, the cache becomes full. Your Web browser automatically deletes old files as you continue to surf the Web. However, if you visit many of the same sites regularly, you can speed up access by increasing the size of your cache in your "Temporary Internet files" section.

Personalize your screen. Most software programs and websites have widgets or icons for instant access that you can install on your computer screen, Web browser, and smart phone. Take the time to personalize and coordinate all three so that you can access information immediately. If you do not want to divulge personal information, downloading free applications and their widgets onto your device, then pay the fee, which is usually nominal, where possible.

Format the resume for easy viewing. Once you have saved a resume as text on your hard drive, you can open it up in MS Word and 1) auto format, 2) use bullets to remove word wrap, or 3) use the "Find and Replace" function to highlight the keywords for your hiring manager's easy viewing.

Refer to a handy Gmail Shortcuts guide in the back section of this book.

Habit #10 – Use Your Brain

"Even if you're on the right track, you will get run over if you just sit there." —Will Rogers

If you find that your current habits are disconnected from the ones described above, consider how your practices deviate from them and whether they uphold or fall short of the spirit behind each habit. So long as you have a prudent practice in place, carry on and perhaps use the commentary herein as a reference point for your activities. You are not a robot, and you can best judge for yourself what are the best means to accomplish your goals.

Chapter 17
Looking into the Future of Recruiting

Many predictions have been made regarding the future of recruiting: Facebook will replace LinkedIn™; social recruiting will rise; Sourcing will become a data dump; ATS will become obsolete; and even specialized onboarding will make recruiters obsolete. Regardless of the widely varying credibility of the previous statements, there is one declaration that is consistently voiced by recruiting experts everywhere: The future of recruiting lies in mobile recruiting.

Section 1. Mobile Recruiting Is the Future

The Oscar-nominated movie *Sabrina* features Humphrey Bogart as Linus Larrabee, a baron of industry who falls in love with the chauffeur's daughter portrayed by the incomparable Audrey Hepburn. What is remarkable about this film, besides the fashion and glamour of old Hollywood, is that it is the first film to feature a wireless telephone, which Linus uses from his chauffeured limousine. This "special effect" was not movie magic. Indeed, the film was released in 1954, but the first wireless telephone had already been successfully installed in an automobile in 1946. For almost 50 more years, wireless telephones would remain a luxury item associated with extreme wealth and exclusivity. Perhaps the single greatest innovation in communication since the "car phone" is the handheld mobile cell phone.

Big Picture: *People once paid for e-mail accounts, yet they no longer do. Today, millions pay for SMS messages and the growing trend is for those to become free, as well. It does not take much extrapolation to see where this is going – that SMS will replace e-mail. Is LinkedIn™ ready to change InMail to InText?*

A Brief Review of the Mobile Phone Landscape

Only in the early 1990s did second generation (2G) digital technology emerge that made cellular (i.e. wireless) phones affordable and available to mass markets. By 1997, there were nearly 50 million wireless subscribers in America. Subscriptions grew to 135 million over the next five years, a 170 percent increase. Another five years later, and the number of subscriptions nearly doubled to 244 million. By 2012, wireless subscriptions had surpassed the 320 million mark. There are an estimated 315 million people in the United States, which means that there is more than one mobile subscription per person in the country (www.census.gov).

Even people who rarely use computers have a cell phone that they use on a daily basis. The fact that more than one in three homes in America have no landline phones demonstrates owners' growing reliance on cell phones. Of course, cell phones now serve greater functions than the basic one that even two cans on either end of a string can accomplish.

Texting

Short Message Service (SMS) is usually referred to as text messaging or texting. Texting is the most widely used cell phone application. Texts are limited to 160 characters per message. There is also Multimedia Messaging Service (MMS), which refers to mobile messages that contain some combination of text, images, audio, and video.

Cell phones are increasingly used for their SMS functions instead of for voice calls. In the U.S., it was reported as early as 2008 that texting is more widely used than voice calls. (http://news.cnet.com/8301-1035_3-10048257-94.html) Currently, 6.1 billion text messages are sent per day, which means 72,085 text messages are sent every second. Contrary to popular belief, it is not just kids who text these days. An astonishing 72 percent of those between the ages of 25 and 49 use text messaging as well as 53 percent of those who are 35 years-old and up. People often respond faster to SMS faster than they do to email on their desktop (www.ctia.org/advocacy/research/index.cfm/aid/10323).

A related message service feature is the ability to employ Common Short Codes (CSC). CSC are short numeric codes to which SMS or MMS can be sent from mobile devices. They are usually five or six digits long, can be assigned to one company or identity, and are commonly "rented" to or otherwise shared with many companies. These short codes facilitate an interactive mobile experience between the consumer and host company. Examples of CSC can be found in voting schemes such as by competitive reality shows or political campaigns. Visit the Common Short Code Administration (CSCA) website for more information.

Internet Access

Another function that cell phones provide in growing numbers is Internet access and browsing. As of February 2012, half of American adults owned a smart-phone, up from 36 percent in the previous year. In addition, on those smart-phones, Americans used more than 1.1 trillion megabytes (MB) of data from July 2011 to June 2012, an increase of 104 percent over the previous 12 months' usage. The mobile audience is growing faster than that for PCs/desktop, partially because smart-phones are relatively inexpensive and easy to use (www.ctia.org/advocacy/research/index.cfm/aid/10323).

Other mobile phone functions less commonly used than texting and Internet browsing but still popular are camera (camcorder, scanner, image recognition, and enhanced reality), email, calendar, video chatting, and media streaming. Mobile applications that incorporate cell phone functions use Wireless Application Protocol (WAP) to customize their services for wireless devices.

Mobile Device Implies Mobile Owner

The central advantage of smart-phones is that owners are no longer tethered to their desktop or laptops in a stationary or sitting position. Smart-phone users are free to make themselves mobile because their infrastructure is also. This central advantage is also not limited to an actual cell phone as more handheld wireless devices such as tablets, e-readers, and game consoles are used as mobile browsers.

Mobile Owner Implies Mobile Workplace

A modern day maxim is that mobile breeds more mobile. Just using their mobile device, on-the-go employees can handle most work responsibilities in the in-between moments as they walk, run errands, go on vacation, or attend meetings about other work. In this way, smart-phone users multitask just as their devices do. Work is also accomplished at all hours because cell phones are frequently the first and last thing users look at each day.

Not all work accomplished using a wireless device is for the sake of convenience to the employee or undertaken in the in-between moments. Historically, certain industries such as healthcare and sales have always required their employees to be mobile, but mobile devices encourage formerly sedentary office workers to migrate far from office complexes and carry out their job functions from home, on the road, or anywhere else business or work style requires. This migratory trend is a substantial factor in the estimation that one-in-three people will work online instead of in an office by 2020 (informationweek.com/byte/personal-tech/science-technology/).

Expanded bandwidth also makes possible Internet activities on mobile devices, and many wireless subscribers elect to pay for enhanced Wi-Fi access. Also notable is the fact that half of public Wi-Fi connections are from mobile devices like the iPhone, iPod Touch, Android smartphones, and Sony PSPs, not laptops. (http://www.mashable.com/2010/02/24/jiwire-wi-fi-stats) Also with increased bandwidth, progressive mobile devices are evolving as remote controls for real-time, cloud-based services that will transform users' experience. (Market Report: *The Mobile Internet Report*. New York, NY: Morgan Stanley, 2009)

Section 2. The Current State of Mobile Recruiting

The ancient Greeks had two notions of time. *Chronos* refers to the actual passing of hours and days, the kind of time that a clock or watch measures. Kairos refers to time in a deeper way. *Kairos* represents the most opportune time or place. Imagine you are at a crossroads and the two roads that lie before you will forever change your path. *Kairos* refers to this moment in time. Recruiters and Sourcers are a kairos. Their employers can both choose mobile recruiting early and be innovators or they can ignore its sway and be laggards.

Companies like Facebook, Google, and Apple have really been the vanguard of mobile computing platforms. Their investments have led to wide approval and adoption of mobile applications. Moreover, these companies have profoundly impacted how people communicate with each other and how they spend their time. Much marketing hullaballoo has been made over the fact that one hundred percent of people who browse the Internet on their phone are intentional visitors, and this key piece of information is causing developers, advertisers, and vendors to re-strategize their methods of reaching consumers and where to spend marketing budgets.

The net result for recruiters is that the mainstream population is already accustomed to and reliant on mobile applications. Consequently, the audiences companies see to reach already expect those organizations to become mobile and will develop negative perceptions of companies without a specifically mobile presence.

This transition does not actually have to be expensive. Free solutions from developers are readily available. For instance, companies can sign up for the mobile services of websites like Weebly.com, Tumblr.com, and getsharesquare.com. Even paid services are inexpensive. These include Movitas and bMobilized. For five dollars a month bMobilized will mobilize your site in 30 seconds and host it.

Most companies that already provide recruiting services online are translating their services into mobile applications. Thus, candidates can now install recruitment and job search apps onto their devices. Recruiting industry websites with social networking capabilities are aware of this shift and the shift it produces in their behavior: Those candidates are now more likely to use mobile apps than PC/desktop versions of the sites. These applications use existing content as the basis for their offerings. The content models of new market entrants are fresh because they rely solely on mobile platforms. Companies like JobKaster and Kauzu link GPS navigation and real-time location-based services to the job search. Basically, any individual can check into a location, access open job postings, and then apply on the spot.

The issue for recruiters to resolve is whether any of these mobile solutions will result in a better talent pool, resolve current recruiting challenges, or create new ones.

Section 3. Mobile Recruiting Is Here to Stay

Top Ten Reasons

#10 Increased Usage

Google has reported a rapid increase in mobile Internet searches and usage continuously since 2008.

#9 Bye-bye Landlines

Over a third – 34 percent – of U.S. households have abandoned landline telephones in favor of mobile phones.

#8 "Snack Sized Portions"

Highly relevant content in "snack-sized" portions are passed around, an example of viral marketing at its best.

- The average response rate to a mobile Call To Action is 12 percent versus 2 percent for traditional media.
- Open rates for messages are three times that of email. Over 90 percent of text messages are read by the recipient.
- Click-through rates are up to 25 times higher than those for email, and the average time to open a mobile marketing message is 30 minutes while email's average is 24 hours.
- Most forms of advertising are experiencing a decline in viewership on traditional computers and notebooks, but the same is not true for mobile devices. Media analysts estimate that mobile ad sales rose in 2010 while ad sales for traditional media outlets decreased 15 percent in the same time period. (jackmyers.com)
- Mobile rich media advertising neared $2.8 billion in 2012, which matters to recruiters because of the axiom, "Where there is money, there are candidates!"

#7 Ubiquity

Mobile devices have become more ubiquitous than traditional PCs. There are four billion mobile phone subscriptions on the planet and only 1 billion PC owners. (gsmworld.com, http://ctia.org)

- Over 50 percent of U.S. mobile phone subscribers use text messaging. More than 76 percent of consumers aged 18-24 communicate via this medium.

- In 1997, there were 50 million subscribers. This figure grew to 135 million by to 2002, and 244 million in 2007. By 2012, it had surpassed 320 million users in the United States. With an estimated population of 311 million people, that means there is more than one mobile subscription per person in the country.
- Mobile subscribers now represent 70 percent of the world's population, and this figure has not yet plateaued.
- Today's teenagers text more than talk. (harrisinteractive.com) In fact, the average teen sends or receives 3,339 texts a month. (nielsen.com/us/en/measurement) These teens are tomorrow's interns and salespeople and managers and CEOs.

#6 Wide Adoption

FierceMobileIT reports that there will be an estimated one billion VoIP (Voice-over Internet Protocol) users by 2017 (fiercemobilit.com/press-releases).

#5 Nielsen Reports

- Text messaging, both sending and receiving, has risen 450 percent in the past two years. In the U.S., 262 million mobile subscribers pay for SMS and send over 75 billion text messages a month or 6.1 billion per day. That's 72,085 text messages sent every second, and not just for kids- 53 percent of texts are from people 35 and older.
- Mobile Internet extends the audience reach of leading sites by an average of 13 percent more than PC traffic alone.
- More than 1-in-10 people (13.7 percent) actively use mobile Internet each month, and 87 million U.S. mobile users subscribe to mobile Internet services (nielsen.com/us/en/measurement/)

#4 All Work AND All Play

By 2020, work and play will be seamless. Well-connected knowledge workers will eliminate the industrial-age boundaries between work and personal time. (http://www.elon.edu/e-web/predictions/expertsurveys/)

#3 Obsolescence

You will be rendered obsolete if you do not go mobile. The mobile device will be the primary connection tool to the Internet for most people in the world by 2020 (http://pewinternet.org/Reports/)

#2 Affordability

Not only will mobile phones be the primary or sole Internet connection for the majority of the world's population, they will remain affordable.

AND... #1 Accessibility

Your prospects use the Web on their mobile phones privately while waiting in line, going to lunch, taking a coffee break, where their employers cannot watch them!

Section 4. Your Mobile Recruiting Launch

In many ways, a mobile recruiting launch will not affect how you do business. You may still use the same vendors that have already initiated their mobile recruiting efforts, or you may simply switch vendors with capabilities that suit your new strategies. At the same time, integrating a mobile recruiting model represents an entire paradigm shift that raises a key question: How will it affect a recruiter's work?

Policy Change

Before any mobile recruiting strategies are operational, organizations must first arrive at the policy decision to adopt them. For early adopters, technophiles who embrace the latest and greatest technologies in their field, this decision is easy, and these managers will quickly mobilize their efforts. For those laggards at the other end of the spectrum, this policy change may appear irrelevant or intimidating.

Small business owners are the most probable managers who will view a proposed policy change favoring mobile recruiting as irrelevant to them. They may have always relied on word-of-mouth or other traditional methods and may not think the shift is worth undertaking because it had never been necessary before to make technology-related policy changes. These owners know they are cutting their access to top talent, but they are content with their relative isolation because they are and always have been satisfied with their current level of business.

Larger companies that are put off by perceived increases in recruiting costs may take such a stand because they are in a weakened financial condition overall. Otherwise, why would they not merely re-appropriate capital?

Other companies that lag do so to minimize current recruiting costs and thus overhead. If a larger company has already invested substantially in their current recruiting strategy that depends on today's most popular

PC-based or limited mobile recruiting presence, they may seek to amortize this cost over a longer length of time. In the latter case, then, it really is just a matter of time when these companies will switch to mobile recruiting strategies.

Individuals within recruiting departments who are laggards may not currently maximize the capability of their own mobile devices, or they may be more comfortable with and attracted to the "people business" aspect of recruiting. These recruiters may repurpose their functions to draw themselves closer to those nexus points where recruiting and human interaction occur, although that may never be closer than a Skype or FaceTime conversation.

The truth of the matter is that change is afoot, and the impending tidal wave of mobile recruiting presents an "evolve or die" scenario. If employers want to remain competitive in the talent search, the decision to institute this policy change becomes an issue of when instead of whether. If Luddites do not embrace or at least incorporate aspects of this change, they will become extinct, even as the community of recruiting professionals transforms itself into a more mobile savvy body.

Resource Allocations

The biggest area affected by a policy change favoring mobile recruiting will be an organization's budget allocations. Before managers can decide where to spend money, they must make several initial determinations dealing with the demographic information of their target audience.

- Who comprises their audience?
- What platform do they use? iOS? Android? Or Blackberry?
- Are they currently mobile? How mobile are they?
- How mobile is the organization? How mobile does the organization expect candidates to be once they are hired?

Next, managers should decide how mobile recruiting would affect individual job duties and responsibilities, which raises all manner of questions that only they can decide. The three key factors are intrinsically tied to the nature of the device itself: Time because access to mobile devices is ever-present, size because these devices have smaller screens, and geography because mobile devices are, well, "mobile". The last factor has particular bearing on Sourcing functions.

Time

Will the pace of communication between prospects and recruiters be so swift that recruiters must devote large chunks of time in a single sitting as they go back and forth with prospects or risk losing their interest because the entire industry's pace has sped up?

Will mobile recruiting require dedicated messengers?

Size

- How will information be presented?
- How will recruiters, historically non-specialists in the skill for which they are recruiting, break down job postings for use on a small screen?
- How much do candidates care about visual style?
- How will technological concerns affect the look of our mobile presence?
- How will we coordinate PC/desktop and mobile strategies?

Geography

- How can we use real-time information about candidates' locations (using GPS features) to enhance candidates' experiences during the application and interview stage?
- Should we provide turn-by-turn directions to candidates and applicants so that they do not have to exit our application?
- Is it possible to provide "orientation" and campus maps or guides to candidates on their interview day?
- Do we even need the candidate to come in for an interview or should we use video chatting to conduct interviews?
- Can we show candidates real estate comps when they apply for jobs requiring relocation?

Outsourcing Mobile Recruiting

It is entirely possible that organizational decision-makers will never have to rack their brains in answering the questions above. For them, they care how much the transition to mobile recruiting will cost, what third party provides the best options, and who in the recruiting department will handle oversight. Not enough data has been collected to know what solutions are best.

Section 5. Employer as App Developer

Despite that the dust has not yet settled, one thing is certain: The rise of mobile recruiting will encourage/coerce more and more employers to become app developers, which they can either accomplish in-house or via an external third party. As an app developer, the issues already common to this world will now apply to employers whose core business may have nothing to do with them already.

User-supplied Data

Employers will gain competitive intelligence (e.g. biographical or other professional profile-like information) and must decide what to do, if anything, with the information.

Social Networking

Employers can enter deals with social networks or other applications already existing on social networks to share information such as people who are mutual connections or who work at the company. In this arrangement, employers do not have to set up their own Facebook page unless Facebook changes yet again the terms of its use. Recruiters will have greater access to users' networks.

Social Check-Ins

When people "check in" to a store or other business location using apps like Foursquare or Facebook, employers can create candidates' consumer profiles or identify suspects based on the places they visit, which has great Sourcing implications. As employers build their base of demographic information, they can then forge strategic partnerships with other businesses either to share information or use the information for company-wide strategies. Social check-ins provide irrefutable data that can form the basis of advanced, multi-dimensional metrics. And obviously, since people check in at venues local to their home area, you can find out where your candidates live.

Branding

A mobile presence is another way to give potential candidates the opportunity to notice and learn about your company. Concurrently, employers can directly monitor sentiment about their company and employment brand. Plus, employers can use geographic information to publicize its important events such as conferences and expos to promote company awareness.

Section 6. Legal Perspectives on Mobile Recruiting

This section is not a comprehensive discussion on all legal matters related to mobile recruiting. Instead, it is intended to give you a one hundred-foot view of your work and to help you think about the corresponding social and policy issues. For that reason, some abstract principles are touched upon. These topics are typically discussed in informal circles over lunch or one-on-one conversations that usually end with the questions, "but what are you gonna do? Well what can you do?" The answers to these questions are not contained herein; rather, they are left to the legislators, policy advisors, legal departments, regulators, and private technological innovators.

"Do not seek to follow in the footsteps of the men of old; seek what they sought." – Basho

It is important to think about these topics for a couple reasons. First, having a basic knowledge of legal issues related to your work increases your expertise. You can better understand the context for trends in recruiting and why crucial mistakes and successes occur. Second, you are also a consumer, and what follows affects you not only professionally but also personally. Nowhere in this text are recruiters presumed to be mindless automatons who lack intelligence or reasoning ability. The fervor behind privacy debates and news regarding perceived breaches underscores the substantial numbers of the population that are interested in these topics.

If you are interested in pursuing the issues presented here further, consult a legal specialist or legal resources, which include myriad textbooks strictly devoted to the fields of labor and employment law and constitutional law.

Labor and Employment Law

The advent of mobile recruiting is not likely to cause any big changes in the field of labor and employment law. In fact, no significant changes in labor laws have been made since The New Deal era when Franklin Delano Roosevelt was president. So, to understand the relationship between mobile recruiting and the law is merely to apply an old law to new constructs, which the courts have done for decades.

When recruiters select vendors that offer their own methodologies to find new talent pools, your service agreement must address a few key issues:

Federal and Local Law Compliance

Be sure to ask the right questions to ensure their models do not discriminate against protected classes that may be tied to certain locations and insert appropriate language in the vendor's warranties and representations.

Liability Issues

Negotiate carefully who bears the liability of cost in the event that a violation of labor or employment law is discovered.

Confidentiality

Determine how the vendor will use candidate information. Ensure that the agreement contains language, which ensures the vendor's policies are aligned with your own.

By addressing these issues beforehand, you can better manage your own risk of liability, and be more confident that you can freely enjoy vendors' services.

Section 7. Privacy

Right to Privacy

As with labor and employment law, there has been no new legislation in several years, and courts will apply the same old laws to new constructs. Basic privacy rights can be found in the

Fourth Amendment to the Constitution: "The right of the people to be secure in their persons, houses, papers, and effects, against unreasonable searches and seizures, shall not be violated, and no Warrants shall issue, but upon probable cause, supported by Oath or affirmation, and particularly describing the place to be searched, and the persons or things to be seized." This amendment only refers to actions by the federal government, but each of the fifty states has incorporated a similar provision into their state constitutions, so state governments cannot violate these rights either.

Just in case you were wondering... Supreme Court Justice John Marshall Harlan established a two-pronged test to determine whether there has been a privacy violation in Katz v. United States (1967). In his decision, Justice Harlan wrote, "My understanding of the rule that has emerged from prior decisions is that there is a twofold requirement, first that a person have exhibited an actual (subjective) expectation of privacy and, second, that the expectation be one that society is prepared to recognize as 'reasonable.'" Again, this test only applies actions by the federal government.

If constitutional privacy rights only apply to actions by governments, then how do private citizens including corporations figure into these issues?

Private citizens can become involved in multiple ways. One way is that the government demands that you give them documents you obtained legally. If the government acted unconstitutionally, it is the bad actor, but that does not mean a person's sensitive information was not exposed nor does it mean that private citizens did not bear the burden, expense, and general hassle of complying the government's demand. In this scenario, private citizens are victims of a government that has exceeded its power. For example, there have been recent cases involving government agencies that improperly obtained citizens' text and email messages. Public outrage followed each time. In these cases, the ease of asking the network or email provider to pony up the messages was too alluring and begs the question: Just because information is easily discoverable using technology, should it be made easily available?

Another way that private citizens can become entangled in privacy issues is when they break laws made by federal and state legislatures intended to protect the privacy of other private citizens. For example, doctors are required by law to protect your medical records. If they do not, they must face the legal consequences of their actions. Another way private citizens become entangled is when users misrepresent facts about themselves or others that lead to negative consequences. In 2012, a prominent film director tweeted the address of a person he thought was guilty of murder except that he posted the wrong address. The innocent residents who lived at the wrong address had to move into a hotel to flee from the negative attention, and the director had to pay a settlement to them to avoid further legal consequences.

As you can see, privacy related issues cover a wide expanse of actions with similar destructive results.

Privacy Issues...Old as Dirt

Since the dawn of humanity, there have arisen issues regarding personal privacy. So long as there was more than one person, there was someone else to interfere in that person's business. Is it any wonder that the U.S. Constitution, the world's oldest living and arguably best form of government, specifically addresses issues of personal privacy? Considering the age of privacy issues, the format adopted here is to utilize the apt words of others that demonstrate the timelessness and universality of the issues discussed, followed by brief comments.

"Who are you? Why do you hide in the darkness and listen to my private thoughts?" — William Shakespeare, Romeo and Juliet

When people find themselves in thorny situations, their first action is usually to conduct an Internet search about it. Before the Internet, people might have visited a doctor or a lawyer, professionals who must keep your information confidential by law, to address their concerns. Now that people turn to the Internet first, the confidentiality of your concerns is backed only by company policy with little force of law. Furthermore, you are entering search terms that are not just stored in company files but can be traced back to your IP address, identifying you. It is more than a little dismaying to consider that some websites may know your every worry and problem. In the defense of large keyword repositories, many companies including Google and Bing have been lauded for their respect for users and their policies intended to maintain your anonymity. Still, there are billions of other websites from around the globe on the Internet with different practices.

"Everyone will be famous for 15 minutes."
—Andy Warhol, Pop Artist

Your every Internet action publicizes your activities to an organization. No matter the device, mobile or PC/Desktop, remnants of you linger behind.

Even if you are careful with your activities, a careless friend or associate can wreck your perfect Internet history with one terrible picture or post. An unknown person can do the same just because someone else has the same name as you. These posts can definitely live on the cloud for longer than 15 minutes.

Colleges are now helping their graduates clean up their online presence by helping them contact the right individuals and post their own vanity sites, so they are the ones that pop up first on any Google search instead of some other piffle. In essence, people are forced to make affirmative disclosures first to protect their image and reputations.

In the free mobile application model, publicity is an essential part of the transaction: You derive benefit from the service for no monetary cost in exchange for their knowledge about you. Often, there is an option to pay for the application to avoid their collecting personal data, but most users do not select it. Think about how much you value your privacy. Then, consider that you gave it away for something that could have cost you a couple bucks. The longer you continue to use free applications, the more personal information you reveal and that is collected from you. Many mobile platforms have user agreements that prohibit malicious use of collected data, but there is no significant legislation in place that adequately addresses privacy issues raised by mobile application technology.

"If you have something that you do not want anyone to know, maybe you shouldn't be doing it in the first place."
—Eric Schmidt, Executive Chairman, Google

Schmidt's quote zeroes in on the fact that many privacy issues are really public scrutiny issues. Sometimes people do not want to face the public scrutiny for their bad acts, and there is something to be said for the notion that people should accept accountability for their actions. At the same time, his words do not sit well. The denotation and origin of the word "should" implies a moral obligation. By using this word, Schmidt implies that people have the moral obligation not to do things they do not want others to know. This is a logical inference with a preposterous meaning. Whether people behave in an ethical manner towards others and how best to carry out ethical obligations are at the crux of religious and philosophical debates and represent deeply personal choices. Even if Schmidt's remark was merely flippant, it nevertheless preys on people's self-doubts, which is the spirit behind a bully's actions.

Moreover, it overwhelms mental capacity if individuals are expected to adhere to this standard for even their smallest decisions.

"You already have zero privacy. Get over it."
— Scott G. McNealy, CEO and Co-Founder, Sun Microsystems

Yet more words from another tycoon of technology. The U.S. Constitution was envisioned as the floor of human rights, meaning states could grant citizens even further protections under the 10th Amendment. The Supreme Court has well established that people should expect privacy, from the federal government at the very least, so McNealy's words are facially at odds with the Supreme Court. But perhaps McNealy is commenting that in practice and not theory, citizens have no privacy. The problem with this interpretation is that his second sentence, "Get over it", indicates that people should discard their expectations of privacy, which are clearly supported by the Constitution, the supreme law of the land.

"The real danger is the gradual erosion of individual liberties through automation, integration, and interconnection of many small, separate record-keeping systems, each of which alone may seem innocuous, even benevolent, and wholly justifiable."
— U. S. Privacy Study Commission, 1977

The U.S. Privacy Study Commission was an ad hoc group of politicos formed to analyze the 1974 Privacy Act. The Commission's purpose was merely advisory, and as such, it had no authority to initiate changes to public policy – only to recommend them. This quote is included here because it embodies the issue at heart of technologically related privacy debates: That when taken together, "separate record-keeping systems" do, in fact diminish individual liberties. Some may wonder what difference it makes and why Americans cannot, as McNealy stated, "get over it".

One possible source that may assist in addressing these concerns is the Declaration of Independence which states, "all experience hath shewn, that mankind are more disposed to suffer, while evils are sufferable, than to right themselves by abolishing the forms to which they are accustomed." Perhaps technology users are so accustomed to current policies that they suffer their "evils" because they are bearable. Plus, users do not right themselves because the policies in place have not yet reached the point where they evince an "absolute tyranny" over them, thus absolutely necessitating their abolishment.

Implications for Recruiting

Most mobile applications raise privacy concerns. When recruiting efforts latch onto mobile enterprises, they likewise affirmatively take upon themselves the risk that privacy concerns will impact them. Despite the fact that new issues have arisen and are quite serious, however, the number one risk of liability to recruiting activities stems from discrimination claims in the area of labor and employment law. Therefore, when implementing mobile recruiting strategies, your first priority should be compliance with laws against discrimination and second comes privacy.

☞ *CROSS REFERENCE BOOKMARK: FOR FURTHER DISCUSSION REFER TO CHAPTER 15, HABIT #1*

> **Nota Bene:** *By virtue of their job, Sourcers must pay attention to privacy laws because they are digging for information not easily accessible. When considering Sourcing and privacy issues, the critical factor here is who has the primary burden to prevent privacy breaches: the program or website that first publicizes the information. The general rule of Sourcing is that so long as information is on a public Web page, it is publicly available information. Thus, the Sourcers' activities are bounded by the privacy policies of the program or website, and this fact will remain true whether the program or website adopts a broad or narrow privacy policy.*

Section 8. Working Remotely

To end a chapter on the future of recruiting, there is no more apt topic than working remotely. Recruiting, particularly Sourcing functions, is a job that can be done from anywhere, lending itself almost perfectly to telecommuting and virtual workplaces.

Reports about the number of workers who telecommute vary drastically because each organization has different biases on what is considered a remote worker. One commonality among all reports is that working remotely is on the rise. Based on a rough approximation of most reports, a generous estimate of U.S. workers who "dial in" to work is about 30 million. About half of these people are road warriors, and the other half are small business employees or self-employed. Of the latter half, almost three million work remotely full-time.

Author's Note: Telecommuting Troubles

Yes - you can skip a shower, work in your pajamas, hit the gym at less crowded times, run to your favorite coffee shop whenever you need a fix, and finish your errands in off-peak hours, but there are downsides to working from home. Indeed, it is not quite so rosy as has been romanticized. If you already work from home, then you probably already know this reality. To help you plan your telecommuting strategies, here are the challenges that are most often encountered.

Lack of face time: Telecommuting really embodies the adage "out of sight, out of mind". Even if your organization does not prize old fashioned face time, being away from the main office can sometimes lead to your being ignored or left out of communications, including vital feedback to ensure tasks are completed well. Thus, you are vulnerable to an impaired communication flow, and that damaged flow of communication can extend into uncertainty about expectations on both sides. Telecommuting recruiters must be vigilant about using direct communication channels, for second or third-hand information is never so clear or accurate as that which is obtained directly from the source. Further, you will also likely have to work harder to be noticed in order to secure a raise, or to win a promotion. For these reasons, it is very important to maintain your own system of metrics and performance assessment.

Lack of focus: Staying on task can be much more difficult from a cozy home setting replete with the entertainment, comforts, and distractions of everyday living. A locked door to a home office is a fortification that children, spouses, and pets can easily penetrate, creating chaos in your virtual workplace. Further, multitasking personal and professional activities is counterproductive and hurts the outcome you achieve in both. So, when you are at home, stay focused on either work or personal affairs at any one time. And finally, beware of letting the "details" of working at home get in the way of your performing at your peak. For example, a computer or printer problem can capture your attention and diminish your focus on your recruiting activities.

Lack of teambuilding: Far less bonding occurs among coworkers when they are physically separated. Quick chats by the water cooler contribute just as much to teambuilding as do happy hours, work outings, or other organizational events that naturally take place by virtue of close physical proximity. Missing even the small lunchtime birthday celebration can leave you feeling disconnected, behind, lonely, or out of touch. Once in a while, it pays to videoconference into random work events, even if it's just to join in the birthday celebration for a coworker in the office. Also help people celebrate important professional achievements by sending a tangible gift such as a floral bouquet or food basket.

Lack of closure: The ritual of exiting an office often allows workers to release themselves mentally from work issues, so they can actually be "off the clock". When your home and workplace have little-to-no separation, however, you never leave your work behind you, and it can be easy to feel as if your work is ever finished. Plus, your computer or phone is often the first thing you reach for in the morning, which can immediately commence the workday - especially because you do not have to break for a shower or your commute. As a result, you end up working more hours than your office-based counterparts. Time passes much faster working from home, and you may find yourself in a 12-hour stretch of work before you realize you have missed lunch and dinner. Therefore, schedule regular breaks, and be careful not to overwork.

Are You Virtual Team Material?

Not everybody should telecommute. Some people like to work alone and can self-impose the discipline to maintain a virtual workplace. Others prefer to have constant direction, enjoy receiving peer approval or accolades, and crave structure, all of which can only be found in a physical workplace. If you view your workplace as a social outlet, then working remotely is not for you.

Success Factors

To make telecommuting viable, you **must** undertake several actions:

- Establish crystal clear expectations with your employer.

- Set goals for what you will accomplish daily, weekly and monthly, so you can track your progress or take notice if you are falling behind.
- Check in frequently with your team via telephone, email, or IM.
- Define boundaries with family and friends to avoid such interruptions as "Since you are working from home, can you walk the dog today please?" If you work from home and you have children or pets, you should still consider the same childcare or pet sitting services that you would have if you worked in a traditional office outside the home. Most importantly, be prepared to enforce the boundaries that you set.
- Use careful email language to avoid miscommunication or engendering ill will. Email is such an opaque medium that you can easily offend or be offended by mistake. Moreover, you can place others in a defensive position without realizing it through the words you choose to use in your messages. Since you cannot walk into coworkers' offices and clarify, explain or read their body language, carefully compose your emails to make your point and convey your thoughts without emotion. In fact, always write in a neutral fashion and wait for the right mood to place calls. When you feel chatty is a great time to make calls. Likewise, when you feel gruff is a good time to avoid social contact. Separate tasks in blocks according to the type or extent of social contact required. If you must make phone calls despite feeling less than social, try one of the techniques from cold calling: Stand up and smile while you talk on the phone.
- Embrace logic to carry you through when your thoughts and emotions are running wild. At home, you have fewer or no "sounding boards" that know the dynamics of your team and on which you can bounce what you are thinking. Left alone with your own thoughts, a vivid imagination can take you to a dark place. Consequently, take the time and care to reason things out with common sense. Furthermore, it may be a good idea to take advantage of good work relationships to identify a couple of individuals who can act as your own work consiglieres. When you find yourself feeling defensive or disconnected, stop and check in with them before you dive off the deep end and respond halfcocked to an email or other communication.

Home Office Requirements

Physical Space and Sense of Place

Maintain the sanctity of your work area. It is far more challenging to telecommute if you do so from the kitchen counter, the living room, or any other place where regular family life happens. At a minimum, you should have a desk or table entirely set aside for work. Invest in a functional desk, and do not pile personal bills, toys, receipts, homework, mail, papers, laundry or other "stuff from home" on your work surface. Buy a real office chair, one rated for 24 hours and not the cheap model on display at your local office equipment store, which is intended for occasional use, not a full day of work.

Never underestimate the impact of psychological factors relating to your workplace. In a perfect world, you have your own room with a door that locks to use as your workspace. The door is important because closing it at the end of a workday is a clear signal that you are finished for the day. When you leave the office, you can close the door and not be reminded of your work when you pass by the office.

Equip Yourself Adequately

Based on years of experience, we know that your "office gear" can be whittled down to a few essential items. What follows is a list of the essential hardware for your office as well as some things you should put in your travel bag.

- A VoIP phone that plugs right into a router, has two lines, can park and transfer calls, has a well built duplex speakerphone, and is headset compatible.
- A VoIP softphone you can run on your laptop. There are applications from Comcast, AT&T, Vonage, eyeBeam and many others.
- A virtual fax. Many solutions exist, including those from faxzero.com, efax.com and j2.com. VoIP providers like iTeleCenter also include virtual fax along with conference lines, mailboxes, and even voicemail transcription.
- A headset. Consider the Jabra GOTM 6470 which is wireless, has a touch screen base, and easily switches between cell phone, desk line and softphone. It has a 300-foot wireless range and six-hour talk time, so is great for lengthy conference calls.

- USB Personal Call Recorder so you can record calls instead of taking notes. This approach leaves you free to focus on asking questions. You can take notes from the audio file, or send it to a very inexpensive transcription service so you will have detailed notes at a fraction of the effort. If you use a softphone, this feature is built in. If you use a hard line you can pick up a call recorder from your local electronics store. Obtain one that plugs in between your handset and the cradle. Note your recordings are for your personal use only; do not share them with others, or you may be in violation of federal and state laws.
- Your health will thank you if you spend less time sitting, and more time standing. With an Ergotron WorkFit Sit-Stand workstation you can smoothly transition from chair to feet in one motion.
- Dual monitors. Install an inexpensive 19" to 23" second monitor and a dual monitor stand. Turn the smaller monitor vertical and use it to read resumes. If you can spring for the luxury of a 27" high-resolution widescreen monitor, simply split the screen into two.
- Webcam. Find something with an ultra-wide field of view, which provides automatic face tracking with autofocus to keep you on screen as you move around and works well in low light conditions such as when you're using a desk lamp rather than overhead lights, Typically, such systems also have a built-in microphone with echo-cancellation.
- Storage. A NAS or network attached storage device is an inexpensive way to store, share, stream, and safeguard your documents. DLink has an enclosure that lets you pop in two cheap high capacity SATA drives and is ready to go. Because it is networked, you do not attach it to a PC.
- Cloud storage. You can share files from your NAS to all your portable devices with services like SkyDrive, Google Drive, JungleDisk, and Dropbox.
- Communication. Subscribe to Skype, MSN, AIM (AOL) and/or Yahoo Messenger. Tools like Trillian will plug you into AIM, Windows Live, Yahoo, Google, Facebook, Jabber, Skype, Foursquare, Twitter, and LinkedIn™ all at once.
- Jott.com sends your voicemail as email or text messages; lets you call a number and add to your To Do list using just your voice; sends texts and emails hands-free; lets you "call in" your Twitter status, and even reads your RSS feeds aloud.

- Time tracking. Measure the time you spend on activities and tasks with applications from manictime.com (for billable hours), rescuetime.com (for time management), and aceproject.com (for project management).
- In-basket. Place your mail and the tasks you have yet to complete in an in-basket, both physical and virtual.

Personal Sanity and Mental Health

If you do telecommute, watch out for your mental state. Go out once in a while. Working from home can become lonely, so find social outlets and do not wait until you are starved for company to do so. Look for organizations in your area where you can interact with other professionals (see Meetup.com). Setting a regular schedule of work or just personal lunches or coffees outside of the house is also a productive way to break the monotony of working solo and keep you connected to the outside world. It may also be helpful to work outside the house on a weekly or monthly basis. For example, perhaps once a week you might head to a local café to complete some work. If you constantly isolate yourself, expect that you may undergo some changes without realizing it. Do an Internet search for the Moa bird to see a hyperbolic representation of what can happen.

Flash Reports

When you telecommute, your manager and your colleagues have no way of knowing if you are keeping busy, so results are more important than your level of activity. It is prudent to send regular updates on status, progress, any obstacles, and other issues that come up. Flash Reports are a short email that is easy to write and read, about 200 words, and less than half a page. It includes sentences or bullet points that answer these three questions:

1. What are the three most important things you accomplished this week?
2. What are the three most important things you will accomplish next week?
3. What do you need from your teammates in order to accomplish these things?

If you are a manager, ask your team to send these reports to you and respond with a brief comment. At the very least, these messages offer a good way to say "thank you" or "good job". They are also the perfect time to clarify or correct the direction of a quickly moving team member, before they spend a lot of time traveling in the wrong direction.

Now get busy. Start Sourcing. Seek and you will find.

Author's Final Remarks

"There are no new ideas. There are only new ways of making them felt." — Audre Lorde

Bright Shiny Object Syndrome plagues the recruitment industry just as it does most others, but there is something different when it comes to Sourcing. Spending time or money on the latest gadget, service, software, tool or technology just "because it's there" can be fatal to a recruitment effort. Not every available solution is appropriate to every environment.

To make matters worse, of course every vendor will tell you their product or service is "the only solution you need". Like snake oil salesmen of old, there is no such thing as a panacea for your Sourcing headaches.

Have we forgotten the practical adoption of appropriate technology? Sourcing and recruitment budgets are under pressure, so do not be bent out of shape when you don't get the budget you wanted for some new toy. Utilize the simplest level of technology that effectively achieves hiring goals, leverage existing internal resources, and be mindful of your target population's cultural and social outlook.

Inexpensive solutions are often ignored in favor of fancy costly ones with big marketing budgets and tons of venture capital investment money to spend. Even when parts of them work very well, these big solutions in turn are ineffectively utilized, not well implemented, or often fall cruelly short of what they promised.

Leaders must formulate integrated strategies that maximize resources already within the organization and make use of a mix of appropriate technology not yet considered. Cost is not the supreme measure of function. Technology decisions should be made based on the best use of resources, not on how expensive they are, how much hounding you received from their sales people, or the design quality of their marketing collateral. Inexpensive solutions can allow companies to hire faster by removing administrative, trivial or repetitive tasks from current recruitment process. Increased speed leads to reduced time-to-hire, which in turn leaves hiring managers more time to focus on critical business needs. Productivity gained from such strategies is difficult to measure in the short term, but becomes painfully obvious in the long term.

"Talent has overtaken risk as top of the CEO agenda." — PwC's 14th annual CEO survey (www.pwc.com/ceosurvey)

If talent is top priority for CEOs, why does recruitment remain reactive and not strategic? Except for in the rarest of organizations, recruitment is relegated to a reactionary role. Operating in sheer survival mode under the unrelenting pressure from hiring managers and job seekers alike, recruiters are inundated with urgent but seldom important requests. This fire drill atmosphere will remain the norm unless business leaders see that recruitment is directly tied to a modern organization's

most critical business imperative: Growth. The top four growth objectives for any business are:

1. Penetrating Emerging Markets
2. Gaining Sustainable Competitive Advantages
3. Innovating for Continued Marketplace Relevance and Value
4. Managing Resources Efficiently, Reducing Cost, Maximizing ROI

Did you notice how hiring is the single largest common denominator for all four? To hire you must recruit. So why is it that during the strategic planning process, leaders take a hard look at their current staff and play roll-the-dice with future headcount by ignoring strategic recruitment initiatives? Why do talent identification, attraction and engagement continue to be an afterthought for CEOs? Leaders in most fields of business consider professional and organizational development to be a paramount need. So, why is it that Staffing and Recruitment leaders are directed to spend the same or less year-over-year on developing their recruitment team?

Recruitment Marketing is a critical component but only one of several needed to be executed with synchronicity and efficiency to achieve greatness in attracting the right talent at the right time. Anything short of an integrated strategy involving all the following components remains tactical, no matter how well they are executed.

Team architecture: Because the primary role of a recruiter is ill-defined, it is nearly impossible to determine the need for dedicated Sourcers, talent community developers, and candidate developers accurately. Centralized, decentralized, or hybrid models all lack strong definitions. There is a great need for team structures that make better use of technology.

Direct sourcing: About 20 percent of critical talent simply will not respond to marketing. Finding talent and making connections is core to recruiting and while not all hires are critical, recruiters must be able to fend for themselves on the few that are. Recruiters need not be master researchers but they should be able to find a handful of critical leads.

Functional analytics: Many people refer to this as "Big Data" to differentiate from other types of analytics. For recruitment purposes, key metrics should demonstrate ROI and provide for a more efficient technology spend, yet the focus of most Applicant Tracking Systems remains risk management. Surveys suggest 70 percent of staffing leaders feel their marketing strategies are satisfactory, yet 62 percent admit to having inadequate or incorrect metrics. How can something be satisfactory when it is not adequately measured? You must be able to find details on every click and forward before investing. To ensure proper adoption and utilization of technology, systems must be capable of tracking every source without requiring manual input or extensive customization and administration. The data is there, but it is not being captured. Your vendors will not capture it accurately, if at all, until you make it clear to them that doing so is a core requirement for you to do business with them.

Career websites: Online prospects expect companies and their recruiters to be Web-savvy and provide a good user experience yet many organizations fail to remove technological obstacles by continuing to use ATS and CRM systems that do not communicate with the HRIS. Applicants demand convergence, integration and portability. Next-generation career websites allow applicants to use them however they want, and connect with employers on their own terms. Instead of making them go where you want them to go, you now have to be where they already are (e.g., Twitter, Facebook, LinkedIn™)

Sustainability: Nobody knows everything, but together we know most of what we need to perform at our peak. What's missing is a place to house our collective experiences and someone charged with managing the knowledge gained, putting it into practice, and creating organizational wisdom. For that to happen, leaders must nurture a center of excellence (CoE) and champion subject matter expertise so it is retained and build in-house instead of rented.

Recruiter development: Time is wasted keeping up with changes, experimenting with dead ends and re-inventing the wheel. Expert advice in Sourcing skills and new media are critical for survival. Most staffing leaders believe that use of the Internet is a key recruitment strategy and a skill set that should be kept in-house, yet almost half of them feel their team is inadequately trained and are dissatisfied with their current Sourcing capability.

Ineffective use of job boards: The Internet population has grown in size and sophistication. Job seekers are more resourceful. They circumvent gatekeepers and use online networking to connect with hiring managers. People are seeking to connect, not just be "talked at". Many recruitment leaders are dissatisfied with their job board performance and most of them plan to decrease the amount they spend on job posting solutions.

But job boards are more than just advertising; they're also searchable databases. The simple minded "enter a keyword and find matching candidates" approach misses talent hidden in plain sight. People describe what they do using language different than what hiring managers use to describe their requirements. Resumes, blogs, social network profiles and other relevant content seldom contain the same language as that found in job descriptions so good prospects go unnoticed. It is the role of Sourcing and recruiting to bridge that gap, yet leaders refuse to invest in the professional development of recruiters as they happily do with other corporate functions.

About the Author

Shally Steckerl is a globally recognized recruiting thought leader and pioneer in Sourcing, recruitment research, and recruitment marketing. He has helped build Sourcing organizations and models for over 250 top employers worldwide including many Fortune 500 companies such as Google, Microsoft, Wal-Mart, Dell, Coca-Cola Enterprises, Disney, and Cisco Systems. He is a Founding Member and Chief CyberSleuth of 4SCT where he also acts as Principal Consultant, advising top recruitment brass on how to embed key Sourcing initiatives successfully into their current efforts, improve the performance of existing Sourcing teams, and establish Sourcing functions from the ground up. An accomplished author and speaker, Steckerl is a frequent contributor to many industry forums and a headliner at leading international recruiting conferences.

Steckerl holds dual degrees from Rochester Institute of Technology and teaches as an Associate Adjunct Professor at Temple University Fox School of Business. Steckerl is originally from Colombia, South America, and currently resides in Atlanta, Georgia, with his family.

For more information on Mr. Steckerl please visit 4SCT.com. Connect with him on Twitter @shally, LinkedIn.com/in/shally, and Facebook.com/shally.steckerl.

Shally's Three Favorite Things

Three Favorite Quotes

- "We cannot solve our problems with the same thinking we used when we created them." –Albert Einstein
- "Set your course by the stars, not by the lights of every passing ship." – Omar N Bradley·
- "The real voyage of discovery consists not in seeking new lands but seeing with new eyes."—Marcel Proust

Three Favorite Sourcing Sound Bites

- Good candidates come to those who wait... but pass by those who source too late.
- Give a recruiter a resume, and you feed them for a day. Teach them how to source and you feed them for a lifetime.
- In recruiting, a little knowledge is a dangerous thing, a lot of knowledge is Sourcing.

Three Favorite Maxims

- There is a difference between knowledge and wisdom. Knowledge is knowing that a tomato is a fruit, not a vegetable. Wisdom is knowing not to include it in a fruit salad.
- If you always do what you've always done, you will always get what you've always got.
- Amateurs work until they get it right; Professionals work until they cannot get it wrong.

Three Favorite Books

- *Freakonomics: A Rogue Economist Explores the Hidden Side of Everything* by Steven Levitt and Stephen J. Dubner
- *The Book of Five Rings* (五輪書, Go Rin No Sho) by Miyamoto Musashi circa 1645
- *Persuasion Engineering* by Richard Bandler and John La Valle

Three Favorite Comic One-liners

- "You cannot have everything. Where would you put it all?" –Steven Wright
- "The only constant thing is change; change is inevitable. Except from vending machines." – Robert C Gallagher.
- "The greatest pleasure in life is doing what people say you cannot do." – Walter Bagehot

Three Favorite Parables

The Turn of the Screw

An industrialist's production line inexplicably breaks down, costing him millions in lost revenue per day. He finally tracks down an expert who with a screwdriver turns one screw. As the factory rumbles back to life the expert presents an invoice for $20,000. Outraged, the factory owner demands to see an itemized list charges. The expert happily obliges:

For turning a screw:	$8.00
For knowing which screw to turn:	$19,992.00
Total:	$20,000.00

The Socratic Gossip Test

In ancient Greece, Socrates was reputed to hold knowledge in high esteem. One day an acquaintance met the great philosopher and said:

"Do you know what I just heard about your friend?"

"Hold on a minute", Socrates replied. "Before telling me anything I'd like you to pass a little test. It's called the Triple Filter Test."

"Triple filter?"

"That's right", Socrates continued. "Before you talk to me about my friend, it might be a good idea to take a moment and filter what you're going to say. That's why I call it the triple filter test. The first filter is Truth. Have you made absolutely sure that what you are about to tell me is true?"

"No", the man said, "Actually I just heard about it and ..."

"All right", said Socrates. "So you do not really know if it's true or not. Now let's try the second filter, the filter of Goodness. Is what you are about to tell me about my friend something good?"

"No, on the contrary..."

"So", Socrates continued, "you want to tell me something bad about him, but you're not certain it's true. You may still pass the test though, because there is one filter left: the filter of Usefulness. Is what you want to tell me about my friend going to be useful to me?"

"No, not really ..."

"Well", concluded Socrates, "if what you want to tell me is neither true nor good nor even useful, why tell it to me at all?"

The Starfish

A man walks along the beach on a beautiful day. The sun shines, and off in the distance he sees someone going back and forth between the surf's and the beach. As the man approached, he could see there were hundreds of starfish stranded on the sand as the result of the tide.

The man is stuck by the apparent futility of such a task. There were far too many starfish, many of them sure to perish. As he approached, the person continued the task of dodging the surf to pick up a starfish and one by one throwing them back into ocean.

As he came up to the person, he said: "Are you crazy? There are thousands of miles of beach covered with starfish. You cannot possibly make a difference." The person looked at the man. He then stooped down to pick up one more starfish and throw it back into the ocean. Turning back to the man he said: "It sure made a difference to that one!"

Hat Tips

Simple kindnesses, like expressing gratitude and the thoughtful act of giving credit where due, are slowly vanishing courtesies in the digital world. They are victims no doubt of a ravenous appetite for content, our predilection for instant gratification, and a penchant to prefer information over knowledge.

Widespread disregard of plagiarism leaves room for unprincipled narcissists to claim credit for others' innovations even when a simple tip of the hat would suffice to acknowledge contributions. Many of the topics in this book are tweaks, offshoots, modifications or improvements resulting from applying lessons hard-learned by others in disciplines sometimes entirely alien to Sourcing and recruitment.

It would be impossible to accurately match each idea contained in this book with its exact point of origin but it would also be conceited of me to let you believe this work is completely novel. I have attempted my best recollection to honor here in alphabetical order the names of all those whose thoughts I have liberally filched.

Alaina Rivas
Amy Suits
Amybeth Hale
Barbara Ling
Bret Hollander
Carl Kutsmode
Carmen Hudson
Cathy Mannis
Charles Bretz
Chris Havrilla
Chris Pritchard
Conni LaDouceur
Dakotta Alex
Dan Kilgore
Dave Manaster
David Carpe
Dean DaCosta
Deanna Geddes
Donato Diorio
Doris Steckerl
Eric Jaquith
Francesco Vianello
Frank Scarpelli
Gale Heritage
Gerry Crispin
Glenn Gutmacher
Gordon Lockenberg
Greg Flowers
Hafeez Khan
Harriet McCormick
Jason Alba
Jim Durbin
Jim Stroud
John Sullivan
John Sumser
John Turnberg
Jon Bryant
Josh Kahn
Judy West
Jung Kim
Karen Hwang
Kate Wilson
Katherine Nelson
Kay Kellison
Kevin Wheeler
Krista Bradford
Laura Stocker
Laurie DesAutels
Laurie Ruettimann
Lizz Pellet
Lou Adler
Mark Berger
Mark Jennings
Maureen Sharib
Megan Calimbas
Michael Glenn
Michael Gray
Michael Guglielmo
Michael Marlatt
Mike Guglielmo
Mike Notaro
Nick Fishman
Nicole Bodem
Nicole Greenberg
Otis Collier
Peer Goudsmit
Peter Weddle
Rabbi Karpov
Ray Towle
Reagan Forlenzo
Rithesh Nair
Rob Delp
Rob McIntosh
Ron Crompton
Ronnie Bratcher
Russ Moon
Saralynn Halsey
Sean Rehder
Shannon Van Curen
Sheila Greco
Stefanie Steckerl
Steve Levy
Steve Rath
Steven Pyser
Suzanne Salsbury
Suzy Tonini
Sylvia Dahlby
Tim O'Connor
Tom Bolt
Tracey de Morsella
Tracy Friend
William Uranga

Appendix

RESOURCES AT A GLANCE

Roadmap at a Glance

It's Not All About Resumes

Finding a resume is clearly a good objective, but it should not be your only one. What you need to fill a requisition is a candidate, and leads to candidates can come from many places, and in many forms besides a traditional resume. For example, home pages, online journals, or blogs can reveal enough to qualify someone as a potential candidate. Once you find someone that interests you, keep digging to pull more information about them and the people with whom they work. Bios, profiles on social networking sites, by-lined articles, groups and associations a candidate belongs to or conferences in which they participated, even news bites that mention them, are all useful data points to help you locate your ideal candidate.

Save Your Formulas

Once you determine the searches that work best for you, hang on to them. Keep them in research form, in your notebook, or as favorites in your browser. In Appendix C there is an example of a research form using Excel that will help you track all the searches you perform throughout the day. Make backup copies of your "search templates" and keep them up to date. Search strings that brought you success before should be used as a springboard for searches later—avoid reinventing your search strings when possible. We also recommend you create your own reference document with a list of prepared searches and formulas ready for each type of search or search engine you use. Just cut and paste your position-specific keywords from the research form and you are off to a good start.

Web Pages Are Public

When a Web page doesn't require you to enter a password or use some sort of security access device that means it's public. Just because the page has information on it that looks like it should have been protected doesn't mean you are doing something illegal or unethical. If the page hasn't been secured but a search engine found it, you can read it with impunity.

Break Down the URL

When you find a page with information that is useful but not exactly what you need, look closely at the address or URL and see what it reveals. Frequently the URL will lead you to another page that contains what you are looking for. For example, if you arrive at a page that happens to be deep inside a website, by going up one or two levels you may arrive at a directory or similar listing. Web addresses or URLs are just like folders in your computer. To go up one level just go to your web browsers address bar and remove the last portion of the address following the final forward slash character ("/"), and you should be brought right to the parent folder of the page you are currently viewing.

All You Need Is a Name

Often you may find potential candidates but they lack complete contact information. There are many ways to find what you need. For example, you could search for the name on one of the metasearch engines or you could go to any of the many white pages websites. If the candidate is someone you want to talk to about your search then just look him or her up on a site such as http://www.zabasearch.com. Do not give up when you have a good looking lead, there are many ways to track down additional information. In this book you will discover some new ways, and as you conduct searches you will discover additional ways.

Make a Connection

When you are busy finding hundreds of leads online, it's easy to forget why they are called leads: Because they lead you to real people. In other words, do not stop there: A quick, friendly email message or phone call to a lead may yield more results. Sometimes the person you find and connect with isn't the ideal candidate but will lead you to someone who is. Make sure you ask for referrals when you talk with people you found online. Thoroughly mining each Internet lead for further referrals helps especially when searching for candidates who wouldn't show up in initial search results because they lack an Internet presence. (While they may possess an email address, they may not have a homepage, online resume, blog, bio, or ever have authored an article.)

One Is Not Enough

No single search engine has yet been able to search the entire Internet. And chances are this may never happen, with the Internet growing faster than search engines can keep up. As a result, it is wise to use at least three of the major search engines for any given search. Because the type of information you seek as a recruiter is contained in hard-to-find pages, it's possible that what you seek is listed in one search engine but not another, so do not stop at just one or two search engines. This topic is covered in detail in its own special chapter because it is so vitally important. Please do not limit yourself to one single search engine when conducting your research.

Be Careful What You Ask

You will not usually find employee resumes listed right on the employer's website. If you were to go so far as to look at every page inside a website trying to find a resume, chances are you would be wasting your time. Each search technique has a purpose. With practice you will be able to apply the techniques appropriately and know when to use a particular method. When conducting a search you may also find that not all your keywords will be on a single page. Just because you have a long list of keywords on your research form, or on the requisition, doesn't mean that all the keywords will appear in one page. Using the right keywords with the right technique will lead you to better results. If a search method yields little, pick different keywords and try again just to make sure you aren't asking for something that doesn't exist. Such a search is jestingly referred to as a seeking a "Purple Squirrel" - a color of squirrel that simply does not exist in nature.

Do Not Give up

The staggering amount of information available online can make it intimidating to conduct searches, especially if you enter a few keywords and the search engine comes back with hundreds of thousands of results. Half the battle is targeting the right kind of information. With dozens of requisitions demanding attention, it's easy to give up and move on to the next set of requirements—but do not. It takes more time to set up search formulas, but once they are established you should be able to obtain search results in less than ten minutes.

Computer Tips at a Glance

Use your quick-keys. Quick-keys are time saving shortcuts. Cannot find your keyword on the resume? Use "Ctrl-F" and up pops a box that asks you what you want to search for. Find a resume you want to paste into an email to your hiring manager? Use "Ctrl-A" (select all), "Ctrl-C" (copy all) then go to your email and press "Ctrl-V" (paste). You can also use" Alt-Tab" to cycle between open windows, saving you from having to point and click on each concurrent task. When entering an address or URL into your browser for a .com website, all you have to do is type in the name, for example, 4sct, then hit "Ctrl-Enter" and the browser will add the "http://www." and the ".com."

View sites in text-only mode. To speed up your search on the Internet, turn off the images in your web browser. If you are using Netscape, de-select "Auto Load Images" under the Options menu. With Internet Explorer, select "Internet Options" under the View menu, then click the Advanced tab. Now uncheck "Show Pictures". If you want to see a particular image, click on the tag with your right mouse button and select "View Image".

Increase your cache. Files you download are stored in a cache on your hard drive; so when you return to a site, you do not have to download the files again— just access them from your cache. After a while though, the cache becomes full. Your web browser automatically deletes old files as you continue to surf the Web.

But if you visit many of the same sites regularly, you can speed up access by caching more of them, by increasing the size of your cache. If you use Netscape, go to the Edit menu, choose "Preferences", and then click on "Advanced". Now increase the cache size. With Explorer, go to the Views menu, select "Internet Options", then click the "Settings" button in the Temporary

Internet files section. Use the slider to increase the cache.

Use the Link bar. You can access all your Favorites folders and sub folders right from the Links bar in your browser. In Internet Explorer there is a Link toolbar, which is hidden off to the right toward the top of the screen. Simply right click on the bar in your browser and uncheck the "Lock the Toolbars" option, then click on the little vertical bar to the left of the word Links on the right hand side of your browser bar, and drag it down one row. Now you can have easy access to your most frequently used folders and links from Favorites. To include a folder or Favorite in your Links bar, just drag it on to the Link bar you just put on your browser, or click on "Organize" from within your Favorites menu.

Choose your own home page. Do not just settle for the home page that came with your browser. Make it the daily newspaper or better yet, a favorite search engine. Select "Internet Options" under the View menu and enter in the address of a page that you would like to see each time you first open your browser.

Use the "save as" feature to save resumes to your folders. The same way you create Bookmark Folders, you should create folders on your hard drive for each position you search. That way, when you run into a great resume you can "Save As" into a folder for future use. You can save a web page as plain text; to save it in HTML in a single page use the "Web Archive, Single File". You can also save a web page as an MS Word document by manually typing a .doc at the end of the file name.

Format the resume for easy viewing. Once you have saved a resume as text on your hard drive, you can open it up in MS Word and either 1) auto format 2) Use bullets to remove word wrap, or 3) use the "Find and Replace" to highlight the keywords for your hiring manager's easy viewing.

Setup an online email account. Use free online email accounts to register for listservs or join chats and newsgroups anonymously as a listener. Some good free accounts are at Yahoo (www.yahoo.com) and Hotmail (www.hotmail.com). Once again, how about Gmail?

KEY(S) PRESSED	WHAT IT DOES
Alt-left arrow	Same as clicking the back button
Alt-right arrow	Same as clicking the forward button
Ctrl D	Creates a new favorite in default folder
Ctrl F	Find text in a page
Ctrl H	Opens browser history
Esc	Same as clicking the Stop Button
Space Bar	Go down a page one screen at a time
Ctrl N	New browser window
Ctrl O	Opens a window to enter a URL
F4	Drops down list of recent sites visited
Alt D	Selects text in an Address Bar

Gmail at a Glance

If you use a company Google Apps account, or your own personal Gmail, here is a collection of my favorite time-saving shortcuts for frequently used actions:

Working with Messages

ACTION	KEY PRESS	DEFINITION
New Message	or Ctrl C	Compose. <Shift> + C will open in new window
Open	O	Open. In conversation view, expands or collapses
Archive or mute	E	e archives, m mutes a conversation so all future messages skip Inbox unless sent directly to you
Reply	R then A	r replies to sender, a replies all
Forward	F	Forwards a message
Save	Ctrl + S	Saves the current text as a draft when composing a message
Delete	#	Moves conversation to trash folder
Send	Tab then Enter	After composing message, this sends it
Undo	Z	Undoes your previous action, if possible (works for actions with an 'undo' link)
Help	?	Displays keyboard shortcuts help menu
Search	/	Puts cursor in search box

Labeling and Organizing

Read and Unread	Shift+I, Shift+U	Marks message as 'read/unread', skips to the next
Mark important	+	+ marks and - unmarks message for Priority Inbox
Star	S	Adds or removes star from message or conversation
Spam	!	Marks as spam, removes it from conversation.
Move	V	Moves the conversation from the inbox to a different label, Spam or Trash
Label	L	Opens Labels menu
Clear label	Y	Automatically removes message from current view plus archives, removes star or removes label
Select conversation	X	Selects entire conversation so you can archive, apply a label, or choose an action from dropdown

Navigating Folders

Browse conversation	U	Returns you to the conversation list
Next message	N or P	N moves to next message, P to previous message
View newer or older	K or J	K moves to more recent, J to next oldest
Archive and next	Y then O	Archives conversation, moves to the next one
Go to Inbox	G then I	Returns you to the inbox
Go to All Mail	G then A	Takes you to the All Mail folder, every message you've sent or received but never deleted
Go to Starred	G then S	Takes you to all conversations you have starred
Go to Contacts	G then C	Takes you to your Contacts list
Go to Label	G then L	Takes you to the search, adds "label:" operator

Go to Sent Mail	G then T	Takes you to all mail you've sent
All or None	* then A or N	Selects or deselects all mail on screen
Read or Unread	* then R or U	Selects all mail you've read, or all unread mail
Starred or Unstarred	* then S	Selects all starred, or unstarred mail

Source: https://support.google.com/mail/bin/answer.py?hl=en&answer=6594

Examples at a Glance

Example Google Searches by U.S. Region on LinkedIn™

Techniques for searching the Web for public LinkedIn™ profiles were discussed in the search methodologies section, under the in-depth look at LinkedIn™. The following is a list of location names corresponding to metropolitan areas of the United States as categorized by LinkedIn™ at the time this book was published. Enclose area names in quotation marks and append them to a search on Google or Bing along with the command site: www.linkedin.com to focus search results on US regions.

Alabama

Anniston, Alabama Area
Auburn, Alabama Area
Birmingham, Alabama Area
Decatur, Alabama Area
Dothan, Alabama Area
Florence, Alabama Area
Gadsden, Alabama Area
Huntsville, Alabama Area
Mobile, Alabama Area
Tuscaloosa, Alabama Area

Alaska

Anchorage, Alaska Area

Arizona

Flagstaff, Arizona Area
Phoenix, Arizona Area
Tucson, Arizona Area
Yuma, Arizona Area

Arkansas

Fayetteville, Arkansas Area
Fort Smith, Arkansas Area
Jonesboro, Arkansas Area
Little Rock, Arkansas Area
Pine Bluff, Arkansas Area

California

Bakersfield, California Area
Chico, California Area
Fresno, California Area
Greater Los Angeles Area
Greater San Diego Area

Merced, California Area
Modesto, California Area
Orange County, California Area
Redding, California Area
Sacramento, California Area
Salinas, California Area
San Francisco Bay Area
Santa Barbara, California Area
Stockton, California Area
Visalia, California Area

Colorado

Colorado Springs, Colorado Area
Fort Collins, Colorado Area
Grand Junction, Colorado Area
Greater Denver Area
Pueblo, Colorado Area

Connecticut

Hartford, Connecticut Area
New London/Norwich, Connecticut Area

Delaware

Dover, Delaware Area

Florida

Daytona Beach, Florida Area
Fort Myers, Florida Area
Fort Pierce, Florida Area
Gainesville, Florida Area
Jacksonville, Florida Area
Lakeland, Florida Area
Melbourne, Florida Area
Miami/Fort Lauderdale Area
Ocala, Florida Area
Orlando, Florida Area
Pensacola Florida Area
Sarasota, Florida Area
Tallahassee, Florida Area
Tampa/St. Petersburg, Florida Area
West Palm Beach, Florida Area

Georgia

Albany, Georgia Area
Athens, Georgia Area
Augusta, Georgia Area
Columbus, Georgia Area
Greater Atlanta Area
Macon, Georgia Area
Savannah, Georgia Area

Hawaii

Hawaiian Islands

Idaho

Boise, Idaho Area
Pocatello, Idaho Area

Illinois

Bloomington/Normal, Illinois Area
Decatur, Illinois Area
Greater Chicago Area
Peoria, Illinois Area
Rockford, Illinois Area
Springfield, Illinois Area
Urbana-Champaign, Illinois Area

Indiana

Bloomington, Indiana Area
Elkhart, Indiana Area
Evansville, Indiana Area
Fort Wayne, Indiana Area
Indianapolis, Indiana Area
Kokomo, Indiana Area

Lafayette, Indiana Area
Muncie, Indiana Area
South Bend, Indiana Area
Terre Haute, Indiana Area

Iowa

Cedar Rapids, Iowa Area
Davenport, Iowa Area

Kansas

Des Moines, Iowa Area
Dubuque, Iowa Area
Iowa City, Iowa Area
Sioux City, Iowa Area
Waterloo, Iowa Area
Lawrence, Kansas Area
Topica, Kansas Area
Wichita, Kansas Area

Kentucky

Lexington, Kentucky Area
Louisville, Kentucky Area
Owensboro, Kentucky Area

Louisiana

Alexandria, Louisiana Area
Baton Rouge, Louisiana Area
Greater New Orleans Area
Houma, Louisiana Area
Lafayette, Louisiana Area
Lake Charles, Louisiana Area
Monroe, Louisiana Area
Shreveport, Louisiana Area

Maine

Bangor, Maine Area
Lewiston/Auburn, Maine Area
Portland, Maine Area

Maryland

Baltimore, Maryland Area
Cumberland, Maryland Area

Massachusetts

Barnstable/Yarmouth, Massachusetts Area
Greater Boston Area
Pittsfield, Massachusetts Area
Springfield, Massachusetts Area

Michigan

Benton Harbor, Michigan Area
Greater Detroit Area
Greater Grand Rapids, Michigan Area
Jackson, Michigan Area
Kalamazoo, Michigan Area
Lansing, Michigan Area
Saginaw, Michigan Area

Minnesota

Duluth, Minnesota Area
Greater Minneapolis-St. Paul Area
Rochester, Minnesota Area
St. Cloud, Minnesota Area

Mississippi

Biloxi, Mississippi Area
Hattiesburg Mississippi Area

Missouri

Columbia, Missouri Area
Greater St. Louis Area
Joplin, Missouri Area
Kansas City, Missouri Area
Springfield, Missouri Area
St. Joseph, Missouri Area

Montana

Billings, Montana Area
Great Falls, Montana Area
Missoula, Montana Area
Greater Omaha Area

Nebraska

Lincoln, Nebraska Area

Nevada

Las Vegas, Nevada Area
Reno, Nevada Area

New Hampshire

New Hampshire

New Jersey

New Jersey

New Mexico

Albuquerque, New Mexico Area
Las Cruces, New Mexico Area
Santa Fe, New Mexico Area

New York

Albany, New York Area
Buffalo/Niagara, New York Area
Elmira, New York Area
Glens Falls, New York Area
Greater New York City Area
Ithaca, New York Area
Jamestown, New York Area
Rochester, New York Area
Syracuse, New York Area
Utica, New York Area

North Carolina

Asheville, North Carolina Area
Charlotte, North Carolina Area
Fayetteville, North Carolina Area
Goldsboro, North Carolina Area
Greensboro/Winston-Salem, North Carolina Area
Greenville, North Carolina Area
Hickory/Lenoir, North Carolina Area
Jacksonville, North Carolina Area
Raleigh-Durham, North Carolina Area
Wilmington, North Carolina Area

North Dakota

Bismarck, North Dakota Area
Fargo, North Dakota Area
Grand Forks, North Dakota Area

Ohio

Canton, Ohio Area
Cincinnati Area
Cleveland/Akron, Ohio Area
Columbus, Ohio Area
Dayton, Ohio Area
Lima, Ohio Area
Mansfield, Ohio Area
Steubenville, Ohio Area
Toledo, Ohio Area
Youngstown, Ohio Area

Oklahoma

Enid, Oklahoma Area
Lawton, Oklahoma Area
Oklahoma City, Oklahoma Area
Tulsa, Oklahoma Area

Oregon

Corvallis, Oregon Area
Eugene, Oregon Area

Medford, Oregon Area
Portland, Oregon Area

Pennsylvania

Allentown, Pennsylvania Area
Greater Philadelphia Area
Greater Pittsburgh Area
Harrisburg, Pennsylvania Area
Lancaster, Pennsylvania Area
Scranton, Pennsylvania Area

Rhode Island

Providence, Rhode Island Area

South Carolina

Charleston, South Carolina Area
Columbia, South Carolina Area
Greenville, South Carolina Area

South Dakota

Sioux Falls, South Dakota Area
Rapid City, South Dakota Area
Sioux Falls, South Dakota Area

Tennessee

Chattanooga, Tennessee Area
Greater Memphis Area
Greater Nashville Area
Johnson City, Tennessee Area
Knoxville, Tennessee Area

Texas

Amarillo, Texas Area
Austin, Texas Area
Brownsville, Texas Area
Dallas/Fort Worth Area
El Paso, Texas Area
Houston, Texas Area
Longview, Texas Area
San Antonio, Texas Area
Sherman/Denison, Texas Area
Texarkana, Texas Area
Tyler, Texas Area
Victoria, Texas Area
Waco, Texas Area

Utah

Greater Salt Lake City Area
Provo, Utah Area

Vermont

Burlington, Vermont Area

Virginia

Charlottesville, Virginia Area
Danville, Virginia Area
Lynchburg, Virginia Area
Norfolk, Virginia Area
Richmond, Virginia Area
Roanoke, Virginia Area

Washington

Greater Seattle Area
Spokane, Washington Area

Washington

D.C. Metro Area

West Virginia

Charleston, West Virginia Area
Huntington, West Virginia Area
Wheeling, West Virginia Area
Greater Milwaukee Area

Wisconsin

Green Bay, Wisconsin Area

Madison, Wisconsin Area
Oshkosh, Wisconsin Area

Wyoming

Casper, Wyoming Area
Cheyenne, Wyoming Area

Example Uses of Filetype: Syntax

Google can index the content of most types of pages and files. When you use the filetype: operator in a Google search (for example, filetype:xml, Google searches for files with the .xml extension, not for files of file type XML.

Not all URLs or pages have the .html file extension. Some pages (like http://www.google.com) have no extension at all, and some have an extension that doesn't match their file type. Limiting your search to a specific file type will return pages with that file extension, and may return fewer irrelevant results. The most common file types the index includes are:

- Adobe Flash (.swf)
- Adobe Portable Document Format (.pdf)
- Adobe PostScript (.ps)
- Autodesk Design Web Format (.dwf)
- Google Earth (.kml, .kmz)
- GPS eXchange Format (.gpx)
- Hancom Hanword (.hwp)
- HTML (.htm, .html, other file extensions)
- Microsoft Excel (.xls, .xlsx)
- Microsoft PowerPoint (.ppt, .pptx)
- Microsoft Word (.doc, .docx)
- OpenOffice presentation (.odp)
- OpenOffice spreadsheet (.ods)
- OpenOffice text (.odt)
- Rich Text Format (.rtf, .wri)
- Scalable Vector Graphics (.svg)
- TeX/LaTeX (.tex)
- Text (.txt, .text, other file extensions), including source code in common programming languages:
    - Basic source code (.bas)
    - C/C++ source code (.c, .cc, .cpp, .cxx, .h, .hpp)
    - C# source code (.cs)
    - Java source code (.java)

- o Perl source code (.pl)
- o Python source code (.py)
- o Wireless Markup Language (.wml, .wap)
- o XML (.xml)

Source: http://support.google.com/webmasters/bin/answer.py?hl=en&answer=35287

Note that other search engines such as Bing and Exalead support many of the same extensions with the filetype command.

Example Text (SMS) and Chat Abbreviations

Useful Text, SMS, Chat, Skype or Instant Messenger abbreviations and acronyms you may encounter:

404	I do not know	A3	Anytime, anywhere
AAP	Always a pleasure	AAR	At any rate
ADD	Address	ADN	Any day now
AEAP	As early as possible	AFAIK	As far as I know
AFK	Away from keyboard	AISB	As it should be
AKA	Also known as	AOTA	All of the above
ASAP	As soon as possible	ATM	At the moment
AYEC	At your earliest convenience	AYOR	At your own risk
B4	Before	B4N	Bye for now
BAK	Back at keyboard	BAU	Business as usual
BBIAF	Be back in a few	BBIAM	Be back in a minute
BBL	Be back later	BBS	Be back soon
BC	Because	BCNU	Be seeing you
BF	Best friend	BFG	Big frigging grin
BFN	Bye for now	BG	Big grin
BLNT	Better luck next time	BRB	Be right back
BRT	Be right there	BTDT	Been there, done that
BTW	By the way	CMON	Come on
COB	Close of business	COS	Because
CR8	Create	CRB	Come right back
CU	See you (also CYA)	CUL	See you later (SUL, SYL)
CYO	See you online	DIKU	Do I know you?
DL	Download	DTS	Do not think so
EG	Evil grin	EOD	End of day
EOM	End of message	EZY	Easy
F2F	Face to face	F2T	Free to talk
FBM	Fine by me	FC	Fingers crossed
FICCL	Frankly couldn't care less	FISH	First in, still here
FOMCL	Falling off chair laughing	FYEO	For your eyes only

FYI	For your information	G	Grin
G2R	Got to run	G9	Genius
GA	Go ahead	GIGO	Garbage in, garbage out
GL	Good luck	GOL	Giggling out loud
GR8	Great	H8	Hate
HAGN	Have a good night	HAGO	Have a good one
HAND	Have a nice day	HOAS	Hold on a second
HRU	How are you?	HV	Have
IAC	In any case	IB	I'm back
IC	I see	ICBW	It could be worse
IDK	I do not know	IDTS	I do not think so
IG2R	I got to run	IIRC	If I remember correctly
ILBL8	I'll be late	IM	Instant message
IMHO	In my humble opinion	j00r	You are (also UR)
JAC	Just a sec	JIC	Just in case
JK	Just kidding	k/b	keyboard
KIT	Keep in touch	LERK	leaving reach of keyboard
LMAO	Laughing my a** off	LOL	Laughing out loud
MSG	Message	n00b	Newbie (neophyte)
N1	Nice one	NBD	No big deal
NE	Any NM	Nothing much/Never mind	
NO1	No one (NE1 is anyone)	NOYB	None of your business
NP	No problem	NRN	No response necessary
NW	No way	OIC	Oh, I see
OMG	Oh my God	OMW	On my way
OO	Over and out	OP	On phone (also OTP)
OTL	Out to lunch	OVA	Over
PCM	Please call me	PLS	Please (also PLZ)
PPL	People	PRW	People are watching
PU	That stinks!	RME	Rolling my eyes
ROFL	Rolling on floor laughing	ROTFL	Rolling on the floor laughing
RUOK	Are you okay?	SIG2R	Sorry, I got to run
SIS	Snickering in silence	SIT	Stay in touch
SLAP	Sounds like a plan	SNAFU	Situation normal all f-d up
SRY	Sorry (also SS)	STW	Search the Web

SUP What's up? (also WU?)
TAFN That's all for now
TC Take care
TIA Thanks in advance
TMI Too much information
TTYL/S Talk to you later/soon
TYVM Thank you very much
WAM Wait a minute
WK Week
WRK Work
WTF What the fudge?
WTH What the heck?
XO hugs and kisses
YW You're welcome
TA Thanks a lot
TBD To be determined
THX Thanks (also THNX THNQ)
TMB Text me back
TTFN Ta ta for now (BYE)
TU Thank you (also TY)
UW You're welcome
WIIFM What's in it for me?
WKD Weekend
WRUD What are you doing?
WTG Way to go
XLNT Excellent
YA Your (also YR)
ZZZZ Sleeping

Example Job Title Study

A statistical analysis of a broad spectrum of software and programming related job postings from major employers over a period of one year reveals vast variations in the use of job titles. Job postings from 30 companies where included in this study:

Accenture	Adobe	Amazon	AOL	Apple
Avaya	BEA	Borland	Business	Objects
Cisco	Cognos	Corel	Dell	eBay
HP	Hyperion	IBM	Intel	Intuit
Macromedia	McKinsey	SAS	Microsoft	Institute
Microstrategy	Siebel	Nortel	Sun	Oracle
Peoplesoft	SAP			

Top Job Titles

Over 1,300 distinct job titles emerged from this study, ranging from 7 to 63 characters long with an average length of 28. Ranked by highest percentage of total jobs, here is a list of the top 20:

Member of Technical Staff	Development Engineer
Software Engineer Staff Engineer	Systems Engineer
Program Manager	Systems Analyst
Test Engineer	Applications Engineer
Product Manager	Software Developer
Hardware Engineer	Quality Assurance Engineer
Software Development Engineer	Software Design Engineer
Manufacturing Engineer	Application Developer
Engineering Advisor	Research Analyst
Quality Engineer	

Example Intake Meeting Form

This form is your place to keep notes from the Intake Meeting. Do not send a blank or partially completed version of this document to the hiring authorities. It is strongly recommended you fill out this form while speaking directly with the hiring party in person or over the phone.

Position Title:	The internal job title
Requisition #:	Job Code in the ATS or HRIS
Hiring Manager:	Name of principal hiring authority
Department:	Division, group or business unit
Location of position:	Where the work will be conducted
Band/Level:	Range of total compensation
Relocation Available:	Level of assistance available if qualified
Degree Requirement:	Minimum education requirements
New Role or Backfill:	Is this a new or previously existing role
Percent Probability of Internal Hire:	It is important you ask like this "Research strategy will vary depending on the availability of internal resources we could tap. Whom within the organization may we approach for guidance on this particular role/function?"
Must Have Keywords:	With each and every one of these verify that if absent from a resume that would completely eliminate a prospect from further consideration.
Synonyms to keywords:	Bring a list of skills & jargon keywords, ask manager to validate, remove from or add to the list.
Preferred or "Nice to Have":	If all else were equal between multiple candidates, which requisition keywords when present on a resume would elevate an individual to the top of the list?
Similar Job Titles and Functions:	Research via Indeed, SimplyHired, and LinkedIn™, what job titles people use when they perform this job function at other companies.
Niche Sites:	Bring to the manager a list of alternative or non-mainstream career destinations for this particular industry segment.

Possible Source Companies:	Use Zoominfo, Google's related: command and others to build a company list. Do not limit to competitors, look for companies that recruit/hire/employ similar talent.
Competitor's URLs:	A list of Web addresses for above listed companies
Organizations, Associations, Consortiums:	Any organization whose members may be prospective candidates including standards bodies or committees
Alternative Degrees, Certifications, Names of Schools or Universities	Licenses, acronyms and abbreviations, educational bodies and organizations that serve this industry.
Names of Vendors and/or Partners:	Organizations which provide services to your client/manager
Off Limits Companies:	Companies who have present employees you are not allowed to recruit.
Tools Used by Target Candidates:	Software, applications, systems, or any other tools utilized by your target candidates. For example, recruiters use an ATS, etc.
Industry Terms, Buzz Words, Jargon:	Related terms and significant action phrases, ask incumbents or previous candidates for terms unique to their role/function that they use in shorthand professional conversations.
Names of Thought Leaders:	Names of prominent people in the industry. Look for speakers at conferences and in local events.
Area Codes and Locations:	Geographic criteria. Include city names, zip codes, regions, neighborhoods, counties, anything relevant.

Example Intake Meeting Executive Summary

Meeting Date	Hiring Team	[NAMES/PHONES/EMAILS
REQ #	Organization	[GROUP/DEPT]
Location(s)	Position	[JOB TITLE

POSITION SUMMARY: This position is liaison between "Games Producers" and "External Stakeholders". Responsibilities include creating/ providing roadmap for paid games distributed through iTunes, Facebook, and Android. This role is responsible for growing revenue from current $2 million to $15 million.

Required: Experienced product manager with heavy emphasis on marketing component and a numbers driven focus. Knowledge and experience in launching technology products particularly in the mobile/handheld segment. Must be well connected to game developers, especially in the casual games (iOS apps & Facebook) market

Similar Job Titles: Business Development Manager, Project Marketing Manager, Business Analyst Example Companies: Popcap, Chillingo, EA, Zynga, Playdom, Playfish, Crowdstar, Contagion, Google

Other Relevant Keywords: Developer Relations/Developer Advocate/ Technical Evangelists

Organizations: Casual Connect (casual games conference)/Touch Arcade Forum/WWDC (Apple conference)/Appdata.com/GDC Games Development Conference, and similar

Challenges: Must be well connected to game developers, especially in casual games market (iOS & Facebook)

Example Candidate Qualification Profile

Candidate Contact Details	
First Name:	Last Name:
Street Address:	
City:	State/Province:
Country:	Postal Code:
Mark preferred method of contact below with an asterisk*	
Work Phone:	Work Email:
Home Phone:	Home Email:
Mobile Phone:	Skype/IM:
Company:	Job Title:
Department:	Work Location:

Executive Summary
Recruiter's take on candidate strengths related to requirements

Resume, Curriculum Vitae, Work History, Bio, Profile
Source URL if found online:
Copy and paste Resume contents below:
Prequalification Screening Questions

Projected availability:	
Current Compensation:	
Desired Compensation:	
Relocation: (Y/N)	Many opportunities require relocation. If adequate relocation assistance is provided for a position would you be willing to move? Choose an item.
If yes above, what are the key criteria that you would need us to be aware of to make an opportunity viable for you? (special relocation considerations, spouse/children's needs, personal needs, etc.):	
If you could write your own job description, describe your ideal role or project?	
Is there anyone you know at this company that may act as a reference for you? Y/N If yes, what is their name?	
Have you ever interviewed with anyone at this company in person or over the phone? Choose an item. If yes, who?	
What would you say is your key professional area of focus, domain or unique specialty?	
What questions do you have for the hiring authority?	
Additional Screening Customer may provide up to five additional screening questions along with correct answers for any criteria not mentioned above.	
1.	
2.	
3.	
4.	

Example Service Level Agreement

A simple commitment that promises "if I deliver that to you then this is what you promise to do in return" and includes everything you need from them in order to effectively source leads. Commits to what you can absolutely guarantee you will deliver if provided what is needed. This commitment can take the form of a Service Level Agreement between Sourcing and recruiting, or between Sourcing and the hiring managers, or both.

1. Keep it simple or it will not be followed
2. Introduce this the first time you meet the Hiring Manager (s)
3. Obtain their "sign off" even if it's a brief email acknowledgement

SLA - Definition of Service

- Who you are, team mission, team description and bios
- Role definition, who does what
- What you do (for example:)
- We specialize in passive candidate identification from specific competitors, organizations or associations based on customer needs.
- Customer's develop these leads and into fully profiled, qualified candidates.

SLA - Description of Process

- Brief outline describing how you do it, typical timeline, and expected results
- What you need from them (for example:)
- To ensure quality and timely work product we require the following from the requester:
- Attempt to contact each lead within 5 business days (10 leads per day)
- Create candidate record and adequately tracking as required by company recruiting process and policies
- Provide Sourcing team with detailed feedback on each rejected lead including why it was not acceptable or unreachable
- What you promise to them
- We will deliver research and identification of up to 50 validated leads for hard-to-fill requisitions. Leads are delivered via CRM/ATS

Glossary

Ad Copy: The text of a clickable pay-per-click advertisement or other online advertising format (e.g., job posting)

Aggregator: website or technology that allows for the convergence of multiple sources or destinations into one access point. For example Job Posting Aggregators collect jobs from multiple sources such as company career websites and commercial job boards, and incorporate them in a single database.

ATS: Applicant Tracking Systems is software that helps recruiters and hiring managers handle the process of hiring, from creating requisitions through making offers.

Boolean: Search engine operators such as AND, AND NOT and OR. These commands tell the search engine which keywords to include. For example, a search for "Tomato AND Sauce" will find websites about where tomato and sauce both appear on the page while a search for "Tomato AND NOT Sauce" will find websites about tomatoes that do not include references to the word sauce. A search for "Tomato OR Sauce" will find a much greater number of websites because it will locate site containing either the word Tomato or Sauce, or both.

Boolean Search: A search allowing the inclusion or exclusion of documents containing certain words through the use of Boolean operators. Not all search engines use Boolean commands the same way. Read each search engine's help file to understand how they use Booleans.

Browser: A Client program (software) that is used to look at various kinds of Internet resources. Internet Explorer and Netscape are the two most common.

Concept Search: A search for documents related conceptually to a word, rather than specifically containing the word itself. For example, searching for the concept Programmer may also find Developer, Architect, or Engineer. Sometimes this is regarded as Fuzzy Search.

Conversion Rate: The percentage of career site visitors who take a desired action as defined by you. This is often associated with the number of applicants who apply for a job on your career site.

CPA (Cost Per Applicant): How much it costs for each application/resume received. If your metrics provide costs broken down by channel, you often find a wide discrepancy in CPA (see ROI).

CPC (Cost Per Click): How much you pay a search engine such as Google or Bing for each time a user clicks on an advertisement you place (see SEM)

CPH (Cost Per Hire): How much it costs to hire an employee, which typically includes more cost categories than those for applicants (see CPA)

CTR (Click-Through-Rate): The total percentage of people clicking on your ad out of the total number of times your ad was displayed. For example, if an ad was displayed 100 times and received 5 clicks, the CTR is 5 percent.

Directory: A human-edited catalog of websites. Sometimes confused with a search engine, a Directory is different in that each website was found and catalogued by a person rather than by software. Closer to a traditional "Card Catalog" than to an actual search engine, Directories are organized by topics.

Domain Name: A unique name that identifies an Internet site. For example, the domain name of my company is 4sct.com.

Filetype: Search engine command that instructs the search engine to look for only files of that particular format. For example filetype:pdf looks for only Adobe PDF files. Others include .doc for MS Word, .xls for MS Excel, .ppt for PowerPoint, etc.

Flip Search: Used to find pages that are hyperlinked to pages that you feel may be good match for what you seek. For example competitor sites, colleges, skill or technology pages, associations, tools sites, or related vendor sites.

Full-text Index: An index containing every word of every document cataloged, including stop words.

Fuzzy search: A search that will find matches even when words are only partially spelled or misspelled.

Hit: "Hit" means a single request from a web browser for a single item from a web server; thus in order for the web browser to display a page that contains three graphics, four "hits" would occur at the server— one for the HTML page, and one for each of the three graphics. It is an often used, but poor, measurement for website traffic given the dependence on graphics, etc.

HTML: (Hypertext Markup Language). The coding language used to create hypertext documents for use on the World Wide Web. HTML looks a lot like old-fashioned typesetting code, where you surround a block of text with codes that indicate how it should appear. Additionally, in HTML you can specify that a block of text, or a word, be linked to another file on the Internet. If you go to "View" in your menu and click on "Source" it allows you to view the HTML of the page.

IM: Instant Messaging, a type of Internet Protocol frequently referred to as Chat. The best-known Chat services are Yahoo, Instant Messenger, AIM, or AOL Instant Messenger, LIVE Messenger, and IRC or Internet Relay Chat.

Index: The searchable catalog of documents created by search engine software; also called "catalog". Index is often used as a synonym for search engine.

Intitle: A search command that returns only words found within the Title tag in HRML <title>search words</title>

Inurl: A search command that returns only words found within the URL or address of pages found by the search engine

ISP: Internet Service Provider. These are organizations that provide Internet access, and often email accounts, to end-users. EarthLink and NetZero are examples of ISPs.

Keyword: The terms or word used when conducting a search.

Keyword Search: A search for documents containing one or more words that is specified by a user.

KPI: Key Performance Indicators – Refers to a set of measurements that help a company determine if it is reaching its performance goals.

Meta Tag: Refers to a tag in the HTML code of a website. The information within this tag describes the content of particular page on the site in which the tag resides.

Metasearch: Search several search engines all at once for very specific, rare key words. This is a simple way to gather multiple results from a variety of sources. It's a very good way to search for names of people, as well as email addresses of known candidates to find similar candidates that may be peers or otherwise related.

Peel Back: Purpose is to analyze the URL to see if there are any other pages within that site that may be of use. You can take off the last part of a URL (the text to the right of the last forward slash "/",) to see which pages may be located higher up in the directory.

Phrase Search: A search for documents containing an exact sentence or phrase specified by a user.

PPC: Pay-Per-Click - placing advertisements on search engines and other content sites where the advertiser would pay each time the ad is clicked on (see "Search Engine Marketing").

Portal: Typically used as a marketing term to described a website that is or is intended to be the first place people see when using the Web. Usually a "portal site" has a catalog of websites, a search engine, or both. A portal site may also offer email and other services to entice people to use that site as their main "point of entry" (hence "portal") to the Web. Yahoo, MSN, and AOL can be considered "portal" sites.

Precision: The degree in which a search engine lists documents matching a query. The more matching documents that are listed, the higher the precision. For example, if a search engine lists 80 documents found to match a query, but only 20 of them contain the search words, then the precision would be 25 percent.

Proximity Search: A search where users specify which documents returned should have the words near each other.

Query-by-example: A search where a user instructs engines to find more documents similar to a particular document. Also called "find similar".

Recall: Related to precision, this is the degree to which a search engine returns all the matching documents in a collection. There may be 100 matching documents, but a search engine may only find 80 of them. It would then list these 80 and have a recall of 80 percent.

Relevancy: How well a document provides the information a user is looking for, as measured by the user.

Robot: Any kind of automated program that executes a series of actions such as downloading resumes, or searching through websites.

RMS: Recruitment Management Systems are similar to Applicant Tracking Systems in that they also help manage the recruitment process, but typically cover additional processes such as management of the internal referral program, and even tie in with the HRIS.

Search Engine: The software that searches an index and returns matches. Search engine is often used synonymously with spider and index, although these are separate components that work with the engine.

SEO (Search Engine Optimization): the process of making changes to your web content in order to increase the chances of being found in the organic (unpaid) search engine results or achieve better visibility within the search results

SEM (Search Engine Marketing): the process of buying paid advertising within the search engines, job board aggregators and social media platforms like Facebook and LinkedIn™ (see PPC)

Site: A search engine command instructing the search engine to narrow its focus of results only to pages within that specific website, domain or top level domain.

SLA Service Level Agreement: A type of "service contract" where recruiter and Sourcers formally define the services they perform, and what is required from both parties (recruiters as well as hiring managers) in order for the agreement to be met.

Spider: The software that scans documents and adds them to an index by following links. Spider is often used as a synonym for search engine.

Stemming: Sometimes referred to as truncation, this is the capability of a search to include the "stem" of words. For example, stemming allows a user to enter "swimming" and also return back results for the stem word "swim". Some search engines offer stemming as a way to search for wildcards.

Thesaurus: A list of synonyms a search engine can use to find matches for particular words if the words themselves do not appear in documents.

URL (Uniform Resource Locator): The standard way to give the address of any resource on the Internet that is part of the World Wide Web (WWW). A URL looks like this: http://www.4sct.com. When searching for something, a good way to find it is to simply type in the URL.

Wildcard: A placeholder character that tells the search engine to look for multiple possibilities. Frequently the asterisk "*" is used as a wildcard. For example, entering "program*" in a search engine that supports wildcard will return results with programmer, programming, programs, etc.

X-Ray: Searches through all of the web pages within a website that have been indexed by a search engine. The purpose is to find pages that may not be linked from the front page or root page of that website. This may access pages that are not obviously liked from the usual places.